SYNCOPE

SYNCOPE

The Philosophy of Rapture

Catherine Clément

Translated by Sally O'Driscoll and Deirdre M. Mahoney

Foreword by Verena Andermatt Conley

University of Minnesota Press
Minneapolis
London

Grateful acknowledgment is made for permission to reprint from the following works: *The Bacchae of Euripides*, translated by Donald Sutherland, published by the University of Nebraska Press, 1968; "Complaint of Time and Her Crony Space," from *Poems of Jules Laforgue*, translated by Peter Dale, copyright 1986 by Peter Dale, reprinted by permission of Anvil Press Poetry; "Eventail de Mademoiselle Mallarmé," from *Stephane Mallarmé: Selected Poetry and Prose*, copyright 1982 by Mary Ann Caws, reprinted by permission of New Directions Publishing Corporation; *Friedrich Hölderlin: Poems and Fragments*, translated by Michael Hamburger, copyright 1980 by Cambridge University Press, reprinted with the permission of Cambridge University Press; "Lost His Head," from Friedrich Nietzsche, *The Gay Science*, translated by Walter Kaufmann, copyright 1974 by Random House, Inc., reprinted by permission of Random House, Inc.

Published by the University of Minnesota Press
111 Third Avenue South, Minneapolis, MN 55401
Printed in the United States of America on acid-free paper

Library of Congress Cataloging-in-Publication Data

Clément, Catherine, 1939–
[Syncope. English]
Syncope : the philosophy of rapture / Catherine Clément : translated by Sally O'Driscoll and Deirdre M. Mahoney : foreword by Verena Andermatt Conley.
p. cm.
Includes bibliographical references and index.
ISBN 0-8166-1977-8 (alk. paper).—ISBN 0-8166-1978-6 (pbk. : alk. paper)
1. Philosophy. I. Title.
B2430.C633S9613 1994
194—dc20 94-7610

The University of Minnesota is an
equal-opportunity educator and employer.

for Jérôme

Contents

Foreword
East Meets West

Verena Andermatt Conley

How to think the *syncope*, a word designating an eclipse, interval, absence, followed by a new departure, is the topic of this book by an author known for her provocative and diverse writings. These include *Lévi-Strauss ou la structure et le malheur*, "La coupable" (The guilty one), in *The Newly Born Woman* (her dialectical, collaborative effort with Hélène Cixous), *Opera, or the Undoing of Women*, and *The Life and Legends of Jacques Lacan*, among many others.

A philosopher with a pedigree academic degree (the French *agrégation*), Catherine Clément became a journalist and founded a politically correct and influential newspaper, *Libération*, that crystallized the utopian spirit of May 1968. She then acted as art coordinator for the socialist government and, more recently, spent extensive time in India. Clément infuses her present book with the practice and knowledge gained from these spheres of her own activities.

The style has journalistic traits, the writing being both serious and ambivalent, even sarcastic. Clément lashes out at some Western philosophers, who "often spend their time plugging the holes in reality with the hems of their dressing gowns." After having impugned class structures in the early seventies, Clément now calls into question intellectual traditions, all the while knowing those traditions well. She does not write out of the sweet bliss of ignorance, and her critique is not that of a quasi-fundamentalist censorship with its binary mechanism of thumbs up, thumbs down. It constitutes a search for an opening and for reestablishing connections lost between India and the Occident.

If Clément summons an occidental philosophical tradition, she herself writes out of one. Formed during the days of structuralism, the French counterculture of 1968, Clément pays tribute to Lévi-Strauss and justly rehabilitates the scope of his writings that many scholars readily dismissed when he entered the French Academy in 1974. Continuing her feminist teachings and expanding their scope, Clément targets the century-old philosophical Western practice of establishing a full subject in philosophical terms one with the advent of metaphysics, the division between subject and object, and the demise of woman as well as nature. This practice eliminates from its purview anything that approaches even in the slightest a vanishment, a gap, or a swoon of meaning that Clément calls the *syncope*. This term, which applies to symptoms as diverse as sneezing, laughing, asthma, or epileptic seizure, is borrowed from music: "The queen of rhythm, syncope is also the mother of *dissonance*; it is the source, in short, of a harmonious and productive discord. . . . Attack and haven, collision; a fragment of the beat disappears, and of this disappearance, rhythm is born."

From one embassy to the other, from Marguerite Duras's Calcutta to Catherine Clément's New Delhi the critique of the Western subject shifts from focus on the gap, the lack, to a tiny interval from which the subject emerges. Like Duras, Clément focuses on an absence of mastery, on an emotion necessary for all creation. And to create is to resist. But Clément—"a woman of the nineties"—is more affirmative. A simulation of death through syncopation constitutes a political gesture—at the level of politics as well as that of aesthetics—that is less tuned in to the past than oriented toward openings and the future.

Both ethnologists and psychoanalysts have recently challenged the occidental concept of the full subject that, on our side of the Atlantic, has found its apogee in a utilitarian American ego psychology, one with the American way of life. By fortifying the ego, the psychologist opens the human condition to violence and endless power reversals. Clément begins her critique of the Western subject by quoting Lacan from the *Écrits*: "It is clear that the promotion of the Ego today culminates, in conformity with the utilitarian conception of man that reinforces it, in an ever more advanced realization of man as individual, that is to say, in an isolation of the soul ever more akin to its original dereliction." And she continues to comment on Lacan: "At each step, Lacan stresses the loss of ritual in modern societies. Without seeming to touch upon it, but with an insistence that continues to address on the sly the 'cultural ahistoricism' that he attributes to the United States.

"Modernity is the 'increasing absence of all those saturations of the superego and ego ideal that are realized in all kinds of organic forms in traditional societies, forms that extend from the rituals of everyday intimacy to periodical celebrations in which the community manifests itself.'"

To the Western promotion of the self, one fraught with cultural ahistoricism, Clément opposes the *syncope* that she theorizes by borrowing from Lacan and Lévi-Strauss. To a lesser degree, she appeals to Freud—the latter being, for her, still too much of a prestructuralist concerned with filling holes—and, of course, to the 1968 champion philosopher, Georges Bataille. She also finds the structure of the *syncope* in Indian thought, in the guise of the *renonçant* (or "renouncing" subject) who leaves the village to go to the forest. This movement is already central to Lévi-Strauss's *Tristes Tropiques*. Social prestige among Amerindian tribes, Lévi-Strauss observes, is determined by excess exerted upon the body. A youth seeks extended isolation in the mountains. Exposed to rain, wind, and cold, for days and weeks he or she deprives him or herself of food. The spiritual and somatic exercise leads to syncope. "It is all a pretext for provoking powers beyond: extended baths in glacial waters, voluntary mutilations" that lead, once the Indian reaches a state of dumbfoundedness, or delirium, to the encounter with a "magical animal" that responds to prayers. In the midst of the ravishment, "a vision reveals to these youths the one that will hereafter become their guardian spirit at the same time as the name by which he or she will be known, and the particular power, held by the protective animal, that will give the youth his or her privilege within the social group."[1] The Indian figure who renounces is quite similar. Clément retrieves an archaic process that produces social cohesion in Indian customs, but like Lévi-Strauss himself, she also reenacts a passage—a departure—and a return in her travel to the East.

Some parallels with E. M. Forster's *Passage to India* may become clear. Clément's experience of the structural condition of the tropical movement and its effects on the subject stands as an extraordinary companion piece, explanation, and sequel to Forster's novel. Written from the standpoint of a person who has *not* lived through the colonial experience of a British subject and who has no part in staging the United Kingdom's reactions in the twentieth century to the legacy left by the empire of the preceding decades, the concept of syncope allows Clément to renew ties between India and Europe. She sees the breakage over which they are knotted far beyond Britain and the nineteenth century. The ruptures are diverse, reaching to the Crusades and the contact with Islamic traditions. To emphasize syncope does not mean to abdicate life and open oneself to passivity. Rather, it has a political thrust and engages a kind of nonagency of agency. By not wanting to control, by not simply reverting to reversals of power relations, the syncopated Indian person acquires political and ecological advantages over the dominant Western technocrat.

As is her tactic, Clément writes a history of philosophy, a negative history of sorts, that deals with what Western philosophers, from the Greeks to Hegel and the contemporary scene, have repressed or excluded. The excluded part is precisely the syncope, which had been perceived as something dangerous by Western philosophers until recently, at least until the advent of Kierkegaard,

Hölderlin, and their French avatars Bergson and then Bataille. In addition to philosophers, psychoanalysts rehabilitate the syncope via the unconscious and the mirror stage that dislocates linear time through notions of anticipation and retrospection. Yet, argues Clément, the real lesson comes from the East. After having stated that it would be too easy to interpret syncope as if it were a lapsus, or simply reject it as a production of the unconscious, she writes: "Neither of these two interpretations would be wrong; I do not exclude meeting Freud, even less encountering Lacan, but it is not enough—or rather, it is no longer enough for me." And after giving a quick overview of her intellectual formation from romanticism, structuralism, the avant-garde of the 1970s with *Tel Quel* and without forgetting surrealism, she asserts that she has found a common moment of "inspiration" (in a strong sense) in direct rapport with the syncope, or a kind of simulated death. She discovers the real art of syncope during her stay in the East. It is in India that she finds the beauty of percussion, the familiarity of death, the charm of amorous poetry, ravishing dancers whose spectacle made her tremble, then imposed an image of, and finally the word, syncope. Readers may wonder whether they are dealing with a travelogue exulting in exoticism or a philosophical treatise. But Clément's conclusion leaves no doubt about the telegraphic genre she has chosen: "I wanted to study this eclipse of thought, this game of following death. A limited rebellion; the political idea is on the edge of weakness."

The book is a turning point in Clément's intellectual trajectory, one that is doubled by a physical displacement to India—a place that, after Mao's China and Reagan's America, has recently struck the fancy of Parisians. There is Clément's previous book, *Gandhi, athlète de la liberté* (1989), or Hélène Cixous and Ariane Mnouchkine's play production, *L'Indiade ou l'Inde de leurs rêves* (1987), also about Gandhi. Yet interpretations shift and the message differs from one work to another. Clément tries to show the ultimate pragmatism—or action—that does not oppose but goes hand in hand with a philosophy of *renoncement* (renouncing), whereas Cixous/Mnouchkine link Gandhi's gesture to the space of an "impossible dream." Where Clément writes of Gandhi as a person who makes possible, and brings about, social change in a postcolonial space, Cixous/Mnouchkine turn the leader into an anachronism, a figure hopelessly lost in a contemporary world of technology and violent politics. But they all declare a need for a link through nature instead of an abstract simple construction of individual subjectivities. This link they find in India more than in Europe. In a period of what geographers and demographers call an extreme compression of time and space and loss of habitat, they have recourse to the figure of the Indian *renonçant* who questions official homogeneous communality and, through erring, opens space.

The first part of *Syncope* comprises eight chapters of a sweeping history of philosophy focusing on the point of exclusion of syncope. As always with Clément, the readings are not systematic. They are journalistic and generally terse. Adepts at close textual work will be disappointed. Clément's merit is in the range of her knowledge and in her ability to bring seemingly separate strands together or to make unexpected and novel connections. Thus, for example, she alludes to a little-known correspondence between Freud and Romain Rolland concerning India. More strikingly, she claims to find a Western counterpoint to Gandhi in Voltaire. Many a reader who has recently chosen to read Voltaire's work through the prism of feminism will be alarmed. Of novel literary interest are the connections and differences Clément points out between the Indian syncopated *renconçant* and Jean-Jacques Rousseau's Julie from *La Nouvelle Héloïse* or Honoré de Balzac's Madame de Mortsauf from *Le Lys dans la vallée*. Despite her praise for Voltaire, Clément launches a critique of a certain male philosophy based on activity and rehabilitates a certain feminine passivity construed not as absence of action but as a different and more valuable type of (non-)action. Symptomatically, the subtitle of *Syncope*, "The Philosophy of Rapture," hints that the book is about an absence or about something that could never be "properly" philosophized.

Clément's overview of European philosophy is classical; the order is quasi—though not strictly—chronological. The hinge between East and West is chapter 9, "The Birth of Identity and the Syncope of the Imago: Lacan." Lacan's concept of the mirror stage dislocates time and focuses on the syncope. It is reversible. In other words, it is always possible to revert to a pre-mirror stage. This psychoanalytic credo—coupled with the distant look of the ethnologist summoning Western obsessions of plenitude, activity, and the integral subject—leads Clément out of the intellectual impasse of East versus West and onto paths that go elsewhere.

The tone is conversational and spunky, at times chatty, its aim openly political. Clément strips philosophy of its aura, democratizes its discourse and empties it of its self-appointed position at the summit of intellectual hierarchies. Clément deinstitutionalizes philosophy by bringing it into a sphere of everyday life. She connects things high and low, finding links between Plato and contemporary filmmakers (such as Bertrand Blier), between abstraction and pragmatism. The irreverence of her position, no doubt, comes out of the countercultural movements of 1968. Questioning Western society and its values based on "idoliz[ing] power and force, muscle and health, vigor and lucidity," she militates for a syncope that "opens onto a universe of weakness and tricks" and that "leads to new rebellions." She believes neither in vehemence of political action nor in that of art. She advocates power through impoverishment *(dépouillement)* and an art that introduces a break, a disharmony in harmony. To find real, spiritual riches in the absence of material wealth and goods is a topos one finds throughout Western literature. Yet it is especially developed in Eastern thought.

The tradition from which Clément writes still believes in art—especially dance, music, but also poetry—as creation that resists the commercial onslaught of a market economy. Real art has a political value. This claim is one that has been submerged by the slogans surrounding postmodernism, and, in a profit-oriented economy, its original ethic may have all but disappeared. From the standpoint of political aesthetics, she finds it productive to locate the Western model of a fully conscious, rational subject in the colonial era, and engage a critique by linking it to expansionism, capitalism, phallocentrism, and the present ecological destruction of the world. She looks for another approach to politics through *renoncement*, strength in weakness, and a decentering of human beings toward living beings. This she finds in Indian thinkers whom she tries to connect to recent philosophical and psychoanalytical gurus of the West. Linking Bergson—who is very close here to Lévi-Strauss—to the Indian *renonçant*, she writes:

> Renunciation in India has conceived of a syncopated staging of social life: suddenly the human world disappears, by means of a death in which the ritual is simulated. At the same time protest becomes possible.
>
> In the history of Western thought Bergson is the philosopher who has most clearly localized the complementary duality of village and forest. From one to the other, there is a "leap," a bursting forth, a branching out of the syncopal order.
>
> The "village" is a society that Bergson describes as closed, comparable to a group of animals. Static and inalterable, the closed society goes about regulating communal life by obeying moral constraints. The "forest," on the other hand, is an "open" society, transformed by the vital impetus, obeying nothing, distracted by newness, and dispersing the group by breaking its social cohesion. These two extremes emanate from a common origin: the strength of belonging and of life in society on one hand; the freedom of the forest, the mystical impetus on the other hand. On one side, time; on the other, rupture.

Bergson has been taken up too by other philosophers, especially Gilles Deleuze, who in his two volumes on cinema[2] uses the theorist of movement and duration for a reading of mysticism in contemporary filmmakers such as Jean-Luc Godard and Marguerite Duras. Though he does not explicitly call it that, Deleuze too develops an ecological view of the world through a heightened state of perception, action, and affectivity. It seems as if the West, saturated with the rational, active subject, has a desire for another, more spiritual rapport with the world. Such a rapport would lead to the creation of new subjectivities based on incorporeal values.

With many of her French contemporaries, Clément shares a taste not only for syncope but also for Romanticism in general, and in particular for the German Romantics. Yet at no point does Clément, unlike some of her contemporaries, advocate the absolute. She makes this quite clear both at the level of the concept and, perhaps, through the prosaic traits of her journalistic style.

Things have changed since the Romantics, when poets committed suicide. Today, in an age of simulation, one survives the syncope. One goes into the forest *and* comes back. We are neither up in the clouds, nor are we completely down on earth. We are between humans and angels, neither quite riveted to the ground nor completely out of reach.[3] Clément democratizes and politicizes the syncope. It is no longer the prerogative of the "happy few" or the elite, but of the ordinary man. She takes Bergson to task: "The creative impetus is not, however, passed on to everyone. It belongs only to exceptional heroes, in whom 'absolute morality' is incarnated. It is they who, Bergson says explicitly, form 'humanity's elite.'" For Clément, unknown to himself, Bergson comes back to the Brahman opposition between village and forest. In the Brahman system, only the elite can inspire the village. Changes are recent: "It was necessary to wait until our century to see the rise of renouncers of more humble origins, when those excluded from elite spirituality come to the fore. I'm thinking of Ramakrishna, a Brahman but a poor peasant, and of Mohandas Karamchand Gandhi, the son of a merchant."

Similarly in the West, the syncope is now available to everyone. One of its most common occurrences, the *coup de foudre*, a violent falling in love, has been popularized by film and mass culture. In the Middle Ages, it was between the rich lady and her unsuitable lover. It is the excluded suitors who started to revolt. Indirectly, syncope opens the way to social change. The troubadours who, according to Georges Duby, can be seen as precursors of the French Revolution, are not without distant echoes of the contemporary Indian gurus advocating social change in their country. In the East, but especially in the West, syncope is no longer absolute as it was in *Tristan and Isolde*. One comes back from it; one can slip in and out of it: "Death is not the order of the day. That is perhaps one of the only elements that modernity changes in love at first sight: it isn't fatal as before. In becoming more popular, it has become more reasonable; one can experience it and survive."

The use of syncope for social change marks one of the substantial contributions of Clément's book. Contrary to many, Clément does not draw an opposition between the "happy few" and the masses or the crowds, but hints at the generalized popularization and democratization of our age. Now, with the syncope in everybody's reach, the syncopating person, the person in love, can be opposed to the "man of action" with his concomitantly bankrupt morality.

Clément finds this kind of revolution through nonviolence more productive than violent action. The Indian *renonçant*, and by extension any syncopating person, is not the center of the world but simply part of nature, of the living, like plants, or animals. It is because of this philosophy of *renoncement*, of a need to leave the village or an urban space and go into the forest, to wander, to leave a fixed domicile and open up to movement and vagrancy, that Clément sees India as more immediately open to ecological movements than the West. To leave the village opens space, erring, undoes confinement, possession, takeover.

Again, the syncope with its resonance of passivity is linked to a certain femininity. But where Western femininity opens onto the desert, as Julie's in *La Nouvelle Héloïse* or Madame de Mortsauf's in *Le Lys dans la vallée*, Eastern femininity opens to a cosmic motherhood, of the forest and the sea. And femininity does not belong to women only. Men like Gandhi do not shy away from being considered maternal beings: Mother of India, not founder of the nation. This common feeling through *renoncement*, a certain erring, in nature is not brought about by an "accord" with the world but a disharmony. That very disharmony makes possible social change, a possibility opened by the moment of syncope.

Clément again quotes from a lecture given by Lévi-Strauss at the invitation of Edgar Faure before the Commission on Freedom at the National Assembly and reprinted since in *Le Regard éloigné*.[4] I share with Clément the opinion of the importance of this text that should be made available to every reader. In it, the ethnologist warned as early as fifteen years ago of the accelerated destruction of the planet. Says Clément: "This idea became accepted. On the other hand, no one has yet thought, as he did then, of the new *cogito* capable of defining man within nature. For if he is thought of as merely a species and no longer as the sovereign king, how does he find his place? And what formula could come to replace the founding master-subject on which the whole of Europe still depends?"[5] If, via Lévi-Strauss, she refers to the place whence she speaks in Europe, her comment on the United States and the political—and ecological—disasters produced by the American way of life subtended by ego psychology had been relayed via Lacan. Lévi-Strauss locates three moments in the history of mankind that succeeded in displacing man as the center of the universe: the Stoics, *la pensée sauvage*, and Indian thought. He concludes with a new definition of the human being: no longer the Cartesian *cogito*, nor the weak though thinking Pascalian *roseau* (reed), but simply "living being." And the anthropologist reminds his listeners that the occidental, anthropocentric, expansionist "moment" is but the product of a few hundred years in the millenary history of the world.[6] Here, the change in attributes from "thinking" to "living" is crucial. White Western man no longer arrogates the right to violate the right of others, that is, to extinguish peoples, flora, and fauna. And Clément concludes in this important moment of her book: "We have all begun to understand today that on the scale of planet Earth, this demand has become, as it is for oral societies, a matter of collective survival."

All of us can fully agree with Clément via Lévi-Strauss. As we have seen, those who renounce their social group endure hardships that yield visions of beatitude unavailable to those who remain fixed to their communities. From this representation and vision there arises the question whether a philosophy of rapture is a means adequate enough to consider shifts in social order that come when East meets West. Like his Amerindian peers, Lévi-Strauss returns from the bush in order, good ecologist that he is, to stay away. Like Lévi-Strauss, Clément also returns, now from India, to preach a renouncement that she knows only as an idea. Thus we must ask how we can articulate the politics of syncope—and whether we have to—with questions of democracy, industrialization, technology, and demography. In other words, is syncope a moment in a history or can it be a tactical tool in an ecological struggle today that also concerns non-Western people? How can we articulate Clément's use of syncope with other issues? Might the syncope be compared to a "passage" of India, whereby the West does not reside or reappropriate its alterity?

European mysticism or philosophy of ravishment proliferated in the sixteenth and seventeenth centuries around what Michel de Certeau—who is mentioned in passing—called a "*collective history of a passage*."[7] The mystics' final appearance and disappearance coincided with the moment of the Enlightenment. Is their return in the twentieth century around writers like Georges Bataille or Marguerite Duras (who despite her connections to India is not mentioned by Clément) a moment of (re)appearance and disappearance before the final onslaught of technology (e.g., Union Carbide) and the disappearance of the forest, the last "resort" for mystical vanishment? And what is the relation of Indian mysticism to contemporary problems of India? Clément writes that Gandhi used mysticism for social transformation. Otherwise, she chooses not to develop the link between her compelling reading of syncope and the contemporary Indian scene.

Clément looks at the world through a romantic filter and despite being "on location," with at times—to borrow from the title of Lévi-Strauss's book she quoted—a look somewhat "from afar." By urging Westerners to displace their selves from those of *thinking individuals* to *living individuals*,[8] and consider themselves not as isolated beings but as living organisms in relation with other living organisms, Clément makes an important gesture pertaining to mental, social, and environmental ecology.[9] In a neoexistentialist vein, many Western social theories still focus on humans as individuals, without ever mentioning their relation with a reassessed nature *in movement*, no longer simple decor. They claim social rights for people as individuals often in terms similar to those that subtended the politics of expansion that brought about many of today's problems. To stress the importance of loss of mastery, of nonagency of agency, and a new rapport of humans and nature, is one of the most important points of Clément's book. Obviously, there is no direct continuity between those textual ideas and action, or the domain of collective political ecology. But if there is a discontinuity between the two, perhaps a moment of syncope, then most certainly correlations abound.

To create is to resist. To philosophize rapture brings together concept and affect. The reminder that one creates out of rapture may be timely in these days when artists negotiate new deals over glasses of Evian water and no longer can afford the state of ecstasy or trance. The book can be read as a personal *renoncement* on Clément's trajectory. She goes East, to the forest, and leaves Paris-village behind. It also points to a general malaise signaling the end of an era of overnarcissistic involvement with the self and lack, and the need for a more active, collective, political involvement. Clément chooses the path of rapture, in accord with her romantic taste, and adapts it to what she perceives to be contemporary needs. What will be the fate of such a neoromantic vision in an age of digital technology, but especially of soaring world populations that are highest where people are poorest, famine, anarchy, pollution, and human-induced environmental disasters that manifest themselves with particular intensity in developing nations like India? Paradoxically, only time will tell.

Translators' Preface

The word *syncope* is rare in English, but it is the only word available to cover the wide array of meanings of the French term *syncope*, and to capture Clément's conceptual use of the word. *Syncope* can mean a fainting or swooning and other kinds of loss or absence of consciousness; an irregularity in the heartbeat; a musical syncopation; a grammatical or other elision. We have followed Clément in translating *syncope* as "syncope" in almost every case, unless one of the narrower meanings was clearly referred to. Clément deliberately moves among and between the different possible meanings, redefining the term.

In the same way, we have retained the French term *jouissance*, in order to preserve its various levels of meaning; in this we are following the general trend of French studies. *Jouissance* can be translated as "ecstasy," "orgasm," or "enjoyment, pleasure, delight"; in other words, it can be physical, intellectual, or spiritual.

In general, we have tried to reproduce Clément's often playful and allusive language in our translation. In some cases, we have included certain crucial French terms and expressions in parentheses in the text so that readers who are familiar with French will be able to appreciate Clément's rich nuances.

Clément often cites sources translated into French from other languages as well as original French texts. Where a direct translation of those sources into English was available, we have used it: the references for those citations are for the English editions. Where no translation was available, we translated from the French: the references for those citations are for the French editions, and we have also given translations of the titles.

We would like to thank Jacqueline Chambord for the clarification of certain terms; Paul Michelman for practical help; and our editor, Biodun Iginla, for his help and patience.

S. O'D. and D. M. M.

Author's Note

The spelling of Sanskrit words poses a serious problem: the works of French specialists give several possible transcriptions for the same terms. Sanskrit has been transcribed into French in several ways, and is in fact often said to be untranslatable; the Sanskrit in texts that deal with India can therefore make them off-putting, especially as far as the use of accents goes.

I am not an expert on India; I do not read Sanskrit; I am merely a philosopher, with a classical training in Greek and Latin. I hope that my friends who are scholars on India will excuse the inevitable errors that they will undoubtedly find. I also ask them to be lenient about my decision to transcribe certain Sanskrit terms into the Roman alphabet without including any of the conventional accents, for the sake of readability and accessibility for a Western audience. Greek terms have been treated similarly, for the same reasons. Average European citizens may from now on be required to read quotations in other European languages (which will soon become everyone's vernacular), but it would be too much to expect them to face two alphabets and two so-called dead languages, even if these are the roots of their own language.

Acknowledgments

No book is ever written by one person alone, this one less than any other. Jean Audouze agreed to read the first half of the text, and did so with extraordinary care. Michel Cassé was the inspiration for "The Angel of Astrophysics." This work would doubtless never have been finished without discussion and suggestions from the following: Cécile Backès, Elisabeth and Gérard Depardieu, Gérard Fontaine, Daniel Larrieu, René Major, Jacques-Alain Miller, Pascal Rambert, Claude Serra, Serge Sobzinscki, Daniel Toscan du Plantier, and Jean-Pierre Vincent. I would like to give special thanks to my first careful readers: Bernard Faivre d'Arcier, André Grasso, Elisabeth Lévy-Leblond, and Sylvie and Serge Plattard. Antoine Vitez brought Meyerhold's *33 Swoonings*, based on Chekhov, to my attention; Emmanuel Leroy-Ladurie greatly facilitated my research.

And finally, regarding India, I would like to thank Pupul Jayakar and Nandini Mehta, and Roger-Pol Droit, whose frequent and helpful comments were always necessary and to the point. Dr. Vigne generously made available some of his unpublished works. Sudhir Kakar, with whom I am now working on a book on Ramakrishna and Madeleine—*Deux Délires Mystiques en Inde et en France* (Two mystical deliriums of India and France)—has been unfailing in his friendship and support, and has also given me several unpublished manuscripts.

Without the affection of Nicole Taché this book would not exist, nor without the infinite patience of A.L.

Introduction
Where Am I?

Suddenly, time falters.

First, the head spins, overcome with a slight vertigo. It is nothing; but then the spinning goes wild, the ears start to ring, the earth gives way and disappears, one sinks back, goes away . . . *Where* does one go?

The subject, says the doctor, is inert, pale, without consciousness. Sensitivity is obliterated. There is no respiration, no pulse can be felt . . . after a necessarily short time, the pulse reappears, as does the respiration; the skin regains color; the sick person regains consciousness. Otherwise, the ending is fatal; syncope leads to death.[1]

Syncope: an absence of the self. A "cerebral eclipse," so similar to death that it is also called "apparent death"; it resembles its model so closely that there is a risk of never recovering from it. The romantic and clinical scenario has usually, in our society, been allotted to woman: it is she who sinks down, dress spreading out like a flower, fainting, before a public that hurries forward; arms reach out, carry the unresisting body . . . People slap her, make her sniff salts. When she comes to, her first words will be, "Where am I?" And because she has come to, "come back," no one thinks to ask where she has been. The real question would be, rather, "Where was I?" But no, when one returns from syncope it is the real world that suddenly looks strange.

Or, if the fainting fit continues, one could, like the Marquise of O,[2] have an unexpected baby, arriving from that "nowhere" one went to. Can we call it rape when the body no longer resists? And what is occupying the consciousness that, at that precise moment, was absent? The marquise's child will be born of syncope and an unknown father. Not completely unknown, however: the young officer who did not resist the charming sight of the beautiful, abandoned woman had appeared to her, just before the syncope, in the form of an angel. She gave herself up to the angel as she lost consciousness.

"Syncope" is a strange word. It pivots from the clinic to the art of dance, tilts toward poetry, finally ends up in music. In each of these fields, syncope takes on a definition. At first there is a shock, a suppression: something gets lost, but no one says what is won.

Suddenly, time falters.

The couple seems to walk rather than dance, briskly, entwined. Who could separate them? But the man takes the woman's waist, and—so quickly that the movement can hardly be seen—bends her at midbody to touch the floor, and there they are, the two of them, overturned, suspended, as if he had stabbed her, maybe, or kissed her. They stop there, as if frozen for an instant . . . He raises her, whirls, starts again. Tango. She is called his partner, his "rider" (*cavalière*); in its day the Church prohibited the tango as indecent. Syncope—here, syncopation[3]—is evident in the backward dip, inherent in the step itself: three steady steps, at a trot, then nothing. Suspense. It is in the missing beat that one can falter. Obscenity.

There is no dance without syncope—without syncopation. The female dancer stops, breaks off the movement, freezes it. The Sylphide's grief, the Bharat-Natyam's mimed prayer,[4] in "barefoot sandals" or reddened feet with anklets of little bells, a swan's mask, a headdress of pearls and flowers—the female dancer, arms crossed, arm raised, leg stretched, leg bent beneath her, accentuates the pause before starting off again, lightly. And the suspended movement—the syncope—will be the most difficult, as if it were its duty to attain, perfectly, a harmonious imbalance, made even more harmonious by being fleeting.

But the female dancer soon catches fire in an unending circle, spinning around ad infinitum, a diabolical, dizzying doll . . . She smiles. The women always smile, that's part of the figure. The spinning must look easy, even though the whirlwind is athletic, a syncope redoubled, overcome: that becomes clear when the white leg, glimpsed under the short tutu, acts as a lever in the mechanics of vertigo. Thirty-two pirouettes, one after the other at the end of the Kathak, the classical Indian dance of Mogul origin: the lever is no longer visible here, but hidden under gold skirts. Only the dress billows, obliterating the woman dancing. Vertigo looms, on the way to syncope. No longer the disordered vertigo of the first discomfort, not the ground falling away. It is a voluntary vertigo, radiating control.

Aside from the rocking motion, there are other ways through which dance, by a perverse turn, can achieve vertigo. Look at the waltz: a minuscule syncope, *one*-two-three, *one*-two-three, a single accent placed on the downbeat; once it is set in motion and the couple takes off, there is no more stopping, no perceptible syncope, just a shared vertigo, so powerful that if the male dancer is skillful, he must turn the dance inside out like a glove, dancing in the other direction to avoid falling. The waltz is like the pirouette: the male dancer, entwined with his partner, plays the role of the lead-off leg, and the couple takes off at breathtaking speed.[5]

Whirling dervishes spin singly, each under the master's control. "The Superior, in a stole and a jacket with full sleeves, claps his hands at the second verse: on this signal, the Monks rise, and having bowed deeply to him, they start to spin off one after the other, pirouetting with so much speed that the skirt of their jacket opens up and fills out like a tent in a surprising manner: all the dancers form a very entertaining large circle." That was written by the traveler Pitton de Tournefort, describing what he calls (lacking other words of his own invention) "this type of play-acting." Black as night is the jacket, symbol of death; white the flowerlike skirt; white the high toque, a sign of the tomb, the color of a shroud. A stamping of the foot, one hand pointing down, the other up to the sky, with the skirt forming the circle: the syncope is swallowed up, then digested by the goal to be reached. Create a vacuum, wait for the master finally to enter the dance and play the role of a sun around which the circle ceremony is performed. The ritual space of vertigo is called *sama*, and the original master's name is Djalâl ul-Dîn Rumi. Hegel cited him at the end of the *Encylopedia of the Philosophical Sciences in Outline*, at the moment when the Spirit, having run out of twists and turns, is reduced to leaving the premises, giving way to the poem:

> Today it's the *sama, sama, sama*
> It is light, ray, ray, ray
> It is love that one obeys, obeys, obeys
> Farewell to reason, farewell, farewell[6]

It spins, it repeats, and the poem says it: farewell to inhibiting reason, make room for confused love! The master represents the love object, and the dervishes are neither alone nor performing; they spin in brotherhood. In the same way, the dancer rehearses love in the backward dip of the tango, and plans it in the first seduction of the waltz. It is essential for the beat to change register, and it is syncope, either visible or hidden, that does the work. From that moment something stops, life perhaps, or habit, the daily routine, even the blood in the veins . . . But the dizzying techniques for attaining love, whether human or divine, are not the only thing. The dervishes' ritual betrays, in one of its details, a little of syncope's secret. Whatever falls out of the dervish's bags or pockets while he dances is not picked up later. This loss is sacred. We shall see why.

It is possible to describe the dance: it is on the order of the visual. Describing musical syncope becomes an exercise in style: either one produces parts of scores, full of staves and treble, bass, or C clefs, which are only understood by those who read music (this is even harder with contemporary scores); or one stumbles into metaphor, and one has to be as talented as Vladimir Jankélévich in order not to sink heavily into shoddy lyricism. It is in the realm of music, however, that syncope is queen. One can see, by way of a beginning, that if melody is often linked, connecting the notes in one continuous stretch, syncope can on the contrary only steal into the rhythm on the rebound. Take the death aria in Bizet's opera *Carmen*. The gypsy, who has just read her cards, finds there diamond and spade, the presages of certain death, which she contemplates. The very exercise of meditation on death naturally leads to a continuous melody, without any sudden break: and in fact, this is one of the few arias of Carmen's role that is *not* syncopated. But even if the sung aria contains very little syncopation, the orchestra never stops stumbling, refuting the meditation, and opposing a shaky tremolo anguish, a subliminal contradiction, to Carmen's fatalistic calm. When the melody itself is disturbed by syncope, the effect is seen even more clearly. If one hums Carmen's first aria, one can feel the difference. "Love is a rebellious / wild bird that no one can tame . . . " A long chromatic phrase, cut in four places by a kind of swaying of the song: "Lo-ove is—a rebellious bird, that no one ca-an ta-ame . . . " It seems ridiculous to transcribe it, but the effect of syncope is magnetic to the ear: the rhythm sways. That is precisely what both the character of Carmen and the composer want. Even more explicit is Marguerite's last aria in Berlioz's *The Damnation of Faust*, which includes some completely syncopated moments, so choppy that they are reputed to be among the most difficult for singers. But the words are simple: "I am at my window waiting all day." Debussy would have joined that together with a straight line, without syncope, but Berlioz makes the sentence gasp: "I am at / my / window / wai- / ai-ting / all / da-ay . . . " The breath is cut off. The song palpitates, suffocates, and finally capsizes in a long cry of unhappiness, deprived of syncope this time, and liberated from its shackles.

Music dictionaries define syncope strictly. An element of rhythm and of accentuation, syncope begins on a weak beat and carries over onto a strong beat. A weak beat between two strong beats, syncope involves several phrases:

"The first part of the syncope," writes Jean-Jacques Rousseau, "serves for the preparation. The dissonance is struck on the second, and in a succession of dissonances, the first part of the following syncope serves at the same time to save the dissonance which precedes, and to prepare that which follows. Syncope is from *sun* (with), and *kopto* (I cut); because the syncope cuts off from each time, opposing, as it were, with the other."[7] The first beat is that of hesitation, the second that of the dissonance that is born as if by surprise when the accent carries the weak beat over—unduly?—onto the strong beat. The queen of rhythm, syncope is also the mother of *dissonance*; it is the source, in short, of a harmonious and productive discord. The process allows some limping before the harmony, however: it is sometimes said that syncope "attacks" the weak beat, like an enzyme, a wildcat, or a virus; and yet the last beat is the saving one. Attack and haven, collision; a fragment of the beat disappears, and of this disappearance, rhythm is born.

The art of poetry is more transparent to writing because it uses words. In linguistics and grammar, "syncope" is the suppression of a syllable, or sometimes a letter. The most familiar language (that is, the most colloquial) produces syncope spontaneously: *m'sieur*, *mam'selle*, *p'tit* . . . There are as many instances as there are syncopated moves. Thus, long ago, words were formed that were later consolidated by the academies; one said "idololatry," but ended up with "idolatry"; "*semimestris*" became "*semestris*." Syncope makes things go quickly, it accelerates: one could say that it is silent through laziness. In metrics, we speak of "*enjambement*." The line stops, one foot in the air, and carries forward to the next line: a step has been surmounted, time has been held back. But one also anticipates. *Enjambement*: we are not far away from the dance, turning the poetic act into a pirouette of words.

Physical time never stops. That may be, but syncope seems to accomplish a miraculous suspension. Dance, music, and poetry traffic in time, manipulate it, and even the body manages to do that by an extraordinary short circuit. "You don't need much of a brain," as the author of an early-twentieth-century medical treatise put it so neatly. People vie to describe the causes of syncope—circulatory, nervous system, neurovegetative; a cure can be found—cardiac massage, smelling salts, a slap. But inside, what is going on? Where is the lost syllable, the beat eaten away by the rhythm? Where does the subject go who later comes to, "comes back"? Where am I in syncope?

Who knows? Philosophers, who often spend their time plugging the holes in reality with the hems of their dressing gowns, do not seem to have come up with any real answers. Imagining the short circuit is working at the limit, or rather *on* the limits, going against the current of Western custom. We are obsessed with the autononomous and aware Subject, and even if nowadays we force it to follow the path of the unconscious (like a policeman tailing a suspect), we never doubt its existence, even less its fundamental validity, without which no democracy, no individualism is even imaginable. Philosophers were determined to master the interruption of time; an intense psychic labor, at least as exhausting as thinking about limits. A beautiful construction dressed up like delirium, which Freud said was related to paranoia. A huge system of avoidance, but avoidance of what? There will be, however, we will see, philosophies just as syncopated as *Carmen*'s *seguedillas*; anyway, they come close to poetry. And they often contain a confused smattering of Eastern thought; that is not an accident.

There—I mean in the East—there is a philosophical practice of syncope. Whatever it may be, Eastern thought is not scared of placing itself at the center of the short circuit, at the center of the heart—that heart beats too well, and it is a question of stopping it. As a poet, Mallarmé guessed it:

Now feel space shivering
Dizzy, some great kiss
Which, wild to be born in vain,
Cannot break forth or rest.
. . . .
The scepter of pink shores
Stagnant on golden eves, *this East*,
This white shut flight you pose
Against a bracelet's fire.[8]
(Emphasis added)[9]

The object is incongruous in a familiar way, and elevated to the dignity of the concept: it is Mademoiselle Mallarmé's fan. Take away the pink of the banks and the gold of the evening; all that is left is the fan that flaps its wing and folds it again. The fan is a syncopal object; in music, the accordion is another. While listening to an accordion playing its part in a gypsy orchestra, watch as well: the interruption running on its path is really up to the other instruments—violin, dulcimer; but the pauses, the breath, belong to the accordion with its pleated bellows. Folded up like a butterfly, the instrument, accordion or bandoneon, skims over the rhythm: when it unfolds and stretches out, it takes the melody, and leaves the breath to the others.

Mademoiselle Mallarmé's fan, the unexpected metaphor of an Orient barely imagined . . . The poets' task, as far as syncope is concerned, is all the easier since the practice of devouring time is one of their professional tools. It is the same for psychoanalysts, who are used to continually negotiating with a time that turns back without warning, disappears, returns disguised as a symptom, explodes, and cheerfully disturbs the mechanics of everyday understanding. Analysts, even if they entangle themselves in misshapen jargon, know more about syncope than do most philosophers. The unconscious, states Freud, does not recognize time; so our good gentlemen are forced to come to terms with that. That is what they are doing by naming the inside of the short circuit as "unconnecting" (*déliaison*), even "unbeing" (*désêtre*). Lacking a better solution, one tries to undo words. Lacking a better solution, one would rather find oneself nude again, without even the philosophical dressing gown as stopgap.

But the "nakedness" so dear to Georges Bataille, who has thought about it passionately, does not declare itself so quickly. Not everyone who wants to can have access to nakedness of thought; bareness is not always regulated. And I am only a philosopher, quick to intertwine the threads of thought around a phenomenon that fundamentally rejects it. All that is left is the way a procession wanders; like an animal, it makes circles around its desired prey, meanderings that little by little draw nearer, perhaps to the heart. That is what philosophers do, and if they become delirious, it should not be held against them, for they are not capable of anything else.

Our first circle will be that of *tremors*, of impacts and falls. The simple bodily signs that suspend breathing belong to the sphere of syncope; they are recognizable because in their extreme state they can give rise to real fainting fits. So it is with the cough, that banal everyday suffocation; banal, yes, but it is spasmodic, and as such provokes a little suspension of being. Paroxysmal, like a fit, it brings on coughing that doctors call syncopal, during which one gets ringing of the ears, vertigo, and loss of consciousness.

"Nasal, pleural, feeble, or barking. That which cannot be silenced; that which is neither yours nor mine, but all of ours, widespread; that which shakes the walls and interrupts sleep, these coughing fits where the unbearable is acted out . . . It gets worse, irrepressible. An access, it is called. Slipping, incomplete and gushing, the belly joins in. Some people cough as easily as one cries, others as easily as one kills."[10]

The sneeze, which is nothing, is less perceptible; yet it shakes us and closes our eyes for the space of an instant so brief that we have already returned from it. In certain Scandinavian countries, sneezing while driving a car is a violation, because sneezing makes one lose control. "Sneezing," says Pascal, "takes up all the faculties of the soul." But how can one prevent it? The enacted law remains powerless; syncope deprives the body of its obedience to the mind.

A wing flaps, and there is the hiccup; the diaphragm leaps, irresistibly. We feel as if we will die if it lasts; to make it stop, we have recourse to fear: emotion against emotion, homeopathic treatment of syncope by syncope. Often, in novels, the hiccup—or gasp—of agony exhales the soul, the last tremor of the living body.

Then there is laughter, but only as long as it is in bursts, unrelenting, an insatiable fire, until consciousness is extinguished. Uncontrollable laughter exhausts consciousness and makes it more tractable, more open to entering other landscapes. Georges Bataille made a frenzied insistence on that, repeating endlessly that laughter is the metaphysical outlet par excellence. Bataille, the essential laugher: "Laughter is an act of knowledge. . . . The principle is: if I laugh, the nature of things is laid bare, I understand it, it betrays itself."[11] A divine jolt, an acceptable spasm, accepted without distrust, laughter has concerned many philosophers; they sense, beyond its innocuous exterior, the seriousness of the thing. Those who have come near to laughter have declared that it springs up from the ruptures, the "differences in level" (*dénivellations*), as Bataille says, or from the short circuits, according to Roger Bastide: risky or deliberate collisions. By tickling, one can aggravate to the point of agony, a form of torture that Fernandel, in Renaissance garb, made famous: a goat licking the soles of his feet with bestial impassivity. It involves getting outside of oneself: however restricted the tickling, there is only a short distance from "the shrill cries of girls teased and tickled"[12] to the unbearable. Laughter intrigues by its course: a short and beneficent ecstasy, it moves toward anguish, accomplishing the opposite trajectory of what Pierre Janet described in an unjustly forgotten book, *De l'angoisse à l'extase* (From anguish to ecstasy).[13] The list of spasms always revolves between these two poles.

Asthma is similar. Bronchi contracted, the asthmatic chokes, wheezes; mouth open like our ancestor the fish thrown on a sandy bank. Queneau: "It is worse than a strangling, worse than an encirclement, worse than a stifling, it is a physiological abyss, an anatomical nightmare, a metaphysical anguish, a revolt, a complaint, a heart that beats too fast, hands that stiffen convulsively, a skin that sweats."[14] Once again, a matter of the diaphragm. In an impressive book, the chest specialist François-Bernard Michel raised two crucial points.[15] The rhythm of respiration is binary (but syncope is not). The Westerner, when he passes out of normal respiration (eupnea), moves into "bad" respiration (dyspnea) and begins to palpitate. The Asian, on the contrary, has learned by tradition to suspend the second phase of respiration, progressively reaching a prolonged absence (apnea) for so long that it has been tested repeatedly without being understood. Legend has it that this practice leads to immortality. This thread is precious; I will not let it drop. Syncope, apparent death, borders on the fantasy of the nondeath; drawn out, stripped of its brevity, it is transformed into something else, something that the East knows by heart and the West has lost.

Later, the chest specialist discovered that the asthmatic cherishes his illness, which he surrounds with a draftproof staging, like Proust near the end of his life, cooped up: asthma rarely kills. One rarely dies in the asthmatic attack; one returns, to start over again soon; but between the two attacks, the pleasure of breathing is intense. The asthmatic often wants to keep his symptom, again like Proust who preferred it to the loss of maternal love. Asthma, says François-Bernard Michel, rather than . . . Or again, asthma in order not to die. This method of stifling immortality is the opposite of Eastern breathing: if one suffocates, ceasing to breathe, one dies without really dying. Sometimes it happens, however, that while doing this, one succumbs.

I will leave the scream to the poet:

> However, there must be some singing
> I can't be only a scream
> This violent thing in me
> Seeks a lack, a crack there
> Where mutiny can pass.[16]

Louis Aragon, in *Le Fou d'Elsa,* calls this poem "Unhappiness Says." But whether it is one of sadness or of joy, the scream does violence to the throat, which is suddenly turned into a hole, as if there were no other way out but to break through a wall. An exit, a rescue, open prison . . . The scream's connection to syncope reveals one of its ends: the *fugue*.

It is the same with tears, struck with syncope when they are accompanied by sobs. Think of the infant who often has only tears at first to let it be known what he needs; then the infuriated sob that ends in a sniffling hiccup, before ceasing abruptly in a satisfied sleep. And since I am on the subject of infants, let me stay there: for the emerging individual, deprived of words, often uses, along with the water of tears, the flux of excrement that burdens him, to escape. Bataille noticed the relationship between tears and excrement; he added laughter to them, as if some invisible substance gushed from its outburst; look at the gripping scene of the gibbon buried alive, whose protuberant hindquarters are the only mound left visible from the outside; "Jésuve," which a rich Englishwoman embraces with devotion, provoked to laughter and tears at the same time, while the gibbon exhales its last breath under the earth, and its last excrement above ground. This scene *confounds* us. That is the right word; it is the desired end.[17]

Screams, tears, tremors, uncontrolled excretion, foaming at the mouth: with epilepsy, syncope joins in. One could say that a wicked genie had gathered all the imaginable symptoms together in this strange ailment. Even before the attack begins, what the doctors call the "premonitory" signs appear, as if by fate epilepsy still came under the prophecy that was, as we will see, its prerogative. Premonitory signs, or "*aura*": this word denotes, as if on purpose, *breath.* Facial spasms, tics, squinting, little tremors shaking one end of the body like lightning, cardiac palpitations, choking, contractions of the rectum, sweating, tears, even tears of blood, cold sweats, tingling, pricking, tickling, cough, wheezing, tinnitus, whispering, auditory hallucinations, visions of whirlwinds and fireworks, mutism, bursts of laughter . . . Collected without any invention in one of the bibles of epilepsy,[18] this dizzying catalogue minutely explores the record of the first circle of syncope—that of suspended time; it opens the interior doors, and gets a voyage under way.

If it is not the great ecstasy that will lead the epileptic to the full staging, with curtain, orchestra, and props, it can be simply a short absence, a gesture that begins and then goes on, but consciousness returns before finishing its work. It is a brief voyage of several seconds, called "petit mal." Two or three essential things are added to the music of the ringing ears, the cut-off breath, the St. Vitus's dance.

First, the smell, peculiarly described as the "rank" smell of cooked turnip. Do not believe that the epileptic hallucinates the turnip; he actually smells of the boiled vegetable; doctors have attested to it several times. This is something to be looked into.

Then, rarely, there is an *aura of rapture*, of which Dostoyevsky is the best witness: "For some moments, I have a feeling of happiness that I never experience in my normal state and that is hard to imagine. It is a complete harmony in me and in the whole world, and this feeling is so sweet, so strong, that I assure you, I would give ten years of my life—even my whole life—for a few seconds of that joy." Others say more soberly: "I feel like a new person."[19] Or they speak of an "attack of annihilation."[20] Is this marvelous chaos really nothingness?

It is impossible to forget the sacred nature ascribed to epilepsy in the ancient world. But properly so: epilepsy figures largely in the story of syncope, for epilepsy long ago lost the consecration that made it divine. What happened to this illness happened later to the very word "syncope": first a loss of repute (a devaluation, as it were), then a clinical partitioning so rigorous that the phenomenon disappears in the process of analysis. Epilepsy, with its paraphernalia, brought together all kinds of symptoms that are now scattered and catalogued elsewhere. Syncope is hardly mentioned any more in medicine: people say "stress" or "collapse" or "lipothymia." Or they call it, in a striking term, "drop syndrome." What strange rain falls on the earth, and what divinity scatters these drops that are men onto the earth, yet makes them fall outside of themselves? This falling of drops gives way to collapse on its way down; nothing remains of the human figure but a shapeless heap. But the term *syncope*, with its connotations of musical science and poetic art, has disappeared.

In the case of epilepsy, as in that of syncope, what was once gathered together under the aegis of the sacred has been separated.

Epilepsy, which was sacred, was recognizable by the fall it brought on: the body on the floor, foaming, convulsed, was the prey of a god. The second circle begins here, the circle of the fainting fit.

There are innumerable scenes where the overwhelmed consciousness disappears in order to let the god speak. It is known that those who are crippled from birth, nature's syncopated beings, are often predisposed to this: epileptics, but also the lame and the cross-eyed. It is enough that the body be affected for the divine function to settle in, as if a fragile capacity for making consciousness disappear could be read in the flesh itself: the cross-eyed man really has not one gaze but two, the lame man syncopates his walk, and the walleyed witch has one brown eye, the other blue. The cross-eyed man and cross-eyedness itself often meet in Bataille's passion for uneven, crooked streets and houses: in French, it is accurate to call those streets and houses "cross-eyed."[21] Only lame Oedipus, the hero with pierced feet, was able to resist for long his vocation as an inspired cripple; he had to blind himself completely to recover his true status as sacred monster. Where there is a limp, syncope of the spirit is not far behind; there is a twist in the air, and something strange at the end of the path.

Curiously, a fainting fit can be called sleep. But is it really sleep? One appears to be asleep; the eyes are closed, the breathing is regular, the respiration has slowed down. *Attacks of sleep* are among the multiple symptoms of epilepsy; they are brutal. What makes syncope is its suddenness. Consciousness goes off to sleep without warning; the awakening is just as quick. Then, during this strange falling asleep, the great sleepers, the Pythoness, the Sibyl, all the prophetesses speak, with a voice that is not their own:

> No, no, Lord, do not take my mouth
> Don't place in it the fire of your tongue, such a terrible kiss . . .
> No, no, Lord do not force me to speak your language
> I am suffocating, I have turned blue from this divine violation, I am near death
> I no longer recognize my voice, I am
> Inhabited by your vengeance, oh sword, and in my stupor I hear
> My face says what I would have preferred to hide
> And my own destruction emerges from me
> No, no, Lord, I do not say it I do not say
> It . . .[22]

This is how the fakir in *Le Fou d'Elsa* (Elsa's madman) is forced, against his will, to express himself. How can one not listen to the voice of a god? No man speaks with that gasp. To achieve it, when there is no predisposition to limping, the fall is provoked, the fainting fit is sought out. One smokes, chews, drinks, pierces the skin, one drugs the subject; but the method is often simpler, without too many contrivances. The list of situations that produce these borderline states is as baroque as that of the signs of epilepsy.[23]

Focus your eyes on the flatness, the emptiness: drive a long time on the freeway, stare too long at a radar screen where an endless line is circling. Empty the body—of sleep, of nourishment, of conversation; insomnia, fasting, and isolation eventually cause one to lose consciousness. The desert does the same thing, but also twilight, dawn, and prayer . . . How do we make sense of it? A harsh shock brings on syncope, but so does repetition; physical disturbances cause syncope, but so does the banal regularity of the sun that rises and sets. Let us look at two or three specific cases. Running for a long time winds you, but it induces a kind of ecstatic weightlessness; the body is suddenly light. Just as the waltz and the dervish depend on syncope and prolong it through spinning, a race makes whatever it is that attaches man to earth fall. *Climbing* does the same thing—to the point where in England, apparently, some workers were clever enough to scale abandoned warehouses, buildings, churches, for lack of peaks within range of climbing. The most radical: the Shoshone Indians, who invented "dynamite parties"; they climbed into a hole not far from where a charge of dynamite was set off. The blast threw them out of the hole, and as we say today, they were "blown away." If classic epilepsy has now fallen to pieces, if it is seeking a cure, the lure of syncope has not ceased; on the contrary, it is renewing itself, modernizing, finding in the urban landscape and modern techniques the necessary food for the disturbing process of devouring time. Repeat "Sama, sama, sama," or "I don't say it say it say it," do violence to your body or give way to the beauty of a dawn; you are caught. The stagecraft of syncope is boundless.

We are in the third circle, the circle of ecstasy. It has been trailing its ineffability for quite some time, in the whirlwind of the waltz or in that of the dervishes where it is the avowed goal; it springs up in the epileptic aura of rapture, it appears at the end of the line of the freeway . . . More than any other sign, ecstasy reveals how impossible it is for language to domesticate it in a given order: ineffable, it refuses to be said. It can be spoken of, often, only in counterpoint, in the negative, saying what it is not, and that it is not what it shows—a god, God, the void, nothing; it is a long internal pursuit, destined to alternate between depressive desolation and sudden illumination. Ecstasy is ravishing; that word has been prostituted so that nothing is left of it but an intense appreciation of a woman's beauty. There one is, *outside oneself*, etymologically. One can drink one's urine and live on acorns as the Tantrics do, or shiver with excitement at the angel's arrival like Saint Theresa. Ecstasy belongs to the madman as well as the saint, to Madeleine, Pierre Janet's patient, a delirious mystic, as well as to Georges Bataille. Ecstasy is always the same: only the ways of achieving it differ, and the staging surrounding it. For Christians, there is only one God; for atheists, there is the *Somme athéologique* (Summa atheologica) planned by Bataille, and the contemplation of the pink, hairy spread genitals of a prostitute made crazy by a night of drunkenness.

Ruysbroeck went straight to the point: "Jesus is a fine funnel / I tend bar with him / he pours good wine for me / always in big gulps." Is this drinking-partner Jesus really so different from Madame Edwarda? Shaken by spasms, buffeted by attacks that have no name, naked under a domino, she reveals her "rags" and proclaims herself God; it is clear enough. The mechanism Bataille invented lacks nothing: neither the "Where am I?" uttered in a "lifeless voice," nor the night, nor the cross-eyed streets, nor the sun that sinks down on her in the end, as if on a child. The author of *Madame Edwarda* was not mistaken:

> The nature of our being invites us of our own accord to join in the terrible dance whose rhythm is the one that ends in collapse, and which we must accept as it is and for what it is, knowing only the horror it is in perfect harmony with.[24]

Bataille is turning up often? Undoubtedly; meticulously, obstinately, lovingly, he has patrolled the pathways of syncope without respite, drawn up his own list of "supreme processes" through which ecstasy is attained—laughter, drunkenness, eroticism, meditation, sacrifice, poetry—he has sharpened words like knives on a lamb's throat and finally considered, as in "Philosophy's such an easy lay."[25] Bataille is indeed a good companion, who will keep coming back.

He noticed that in India and more generally in the East (the Far East and Asia), the techniques of ecstasy have achieved a degree of perfection with which the West cannot compare. Not that the results, I repeat, seem so different; but the stagecraft, shaped by millennia of practice, is—despite its variations—completely different from ours. Inscribed in a system whose rule is the suppression of consciousness, ecstasy burns the world and man. Breathing *is* the art of rapture: there is no need for any expenditure other than the retention of breath and of semen. The Eastern propaedeutics of syncope is miserly; ours is extravagant. There, they hold back, economize; here, we let loose, unload. And the key to this difference is the very same one that separates, enduringly, East from West.

Here, ecstasy is sometimes produced in those protected, well-lit places we call theaters. And in these theaters, nothing is closer to ecstasy than the rapture sought by opera. Singing turns the head a little; and bel canto training produces in the singer—or so they say—a special drunkenness, a fairly violent vertigo. The lungs open up, the sounds resonate in the cranium, which is transformed into a fairy grotto; the voice is as it were liberated, a prey to the climbing known as vocalization. The singer looks after his organ with as much care as the climber his ropes and crampons; singing is an interior athleticism, and the difficult utterance is a feat. It is not surprising that the spectator comes to share the drunkenness, pouring it into his hearing, and from afar, but fervently, in turn, gets out of himself. The innocent fanaticism of opera buffs seeks a syncope without risk, framed in golds, velvets, unveiled by the curtain; it pursues a domesticated syncope, authorized to whistle, to boo, to dance with happiness and cry with joy. Opera is made to stun; often, it achieves that.

But not always. When syncope becomes the object of an art—mystical technique or stage art?—it is not bound to occur. The contemplative can await ecstasy his whole life without achieving it; opera can become a monument to boredom. It is not a question of perfection; on the contrary. The entire art of syncope consists in preparing surprises; and when technique is abandoned, the fainting fit occurs when one least expects it; it is an accident; and no one can foretell the day or the time.

The fourth circle is also the last, coming closest to death. The phenomenon, though familiar, looks so much like it that it is sometimes called the "little death"—but also "seventh heaven," for example. *Orgasm*, like music and ecstasy, seems indescribable; there are few words to depict it, always the same ones: explosion, eruption, earthquake, ascent, rending, bursting, vertigo, and the stars . . .

> All throats were strangled by raucous cries, by impossible sighs, and, from all sides, eyes humid with the brilliant tears of vertigo.[26]

That is Bataille again, excuse me . . . And this is still him, describing Madame Edwarda's *jouissance*:

> From her stare, then, at that moment, I knew she was drifting home from the "impossible" and in her nether depths I could discern a dizzying fixity. The milky outpouring travelling through her, the jet spitting from the root, flooding her with joy, came spurting out again in her very tears: burning tears streamed from her wide-open eyes. . . . And everything swam drowned in that dreaming

> stare: a long member, stubby fingers prying open fragile flesh, my anguish, and the recollection of scum-flecked lips—there was nothing that didn't contribute to that blind dying into extinction.[27]

Human jouissance[28] requires that one lose one's head; that is the foundation. That is the only way to attain the simulacrum, the moment when nature's harbor is reached, where the mooring ropes that hold fast the subject—consciousness, its *cogito*, its history, and through that everyone's history—are cast off at last.

The famous death of Isolde on the opera stage represents this as far as is possible: the slow ascent through chromatic waves, a sweet climb toward a sung nothingness like an ocean of light, it ends in perfect harmony. No syncope: a flawless continuity, an illusory death, a perfect icon of impossibility itself. We know, however—it is practically all we know—that the crossing over to death is not accomplished without conflict.

The ideal death in the East prolongs the highest ecstasy, of which it is the desired completion. Legend has it, for example, that Vivekananda, in nineteenth-century India, decided on his own death and planned his final ecstasy; his disciples left him in the evening, meditating. In the small hours of the morning, they found him dead; he was forty years old. Dying in ecstasy is no longer exactly dying; it is simply detaching mind from body, and abandoning this unimportant refuse; it is prolonging a light obtained through asceticism and artifice; there is no more break; there is no longer any crossing over. It is simply a breath that is not taken again. In Europe, the ideal death is unexpected—the death that takes someone in their sleep, or by surprise, all of a sudden. It is the same idea: he didn't suffer, people say; or again, he didn't feel it. Our farewells evoke "eternal repose"; Indian farewells insist that the deceased have simply "entered into ecstasy." In both cases, the event is neutralized; it is a matter of passing beyond the final syncope, the gasp of agony, the last one. The last crossing must be evaded. Syncope seems to simulate it, and to anticipate it: is that not all death is, a narrow, shifting corridor followed by an intense happiness?

But the advantage of syncope is precisely that one always returns from it. Asthmatics, epileptics, lovers they recount explicitly how wonderful it is to breathe after the attack. How ravishing the moment before it is! Syncope is like asthma attacks: one play-acts death, but in order not to die; one passes beyond consciousness, but returns with a dazzled memory. We do not go as far as the moment where physical time continues its work and nature continues its decomposition; I'm speaking for Europe. We place ourselves in the *before* death, in the *after* death. The real crossing is forgotten.

But have I surveyed all the scenes of syncope? Have I really unrolled the thread that the spider brings out of its stomach to spin the web? I have hardly mentioned alcohol; barely skimmed over catalepsy and its retinue of phantoms risen from the grave where they had been buried, so strong was the illusion of death—oh sickly heroines of Edgar Allan Poe's fantastic tales: Berenice, Lady Usher, beautiful princesses like the inspired automata created by Hoffmann . . . I have barely begun to tackle the vast repertory of trances, and the shamans' imaginary voyages. I was even about to forget the sigh, that hint of an accentuation on a single beat, sadness barely breathed out . . . And at the other extreme, gambling, a contradictory passion of surprise and anticipation that "burns" the player,[29] suspending the course of his life on this other world steeped in secret divinities and sudden inspirations; gambling, where we recognize those who have a desperate hunger for the moment. I have not yet spoken of love. It is time to deal with that serious accident. Love, the most perfect of syncopes, starts with love at first sight.[30] A shared syncope.

We say that we fall in love; we fall as we would stumble; it is a dizzying drop. Is it sudden? No. The apparent characteristic of love at first sight is to be thought of as staggering, although it is not. It can begin with indifference, or with repulsion—the first time that Aurelian saw Berenice, he frankly thought her ugly. It starts with a declared hostility, a violent social antagonism—Iseut hates Tristan;[31] before loving him, she raises her dead fiancé's sword against him. It can settle in with little noise and crystallize in silence. Love at first sight seems to have been invented for the cinema, the only art that can show slow motion. Think about the process of slow motion: it stretches out time, analyzes the slowness of attraction, dives into all syncopes and makes them manifest. But off camera, in real life, what is it that projects onto love at first sight this taste for abruptness, this flavor of suddenness?

The gaze. It is always the gaze. A glance that lingers and does not move again from the settled point where it rests from now on. To find a woman ugly is already to look at her; the gaze that Tristan turns on Iseut brandishing the sword is enough to link them together. And since cinema is a good place to exhibit syncope, let me mention Bertrand Blier's film *Too Beautiful for You*, a story of ordinary love at first sight. There is the boss, a handsome guy, a husband overwhelmed by a wonderful wife; and there, behind him, separated from him only by a pane of glass, is a temporary secretary—without grace, elegance, or charm. The audience guesses love at first sight from the moment they cannot stop looking at each other. "Can someone tell me why I want to smile at this woman? She's so dowdy! Why am I looking at her? I've been looking at her for three days now," he says. "If he looks at me again, I think I'm going to faint," she says.

And he looks at her. "There's something wrong, there's something wrong—this feeling isn't normal," he says again.[32]

Too late. For that matter, once the anomaly has been established, it is already too late. The thunderbolt that makes the lovers give in to the happy illusion of Completeness is almost upon them. A Completeness that is no longer "shared," not even "exchanged," since the gaze and the pressure have confused two individuals. "A celebration of the return to original Oneness," writes Bataille; and it is a celebration that annuls the passage of time, inverts the order of daytime and makes the night reign supreme, overturns the family, society, the world, even God if necessary. The syncope of love immediately rehearses eternity; lovers want it now, forever, it is the sea going off with the sun . . .

The difficult thing is to live it. It is a daily feat. Whether it is recounted in vaudeville or torn apart in tragedy, love at first sight, like every syncope, is athletic, takes up an incredible amount of energy, and does not cease to exhaust the lovers. Death is one fatal and easy resolution: a "single flash of lightning," and they die together. Usually, death from being struck by love takes time, and chars each of the two partners, who find in this pain their real identity, from now on separated from each other. But they will have earned some scars, like those the biblical angel inflicted on Jacob while they fought. To be struck by love is absolutely necessary for anyone who truly wants to relish duration. It is the lameness of life.

The mythologies of love at first sight are often radical and explicit. The young Selene, beloved by Zeus, wanted to see him in all his majesty while she was already carrying the king of the gods' child. Finally, Zeus agreed to reveal himself; but his light was so bright that it burned Selene right down to the bone. Only the fetus was not consumed, and the god sewed it up into his own thigh so that it could go to term. Thus was born Dionysus, the god of syncope, son of a mortal woman and a bolt of love. In the universe of the gods, the bolt of love really is a thunderbolt. The God of the Jews and Christians does not escape this terrifying power; when he reveals himself to Moses, it is in the middle of a storm, amid thunder and lightning, on top of a mountain. When he wants to conquer Paul of Tarsus, he overcomes him, blinds him, and cripples him grievously. The gaze is often fragile; no one looks directly at the sun without burning their eyes; how could one look death in the face? That is a characteristic of the gods: to look directly at them is to expose oneself to the thunderbolt. The desire for the impossible confrontation persists in human love at first sight: if they can look at one another, even if it entails being charred at the same moment, then they have both become gods.

Freud has no hesitation about confusing love and hypnosis; he even suggests explaining one through the other. "The same humble submission, the same docility, the same absence of criticism toward the hypnotist as toward the beloved."[33] The only difference is that hypnosis has no avowed sexual goal. The comparison is not, of course, completely convincing, for it does not take into account the way the two lovers are swallowed up together in the same fascination; but it displays the submission, indeed the passivity accompanying the state. And it brings into the analysis of syncope the tactics of the pendulum, the bright point, the shiny ball, the hypnotizer's eyes, eyeballs fixed and blinding. With the pendulum, attaining syncope through hypnosis makes the *illusion* manifest, the driving force behind fainting away.

There is more. Hypnosis is not only for humans; it also occurs in the animal world. Lapwings, little waders that nest on the ground, have a marvelous system for protecting their young, which cannot fly for several weeks. They fly off, uttering cries of alarm. Immediately the fledglings sink down and do not move. If you approach them, they are in a cataleptic state: it is not a matter of play-acting, but a far more complex phenomenon. It seems that with animals, the perception of danger and the terror this produces provoke a cataleptic immobility; it seems, moreover, that this strategy of syncope may be, for the animal threatened by a predator, the most effective one.

Hypnosis, in syncope's catalogue, is a point thrown between the sphere of animals and our sphere. But how should we really think about it? These magnificent creations—music, poetry, and dance—that start off the Completeness, the ecstasy, the delirium, and then finally love itself: what connection do they have with the animal world, which seems so far from us phylogenetically, a giant leap backward? Or should we instead consider syncope to be an innovation that belongs to what is most highly evolved about our species?

An abrupt suspension of time, syncope contradicts time's natural progress. Through syncope the motives of desire are swallowed up: passivity, love, the other, God, emptiness, and destruction are there—all mixed up, in the heart of a confusion that one could say was planned. This jerky tremor suppresses the subject's consciousness. But it is also what sets music, dance, and poetry working. This suppression moves us; this passivity is productive. That is the paradox that must be explained. Why is the last beat of musical syncope a "salvation," as Rousseau said? What is the point of this little leftover piece of the beat?

It would be too easy to interpret syncope as a lapse, a failed act; in short, it would be premature to put it in the huge cupboard of products of the unconscious. At best, that would be so true that it would not risk being false.

It would be easy to collect all the accidents of thought, language, and deed in Freud's work, and to include syncope with them as a psychosomatic phenomenon, with hysterical origins, rehearsing a forever unknowable primal scene. It would be easy to find in Jacques Lacan's work a series of signifiers covering up emptiness, lack, internal twisting, and to treat syncope as a punctuation mark in life. Neither of these two interpretations would be wrong; I do not exclude meeting Freud, even less encountering Lacan, but that is not enough—or rather, it is no longer enough for me.

I adore Romanticism—the real thing—love stories and opera. My youth was spent in respectful apprenticeship of structuralist methodology, whose goal was to explicate the outlying regions of fainting phenomena, at the edges of thought, with a rigor that became increasingly arid in the process, and from which arose in counterpoint the emotion we pursued. True outpourings are indeed born of a certain aridity.

There is something else; I had the great luck to have lived through the avant-garde period of the seventies—I mean *Tel Quel* and the movement that this journal inspired. It had everything: radicalism, excess, the necessary annoyances that any serious avant-garde provokes. It had everything: violent polemics, anathema, unbridled support for some of the group and insults for others, a continual atmosphere of jousting, of derisive chivalry, of dubbings and affiliations. Nothing was missing: especially not the mutiny that I believe to be the source of syncope. Today—and this is one of the things that encourages me to write this book—there is no visible avant-garde in France, perhaps not even in Europe, and the mind is rebelling elsewhere.

It is in France that Surrealism was born, however, and where its revelatory productivity was carried out. Avant-gardes are indispensable, even more so because—and we shall see that they are not the only ones to do so—they manage to sublimate the attitude and vocabulary of war for the pacific productions of the mind. This is what André Breton said about inspiration:

> We can easily recognize it by that total possession of our mind which, at rare intervals, prevents our being, for every problem posed, the plaything of one rational solution rather than some other equally rational solution, by that sort of short circuit it creates between a given idea and a respondent idea. . . . In poetry and in painting, Surrealism has done everything it can and more to increase these short circuits. It believes, and it will never believe in anything more wholeheartedly, in reproducing artificially this ideal moment when man,

> in the grip of a particular emotion, is suddenly seized by this something "stronger than himself" which projects him, in self-defense, into immortality.[34]

There, beautifully defined, is the object of any avant-garde: the search for an inspiration, for everyone and for all the members of the same group. It goes without saying that inspiration, that first moment of the respiratory exercise, maintains the closest connection with the syncope that is so dear to me.

Finally, I have lived in India. Perhaps some other change of scenery,[35] in the true sense of that term, would still have provoked the idea of syncope and its aporias. India, however, brings a certain illumination to this terrain that is hers alone: the endless beauty of her percussions, their incredible melodic capability, their science of pauses; the daily contact with death, familiar, lived, and without terror; the charm of the *ghazals*, the power of this love poetry, even more enchanting because I did not know its language, Urdu;[36] and the ravishing dancing women whose repeated performance finally thrust on me the shock, then the image, and finally the very word "syncope."

I wanted to study this eclipse of thought, this game of following death. A limited rebellion; the political idea is on the edge of weakness.

Surprisingly, this glaring weakness contains a raging force. This prostration is creative; from its disorders unknown energies are often born. Sometimes men, aware of this secret force hidden within syncope, have even used it to conduct rebellions and to free peoples from their oppressors. I am not speaking of riots or of revolutions; I am speaking of politics in the long term, in which calculation and thought depend on syncope, or rather on the force that it contains, restrained, planned, thought out. Exceptional stories? Perhaps; I am not sure; but they are often forgotten. The world in which I have lived until now idolizes power and force, muscle and health, vigor and lucidity. Syncope opens onto a universe of weakness and tricks; it leads to new rebellions.

The product of this venture is the brand new, in all its freshness.

But how should we begin this venture? In the world that we call modern, the rituals that regulate it have disappeared; others appear, which we hurry to nurture. And though we tolerate the ecstasy of rock and roll, we fight against drug use and we do not deal very well with the depressive *raptus*. The voyage begins with this violent desire for night: depression is the current end-point of a long genealogy of syncopes, which we once knew how to manage. Now, they seem overwhelming.

The history of our classical philosophy, as it is now taught, shows this:

Western thought has been busy filling this hole in life. For a long time, it has worked desperately to include syncope in the ranks of unfortunate accidents, sources of disorder, unhealthy disturbances, private and public fanaticisms. It is not until the dawning of Romanticism that this surprise, in all its liveliness, finally finds the position that it had occupied elsewhere, although not in philosophy. When it arrives in thought, it does so with a vengeance, but in poetic forms, with Friedrich Hölderlin, Søren Kierkegaard, Friedrich Nietzsche, like youth finally cured. That is how it acquired its rights in the philosophical world at the moment when it passed, medically, into the realm of madness.

But we stay on the sidelines—Bataille more than anyone else, with an extraordinary stubbornness, and words held in suspense. For how could one succeed in describing the inside of ravished time?

In the East, the abyss where the fan beats like a wing, this chasm where the West has so often got lost, one can succeed in this description. The detour through India makes us discover a philosophical science of syncope, the consummate art of its practice, a comprehensive consideration of its secret powers. By starting in the East, we can then return and rediscover the enclaves into which the art of this dissension has slipped, through the meshes of a tightly drawn net.

There is still one thing, however, that the West has not dared touch, except in those countries where tyranny has temporarily taken over. That is creativity; there are artists whose work reproduces the scenario of syncope: a surprise, a delay of life, a violent anticipation, and a slow return to what one calls the "self."

There will be a scandal, for syncope is a warning; it demands attention. It is true that by intruding, it cheerfully breaks the laws of the world. And if it simulates death, it does so the better to fool it.

Joyfully, between laughing and crying, between ecstasy and agony. Joyfully, between the pleasure of orgasm and the happy sadness that follows. Joyfully, playing with our most deeply held beliefs, which, in the space of rapture, no longer exist.

1
Choosing Night

True night does not exist.

No, the black night, the primal one, will never exist. To have access to its flawless opacity, perhaps one needs the sudden gap of anesthesia or the experience of syncope. In those moments there is certainly darkness. As one says in the theater when one wants to achieve the effect of time passing or of spatial displacement, "Lights out!"—and everything is extinguished.

It is impossible. One can never extinguish everything. In the theater one never succeeds. Thomas Bernhard's protagonist, the Theater-Maker,[1] demands, when he acts, *true* darkness; it is absolutely necessary for the fire-exit signs to be extinguished. But that is forbidden, for safety reasons; then the fire chief has to be asked . . . And finally when they give in to this eccentric's need for darkness in the theater, the planned play does not take place. There will be no total darkness; the fire-exit signs stay lit, tiny bright spots that remind the mad idealist of the bounds of human community and the laws of protection. Darkness in the theater is utopian.

Impossible to represent, it is equally impossible to *re*-present; we retain neither the image nor the memory of the darkness of anesthesia, of a physiological syncope. Language can evoke it; but thought comes up relentlessly against this nothingness that rejects it violently. Let us not delude ourselves that we will be able to enter this darkness; one would have to be mad, or God, and it is to attain this that those who are mad for God seek ecstasy. In terms of physiological syncope, we are in the same position as the Theater-Maker was with the fire chief; for reasons of safety, it is impossible for us to go in there with words, with language. We will do what the stage directors did; we will be just before, or just after, in the rapture of the aura that precedes the attack, or the calm that follows orgasm; we will cheat with the shadow's shadow. And we will start by studying our nights.

Our true nights are modeled on the theater; they are full of light. They are starry, fiery, stormy, and streaked with lightning; they are sometimes white, or blue, and perforated by bombs.[2] They are sacred, lit by processional torches. They are inhabited by a clarity that is not the light of the sun. And whether it is the crescent moon or the swarming planets, whether it is the footlights or the veiled streetlamps, the writer's lamp or the glittering globes of the dance halls, there is never darkness.

Night owls seek out the twinkling half-light. Those who reject daylight know the art of finding night lights. Whether they be lovers or revelers, what they do not want is natural light. Too crude, it allows them to be recognized; too bright, it obliges them to be themselves. At night, one is no longer completely oneself; one has already started to leave oneself behind. One can confuse oneself with the other: this is where humanity's real night begins, beloved by poets, mystics, and lovers.

Once, this need was recognized. The social order scrupulously organized great nocturnal transgressions, feasts with a set date, nights of Saint John or mysteries of Eleusis, to acknowledge the chiaroscuro. Confusion was allowed, the breaking of taboos was prescribed. Night feasts sanctioned the uprising of planned discord: masquerade parties where one could carry on in hidden thickets, a sacrifice where human flesh could be dismembered . . . Enough of the city's laws, enough of the taboo against cannibalism, enough of the daylight order. And to help each one to cross the stages of life without any mishap, there were initiation ceremonies. Almost nothing is known of the mysteries of Eleusis; enough is known, however, to understand that the initiate had to pass through "darkness" before reemerging, as if brand-new, refurbished by his rebirth.

Passing through the darkness of initiation, whether it involves being shut up in a dark place, being buried underground, or being momentarily blinded by a black band put over the eyes, delivers a very precise message. One passes through death, goes beyond the last outpost. At that moment one feels contradictory sensations: the childhood terrors and fear of the dark return, and one's thoughts free themselves, and start to run away, split apart. Then contradiction itself fades away; daytime logic is no longer appropriate. One has entered the logic of nighttime; it is a different logic, one of syncope. A liberated logic.

Today's world watches with jealous care in order to limit these crossings over into nothingness. Everything is done to make the tests less dramatic; momentary suffering is proscribed; we no longer speak of old age, and agony is avoided. They want to make school examinations painless; it was not so long ago that they wanted to do away with them; and they have just forbidden the hazing of freshmen, because, it is true, it involved playful cruelty. The work ethic and the energy invested in it take over benevolent night's territory; retirement, where the senses once sheltered from thought, now resounds like a bell with productive activity.[3]

And when the desire for night becomes too strong, they attempt to cure it.

Depression is that solitary, initiating exercise of the desire for night. It may seem strange to consider depression as an exercise even when it sweeps down on the subject like a vast, uncontrollable shadow. In appearance, it is a collapse; a despondency so radical that doctors speak of a "depressive *raptus*." The subject who is prey to a depression has actually been stolen from the world; he is the object of an abduction. We forget that the words "abduction" (*rapt*) and "raptus" come from the same root as "rapture"; we ignore the fact that the depressive is also enraptured.

It is a fearsome regression, an echo of those lost initiations. The depressive goes to ground, has no more taste for social life, refuses to go to work, and hates everyday life; he takes refuge in a state of passivity and grief. The least contact is exhausting; he seeks irresponsibility at any cost. He wants to depend on someone; it could be the mother, the wife, friends, the psychiatrist, the psychoanalyst; they will take care of everything. What else could they do? The depressive is too tired to live. Someone else will have to live in his stead; he has become too stupid for this task.

But depression is also a retirement, a retreat.

Hard-working modernity denies this retirement to the social being. To "take a breather," as we say, vacations were invented; but they are the other side of working; they are an authorized interruption. One could call them the diastolic of the social heart, which contracts and then relaxes. True retirements, as one used to make them before, didn't give warning; only internal need directed their course. Today, to get access to retirement, the social being has to prove that he is no longer fit to function normally. He must declare himself old. It is impossible to go *on retreat*, as one used to say. Now, one does not *go* on retreat, one is *retired*; it is a state, old age, uselessness, a social shame. The depressive prefers to live as an invalid, and gorges himself, in order to treat his rapture, with pills for sleeping, more pills for waking. He looks after this social syncope and does not even have the time to abandon himself to it.[4]

As if one had to demonstrate the desire for night, depression is first signaled by sleeping disorders. The depressive awakes before dawn, almost in the middle of the night, and does not go back to sleep. This is how, although he does not always know it, he makes himself unfit for work and tires himself out. This "phase-displacement" is a strange signal: as if it were necessary—at the cost of daily life, which has become an exhausting pain—to keep one's eyes open and celebrate the night all alone. Wandering in the streets at night brings on an identical fatigue: but one must have the courage, the inclination, the vocation for it. The depressive wanders in his bed at night, and he resists getting up. His whole life is upside down; there is no longer either a right side or a wrong side.[5]

For him, the alternation between waking and sleeping is completely disturbed. Doctors have studied this phenomenon; with depressives, they say, the circadian rhythms are disrupted.

The study of biological rhythms begins with the heliotrope. As its etymology suggests, this flower moves spontaneously toward the sun, *helios*; it has a penchant for the sun, a tropism. Dortous de Mairan had the idea of isolating a heliotrope and keeping the flowerpot in the dark. Surprisingly, the plant, in the dark, deprived of its favorite, the sun, continued to turn its head and to open its leaves in its master's absence. In 1962, the cave explorer Siffre played the role of the heliotrope; he undertook to stay with a group of researchers in a subterranean chasm that had no light. There, in the entrails of the earth, they found almost absolute darkness. The pioneers of human biological rhythms were given no instrument for measuring the course of time. Each fell asleep when he felt like it and woke up spontaneously.

The vocabulary that creeps into these studies is strange. These experimental excursions of the living environment and the plunge into darkness are called "free flows."

The constraints of daytime and the liberty of nighttime could not be better expressed. Left to themselves, however, the experimenters showed when they returned that they had obeyed precise rhythms; independent of light and dark, the circadian rhythms are of twenty-five hours and about twenty minutes. Two "oscillators" regulate the movements of waking and sleeping, thanks to hormonal secretions produced during sleep. Body temperature, which had gone down during the first phases of sleep, increases progressively; the organism anticipates waking, and on its own manufactures a magic potion, which contains growth hormone. Upon waking, one is ready for day, even if one is in darkness and in free flow. The body is readied for diurnal activity.

Not surprisingly, the depressive no longer knows anything about these habitual mysteries. With him, the circadian rhythms are disrupted to the point where even the growth hormone is no longer on time. Instead of increasing during the night, it increases during the day.

Among the lucky finds of these vocabularies are those superb inventions of language, the "synchronizers." These are variables in the environment that allow the organism's relative adaptation to social time according to the circumstances of life. The German language adds another: *Zeitgeber*, "giver of time." In French, the triggers of hormonal secretions for the day's activities are satisfied with being "in good time"; in German, they do more: they *dispense* time.

To these still embryonic discoveries are added the cards dealt to you by modern life. Night shifts, those three-eighths rhythms, have already produced significant problems; but transmeridian plane flights have opened an era of confusion. We call this playing with space "jet lag";[6] it stretches or compresses what we are used to calling time. Complete confusion: even if one barely exceeds two hours of flight, one no longer has an hour or a time. What is more, flying west, the problem is resolved; by compressing time, one is at less than the twenty-five hours and nineteen minutes of the circadian rhythms. But flying east, time stretches out; the cycle is exceeded. One is no longer inside the circadian rhythm but overshoots it. Modern people are used to treating jet lag like a windfall: going west, at least, one "gains" time. Going east, one "loses" it, in return: one "lags behind" on life. Westward flights are more easily dealt with; as for eastward flights, they are so formidable that a noticeable rise in the number of suicide attempts has been seen afterward; they are not so easily resolved. Beyond the game of win or lose played by part of flying humanity, it is clear that the deep rhythm balks, and doesn't like having its time synchronizers changed.

What is the time that is given in this way? Are the synchronizers really givers of time? All calculations seem to be measured on the muffled rhythm of the social day and the social night, of work and rest. The time that the synchronizers prepare us for is work time, it is not relaxation time, or time for erotic epiphany. It is for neither ecstasy nor agony. For *those* moments, stealing time is not enough; one has to go further and *suspend* time. That is the function of the short syncope: a sudden flight into nonexistent time. That is also what the depressive does when he displaces the night by prolonging it into day. Sleeping during the day, or making oneself drowsy and unfit for work, is a silent revolt against the constraints of light. It is choosing night, a happy confusion of genres. If the depressive suffers, it is from having to painfully simulate a sham diurnal activity that is suddenly senseless. Meaning, all meaning, has suddenly gone into the night.

Only night actually banishes limits, distances, behaviors, and identities. Night wipes out the skin color of the African, and sanctions Othello's embrace of white Desdemona; night takes away Tristan's identity as nephew of Queen Iseut, and opens the road to merging with his beloved. Extinguish that torch that was calling the lover! It gives too much light. It is nighttime that lays down, at the feet of sleeping Boaz, a lowly gleaning woman, a Moabite whom he makes his companion; it is in the midnight hours that hybrid dances are born—the tango in the brothels, the java in the Parisian dives; you dance, you mix, you blend the skins and their colors, origins, and destinies. You kill me, you do me some good: that is night logic.

But what awakenings!

In a short fragment, chaotic and unfinished, Georges Bataille considered the night. Here is the extract that was crossed out, not finished: "Night, when are swallowed up as futile not only the objects of original desire, but every object of knowledge, is first of all horror itself. In it every value is obliterated and as one enters it [*crossed out*: only enters it] at the peak of desire, it [*crossed out*: one can only welcome it in] nausea."[7]

The accidents of the struck-out pieces of a broken text produce a beautiful image of the effect of night: "nausea." I do not know if Bataille was evoking night itself or disgust at having to leave it; but the depressive is not the only one to feel the nausea of this crossing. At the depth of love's ecstasy is a certain loathing.[8] We should take this word seriously; one actually has no more heart, it has been passed on to another entity, a double, nonexistent, who has taken it from you completely. I've had a change of heart, said the epileptic, speaking of the rapture of an attack. Yes, it is a matter of dis-heartening. The body is also "all upset"; that is the choice of night—it dis-heartens.

A hypertrophic poet—that is, one whose heart is overlarge—wrote a strange complaint one day. Time and his crony, Space, became lovers; Time is the man, Space is the woman, of unlimited dimensions. Then Time gets tired:

> When've I made you pregnant? Oh, that must have been
> An interesting spasm! What purpose had I seen?
> I have you, you me. Where? Everywhere, always. Joy, that,
> Which, when one's Time, becomes a trifle old hat.[9]

We must be done with this. Or choose endless night.

And if one has ever experienced ecstasy, whether it is love at first sight or wild bacchanalia, syncope or music, it is difficult to let it go. Going back to daytime produces a shock as serious as that of the first shock of syncope.

Euripides tells us about the terrifying awakening of the bacchantes.[10] Agave was queen and an initiate of Bacchus's cult; during a night of drunkenness, she attacked her own son, whom she took for a lion. She tore him apart alive, ripped off the head of King Pentheus, to whom she had given birth.

Her father was there, saw her coming from far off. It was dawn. Queen Agave smiled like a child, still in her bacchanalian night. Laughing, she held out the bloody head and cried out loud proudly: "See how brave we are! We have killed a lion!"

Agave's father asked his daughter to look up into the radiant blue. Then he forced her to look down at her hands. And in the hollow of those hands, her gaze cleared by the sky, the mother suddenly saw the head of her dead son, which she herself had torn from his body. That is the reality of daylight: it enlightens.

The Greek term Euripides uses for the glance in which Agave finally recognizes her son's head is *skepsis*. "Skepticism" is derived from the same word. The philosophy of the time was, as a matter of fact, skepticism: it scrutinizes, it examines, it makes distinctions—yes, it sees clearly. It does not let itself get confused; it does not let itself get caught in night's traps. And to protect itself, it looks at everything with the same eye: in the full light of day, when the shadows are at the shortest and everything is flat. It will make use of delay and doubt, if need be; and the need is actually so often felt that the skeptic no longer believes anything he sees. One never knows . . . Even clarity hides mysteries, and who knows but that the gaze can be endlessly mistaken. The skeptic does not risk choosing night; and more than anything, he dreads the illusory and unreal syncope. Rather than let himself be surprised, the skeptic suspends judgment. As for everything else, he is on guard, with the vigilance of a wolfhound. One never knows.

In 1917, a substance was discovered that regulates the secret mechanisms of falling asleep: melatonin (whose name harks back to the darkness of night) induces sleep, inhibits public outbursts, and regulates mood swings. Our excitations and listlessness depend on it; moreover, it was hoped that it would enable us to clear up the pernicious effects of jet lag. For a while, it seemed as if we were going to be cured all at once of our loves, our passions, and our circadian rhythms. This wonderful futuristic substance is secreted by the pineal gland. The little gland had seemed almost deprived of functions: it was not much understood what it was doing inside our skulls. Bataille, visionary that he was, imagined the pineal gland as the visual organ of the celestial vault, a virile gland pointing vertically up; erect to look straight at the sun. We are not yet there. Although it was built on anatomical ideas long out of date, scholars are today doing justice to Descartes's intuition that nevertheless attributed to the pineal gland the supreme function, that of being both the main seat of the soul and the mover of passions.

Descartes wrote the *Treatise on the Passions* to teach a sad princess how to protect herself. Nothing acts more immediately on the soul than the body.

One desperately needs to know, then, how the soul is joined to the body: it is "united to all the portions of the body conjointly."[11] But the soul has a single dwelling in the body, which belongs only to it and which allows it to perform its functions on the body. This dwelling from which it functions is, specifically, the pineal gland.[12] If the philosopher chooses this precise place, it is first because the gland is very small; then, it is in the middle of the brain; finally, within the brain it is the only unique element. We have two eyes, two hands, two ears, whereas we have only one thought at a time; this unity of thought must correspond in the cranium to something single, a piece of the body that is the seat of the union between soul and body. There is an additional reason: the pineal gland is in suspension—so much so that it is highly mobile.

Cartesian anatomy lays out a system of cavities through which, in the blood of the veins, the animal spirits circulate; these are very small, very mobile particles that are "the most animated and subtle portions of the blood."[13] This is the enemy: these spirits move *too quickly*. They have to be counteracted if the philosophical ideal is to be reached—that is, tranquillity of the soul. This restless heat, too scalding, that "nourishes" the whole body and inflames it has to be cooled off.

The little gland will be the battlefield of heated debate:

> There is here no strife, excepting that the small gland which exists in the middle of the brain, being capable of being thrust to one side by the soul, and to the other side by the animal spirits, which are mere bodies, as I have said above, it often happens that these two impulses are contrary, and that the stronger prevents the other from taking effect.[14]

The soul, to protect itself in its dwelling place, uses willpower and hard work; it is up to the soul to push harder than the fiery animal that courses through the veins and rushes headlong through the brain's pores to take possession of it. Through artifice, I can turn aside the natural joining between the movements induced by the gland (itself pushed by the hot little animal spirits) and those of my will. I raise my hand to strike in a fit of rage; it is the natural joining of a specific wish with the movement produced by the pineal gland. I stay my hand, through habit or willpower; I have contradicted one force with another. One can, says Descartes, "separate in itself the movements of the blood and the spirits from the thoughts with which they are usually linked."[15]

This is philosophy in action: it curbs and delays natural movement. It suspends it, as the skeptic does with his judgment. There is hardly a philosophy in the West that is not concerned, however, at some point in its course, with taking control of the body, with delaying the coming of passion. The philosophical result of this delaying action often takes the name of freedom.

But this delay chooses daylight and clarity. It is no longer a question of teetering in the darkness of night, but of avoiding losing the spirit. Passion is suspended indefinitely; it never recovers its original spark. In the movement of syncope there is indeed a delay; but immediately, like the note in musical syncopation, this delay rushes into anticipation. The philosophical act rushes nothing; on the contrary, it curbs, it slows down, it suspends without hope of return.

And yet how it burns, this desire for ecstasy! The flame of animal spirits runs between the lines, and so does the passion for succumbing to passion . . .

Philosophers, like mystics, are aware of the flavor of illuminated nights. They know the flash of wit and the violence of ideas' appearance, daughters of wakefulness and of fever.

Let us stop at the most illuminated among the philosophers, and the wisest also: Pascal, a man of suffering and of syncopes. He is the one, however, who, obsessed with equilibrium and balance, was the best doctor of his time, the most gifted. What is known through his sister[16] of his childhood shows a child that one would now call precocious; very young, "he wanted to know the reason for everything."[17] His father was terror-stricken. But at eighteen, the age when serious life begins, his suffering began: not a single day without pain. There were convulsions, migraines, toothaches, flux, colics, the vapors; at those moments the extraordinary wheels of his thought were forcibly halted. To cure him, the doctor sent him "into the world"; he was supposed to have "normal conversations."[18] He supposedly needed people who were not geniuses—normal people, in short, who would lead him back to the world that he undoubtedly did not like. He called the world a distraction, and left it at the age of thirty to go to the country, into retirement, into retreat. For Pascal, the word "retreat" takes back some of its military connotations; the army of everyday forces was actually in a rout, it fell back. Only the interior forces mattered, those of the thinking mind. For however weak the reed is, it bends but does not break; he thinks.

But when anyone came to visit him, he placed on his bare skin, around his kidneys, "a belt of iron full of spikes."[19]

And to make sure that he would not surrender to the brilliance of his own eloquence, when these visitors were talking to him for quite a long time, he gave himself little jabs with his elbow; the violence of the pricks would remind him that his wit was too lively. Madame Périer, his sister, understood what was happening:

> and to keep himself aware, it was as if he had incorporated this voluntary enemy who, by pricking his body, endlessly provoked his mind to keep it in a fever and so gave him the means for certain victory.[20]

When he was about to die, he repented. What transgression had he committed? He had not taken the time to come back into the world and take care of the poor. He occupied his time quite differently—or, to be more exact, his nights. For he didn't sleep; he discovered. "Multitudes of thoughts" came to him in his long hours of wakefulness; it was at night that he discovered his explanation of roulette. It was at night that he wrote down with all possible speed, at lightning pace, his inspired brainwaves. And it was during the night of November 23, 1654, that ecstatic illumination finally came to him full force, a syncope of everyday time that lasted two hours. "Fire" was the first word, the fire of lightning. Then: "God of Abraham, God of Isaac, not of philosophers and the learned."[21] Thus he died, erudite man and philosopher, to abandon himself to a God who demanded of a father the sacrifice of his son.

When he wrote *Outline of the Life of Jesus Christ*, he was talking about himself. Jesus, in the desert, fasted for forty days, "trembling in his spirit"; Jesus stayed awake in the garden of Gethsemane while all the others, who were ordinary men, slept; Jesus, in agony, sweated blood. And when he finally gave up his spirit, his final cry, at that instant, could not be natural, writes Pascal: "for those who die of weakness lose their voice long before."[22] When he lowered his head, it was not out of weakness, either, but of his own will. It is only man who lives weakly, not God. Only man is weakness, except for thought. And if it is necessary to punish thought for being too swift, if it is necessary to keep it at a respectful distance with dreadful jabs on the body, it is no less the grandeur of mankind, in search of a center.

Jesus Christ is this center for mankind that Pascal sought in physics and in metaphysics. Jesus is "the fixed point through which man can find his place,"[23] his balance; he is "the center of the center, the middle of the middle."[24] Without him, there is no balance between world and retreat, day and night, childhood and old age. "When one is young, one judges badly; when one is old, the same. If one does not think enough, or if one thinks too much, . . . It is the same with pictures seen from too close or too far away; there is only one indivisible point that is the right place . . . "[25] Pascal, the doctor, calculates this center without much effort; too easily, one might say. With the obstinacy of a philosopher he affirms the grandeur of mankind, the capacity to raise oneself to the idea of the center. "All of our dignity consists in thought. It is from there that we must raise ourselves, and not from space and time."[26]

The iron belt was a well-guarded secret that was not discovered until after his death; likewise the collection of the *Pensees* and *Mémorial*, which he sewed into his clothes, carefully unstitching it at each change of garments, those worldly skins. The revelations of the punishments he inflicted on his too-quick wit, on his endless hours of wakefulness, were posthumous; the irrepressible call of the night was posthumous. Pascal was an ascetic philosopher; he was what India would call a renouncer. Renouncers, we shall see, have syncope as their vocation. The retreat from the world, the mortifications, the use of the spiked belt, the exercise of controlling his screams, are all found in India as erudite methods for domesticating syncope to the point of ecstasy. What will not be found there, on the other hand, is the need for the center and for the grandeur of mankind. Mankind, these surroundings, will not exist anymore.

Allow me to take a detour that has been anticipated by the mention of India; just enough time to see where this difference leads. Jesus Christ is dressed up, in India, in an extraordinary legend. There is no doubt about his existence; he lived in Palestine and was condemned to death. But he did not die; that is to say, he did not give up his spirit; he did not expire. He had spent the mysterious time of his long adolescent absence in India, where he was trained in yoga techniques. There one learns to hold the breath long enough to plunge into a cataleptic state. You understand: Jesus on the cross let out the cry of a yogi and put himself into catalepsy. He simulated death.

By the same token he did not rise from the dead, because he was not dead. His Essene friends, also great yogis, woke him up. Jesus Christ ended his days in Kashmir, in a valley that has actually always been called Paradise. Today his tomb is pointed out there, along with that of his elderly mother who accompanied him.

Beyond these extravagances, Indian thought is in opposition to Christianity on some crucial points. A god never dies; a body cannot be resurrected. The soul is reincarnated in another body, and that is something very different. At all costs the *very idea of mankind's grandeur* must be fought. Jesus Christ, man-god, is for Hinduism an outrage against metaphysics. If one is a god, one is immortal; and if one is man, one cannot do better than to hold one's breath to put out the body's fires. The Indian version shows us a Jesus who holds his breath but does not die; the Christian version shows us a Christ who gives up his last breath and dies.

As for the dizzying thoughts that cross the night of the consciousness like so many shooting stars, they must be held with the help of the cut-off breath; transients, they are less important, says India, than the concentration on a fixed point that is intended to *disintegrate* consciousness rather than *exacerbate* it. Our classical philosophy does exactly the opposite.

These ideas are so sudden that they crystallize worlds of thought that philosophy feels it can do nothing with, for the moment, except receive them. Something else is needed to *have* them, truly, in mind. It is necessary to get out of this philosophical syncope in which enlightenment skims obscurity, where the idea, like mankind, could faint in its turn.

Ideas, those daughters of the night, have to be educated, presented. The philosopher will have felt them being born in his brain, off the beat, against the light. It will be necessary from now on to separate them, as one separates the movements of the consciousness and the will. The philosopher will do anything to avoid new collusions with the moment.

There is everything to be done: elaborating meticulous methods, suspicious and resolute confinement, *cogito*, dialectic, critique. There is everything to be done: forget nothing of what can be thought, for fear that something might escape and go off to choose night, that pagan and lacerated night. With syncope, with that swooning in which Descartes saw nothing but the extinction of the fire in the heart, there is only one hideout left. A lair for animals: a cage, a niche, a logical cell-like place for avoiding flight.

But make no mistake about it: nothing demonstrates the power of syncope better than the philosophers' desperate building fury to reduce and imprison it.

Sartre against Bataille: No, Not the Night

There is delay everywhere. Lovers, choosing the night, are out of sync with daylight and with their society; mankind's circadian rhythms are at variance with the alternation of night and day and go to help out love; the depressive, refusing daylight, unduly extends the effects of nighttime and encroaches on his daily work time; and the philosopher Descartes attempts to neutralize emotion with a voluntary delay. Human time is definitely limping, unruly.

"Night," says Bataille, "is youth and drunken thought: it's youth and drunken thought to the extent it's night, to the extent that it's violent discord. If humanness is discordancy in terms of itself, in its vernal drunkenness it's night."[27]

So choosing night is choosing to *ensure* that one is at odds (*désaccord*). Intoxication, youth: to be at odds with the world. Lovers are at odds with their surroundings the better to have an agreement so complete it ends in fusion, necessarily fatal to their identities; the depressive is at odds with himself, and loses what he had always thought of as "himself" the better to have an uneasy decline, but also to have a deep agreement (*accord*)[28] with an abandonment he finally accepts. Only the philosopher protests, and tries to break the blissful disagreement. The order of thought is to be restored.

Jean-Paul Sartre, for example, is angry with Bataille precisely about the subject of night. Hoax, bad faith . . . Sartre doesn't go easy on him:

> What M. Bataille forgets is that he has made with his own hands a universal object called Night. And now is the time to apply to our author what Hegel said about Schelling's "absolute": "At night, all cows are black." It appears that this abandonment to night is ravishing. I am not surprised. It is a certain way of dissolving oneself in nothingness. . . . With the words "nothing," "night," "lack of knowledge" that "denude," he has simply prepared a nice little pantheistic ecstasy for us.[29]

Why this anger? Because of the *transcendental*. Bataille can protest, invoking in vain his hard-core atheism, it will be to no avail. "M. Bataille does not want to see that lack of knowledge is *immanent in thought*. A thought that thinks it does not know is still a thought."[30]

Bataille's effort collapses. Sartre's cry is of an almost corporatist nature: don't touch thinking. It is based on professional autonomy, and on immanence, that is, the possibility of being impounded by the subject. The suspicion of transcendence, be it confusedly religious or vaguely mystical, takes on in the philosophical mind the proportions not of a crime against consciousness but of a crime of high treason. A thought that thinks it does not know is still a thought: nothing is more Cartesian than this brutal repetition of the *cogito*'s founding gesture. It is a total block!

Sartre against Bataille: but also Kierkegaard against Hegel, or Socrates, Descartes, Kant against themselves within themselves. Socrates, perpetually cheating against his familiar daemon, busy mishearing it, except for twice in his life. Descartes, doggedly suspending, delaying, stopping anything that could go beyond the limits of thought, obsessed with the speed of affects, and suddenly leaving everything in peace to console a princess in exile; and then Kant, classifying, dividing, separating, succeeding somehow or other in throttling music and laughter by finding in them a limited usefulness that is as safe as possible. When the philosopher refuses to be a poet, he doesn't like to be surprised. Lacking anything better, he tries to put up some protective barriers. Philosophers constitutionally hate syncope and everything that resembles it—the upheaval of wit, the unruliness of passion and anger. And since delay exists, at least its practice will not escape philosophy. The philosophers' true goal is control: to control the rhythm of thought, its stops, its hesitations, and even what are commonly called its ulterior motives.

2

Philosophers and Their Daemons

Socrates, who had nothing of the bacchante in him, was nonethless troubled by a daemon. Later, in a different system, it would have been called an angel, or maybe a devil. But Greek daemons are not devilish; they are simply slight emanations from the divine world, in charge of warning mankind to be on the lookout. You have to have an acute inner sense of hearing to feel their effects, which are mere shudders, little signals from the soul. Almost nothing. Enough, however, to stop Socrates in a philosophical move. Yes, that nonstop talker, that unrepentant dialoguer, who was capable of defying the powerful men of this world to the point of risking and losing his earthly life, this Socrates who was called a corrupter of youth, stopped at least twice. The first halt caused by the daemon took place at high noon, the second at sunset.[1]

The first time Socrates stopped, it was right in the middle of a discourse that was going very well. Phaedrus, one of his disciples, whom he had run into by chance, had taken him off for a walk outside the city walls; they went on their way together until they reached a place that Socrates thought beautiful: there was a plane tree for shade, a spring for coolness, grass for softness. And Socrates, who did not often go into the country, Socrates the townsman who said that fields and trees had nothing to teach, Socrates allowed himself to be seduced all of a sudden, like a stranger, by the spirit of the place.[2] He was drugged, he said to his companion Phaedrus. Drugged by nature, all of a sudden. No doubt it was this subtle drug that inspired him to a discourse on love, a subject that Phaedrus wanted to debate that day. And the discourse went well; so well that Socrates was astonished by it, by this emotion that animated him to something supernatural, which was not his ordinary style. There he was, talking about excessiveness, saying nothing bad about it, even though it is the preeminent fault . . . Yes, the supernatural must have been present at this meeting. Socrates went into raptures and then suddenly stopped short. Not another word. The daemon:

> At the moment when I was about to cross the river, dear friend, there came to me my familiar divine sign—which always checks me when on the point of doing something or other—and all at once I seemed to hear a voice, forbidding me to leave the spot until I had made atonement for some offense to heaven.[3]

An offense, but what offense? Yes, Socrates was offending, doubly so. He dared to speak of love without saying that love was of divine origin. That was the first offense. And he was able to commit it with such lack of concern because he had let himself get carried away by a danger that he knew well and had often fought against: rhetoric, that seductive rhetoric that chats away all by itself, that talks without saying anything and poetizes in order to scorn philosophy. Socrates allowed himself to be stirred by these words, and that was the second fault: he forgot the divine part of it. There was only one way to put himself in accord with the daemon's strange signal: start again with a new discourse, cancel out the first one, and speak about love again, in the shadow of the plane tree, philosophizing it. The conspiratorial obliteration of the first discourse by the second is called a palinode; it is no longer quite noon; the sun is already shining a little less brightly. Philosophy regains its rights.

But the dubious inspiration of the stream and the nymphs it shelters is not far off. So Socrates opens his palinode, his second discourse, with the art of delirium, as is only right. And prudently doing justice to the prophetesses of Greece, the priestesses of Delphi, of Dodona, who can only be useful to Greece through their delirium, "whereas when they are completely rational, they can do little or nothing at all." One has to be "honestly possessed, honestly delirious," or not at all. Then, having paid his dues to the thing that disturbs him more than anything, Socrates can at last do some philosophy, and give a discourse on love that culminates in a description of love at first sight.

The soul is in the form of a two-horse carriage, driven by a coachman. The first horse, "white, with black eyes," obeys the coachman; the other—ah, the other horse!—"crooked of frame," with a snub nose, gray, with bloodshot eyes, it rarely obeys. All the unhappiness of desire is the result of the imbalance between the first horse and the second. When the soul sees the object of its love and is suddenly completely aroused, it is the second horse—the syncope-horse—that runs the risk of overturning the carriage. One has to keep an eye on that one; it mustn't upset love. The coachman throws himself backward to pull harder on the bit; he makes the impudent tongue of the snub-nosed horse bleed, he makes it drop its hindquarters to the ground; he "deliver[s] him over to anguish."[4] Then the rotten beast gives up its excessiveness; the syncope-horse is broken in. It becomes so well disciplined that the coachman will be able to make it undergo the test of love held in check (counterlove); when the lover is lying by his beloved's side, he resists the snub-nosed horse, and does not proceed to the act.[5] Careful reserve; love held in check, suspension of desire . . . We will find the great proof of suspended desire in other times, in other places: in European courtly love as well as in the erudite ascetic practices of India. It is a matter of control, a return to a wise dialectic. Delirium and the daemon leave that place. The sun is already getting lower, and Socrates, having got under control as best he could the danger and the charm of nature, which is foreign to him, can leave, finally, and go back to the city.

But not yet. It is important to pray to the god who is hidden there; does one ever know?[6]

For in the end, if Socrates allowed himself to be seduced by the poetic dithyramb, if he succumbed to the enchantment of the place, it is because there really was magic there! And so strong was it that it would not have taken much more for Socrates to go away suddenly, leaving his companion in the lurch and crossing back over the river right away . . . That imprudent friend, suspected of having delivered Socrates to the nymphs "with premeditation," only obtained a respite thanks to the midday heat; for truly, "time is leaden." When Socrates had settled his accounts with eloquence, rhetoric, and his friend Phaedrus, there was still one piece of business to put in order. The gods are susceptible and the daemon is watchful, so one must make a little prayer to the spirit of the place. And this god, who had not been named until then, is now worshiped: it is Pan. Pan whom Victor Hugo, thousands of years later in the midst of the Romantic period, made mankind's divinity, the badly brought-up faun who made eyes at Venus on Olympus, the red-furred satyr who, excessive, suddenly fills up all the space and brings Jupiter to his knees. Pan, that is to say, All:

> His hair was a forest; waves
> Rivers, lakes, streamed from his broad haunches
> . . . .
> He cried out: . . .
> Make way for the endless swarming of black skies,
> Of blue skies, of noon, dawn, evening!
> Make way for the holy atom, that burns or flows!
> . . . .
> Make way for Everything! I am Pan; on your knees, Jupiter!

Sartre would have detested it, and Socrates is wary.

The second time Socrates stopped was on the evening of his death. He had already been in prison for a long time. He was supposed to have died sooner, but the sacred boat that went each year to Delos to thank Apollo for having saved the young people of Athens, through Theseus's aid—this boat had just left, and the city could not be polluted with a capital punishment until it was back. So Socrates was imprisoned and chained. The boat returned; Socrates was untied.

He was told that he was to die. His disciples were there in full force, divided between grief and astonishment, for Socrates seemed happy. Moreover, from the very day he was imprisoned, he had indulged in a practice that was not habitual with him, and which he had even rejected. Socrates wrote poetry; he set to verse some of Aesop's fables and drafted a "Prelude to Apollo." The disciples could not believe it; but after all, since Socrates was just as approachable as usual, since he was visibly willing to hold his habitual dialogues, one of them asked him the question: Why, Socrates, why, after having attacked poets so strongly, are you writing poetry?[7]

The daemon. And it is not the first time that it has manifested itself like that. This time it is a dream; but all through Socrates' life it was a voice that had given him the same command: "Make music! Produce!" During his lifetime, Socrates tried to outfox the daemon, and extricated himself by regarding music as, all things considered, the highest philosophy. Since Socrates was a philosopher, he turned a deaf ear and ignored his daemon. But on the day before his death, it was appropriate to be more prudent: and what if disobeying the daemon was impious? And what if it was necessary—one never knows—to compose just this once, the last possible time, to make music? Socrates yielded and complied, before the city took charge.[8] Alone in prison, chained, he composed. At last.

For his whole life Socrates had been called by a poetry daemon, and did not obey. Holding firm against inspiration, he preferred philosophy and said so. Philosophy contradicts music, poetry, and even the Pythoness's delirium. It labels all those things "weakness." Those things are a collapse of the mind, suitable for weeping women whose funereal howls exasperated him in his prison to the point that he sent his wife, Xanthippe, out because she was screaming and hitting herself on the head. All of that, all of that was a reprehensible weakness in the philosopher's eyes. And to prepare himself for death in a dignified way, he started his final dialogue.

Then the sun sank lower; it was the hour of night; the hour also of the execution. Oh, his disciple Criton tried very hard to thwart it; after all, one could dawdle, one could delay taking the hemlock; some waited for the first beginnings of dawn, they lived it up one last time, made love with their lovers . . . [9] But Socrates was an honorable man; the night's celebrations must take place at the right time; when there is no more time, when one is ready to die, one drinks the hemlock. He drank, and became numb little by little. The cold reached his belly; he covered his head. Then suddenly he uncovered it for a last word, a last precaution. He had forgotten a rooster, an old debt to the god Asclepius. So, having settled his debts to the gods and his daemon, Socrates could finally leave the world.[10]

All his life he regretted not being a cicada. It was right in the middle of the dialogue with Phaedrus that Socrates told the story of the cicadas.[11] Once, there were some men who knew neither of the Muses (who were not yet born) nor of music. Then the Muses appeared, and with them the wonder of song. So the men started singing, with such joy that they forgot to eat and drink, and they died without noticing that they had. And thus were born, following the Muses, the cicadas, who do not eat but chirp from birth until death. The cicadas are former men who, by dint of singing, set themselves "outside themselves." Socrates is never outside himself, except when his daemon suspends philosophy, that ant, and stops it. Twice, at least. Time enough to chirp a bit and to write poems.

On a November night in 1619, Descartes discovered in a kind of sudden flash the intuition that was to support his whole philosophy: there was a basic agreement between natural laws and mathematics. It was the night of one's dreams, a night tremendously full of dreams. From that moment, Descartes became the most cautious of philosophers, as if he wanted both to recover the terrifying light of that nocturnal truth and to reconstruct it, but step by step, with a slow and gradual patience.

There is not a single one of his published texts that does not demonstrate prudence. Danger is everywhere: in the schools, in books, in rhetoric, in poetry, in theology, in philosophy—everywhere, he tells you. And in the war torn era when this paragon of modern-day philosophers lived, the wisest path was to construct his own truth, rejecting straight off those that had already been taught. The worst thing would be to fall into error: that would be the major lapse, a vertigo on the order of the unthinkable; anything rather than be mistaken. The remedy is in the first rule of the *Method*:

> to accept nothing as true which I clearly did not recognise to be so: that is to say, carefully to avoid precipitation and prejudice in judgments . . . [12]

Against the chiaroscuro of received truths, of revealed truths, the glory is in slowness. For eclipses of thought are as quick as lightning, and swiftness is their preferred speed. Our philosopher knows something about this, since he himself was originally illuminated. And yet this is the same gentleman who refuses to hurry:

> But like one who walks alone and in the twilight I resolved to go so slowly, and to use so much circumspection in all things, that if my advance was but very small, at least I guarded myself well from falling.[13]

Falling: an obsession. It leads him also to block his way with the shadows of some precepts of abstraction: dividing difficulty, going from the simple to the compound, and in order not to forget anything, recapitulating without a break. In short, cross-ruling thought; in a sense, surrounding it with wire netting and preventing it from escaping. The harmony dreamed in the middle of the night has such great importance that it deserves some prophylactic measures.

The first application of illumination and of its contradictory methodological consequences consists of a long wait. Descartes was twenty-three when he spent his famous night of the revelation of the "wonderful science." He waited patiently for maturity: not too old, not too young. Just right. Long years of slow trudging. The philosopher's first distrust is of youth: the same youth that Bataille saw as the characteristic of night. Descartes does not want this youthfulness of thought:

> As this enterprise appeared to be a very great one, I waited until I had attained an age so mature that I could not hope that at any later date I should be better fitted to execute my design.[14]

Not the prime of life, but maturity.

The second application is isolation—an isolation that, in the first *Metaphysical Meditation*, takes on resolutely delirious proportions. Certainly, this delirium is premeditated and controlled; still, it is a delirium, and it makes the Method look like an authentic paranoia in which the stakes are truth; menace rules, absolutely everywhere. Let us not speak of the prejudices dwelled on by other people; the philosopher is alone in his room, near the fire. But wait, this fire, this dressing gown, this body wrapped up in it, are they real, or are they just illusions such as madmen have? And what if the philosopher were dreaming? That could be; so the fire, the room, the gentleman himself will not be trusted. All that remains is that three and two make five. That is what resists all eclipses, "whether I am awake or asleep." Unless . . . what if by chance this good God, the idea of whom spontaneously came to me, what if he were tricking me too, and profoundly? To ward off the blow that the mind brings on itself with that hypothesis, the philosopher will imagine that in place of a god an evil genius has plotted everything. This great devil of thought destroys everything in his path:

> I shall consider myself as having no hands, no eyes, no flesh, no blood, nor any senses, yet falsely believing myself to possess all these things.[15]

Madness, is this last fabrication nothing but madness? Yes. But anyone who could now dupe the lonely person by the fire would have to be very smart. And since the process is difficult, the philosopher goes to bed, sure now that his slumber, however full of illusions, will not shake the certainty of his doubt.

The next day, as if he had fallen into "very deep water," he invented the formulation of the *cogito*. This hypothetical evil genius,

> let him deceive me as much as he will, he can never cause me to be nothing as long as I think that I am something. So that after having reflected well and carefully examined all things, we must come to the definite conclusion that this proposition: I am, I exist, is necessarily true each time that I pronounce it, or that I mentally conceive it.[16]

That was the important step. The first certainty was gained at the expense of a *total eclipse of the world*, in a nighttime darkness no longer inhabited by anyone. It is the opposite of syncope: everything is eclipsed, except for the subject who remains, the only fixed and sure point. At least I am, I exist. What then?

Then things get more complicated, from the moment when I have to regain the real. Start with this "I" that I affirm, and of which I know nothing with any certainty. Let us not speak of the exterior world: as soon as I glance out of the window, the delirium of doubt can begin again. There are some men passing in the street;[17] no—those are coats and hats, that's all, and who is to say that they are not phantoms, or automatons? Things are not so simple. The philosopher has succeeded in a marvelous operation: the subject has eclipsed the world. But certainty is so fragile that it turns into an extended syncope.

The world, however, must not stay absent forever. On the contrary, if the philosopher takes his time, it is the better to think about it, slowly, patiently. But the operation of the *cogito* is so cut off from the real, so strained that Descartes temporarily appears to run away from it. That is what Bataille says:

> Descartes' small affirmation is the most subtle of escapes. . . . I am in anguish and I think; thought in me *suspends* anguish; I am the being gifted with the power to *suspend* within him being itself. Existence is put off until later.[18]

Existence will not take long to come back; nor will God, who upholds the affirmation of the *cogito*, and guarantees it by the continuity of a permanent creation. Anguish—but was it really anguish?—gives way before this body that is definitely mine, this fire that warms and these flames that burn, and this world "for real," as children say. For it is like a children's game: one can play at not living, one can play hide-and-seek with the real, until fatigue (of which Descartes often speaks) is the end result of this extreme tension. The game, suspended, will only have lasted an evening or two, the time of the eclipse. Bataille's undertaking, and inner experience, move on the contrary at top speed: "Inner experience is the denunciation of the truce; it is *being without delay*."[19]

Negotiating delays: that is what Socrates does, that is what Descartes fiercely adheres to. One could say that they know the threat of the raptus, and the fragility of all systems: that is what paranoiac delirium does, when it builds an impregnable fortress of suspicions around itself. The Other is a threat. Descartes pushes philosophical suspicion as far as it can go. One could also say that philosophical thought's only success is knowing how to delay. To delay itself. But in doing this, it traps itself, and brings itself to a standstill, entranced by its own gesture. I am, I exist, and then what?

Then the impure, the motley, the out-of-tune regain ground. In vain I divide up into as many parcels as seems appropriate, count and re-count and dis-count the links of Reason, looking for the simple; I will still bump up against the passions, the fires of love, anger, spirited impulses, against everything that I hate for its speed, and that will always escape me. For example, when it is a question of mankind, I imagine, not to be mistaken, that in the beginning God formed a human body without a reasoning soul or a vegetating soul. But in my heart I have to admit something. An excitement, "one of these fires without light," which I can only imagine as "that which makes the hay heat when shut up before it is dry, and which makes new wine grow frothy when it is left to ferment over the fruit."[20] I really have to surrender to the mysterious fermentation. These overheatings are found everywhere as soon as Descartes discusses the body! And the care he takes to find simple causes for emotions that—one never knows—could become uncontrollable. . . . "What is called a 'sardonic' laugh is nothing other than a convulsion of the facial nerves."[21] The sigh, in turn, can come from the passion of sadness or of desire, but it can also come from reassuring habit or, *melio encor*, from a full stomach. It is not a trifling business; on the whole, the process of the *cogito* is easier to master.

November 1646. Descartes writes to his beloved princess, Elisabeth of Bohemia, the aging philosopher's sensible and amenable pupil. Is it to comfort her in her many problems? Our man is in the grip of strange thoughts: "I dare to believe that inner joy has some secret power for making fate more favorable." If it weren't a question of a philosopher/noblewoman, Descartes would not take such a risk. "However, I have an infinity of experiences, and also Socrates' authority, to confirm my opinion. My experience has been that I have often noticed that things I have done with a glad heart, without any internal reluctance, usually turn out well, just as in games of chance, in which fate alone rules, I have often felt it to be favorable." Games of chance, indeed!? Heavens! We must be dreaming. But we are not dreaming; witness the following: "And that which is commonly called *Socrates' genius* was undoubtedly something else, probably that he was used to following his *inner inclinations*, and believed that what he was undertaking would turn out well if he had some feeling of happiness, and, on the contrary, would turn out badly if he were sad."[22]

Farewell to Method, farewell to prudence . . . Long live inspiration, inner inclination, and the hay of metaphysical suspicions. The evil genius of the *Metaphysical Meditations* is transformed into a benevolent genius, a little inner daemon, gay or sad, which one does well to listen to. So! Descartes could also love Being without delay, and could play games of chance.

In his youth, he was so sickly that he was allowed to get up at whatever time he wanted to; so he got into the habit of meditating for a long time in bed. Meditating, or dreaming? No doubt it was a mental safety valve.

Christine of Sweden, the far-off queen of the cold countries that so terrified Descartes, had him come to her to be her master of thought. She took her lessons at five in the morning; that is what queens are like.

He no longer had his meditative dawns to himself. It was said that he took cold. He died of it.[23]

Kant tirelessly classified and divided. If there was ever a philosopher who knew how to give the term "criticism" its original meaning—that of discrimination—he was that man, who wanted obstinately to protect Reason against all the dangers that threatened it: the illusions of metaphysics, the exaggerations of fanaticism, and the confusion of genres. And as far as the bacchante's awakening is concerned, none gazed more steadfastly at the daylight than this enlightened philosopher.

The battle against metaphysics produced the first two great "critiques," *The Critique of Pure Reason* and *The Critique of Practical Reason*. Reason must not be "mixed up"; it must be distinguished from sensibility on one hand and from understanding on the other, and both must be integrated in one work of knowledge, related and limited. Reason, if isolated, could fill a whole work by itself, that would deal with the workings of the Infinite, produce the idea of moral law, of the greatest good, of the ideal city, and of the abstract God who governs it all. On one hand, Kant describes mankind's ability to decipher the world and nature; on the other, he makes of him the only being capable of constructing a new moral and ideal world. But in any case, mankind has to be torn away from nature: whether he understands it or diverts it, he separates himself from it, and that is his philosophical privilege.

At the end of *The Critique of Practical Reason*, everything is as clear as the day that makes the head of the bacchante's son visible in her hands. Two key words are engraved in the mind: "the starry sky above my head and the moral law within me." The starry sky is the knowable; the moral law, that is the infinite that Reason lays down in an unquestionable gesture.

Between me and the sky, however, things become newly complicated. For I can look at the starry sky with a connoisseur's eye, and

> then [conceive of] the bright dots that we see occupying the space above us as being these worlds' suns, moved in orbits prescribed for them with great purposiveness.[24]

But the philosopher knows quite well that that is not how one feels the contemplation of stars at night. Between the sky and the moral law, there is a bulky obstruction: the body, that instigator of disruption. The passions, the affections, and the raptus. Kant pays even more attention to them because he pursues fanaticism with a legitimate philosophical hatred; he is even more demanding of his own thought because he understands the function of the aesthetic, and because that too has to be classified. That is the goal of *The Critique of Judgment*, which he says is the completion of all his critical work. It has to be done quickly:

> I shall proceed without delay to the doctrinal [enterprise], in order to snatch from my advancing years what time may yet be favorable to the task.[25]

Doctrine, then, and classification. *Three powers of the soul*: the power of cognition; the feeling of pleasure and displeasure; the power of desire. *Three powers devolving on the understanding*: understanding; judgment, which concentrates on pleasure and displeasure; and reason, which takes charge of desire and turns toward the highest good. *Three principles*: conformity to the law, which is the rule for understanding and science; finality, which is the rule for aesthetic judgment; and the final purpose, a mysterious entity that regulates the activities of reason. Finally, *three spheres of application*: for the power of cognition and understanding, Nature; for judgment, pleasure, and displeasure, Art; for desire and reason, Freedom. Everything is in place.[26]

Now into the picture comes a feeling whose characteristic is disruption. It is the sublime, which does not let itself be so easily classified. What is it? As usual with Kant, that depends. If it is connected with mathematics, it has to do with that which is completely large, in comparison with which everything else seems small; Pascal's reflections on the two infinities would be on the order of the mathematical sublime. Even though . . . Does one ever know? The other sublime, the "dynamic," aroused by the imagination, could also join in the game. And this game is strangely ambivalent.

Beauty is unambiguous: it pleases, calmly. The *sublime*, on the other hand, is not calm; it is agitation. And this emotion is a vibration: "that is to say," says Kant, "with a rapid alternation of repulsion from, and attraction to, one and the same object."[27] Horror and seduction; fear and attraction. Rather, the emotion is so strong that it *stops* something in man.

Let us look at this text, which talks of a syncope already mastered:

> But the other liking (the feeling of the sublime) is a pleasure that arises only indirectly: it is produced by the feeling of a momentary inhibition of the vital forces followed immediately by an outpouring of them that is all the stronger. Hence it is an emotion, and so it seems to be seriousness, rather than play, in the imagination's activity. Hence, too, this liking is incompatible with charms, and, since the mind is not yet attracted by the object but is alternately always repelled as well, the liking for the sublime contains not so much a positive pleasure as rather admiration and respect, and so should be called a negative pleasure.[28]

In a few words, Leibniz said: "Comfort eats away at us." But our philosopher, Kant, wants to arrive at two very precise things. The first is that there exists in sensibility (of which he is extremely wary) a sensation that seems to suspend life; it could therefore be very useful to a philosopher who wants to tear mankind away from Nature. The second is that the sublime is a feeling of displeasure that after a momentary suspension turns into a delighted effusion. That is the "sacred thrill," he says, that takes hold of you in front of a mass of shapeless and chaotic mountains, or unleashed waters, or shadowy forests, or the stormy ocean,

> a clear mirror of the water bounded only by the sky; or, if it is turbulent, as being like an abyss threatening to engulf everything.[29]

For the first moment, the senses fall back, appalled: "suspension." Then something prevails over the displeasure and turns it into rapture. The first motion is one of powerlessness; the second, the inrush of a faculty of the soul that is capable of resisting the senses.

The delightful shiver that runs up your spine before the spectacle of Nature's menace comes from the *transcending of the senses*. This displeasure is overcome in order to hold one's own, properly speaking; it is a glorious transcending of your spontaneous fright. You delight in saying "yes" to fear at first and then "no"; only the "no" will be that of the philosopher. It is not a "no" to Nature, or a "no" to Reason; it is a resolute "no" to feeling.

The last corrections that Kant made to *The Critique of Judgment* date from 1799. In 1797, he drafted the letter-program of the "first romanticism," *The Athenaeum*. The spectacles that the sublime mastered in Kant's philosophy were to overflow Reason and its cautiousness and sweep it all away with *Sturm und Drang*.

We are not yet there. In a while, and since it is art that breaks down the compost of pleasure, our philosopher is going to grapple with music.

As he says perplexedly, music is "more a matter of enjoyment than of culture";[30] he prefers—of course—poetry, which strengthens the mind; it does everything to please, but has a "wealth of thought"; nothing better could be dreamed of. But music! That is something that disturbs the soul.

At the forefront of all the dangers that lead to fanaticism is enthusiasm. It appears innocent; but alas, it is seriously affected. Affected, simply; affected in every sense. Now, affection is always blind; it never satisfies the demands of Reason; it prevents freedom of expression. Only one affection escapes the misdeeds of this daemon of wildness: *apathy*, whose name means the absence of *pathos*, that is to say, in Greek, the absence of affection. Only of apathy will Kant say that it is a "noble" emotion, which allows the mind to pursue its "unchanging principles": apathy, you understand, does not get excited, and is the philosophical emotion par excellence. Everything else is not noble, or, to put it differently, ignoble.

Let us talk, then, of music. If it has "less value than any other of the fine arts," if its repetition bores, if its work is nothing but a "purely mechanical association," if it plays only on the feelings, if mathematics definitely has no part in it, if indeed it holds the "lowest place" in the classification of the fine arts as far as culture goes[31]—if, in short, Kant does not like it—it is because it approaches the ignoble; it is because it agitates, it is because it goes into raptures and provokes. Uncontrollable. Now, that is itself the unthinkable.

All the same, the philosopher concedes that, if one were to classify it in terms of pleasure, music could—perhaps—be of the first rank; one never knows. But Kant wants nothing to do with an art that pleases, simply and without explanation. There has to be Reason somewhere, and it is hardly to be found in music.

So to say his final word on *pathos*, he invents, in an astonishing "Comment," another classification;[32] by classifying one already has the illusion of mastery. It is a classification of games. Indeed, Kant knows that "any changing free play of association . . . gratifies us." And as he knows at least "that," it is in the classification of games that one finds music, debased but in familiar territory.

There are three (of course three) types of games. The *play (or game) of chance*, which is only of interest in its purest form, under the pretext of profit or vanity; the *play of tones*—music; and the *play of thought (or of wit)*, which produces laughter.

These three games have in common that they belong to what Kant neatly calls "our evening parties"; and I guarantee that the same music that makes his flesh crawl is the one that makes people dance. Now, that annoys him, but the philosopher is obliged to note that no society can do without games. The verdict is resigned: "There is no beauty," he says. And to music and laughter together he links amusing movement games, which ensure good health thanks to "an intestinal agitation."

Here he is, set on the intestines. Shaking of the diaphragm, vibration of the internal organs, alternating tension and relief running from belly to lungs . . . he will spare nothing to ensure that music and laughter have the most physiological of explanations. He goes as far as bringing up tickling, a model of little shivers of pleasure. And finds, for all those excesses of irrational emotions, a reassuring salutary goal. Laugh, tickle yourself, or make music: it is good for your health. For all that counts is

> an agitation that is good for the health. It is this agitation alone, and not what goes on in the mind, that is the actual cause of our gratification in a thought [by] which [we] basically present nothing.[33]

There we are. The agitation of the intestines, of the diaphragm, and the lungs certainly does not take place in the mind. The pleasure it produces depends on a peculiar kind of thought that represents nothing. Now, if it represents nothing, it has no importance. How could a gratuitous thought exist, like that, for the sake of laughing? All of this vast edifice must exist for something—even if it is a matter, as for Beauty, of a finality without end, a project without a object and of a goal without content.

Thought, for Kant, has hardly any breathing room; it finds some with great difficulty in the triple parlor game: the game of chance, music, and laughter. Kant evidently thinks nothing good of games of chance; *he* will not let himself be tempted by the daemon of Socrates and Descartes. Of music, it would be preferable to say he thinks nothing; but it must be recognized that he sees it as an amusing and sanitary art, not, as Claude Lévi-Strauss says today, the "supreme mystery of the science of man."[34]

That leaves laughter and the sublime. Kant gives quite a good description of the mechanism of laughter: "Laughter is an affect that rises if a tense expectation is transformed into nothing."[35] There is really nothing there to involve the understanding, but this lively rejoicing, like the sublime, *comes indirectly from an equilibrium of the vital forces*.

Anticipation, dread, horror: these are the first sensations of the sublime and of laughter. Then nothing, syncope, a brusque halt, in laughter just as in the sublime. Finally, this draws to a close: in the sublime, through the pleasure of powerlessness recognized; in laughter, through the annihilation of anticipation. Going a little further, we could join the two ends, and laugh before the ocean, the mountain, or the clouds; we could laugh and sublimate everything together, in front of a lake at noon, as Nietzsche was to do.

Kant does not take this step. It is already enough if he will allow to pass, by detouring through a scrupulous and honorable analysis of the feelings and the arts, a little syncope in the sublime and a lot in laughter. For we must make the best of the intestines and the tickling, find pleasure a place in the sun without allowing it to be engulfed in the night. But great care is taken not to let it spill over. We will not let it out as it likes; we will go out into society, at least to give the illusion of well-being. For ourselves alone, on the other hand, we keep as a rule one of the definitions of the sublime: "*Sublime* is what, by its resistance to the interest of the senses, we like directly."[36]

We keep our reason; we face up to the little shudders and the large syncopes. We keep our heads; and so—in spite of music and affected intestines—we keep cool.

The Last Drop

When a woman washes her hair, if it is long, when a laundress washes linen by hand, both of them, when they are done, twist the braid, the sheet, to get the water out. That is called wringing; to expel the last drops more thoroughly, the damp mass that has to be dried is twisted in the other direction. Sometimes, one slaps it as well; look at the long lines of washerwomen beating the washing furiously on the banks of Indian rivers. Systems of thought are similar: one could say that they make use of all the twistings of the mind to expel something from it. But what? What is this water that has to be got out? Desire, impulse, tremor, spasm, affect—which dampness disturbs the philosopher? What dryness is he aspiring to?

To observe philosophical systems, starting, as I have tried to do, with the last drop, with superstition, nonsense, weakness of thought, is to put oneself deliberately (as Hegel said about great men) in the position of a valet, for whom the master is always petty. This gaze of the chambermaid, with its erotic inquisitivenesses, its taste for keyholes, and its shady chuckles, actually says a lot about the philosophers' shortcomings; it is not a question of contradicting their underlying attitudes, nor of unveiling the social unconscious at work in their ideologies. But one sees them in their dressing gowns: Socrates with his daemon, Descartes with his taste for gambling (which is mixed with the superstition about luck that characterizes the true gambler), Kant buried in music's intestines. It is through keyholes that one can see other people's love affairs: that is the primal scene, with the child thunderstruck by its own parents' naked embrace. This gaze, the tiniest bit perverse, half-child / half-witch, is the one that Freud assigned to the drive for knowing: to know, but first to know where it is going, that last drop of pleasure thanks to which one is born into the world.

These philosophers want, then, to express the last drop of fear. The great mortal and banal fear that surrounds the fate of the body after death. In India, where the corpse is burned, the fear of death is no less than elsewhere, but all the activity of Hindu thought, from the simplest rite to the most sophisticated metaphysics, consists, as we shall see, in an eternal combustion. The subject is in difficulty and has a hard time burning spontaneously, so it has to be forced to an intellectual combustion. In our country, we bury the dead; the imagination weaves and reweaves interminable *danses macabres* on decomposition and its funereal worms. Philosophers, like everyone else, want to protect thought against decomposition; but unlike everyone else, one could say they are afflicted in this matter with an odd phobia, age-old in European history.

Death, if it is to be mastered, must be tied and retied. Tie the soul and the body: a stubborn connection persists across the centuries, including the centuries in which atheism exists. The soul and the body: first the philosopher wants to demonstrate their union, the better later to unfasten the soul from its body, and thus to preserve it from corruption, that moldiness so appalling to the mind. Whatever the metaphysical solution, it will always attempt to neutralize the brutal halt. If one can succeed in demonstrating that there is no halt between life and death, the desired connection and disconnection will have been secured. The characteristic of Western philosophers up to the Romantic period is the desire to dry up the subject at the same time as the soul. It is kept in the house, dry, deprived of the dampness of nature. In India, as we shall see, the subject is all burned up, charred; there is nothing left.

With us, every disconnection, every rupture that would take consciousness by surprise would threaten the idea of the subject. The soul and the body are kept together. Beyond this union floats another, wider union; that of the city, then of the nation, the souls of the collective; and just as the union of an immortal soul and a corruptible body preserves the subject from physical decomposition and assures its permanence, so this confused union, the city, protects the image of the social body from its political decomposition and its moral corruption. Fanaticism is a dampness of the feelings that governments use to corrupt the collective heart. Music and joking, duly kept in the background, touch the disagreeable sphere of the intestines, elastic and sticky. Descartes dreads the humors; Plato distrusts Nature; Socrates is frankly allergic to it, suddenly afflicted with unforeseen poetic hives. And when finally Plato, Descartes, and Kant admit that one has to pay one's share to weakness and stop the thought processes in midmotion, it is done begrudgingly; it is for health's sake, it is to breathe a little, it is because of distrust of the gods. This salutary repose for the being is not without ulterior motives.

This mastery demands incredible efforts of philosophy, and an exhausting expenditure of energy. Connecting thought, keeping it tied up, preventing it from escaping is a difficult enterprise. However tight the tie, thought escapes, flees . . . In vain one wrings out the system, there will still be, as in the damp hair or the washerwoman's sheet, always a last possible drop of water, a living dampness that will not leave except of its own accord, or because of the wind or the sun. There will still be the sleep of reason, from which, we know, monsters emerge; there will still be love, that uncontrollable inflammation, and the snub-nosed horse that rears up. Syncope is not easily expressed; there is even some danger in the operation. But patience: we have hardly begun to wring out the linen.

3

Depriving the City of Spices: Plato Purges the Republic

One day a stranger met a young man.[1] He told him a story, one of those symbolic stories in which thought lets itself move toward a touch of wildness, yet still maneuvers a secret logic that never loses its rights.

At that time, old people didn't age anymore. When they had reached a certain threshold, their hair changed from white to dark; their hard beards softened and turned downy like children's again, and then disappeared entirely. Adolescents grew shorter and even younger. And if one died—there was no other way to die than by violent accident—the corpse itself disappeared from the earth within a few days. Then suddenly, without warning, the movement reversed itself. The dead came out of the earth at the same spot where the bodies had disappeared, and since they had become children again, they reappeared as infants. They were and still are called the "Children of Earth."[2]

It was a pendulum that caused this forgotten era: the pendulum of the world, which organizes the contrary cycles, first in one direction—from aging to youth—and then in the other—from birth to aging. It is a twisting pendulum, which rotates first to one side and then to the other, eternally, held by the invisible hand of a kind of god.[3]

This deity hardly stirs. That is its privilege. Among all beings, it fell to the lot of this one to have "the least possible variation of its proper motion." A fulcrum, in other words, a fixed point, an important obsession in philosophy to which Descartes would later succumb when he was searching for the lever that would allow him to raise up the whole universe.

It cannot be said, however, that this generative god does not move at all. No: it moves, in fact, but "its movement is uniform, invariable, and in one place." Nor can it be positively asserted that this deity is completely divine, for even if its movement is only slight, still it pivots, and this minuscule shudder reduces this god to a bodily nature. Complete immobility is an attribute of the highest gods, the true gods; beings that remain ever the same, without movement. But without movement there is no world, and it is the world that the dialogue called *The Statesman* undertakes to explain.

This same principle stirs the dervishes and the waltzers: turning, but with the illusion of a uniform movement in one place; turning, but in such a way that the world is not affected; preserving both the immobile and the mobile, the stable and the unstable, even the impossible. Thus is achieved the disappearance of the too-real world in which children grow old. The stranger's myth is about immortality itself.

But in this game one can fall, and one's body, unbalanced and overcome by vertigo, may swerve from its own orbit, to one side or the other. Something like this happened to the dervish deity, who suddenly stopped directing the whirlwind of things after the world had turned thousands of times. The demigod retired, says Plato, "to his conning tower in a place apart."[4] And he waited. Immediately, the world started to drift into a tremendous noisy riotous agitation; left to its own course, the world needed time to find its rhythm again. The state that comes after vertigo, this return from the syncope, compelled the world to rediscover by itself the slow progression of history. And we are still positioned in this same progression, from infancy to old age.

The god suddenly releases the spindle that controls the revolutions, and retreats. The world falls. There is syncope in cosmology: to dream of the gods is also to raise one's eyes to the clouds in a high wind, and see them fleeing as quickly as the earth turns. Think of that wonderful moment in *War and Peace*: Tolstoy shows us his melancholy hero, Prince Andrei, taken by surprise and mortally wounded on the battlefield. Without any transition he is there, stretched out, almost nonexistent, strangely weightless, and overcome with joy. Look at the whole sky turning slowly, the ground giving way deliciously, the unconscious body . . . The unreasoned happiness that fills a man in this meditative moment is the first sign of a deathly detachment. Dreaming of the gods gives rise to a vertigo that Plato, in *The Statesman*, transforms into a mythic theory.

Yet myths can be poisonous! Look at how energetically Socrates hunts them down; yes, this same Socrates, whose mouth is florid with legends and stories, pitilessly finds fault with them when it comes to training the Guardians of the ideal city, or the poets and the musicians.[5] What is good for an old man (since a man close to death pays more attention to what lies beyond him) is bad for a child. Oh, we know that myth carries symbols within it; that is why it is useful. But youth is not capable of this discernment. When his follower Adimantus insists naively that certain fictions can be an aid to virtue, Socrates' dry response admits of no reply: "Adimantus, we are not poets, you and I, at present, but founders of the State."[6] The door to censorship is open wide, and censorship makes a bold beginning.

First of all, Homer, that greatest of all poets, has to be mutilated. Homer in particular, who recites all kinds of nonsense about death: souls disappear underground with a little scream, the realm of Hades, god of the dead, is a putrescent place that chills even the gods with fear . . . in short, "all other terms of this type, whose very names send a shudder through all the hearers"[7] must be struck from the corpus. Poetic excess is incompatible with the city's stability: wailing and lamentation are just as dangerous as the depiction of irrepressible laughter. Do poets love to describe the "inextinguishable laughter" of the gods?[8] Well, then they must be kept out. Danger. If the poet is allowed into the city, he will be under surveillance. The list of topics he will not be allowed to treat is, in essence, a catalogue of excessive syncopes.

When it comes to women, take care. The poet will not have the right to describe woman in all her phases: not in anger, nor in great happiness—"loudly boasting, fortunate in her own conceit"[9]—nor miserable and weeping with sorrow, nor sick, nor in love, nor in the act of giving birth. Then come the slaves, the wretched, and the delirious; but also the blacksmith, because he strikes, the oarsman when he gives a stroke to the trireme, the man who spurs on the cohort of oarsmen, and even the neighing horse, the bellowing bull, the lapping of the river, the noise of the breaking wave, and finally the thunder . . . The lesson is obvious: excess—that is, the breaking of the rhythm—must be forbidden. In fact, that is the only point that the wave and the woman, the thunder and the wretch, the bull and the delirious man have in common: the scream, the momentum, the fracture, the breach. And if by some chance a poet appears who is talented enough to describe all these forbidden phenomena, "we should fall down and worship him as a holy and wondrous and delightful creature, but should say to him that there is no man of that kind among us in our city, nor is it lawful for such a man to arise among us, and we should send him away to another city, after pouring myrrh down over his head and crowning him with fillets of wool."[10]

The poet is not killed, nor hunted; for—one never knows—the daemon of inspiration that Socrates yielded to twice before still haunts his philosophy, and does not let go of his consciousness. But the poet is a carrier of the potential for delirium, and by neutralizing this, one is purged; one immunizes oneself. Then the process is repeated for music. Soft harmonies are dismissed, the ones that are "suitable for banquets" and incite drunkenness: these are the Ionian mode and some of the Lydian modes that are—with good reason—called "lax." Then the satyr Marsyas's instruments are driven away, Marsyas who dared to compete with Apollo and was flayed alive for this crime: therefore, no harps or flutes. All that is left are the wise lyre, the cithara, and for the shepherds who look after the flocks, a "little piccolo." Thank you for those. Socrates also expels excessive love, and regulates the quality of the kiss a lover can give his beloved; then—a terrorist because he is not more than a philosopher—he *forbids spices to the gymnast.* Here, like a watermark, the dangerous *pungency* of the syncope shows through:[11] the piquancy of sudden attachments, the contrast of ecstasy, the sweet and sour, the spices of the heart.

"And by the dog," he concludes, "we have all unawares purged the city which a little while ago we said was luxurious."[12]

All unawares? By the dog! This is the philosopher going into action, breathing deeply, with a calmness that I would not dare call supreme for fear of offending Bataille's memory, with that victorious aura of repression that is called wisdom. In it appears the hatred of anything wild in all its forms: let wildness be expressed through the screams of women in labor, let it appear in the stark features of the slave who does not even resemble a man, let it be read in the anger of the wretch or in the rage of the delirious, let it be heard in the blast of the blacksmith's forge or the sung rhythm pushing the trireme forward on a sea that is bearable when the waves are steady but unbearable when the waves crash down heavily, let wildness burst out in the neighing of the horse, the bellowing of the bull, or the thunder—that is the essence of unruliness. Wildness is the Nature that is so foreign to Socrates, the city-dweller. Wildness, the frenzy of a kiss that is too passionate; wildness, or love. In *The Republic*, Plato reveals through Socrates that he too fears syncope: the syncope in Nature. The philosopher, whose calling is to educate, seems born to set this straight.

Later he defines the qualities of a true philosopher: a true philosopher is not one of those sophists who arouse the crowd's shudders and applause; that is just a din. The true philosopher, on the contrary, loves a reality that "is not wandering between the two poles of generation and decay."[13]

Generation, decay. The two connect across the taboos. Looking at or touching what happens to a body after death provokes horror and nausea. But the prohibition against cadavers is not isolated, it relates to generation: the place where excrement is expelled is close to the place where the child is expelled, "*inter faeces et urinas*," between excrement and urine. Excrement itself is close to the putrefying cadaver, and to fermentation, which Descartes acknowledges only reluctantly:[14] the fermentation of eggs, of grubs, of seeds, of the worm or the grape, that turns the stomach with disgust.

"One day this living world will swarm in my mouth," said Bataille on the other hand, and then: "We have a shameful attitude toward the life of corruption, and the death that brings us back to it is no less revolting than birth."[15]

Then there is the smell of death. Immediately recognizable, immediately stinking. The uncontrollable smell. Think of the stench of boiled turnip that the epileptic gives off before the crisis, as if a man struck by the sacred disease suddenly became the object of a deadly ploy (*mortelle cuisine*), oddly instantaneous; one could say that the attack transforms him into a witches' caldron. And if it is not the smell of death, it is a stench that anticipates it, repulsive, enough to make one flee. When we get to the mystics, saints from all over the world, we shall see that their final miracle consists in transforming the stink of their dead bodies into the smell of roses. It is so strong, this passion for God, that it can transform corruption into its opposite. The corpse of a saint gives out a fragrance; it is a spontaneous embalming. But if one is not a saint or a mystic or an Indian, if one is only Greek or European, one is terribly afraid.

We are afraid of corruption in all its forms; we are also afraid of generation. A woman in labor or a putrefying corpse, there is an oscillation between these things: this shudders, this ferments, too naturally. The philosopher, on the contrary, tries his hand at not oscillating in order to face *the great crossing* without dread. The great crossing has to do with birth as well as death, and reduces the threat of generation and decay. But to do that, it has to reduce the piquancy of life, the spice of thought, and it drives out anything that resembles syncope. According to Plato, the philosopher is a "well-ordered being" who has driven out all discord, all *pathos*; he resembles the widow in India, who has no more right to jewelry, parties, her hair (which she has to shave off), or brightly colored clothes—and who is never again allowed to eat salt and spices.[16]

To demonstrate the immortality of the soul, no proof is satisfying. In *The Republic* as well as in the *Phaedo* Socrates continually finds new forms. It is like the story of the caldron. A man cannot find his old caldron, and suspects his neighbor of having taken it. But the fellow defends himself; first of all, the caldron is old and worn-out; then it is not true, he did not take the caldron. And then finally, well, he was just borrowing it . . .

First the caldron was old and worn-out; it is the same with our bodies, that wear out during our lives while our souls do not. Then the caldron was only borrowed, just a loan: it is the same with our bodies, which the soul borrows, life after life, remembering this later. Finally, we are told, we never had a caldron; our bodies do not belong to us, for only our souls belong to us, and will go on traveling after death in the infernal world, where there is the principle of the twisting pendulum.

The goddess Necessity sits there; in her lap lies the spindle that orchestrates the world's turning. At her sides are the Fates, her daughters, who weave, spin, and cut the lives of men; but one can also see strange Sirens, perching on the ring of the spindle of the universe. Eight rings, eight Sirens; the function of each is to emit a single note, held indefinitely, an unchanging, drawn-out note, so that the eight of them form a "consonant" harmonious accord. This is the music of the spheres, and the image of the monstrous young woman who sings on a single note. In the underworld, in any case, the feminine principles are not those of commotion; the strange female divinities take the position of immobile purveyors of future lives. Mistresses of ceremonies, they set about the great game of chance where souls have to draw lots when it comes time to choose, from among a pack of lives spread out like playing cards, their next existence, as well as the personal daemon who accompanies them on earth to remind them of the infernal order if the souls forget, for example, to make poetry.[17]

When the souls have chosen their future lives, they undergo the crucial passage of forgetfulness. First the gods make them thirsty by making them cross the wide plain of Lethe, a scorching, parching desert; then the souls pitch camp along the Ameles River, whose name means "carefree," and whose water cannot be held, not even in cupped hands. One must drink this water—but definitely not too much. The water is a narcotic; it sends one to sleep. Then one is carried by an earthquake that pushes one, at the speed of a shooting star, toward birth—that disgrace.

This is the turning of the spindle, but the spindle is deep in the hollow of a goddess's lap. There is a single note, but also a chancy lottery. There is a thread that twines itself around the soul, but one has to drink the water of forgetfulness. The myth puts everything in its place: Necessity's lap, the lottery, the forgetfulness, and the earthquake change the unmoving balance and the circle of revolutions, just enough to provoke the little shudder of birth. Just enough for the soul later to be able to remember this infernal syncope from which it was born. And if above all one must not drink too much water, it is so that one can remember in the future.

That is what happened to the Armenian soldier, Er.[18] He was on the battlefield, apparently dead, and was carried onto the pyre to be burned; the moment the fire was lit, he woke up. He was then able to tell how he had just seen the underworld, all the better because the goddesses had prevented him from drinking a single drop of water from the Carefree river. He was able to tell the whole business. In Platonic thought, it is thanks to this soldier left for dead that mankind knew from then on that knowledge is never anything but remembrance. That generation and decay do not prevent the soul from being immortal. And besides, this lost caldron, the old caldron of the body, is of no importance whatsoever.

This very old story, told in *The Republic*, can still be put to use.

The West knows a lot today about the funeral rites of the past. The plague brought the *danses macabres*, and the grimacing smile of metaphysical skeletons; kings died in public, with great ceremony. Death was a significant and dignified event. Then the meaning of death became so indecent that people only spoke of it in whispers. Finally, no one spoke of it at all, unless as of an unexpected accident, a serious obscenity in these days when technology can do everything. Yes, it is true, in a time when wise men know the secrets of schizogenesis and cloning, how can one dare speak of death out loud? The West invents thin artifices, minor technology for preparing corpses, putting makeup on them, making them more suitable for the living to see. But the West hardly does any better than the ancient embalmers of Egypt.

The West adores youth, and drinks enough of the water of the Carefree river to forget death completely. At the moment when old age itself began to be hidden from the world, and because this wealthy society let its old people die in a corner like dogs, doctors and nurses recalled the myth of Plato's soldier. That is today.

For we can see this myth of reincarnation, this enigmatic sign, coming back in the West today, arising out of the technology of resuscitation. We know how to restore the almost dead, a little better than before. Enough to make them come back to themselves. Accident victims are more often brought back to life. When they wake up, they do not say, "Where am I?" but rather, "I did not want to come back!"[19] And they all recount an identical myth, of narrow tunnels followed by a dazzling light and great happiness. The frequency of these tales, their exact similarity, made the seed sprout, the seed that had been long buried underneath the stones of reasonable pyramids.

An acronym has been found for this new genre of resurrections, as is usual across the Atlantic where the myth arises more spontaneously than it does in Europe. They are called NDE: Near-Death Experiences. And let us remember that the first of them was Plato's hero, Er the Armenian, who was momentarily dead and came back to recall his experience from beyond the grave, or rather, from beyond the pyre.

Plato, or the fight against Darkness. The struggle is endless. The shadow of the daemon always threatens, as does the whole shadow of the gods, which demands caution and steadiness. If Socrates wisely prays to the god Pan, if he pays his dues to Asclepius, it is because one never knows. The evil side[20] of the gods can always attack a man, turn him into a tragic hero, an aborted god, a monster, inhuman in his lack of restraint and human in the suffering that overwhelms him and that he understands in darkness.

The same Greek word, *hubris*, indicates excess, pride, and the fermentation of wine. That is what pushes "the beastly and savage part" of the soul, gorged with food and drunk with liquor, to "gambol."[21] *Hubris* is alcohol, a bursting, absolute passion. The French word, *démesure* (excessiveness), does not convey enough of the muffled effervescence of the bunch of rotting grapes; perhaps the drunkard's getting plastered conveys the movement better. Plato hates all that, but he has little recourse against the powers of these syncopes: the deprivation of spices, the refusal of excessive rhythm, the slow disconnection of the soul from a transient body.

One must go slowly. The method, very restrained, that allows one to connect the mind and to disconnect the body is called dialectic. Syncope draws the soul toward turmoil; dialectic draws the soul toward a progressive calm. The philosopher knows very well, however, that the dialectic recourse is vulnerable, perhaps to the murmuring of a stream under a plane tree; he knows that words in a language have two uses. He knows that they can be used to inflame the heart to the point of syncope, or on the other hand they can be guides toward reserve, mastery, control.

The daemon will not let it go. That is understood. He will be given his due when it is time to die.

Stimmung; *or, Granting Trust to Chaos*

Mastering the oscillation between the "daemonic" and thought has had an unlucky history as a philosophical enterprise. Philosophers, those crusaders of time, have manufactured as many pieces of armor as systems. Hegel, for example, rediscovers the dialectic method and perfects it to an extreme, squeezing the oscillation as tightly as possible by using, instead of slowness, a mastered speed, as we shall see. Leibniz, on the other hand, leaves no place for death, no space at all, no hole through which it could be thought. Leibniz trains on mankind and the world a light so blinding that even death disappears in the extravagant jubilation of a metaphysical game from which absence is absent. And Hegel swallows everything, even the historical defeat of the Enlightenment, like a metaphysical whale who will not let Jonah out until he has been reunited with the god who threw him in the monster's mouth.

But between Leibniz in the eighteenth century and the nineteenth century when Hegel was thinking, a whole world collapsed. After the *Aufklärung*, after man had been exposed to the burning lights of Reason, after the philosophers who had so passionately battled against mysticism and its dark religious impulses, its *Schwärmerei*, had seen universal liberty produce the Terror in its turn, a whole generation of youth chose to abandon itself to chaos. The philosophical era of syncope began.

The Romantic avant-garde was very young and thought fast. A group of very young people, bound together by loves and rules, surrounded the beautiful heroines to whom they gravitated, star-women, whose liberation they, like all avant-gardes, would sing. Those people did not deprive themselves of the spices of the heart; they drank copiously of the tenderness of dead young women, of their sisters, their lovers, Caroline Schlegel, Bettina Brentano, Henriette Vogel with whom Kleist committed suicide; and they chose poetry and chaos together.[22]

Through poetry, the German Romantics pushed time headlong and breathed infinity. They searched passionately for syncope, in the dazzle of the sunset, in that of the snow on the top of lonely mountains, in unleashed tempests, in *Sturm und Drang*.

They did not settle, they traveled; they wrote fragments, scattered pieces, crystals of language, they looked for syncope in wit, the *Witz*, breaking up meaning and bursting into laughter.

They also searched in the widened illumination of the ecstasy of love and in the supernatural calm of the embrace. They preferred women and raised them to the level of inspirational goddesses; they chose the *pathos* of the breaking wave.

How well they understood Plato's philosophy!

For in their eyes woman is the very incarnation of the daemon. The daemon changed behavior with Christianity; no longer the enchanted voice that stopped Socrates in the middle of a discourse, it is a gloomy devil that rose from the Christian Hell. Caroline Schlegel was called "the Lady Lucifer." Schleiermacher wrote, for the use of "noble feminine hearts," a "Catechism of Reason" whose fourth commandment is deliberate sacrilege: "Observe the Sabbath of your heart: free yourself or perish."[23]

Novalis called this liberation *Stimmung*. *Stimmung*: the tuning of an instrument, and metaphorically, of the soul. But it is a steady harmony, made up entirely of harmonics, those echoing sounds that one produces by, for example, caressing the strings of a violin. Novalis writes: "The word *Stimmung* refers to or is a harbinger of the psychic conditions of musical nature. The acoustics of the soul are still an obscure field but perhaps a very important one."[24] The analogy between music and the workings of the "soul" (mind, affect, subconscious, thought?) arouses strange Asiatic images: the ascetic exercises in which one lets a single sound resonate for a long time, so that it fills the hollows of the throat, the mouth, and the nose until it strikes the forehead like a direct hit; the single note sung by the enigmatic Siren who sits at Necessity's feet in Plato's *Republic*. A single note is never alone; it carries with it a procession of harmonies, harmonious vibrations—or discordant ones. *Stimmung*: first a state, not an action. *Stimmung*: a note held without reason for one's whole life. *Stimmung*: first set life out of tune, in order to find the harmony more easily.

Fainting in chaos as one chooses to faint in the arms of a nurse who rocks one, the Romantics return to the holy nights of Greece, to pantheism; they return also, in an illusion of the epoch, to a ideal end to the wars of religion.

"With us," says the painter Otto Runge, "something is in the process of disappearing, we have reached the final stages of all the religions that emerged from Catholicism, abstractions are dying, everything is more airy and light than before; everything is springing up in the countryside."[25] A joyous, resurrected paganism. That is the "daemonic" when it no longer stops: an absolute syncope of reason, a flight of understanding, a "granting of trust to chaos," as Albert Béguin said in 1947, emphasizing the mortal dangers.[26] That is how syncope acts to escape the law of religion, to achieve immediate illumination without intermediary priests. Or to flee from morality: the bourgeois sleeps at night. The Romantic hero, on the other hand, stays awake, and passes through the day like a sleepwalker. It is as a sleepwalker that the prince of Hamburg dreams of his victory, as a sleepwalker that Penthesilea hacks her dear Hippolyta to pieces. But the Romantic bacchante does not wake up from her ecstasy; she stays there. The rhythm is broken forever.

When Romanticism ends, as avant-gardes end, with quarrels, suicides, fizzling out, reasonable conversions, then comes a philosophy that puts it in prison.

> In the bacchanalia, Greek women were given room to express their pent-up passions. Their physical and emotional exhaustion was succeeded by their peaceful return to the realm of their normal feelings and their accustomed lives. Outside the festivals, [the rest of the time] the savage Maenad was a rational woman.[27]

Hegel was the one who was needed to control the return of the bacchante to the bosom of the family, and to take care of the "rest of the time."

4

The Owl and the Nightingale: Hegel and Hölderlin

Frankfurt, 1797: at twenty-seven, Hegel plunged into a profound crisis. He no longer knew what he thought; he no longer knew what to think. The republic and the revolution had collapsed under the repeated blows of German history. Several years later, Hegel would speak of this episode as an attack of "hypochondria." *Hypochondria*: literally, under the cartilage of the ribs, with one's heart cramped. When the perception of the world is too closely concerned with chaos, the heart suddenly, without any reason, sinks. Without any reason: one might say that reason gets muddled. Look closely at the letter in which Hegel, at forty, describes the crisis that overcame him in Frankfurt:

> I suffered from this hypochondria for a number of years to the point of total exhaustion; no doubt every man experiences such a turning point in his life, *the nocturnal point where his whole being contracts* and he must force himself through the narrows until he becomes secure and certain of himself, secure in ordinary daily life, and if he has already made himself incapable of being fulfilled by that, then secure in a more inward, more noble existence. (emphasis added)[1]

Here then is the eternal philosopher, just as one says "the eternal husband," in the humility of his confrontation with the depressive epoch. And here, clearly described, is the radical initiating rite: a narrow crossing, under coercion; night; the contraction of the ribs; and a point—the nocturnal point of the body's contraction, from which the initiate emerges later, reassured. Out of the crisis, once it is overcome, emerges the long philosophical rite that is *The Phenomenology of Mind*, an adventure of consciousness across repeated contractions. The logical *contradiction* allows the *contraction* of syncope to escape.

Hegelian dialectic is caused by a depressive spasm: logical movement goes forward by jolts, haunted by the syncopes that are always possible and that would perhaps halt the logic of history. Suddenly, the outcome of the battle between master and slave is held in suspense for a dangerous eternity: no one knows which of the two men who have set upon each other in a fight to the death will be the master, which the slave. Suddenly, Antigone goes to scratch up the sand with bare hands to bury the cursed brother, who was condemned to rot in public beneath the walls of Thebes, without a tomb; no one knows who, she or Creon, will impose the law, no one knows anymore who is the law.[2] Suddenly, yes and no are tangled up, and the no of no destroys the meaning; suddenly . . . Hegel's thought is shot through with these syncopes, which, on the evidence, he has remembered and enjoyed, like an owner proud of his beautiful brand-new mind.

But one of the men is afraid, falls back, gives way: he will be the slave.

But Creon imposes the law of men, and Antigone will be defeated.

But the negation of the negation fulfills its work of circuit breaker (*échangeur routier*) and meaning gets under way again. The crisis has barely been reported, and already it has disappeared; the fainting spirit has barely sunk down and already the system has set it upright again: the logical guarantees have acted quickly to avoid the slowness that alone would authorize a true eclipse. Dialectic's rapidity regulates the question of syncope. There is no question of abandoning oneself any longer. One is "fortified": the dialectical crisis is an impregnable fortress.

The philosopher, however, is a strange bird. During the day, while others work and live, God alone knows what the philosopher is doing: he dreams, he faints, perhaps, he sleeps . . . One never knows. But when his peers go off to bed, the philosopher, like a methodical depressive, a true resister of anguish, opens his eyes and starts to keep watch. "Minerva's owl rises at dusk," said Hegel when he wanted to justify why philosophy was behind the times.

At the end of his hypochondriac crisis, Hegel wrote an optimistic poem, in the form of a resurfacing:

> . . . Strive for, aspire to more than today and yesterday
> Then you will not be better than the age, but the age at its best.[3]

To incarnate one's epoch, that is the beautiful obsession of Hegelian philosophy. But the philosopher, alas, will always keep watch too late. Any coincidence with any event whatsoever is impossible; or rather, *unthinkable*. Thought can never be anything but *twilight*; it is at nightfall that the eyes open, to watch, fixedly, what still remains hazily in the gray shadows. With the gaze riveted on blurring shadows, the philosophical owl that Hegel dreamed of gathers in, classifies; it *recapitulates*. By dawn, it will also have anticipated the future, and will close its eyes. The entire Hegelian dialectic can be read as hard labor that links the recently disappeared past with the burgeoning future. Of syncope, nothing; it is a matter of linking without any break the reflexive delay and the anticipated dream. The choice of Minerva's bird is not that of disintegration. It is that of the watch patrol, vigilant and policing; it is the cry of the watchman who goes through the city streets and reassures the sleepers at each stage of darkness: "It is three o'clock: sleep in peace, good people!"[4]

If the owl amasses things, the nightingale, the lovers' bird, sings all through the night, and does nothing else. It is a wild and abandoned song; as long as it can be heard, the night that frightens the bourgeois protects love's rebels. Nightingale or skylark? The first lovers' tiff between Juliet and Romeo centered on the interpretation of a birdsong. If it were the nightingale, there would still be time for nuptial caresses; but if it were the skylark, Romeo, the secret husband, would have to leave Juliet; daytime reasserts its citizen's rights. Nightingale or lark? The choice is between love and life.

Owl or nightingale? These are both birds of the night. One hoards; the other dispenses with reckless cries. Nightingale or owl? The nightingale is called Hölderlin; the owl is Hegel. Hölderlin the nightingale knew just what to think of the owl. This, for example:

> . . . And the owl, familiar [with][5] Scripture, speaks
> Like the wail of women in devastated towns.[6]

The poor owl. Forever alone in the ruins of dead towns, and unable to sing clearly . . .

1836. Hegel has been dead since 1831, victim of a cholera epidemic; a revered professor, discoursing in the universities, he had come to incarnate his epoch, to represent the epoch better than the epoch itself could. Hölderlin, his friend since childhood, was living as a recluse with a cabinetmaker, in a little tower on the banks of the Neckar. He hardly wrote anymore, and when he did, he signed it "Scardanelli."

He had been cut off from his time for almost thirty years already by what it suits us to call madness when he received a visit from the writer Gustav Kühne, who left this testimony of the meeting. Prudently, the cabinetmaker introduced Kühne to the poet as a spinet tuner come to repair the instrument on which Hölderlin only ever played a single tune now, always the same one. The cabinetmaker had reached the point of banging harder and harder to stifle the refrain. Hölderlin came in and saw the fake tuner, who introduced himself and offered his services. "Useless, useless!" said Hölderlin, in great haste. "There are other ways to take care of tuning. That's good, that's good. I have known you for a long time. Your Grace has been known to me for a long time.

And if everything continues to go badly for me today, Jupiter will have a meeting; even his sister will not be spared. Yes."[7]

Hölderlin the nightingale had survived Hegel the owl. But nothing remained of his inspired outpouring, except for the embers. And in the old madman's last words one still hears something of his search for syncope. The spinet's being out of tune is not a restful state.

The cabinetmaker could do nothing about the out-of-tune instrument. Nor could the visitor; had he been the most professional of spinet tuners the result would have been the same. The cabinetmaker and the visitor were men, after all; and Hölderlin's madness kept men apart from his dealings with the gods. Poets have always spent time with divinities; they have always escaped from our world and wandered in the other, the True, the Ideal poetic world where the poet is the gods' regular visitor. He holds men in respect with some courtesies—always excessive, as the attentive cabinetmaker noted; but what can men know of conflicts with the gods?

The spinet suffered from being out of tune;[8] that is not a matter of acoustics, it can only be a metaphysical accident. To tune the spinet, one needs the intervention of the king of the gods, who will not spare his own sister. Was it Hera or Demeter who was involved? No one will ever know. But it is certain that it was she who put the spinet out of tune. Discord is a matter between a god and his sister; the spinet was caught in this conflict, and with it the poet.

"Like lovers' quarrels are the dissonances of the world. Reconciliation is there, even in the midst of strife, and all things that are parted find one another again,"[9] Hölderlin wrote. It is *desperately logical* that a spinet's being out of tune should signify a lovers' quarrel. The goddess's brother, the king of the gods, no doubt knows how to reconcile the poet and his divine mistress.

Gustav Kühne, contemplating the old poet, saw nothing but disaster. "Suddenly," he said, "he fell silent and looked straight ahead with a calm gaze. His face reflected the peace of battlefields. Ruins, all around: all willpower collapsed, burned to ashes; all muscular tension relaxed . . . "[10]

But of the nightingale and the owl, who won, and what was the gain? The nightingale went all the way to syncope, and sank down into madness. The owl skirted around syncope, and was a philosopher.

At this Romantic dawn when Germany was looking, as now, for its shape in the accord of nations, it is enough to see how each poet confronts the question of tragedy.

This is the nightingale's complex version:

> The presentation of the tragic rests primarily on the tremendous—how the god and man mate and how natural force and man's innermost boundlessly unite in wrath—conceiving of itself, [rests] on the boundless union purifying itself through boundless separation.[11]

An instantaneous coupling that brings together god and man in one same being, tragedy is a brutal fusion, without interval, without distance. That is the mystical short-circuit, destroying with the same bolt of lightning the individual subject and the god he searches for. "At such moments," continues Hölderlin, "man forgets himself and the god. . . . Inside it, man forgets himself because he exists entirely for the moment."[12] Nothing could get closer to syncope: man has blacked out in the moment of coupling. It is the orgasm of the soul, ego orgasm.

Hegel's version is, on the contrary, wise and learned. Tragedy produces "universal individuality"; the tragic hero is uncommon, unique, but he represents the whole human race. The unbearable is already no longer there. Everything keeps its head; the conflict between the hero and the city is productive, the tragic hero gives birth to the idea of the individual, and his confrontation with the gods brings autonomy to humans.[13]

Moreover, the first character that Hegel thinks of is not the hero but the tragedy's chorus. The chorus is the age of maturity, a little powerless, worshiping first this, then that, willingly opportunist, dull, devoted to the "empty peace of resignation." Not very uplifting, but very useful, the chorus. The rights of the people are indefeasible. The people, when all is said and done, or the tragic chorus, are similar to the worthy cabinetmaker who takes care of Hölderlin in his madness, and who kindly repeats to all who will listen, "You have to treat him like a child."[14]

When it comes to the tragedy of Antigone, the divergences between the nightingale and the owl are even more obvious. For Hölderlin, Antigone incarnates rebellion. But even more, since the poet adds to it that "patriotic [primal] reversal[15] is the reversal of all modes and forms of representation."[16] If one understands why Antigone actually turns against the remonstrations of her own city, since she is violating its enacted laws, the word "primal" is more obscure.

"Primal." As if it were a question of a return to, of a sudden and compulsory step backward. Hölderlin says again of this reversal that it is "without restraint," as if he wanted to evoke a young girl stripped, lewd, tormented by an extreme wildness. Antigone rebelling is not satisfied with revolt; she returns to her birth. And in fact Antigone's birth is shameful: it is incest, the horror without restraint. There is blasphemy in Antigone's rebellion; she is a sacrilegious rebel who displays her brother's and her own scandalous birth with a public gesture.

Hegel does not present Antigone as a rebel at all. She is a good daughter, and a good sister. She is Oedipus's daughter, a daughter of whom one knows that she would accompany her old monster of a father to the sacred wood where he mysteriously melted into the shadows. And she was a good young girl who wanted to bury her brother. The owl, gazing fixedly at the tragic stage, sees only one scene: *brother-and-sister*. That is the ideal relation between men and women! Between husband and wife, as we know, things do not always go well; the combination is not designed to succeed: either things balance out more or less in a marriage whose purpose is procreative and social, or the combination reaches its point of fusion in love, and implodes. Between brother and sister, however . . . that relationship, says Hegel, is "unmixed." "They are the same blood, which, however, in them has entered into a condition of stable equilibrium."[17] Not a word about the incest; not a line about eventual conflicts—after all, Antigone is not the only sister of her brothers, and little Ismene does not make the mystical choice of suicide in honor of her vanished brother. When Antigone appears in the *Phenomenology*, "the brother" emerges at her side; for the two together, freeze frame. Pause. Something stops in the infernal dialectical movement that, from affirmation to negation, and from negation to negation of the aforementioned, carries the mind along without stopping. Something quiets down. "The brother, however, is in the eyes of the sister a being whose nature is unperturbed by desire and is ethically like her own."[18]

Beyond the tragedy of Antigone, Hegel "fixes" femininity. Femininity, he says, is always quarrelsome, the enemy in the interior of the community, its "eternal irony."[19] Daughter, spouse, mother—all of these stir, arouse pathos, and annoy the philosophers, as much Hegel as once Plato. But if there is a brother in the family photo, then the femininity-sister holds still: she cannot want sex from her brother, she cannot want the city from him. We are of the same blood, you and I. Peace can at last be seen—*there is peace*.

The possible misogyny of one philosopher more or less does not matter very much. What counts is the abyss dug by the nightingale Hölderlin. One cannot say, however, that Hegel has not read Sophocles' *Antigone* well. It is true that for all the argument, when the chorus questions her on the choice she has made for her dead brother rather than for her live fiancé—for she is loved, and she loves—she explains: a spouse can be replaced by another, a dead child by a new one, but one can never hope for "the birth of a brother." Hegel is obsessed with the frozen image of the sister and the irreplaceable brother, a strange familial stopping place in the dialectic. He does this at the cost of some forgotten minor details: Antigone has *two* brothers, and chooses the rebel who is rotting outside the walls; from that moment on, her act only has a foundation provided that it takes the side of the gods' law against the law of men enacted by King Creon. In Hegel's reading, her rebellion has disappeared.

This then is the paradoxical fable of the owl and the nightingale. Hegel, who perfected the mechanism of the dialectic right up to the final touches of the return, does not see it in Antigone and forgets the heroine's rebellion. Hölderlin, poet of the amorous syncope and of the unifying reconciliation, on the contrary sees in the young girl only rebellion and "patriotic reversal."

Hegel's owl is far-sighted. To capture the taste of young girls' rebellion, one must plunge into the universe of syncope; hysteria, coughing fits, little cries and sighs, and great rebellions cannot be evaded. One must be able to be in love. Now, what interests the owl Hegel in the young girl is her procreative future, and the child to whom she could give birth. The syncope-Antigone who quivers beneath Hölderlin's pen does not exist in the Hegelian dialectic of tragedy. Nor does the family know of the incest that from birth pushes the young girl toward her *Ate*, her complete curse. Even though she could have signified the very essence of impossibility, under Hegel's eye Antigone is transformed into a proper little person. In complete conformity with what a sister must be for a brother: "*a good sister*." And tragedy's veil is drawn over her headdress.

Emerging from his hypochondriac depression, Hegel wanted to produce, and to produce with a calculated rapidity. Produce thought, logic, philosophy of history, whatever one could want, and even, in the *Encyclopedia of Philosophical Sciences in Outline*, produce thought from the infant's excrement;[20] in short, producing and not stopping. That is where the sister's calm is unusual; that is where it is questionable to dissimulate love itself, the love of the sister-wife, the leading romantic heroine, who exists nowhere but in the owl's universe.

What does woman actually do in the dialectic? She is like stone, and remains immobile, at home. Opposite her, man is on the contrary the force that moves, leaves home, goes to work, or makes war. The woman produces the child, the synthesis of the couple. Later, after the war, she will be the gravedigger, who takes care of the soldier who has died after returning home—father, son, husband. This side of Antigone the gravedigger partakes of the eternal feminine, made to maintain the flame of the unknown soldier. The other side of her titillates the city, battles against Creon. But the passion of rebellion has disappeared; the patriotic reversal has disappeared; at the most one can guess that Hegel has a certain tenderness for Antigone: she is a woman, but she behaves with the courage of a man. She is a woman, but she takes after men—a halfway point between the sexes.[21]

When Jacques Lacan took it into his head to talk about Sophocles' *Antigone*, it took him a long, long time. He announced it several times, and never got to it. When, however, he came to it, backward, he found the image of the nightingale—not of Hölderlin, but of the bird. The chorus describes Antigone in the night as a nightingale, when she covers the rotting body with sand, with little plaintive cries, the moans of a bird trying to protect its brood. And in one of those strange visions that took him by surprise, Lacan "saw" Antigone metamorphosing into a nightingale.[22]

He even saw there the symbol of pagan metamorphosis. In the lost world of defeated paganism, metamorphosis was common, if not commonplace: Philemon and Baucis became trees; Adonis, a blood-colored flower; Daphne, a pink laurel; Arachne, a spider; Niobe, a streaming stone[23] . . . however slightly one contravened the capricious command of a god, one disappeared as a human being and became animal, vegetable, or mineral. Metamorphosis is closely connected to that patriotic reversal that Hölderlin loved; it is one of the enduring characteristics of the universe that syncope opens up. When the subject blacks out, it is always possible that he might find himself elsewhere in another form—that of a nightingale, a serpent, or a wolf. In the "one never knows" of syncope, all metamorphoses are allowed. Hölderlin's metamorphosis into Scardanelli is no exception.

The "one never knows" must still exist. On the evidence, Hegel excluded it from his field of vision. To be the bird that rises at dusk, his philosophical owl becomes a little like a panopticon: see all, hear all, know all—except the eclipses of being, and the violence of young women.

Asia, the Abyss

Hölderlin, once more. *Hyperion*, or mad love. Hyperion writes to Bellarmin and tells him about a walk that he took in the near end of a garden, with his beloved.

It is not just an ordinary garden, however. When the lovers find themselves alone—I dare not say "at the far end of the garden," which would sound too much like a kitchen garden—when the lovers are, then, at the near end of the garden, there is Diotima, also called the Ravishing, leaning over the parapet. She is nearly falling into a landscape equipped with all the scenery of *Sturm und Drang*: a cliff, a sudden terrifying depth, shadowy forests, chaotic rocks, and stormy torrents: and this is at the far end of the garden, moreover! In this erotic enclosure Hölderlin suddenly sees Asia: "Now we were standing close to the summit's rim, gazing out into the endless East."[24]

That is how Diotima, the young woman on the edge of the parapet, was. Diotima, instant access to the East. That is how Asia crops up in Hölderlin's poetry. It is mysterious, accessible through a young woman's blooming grace; it bursts out on the forefront of a poetic interval. Asia, isolated, dazzled.

> You opened up to me like a flower
> Asia![25]

Or this:

> Like brooks the end of something sweeps me away, which expands like Asia. Of course, this affliction, Oedipus has it too. Of course, that is why.[26]

Asia: immediately accessible in the syncope of a poem. Spread out, boundless, the land of "yes." No "no" envisioned there; no negation. And a "naturally" Eastern Oedipus. The poet moves naturally toward the East: toward the most difficult rhythm, the bearer of fascination.

Among the German Romantic avant-garde was a woman who had a vision. It was at night; Karoline von Günderrode immediately wrote down what she had seen; several days later, she chose to take her own life—to meet the Asia of her vision:

> I stood on a high rock in the Mediterranean, and before me was the East, and behind me the West, and the wind was resting on the waters. . . . I saw a vast ocean before me, that did not touch any shores, not to the north, nor to the south, nor to the east, nor to the west. Not the slightest breeze stirred the waves, and yet this immense sea was troubled in its depths, as if by an internal fermentation.[27]

Reaching Asia, the horizons disappear. All that is left is that pure fermentation that Karoline von Günderrode calls *Stimmung*, a name that evokes vibrations, abandonment to chaos, the waves of the matrix.

Then she went to die.

It can still be seen today, in the footsteps of the hippie generations and flower power, Hölderlins of all nations who go off to Asia just as the Romantic poet lit upon it: whether they are drugged to the eyebrows or simply a little cracked, the inconsequential leftovers of a system they do not fit into, that is where they go without purpose or goal, bearers of an absurd "yes" that often leads them to an unexpected physical death, from unforeseen, disconcerting accidents. This is far from over, this business of Europe, this long, twisted history of Europe dreaming of Asia. The banks of the Neckar are just as mad as the banks and the whole course of the Ganges, from its source in Ganjoti to the estuary of Bengal.[28]

The Asia of reality, at least the one I know, treats these emigrants from Western metaphysics as it pleases: as bearers of currency. There are innumerable cunning businessmen who have made money off the scenography of Romanticism. The business of ecstasy is saved for the West: there are specialists in ashrams, successful marketers of Asia who do neither good nor evil but are simply making a living, an import-export business in the techniques of the moment. Who can criticize them? It is Asia's revenge on Europe. Among the figures who embody this reversal of history can be counted some legendary women, all Western, and all hoisted into the ranks of true saints. They are upstarts, but after all they got "there," to Asia. Look at those who devoted themselves body and soul to the major spiritual leaders and the leaders of the independence movement: with Vivekananda,[29] the woman he called "sister Nivedita." With Gandhi, the astonishing figure Madeleine Slade, daughter of an English admiral, whom the Mahatma called "Mirabehn." And with Aurobindo, after he had a brush with terrorism and took refuge in the French territory of Pondicherry, the strange Frenchwoman revered by her disciples by the name emblematic of all the others: "Mother."[30] They were women: organizers. Diotimas who would have become bankers.[31]

Hegel infinitely mistrusted the "yes," the immediate, and Asia in general. And moreover, when he valiantly set out on the long journey that recapitulated the universal history of the world, he started with the East and proceeded to the West. The owl was not mad; he took the path of least resistance. The owl wanted nothing to do with madness; that is why he could not be content with the ecstatic "yes," the "yes" that accepts and glorifies Oedipus's pain, the "yes" that challenges, in Hölderlin's last words to Gustav Kühne, his belonging to humanity: the "yes" of the gods.

Hegel begins the *Philosophy of History* with two countries that, he says, stand outside universal history: China and India.[32] The "*real theater*" of history only starts with the European zone, as if the mixture of heat and cold, of wind and sun, the alternation of weather, were necessary to establish a temperate dialectic. China and India are neither theatrical nor temperate. And if China, according to Hegel, is the land of the unchanging era of the patriarchal family, then India is the realm of divine intoxication, "the dream of the boundless mind itself."

Hegel's portrait of India, however, lacks nothing to make it match Hölderlin's Asia: there is the special beauty of the women, the immediacy of ecstasy.

Hegel describes the beauty of Indian women with a diabolical intuition. It is a soft beauty, lit up by an internal inspiration, comparable to the beauty of a woman who has just given birth, or to that of sleeping or sleepwalking prophetesses, comparable, indeed, to "dying Mary, whose spirit is already rising to the regions of the blessed, but once more, as it were, lights up her dying countenance for a farewell kiss."[33] It is a woman's beauty, then, but on condition that it is affected by weakness: women are beautiful when they are exhausted, asleep, or dying. They are beautiful when they are the Mother in agony. But, he says, that is how the soul got a head start on understanding.

He had better not—precisely—yield to the spell of this unique moment, this birth, prophetic sleep, or agony. *The sphere of understanding does not exist in India*: let that be a given. That is why India, the weak woman, has always been conquered: that is what you were told. As for the perception of the divine, it does not escape from the harsh law of the antidepressive dialectic. Hegel dares to say shamelessly that the divine in India is "defiled and made absurd."[34] The philosophical owl with its fixed gaze can no more see India than it can see Antigone's rebellion. There is something irreparable there: the horror of immediate ecstasy is so great that it generates the immense system that flees it.

But when the dialectic finally draws to a close—as everything draws to a close, because one day one is too old to think—then something happens, gently. One has to have gone all the way to the end of the road, traced the whole course . . . Then, only then, the knot of thought unravels, then the violent hurry of logic halts. Then perhaps one glimpses a kind of suspension, a shadow of syncope, a thought that finally stops wanting, desperately, to answer all questions, to stop up all gaps. A *détente* of thought: that is what Bergson, who was a great aficionado of mysticism, called (probably in a paradoxical spirit) dialectic.

5

Loves Me, Loves Me Not; or, The Love of Dialectic

Suppose we abandon the methodical reading of Hegel's *Science of Logic*. Suppose that, instead of making our way through a dialectic that we know academically raises first the question of the One, then the negation, then the negation of the negation—let us suppose that instead of this somewhat military route, we choose a less studious and more speeded-up reading, the way a cartoon film could show it. Let us imagine that a mad filmmaker had decided to bring *The Science of Logic* to the screen.

At first, *that* (*ça*) does not move: that is the "appropriate" relation of the One to itself. Then, all of a sudden, it comes to life. Like a birth; like the division of cells; or like one of those sea anemones that spreads its tendrils with a voluptuous delicacy. A kind of octopus, similar to the one Valéry describes at length to conjure up dancing. Multiple tentacles emerge from the octopus, each endowed with autonomous life: "the one repels itself *from itself*,"[1] writes Hegel, and that is how it places itself "from itself": logic begins like an animal withdrawn into itself. The next moment, the One has become "many ones." Hegel calls that "repulsion": that is a completely mechanical word—the simple fact of pushing something away—and a violent one. It is a departure and a hiccup; a logic, and a nausea. Hegel says it a little later: repulsion is also exclusion. "Repulsion is, although negative, still essentially *relation*; the mutual repulsion and flight is not a liberation from what is repelled and fled from, the one as excluding still remains *related* to what it excludes."[2] I push you away, but I love you.

Right away—one of logic's attributes is to be in a hurry—repulsion has already become *attraction*: it is enough to seize the extension that goes from the tips of the octopus's tentacles to the body of the animal. Brush against the sea anemone, and it closes immediately. The mother expels the child from her belly, and there it is in her arms, attached by the cord:

> The one as such, then, is a coming-out-of-itself, is only the positing of itself as its own other, as many; and the many, similarly, is only this, to collapse within itself and to posit itself as *its* other, as one, and in this very act to be related only to its own self, each continuing itself in its other. Thus there is already present in principle (*an sich*) the undividedness of the coming-out-of-itself (repulsion) and the self-positing as one (attraction).[3]

If it were really a cartoon film, we would see the metaphysical beast beginning to throb like a heart, a tentacle, a newborn baby, or love.

Almost imperceptibly, the movement *will have occurred.* Already. So there are two movements, the first by which the One sets itself apart and expels; the second, the attraction, by which the One reassembles its scattered multiples. So there will have been movement; or yet, it is still to come. Of the Twice-Negated: negation of the negation, which begins with the hiccup. After that, everything can be imagined.

Let the tip of an anemone's tendril turn into a warrior and attack the One, and then there are two combatants, the future Master and the future Slave joined in a fight to the death. Let another fragment of the image begin to resemble Antigone, and let the One take on the appearance of Creon; let another tentacle become woman, and the One man, or the other way around. The animation has started, and will not stop. Besides, it must not stop; for (and he says it unequivocally) Hegel thinks the unthinkable, and knows it.

> On this point, formal thinking lays down for its principle that contradiction is unthinkable; but as a matter of fact the thinking of contradiction is the essential moment of the Notion. Formal thinking does in fact think contradiction, only it at once looks away from it, and in saying that it is unthinkable it merely passes over from it into abstract negation.[4]

That abstract negation is nothing other than the dialectical animation, moving past frame by frame. It is a question of speeding up, or slowing down.

That thought, despite its methodical premeditation, depends only on its speed: stopping and slowness are impossible. The dialectical route in the course of which Hegel develops the functions of repulsion and attraction is placed exactly where one would expect a jolt, a suspension, a hesitation. But the hiccup, if it exists, reintegrates immediately what it has regurgitated; no expulsion is complete, and nothing would ever be able to stop as long as the dialectic is in operation. This reintegration of syncope into logic is called the "turning point." Here is the text:

> Now the negativity just considered constitutes the *turning point* of the movement of the Notion. It is the *simple point of the negative relation* to self, the

> innermost source of all activity, of all animate and spiritual self-movement, the dialectical soul that everything true possesses and through which alone it is true . . . [5]

On the picture screen, the tentacles have drawn back to their original animal, after scattering a thousand figurines, which were roused by a thousand battles; the beast itself has been reduced to a single round blot, what one could call a *point*. There is no real separation, no true absence. The negation of the negation blocks all exits. A "no" closes off the route to syncope from the very beginning. There is no crack at all. The One always keeps contact with its metamorphoses; everything is connected. Whatever has been expelled is never entirely so; it is caught in the corner of the concept by the centripetal force of a dynamic similar to that of the waltz. The most serious danger is that thought would stop, and would imperil the dizzying spinning from which it draws its characteristic movement.

One of the moments of dialectic between repulsion and attraction resembles the principle that propels the dance, and its essential speed: *anticipation*. A vertigo of thought. A logical waltz, in order to avoid the fall that the slightest pause would provoke; a waltz to stun reality, to the point where seeing the walls of logic, the floor of awareness, the ceiling, the earth and the sky in constant motion, one would actually like to get all that back on its feet again. It is understood that Marx wanted to "get dialectic back on its feet again," attach the tentacled animal once and for all, and prevent it from floating freely.

Dialectical anticipation, however, is like the anticipation of the next turn in the waltz: one turns around *oneself*.

When Hegel assigned philosophy its task in the preface to the *Philosophy of Right*, he specified its limits: those of the era itself, of "the time." Everyone is a product of his time—the best of the era, or "the age at its best"; it is the same with philosophy, which epitomizes its time in thought; a recapitulating owl, but definitely not more than that. "It is just as absurd to fancy that a philosophy can transcend its contemporary world as it is to fancy that an individual can overleap his own age, jump over Rhodes."[6]

"Rhodus," Rhodes, where the colossus stands, whose huge legs one has to go through to enter the port. "Rhodus": any impossible crossing can be called Rhodus. "*Hic Rhodus, hic saltus*" in Latin means: "Here is the port, here is the leap." This means that by declaring as mad the philosophical enterprise that wants to think about the contemporary world and go beyond it, Hegel forbids one to look ahead, to dream about the future, to prophesy. He says that, but stoops to predicting; he says that, but the temptation of philosophy is also to go beyond its time. And having cited the Latin expression "*Hic Rhodus, hic saltus*," he proposes changing its terms. Not a leap, now, but the dance; not the port, but the rose. "Here is the rose, dance thou here." It is exactly the opposite, it is thought's dizziness. Like the waltzer or like the dervish, Hegelian dialectic whirls around itself until it *loses consciousness*. And that is what happens when, finally, thought must stop and one must finish summing up time.

For there is an end point, or rather a last *glissade*. The final gesture of philosophy concerns the essence of philosophy itself, and is called the "Absolute Mind."[7]

All the figures have been set out, pushed away, pulled back; all the struggles have taken place, and every victor will have known the slavery of his victory. There will have been, in short, all the "rest of the time": this "rest of the time" for the bacchante when she stays at home waiting for the moment of her drunkenness. The time to run through the logical generation, the adventures of consciousness, the emergence of the individual in the city, the history of history, and of art forms, to arrive, at last, at philosophy, where the waltz should stop. The time to imagine everything without leaving out anything that could have slipped out of range. It is the last series of images, after which there will be nothing on the screen but a "That's all, folks" that sends everyone back home, where it is up to them to start the totality again at zero.

So it is important to appraise one's totality once more, and to establish it well, for that is the last lesson. It unfolds in three syllogisms; each lays out its own three elements: the first is the starting point; the second, the middle term, is the mediating factor; the third is the product. And what is seen?[8]

The first syllogism of the Absolute Spirit as Hegel lays it out has for a first term *Logic*, as a middle term *Nature*, and as a product *Spirit*: Logic becomes Nature, which produces Spirit. Logic-Nature-Spirit. Immediately, *Nature* becomes the first term of the next syllogism, and activates it: Nature produces *Spirit* and reconnects it to *Logic*. *Nature-Spirit-Logic*. That leaves the final syllogism, and it is *Spirit*'s turn to begin. A surprise: instead of producing Logic, as this game of final tease might lead one to believe, it is *Reason* that arises, unexpectedly, which gives rise to *Nature*. *Spirit-Reason-Nature*.

Logic has disappeared, and with it, dialectical movement; all that is left is Spirit, defined as "the primarily conceptual activity of the Idea" and as by-itself, and Nature, defined in turn as "process of the objective Idea" and as in-itself. This is how the encounter is described:

> These appearances are suspended in the idea of philosophy, which has self-knowing reason, the absolutely general, for its middle term: a middle which divides itself into spirit and nature, with the former as its presupposition, and

> the latter as its general extreme. Thus immediate nature is only a posited entity, as spirit is in itself, not a presupposition, but rather totality returning into itself. In this way the middle term, the self-knowing concept, has as its reality primarily conceptual moments and exists in its determinacy as general knowledge, persisting immediately by itself.[9]

And that's all, folks: nothing else moves. The dialectical logic has stopped at last.

As the philosopher also says in the preceding pages, it is the same with thinking as with "eating." Eating is truly a thankless activity, for one absorbs the thing to which one owes one's existence. "In this way," he adds, "thinking is no less thankless": it devours experience, reality, to which it also owes its existence. The dialectical creature is driven by a deeply digestive activity; and when it has digested everything, when it has vomited up everything, regurgitated, expectorated, reintegrated, it falls asleep, like the dragon Faffner on top of the Rhinegold, at the back of a cave.

For there is a falling asleep in Logic's vanishing. It is no longer turning; it no longer has any movement other than from one to the other, from the other to one, by itself, in itself, by itself, autogeneration and jouissance equally guaranteed by the absolute autism of that which is no longer, from that moment on, dialectical thought. Here is the rose, here shalt thou rock; here one nods, in the manner of the childish motions of those great thinkers who have been marked by deep thought, those who are called "idiots," and who sway in order to survive. Take, for example, Saint Anthony, whose long journey through the temptations of the flesh and the spirit was written about so superbly by Flaubert; the philosopher, having succumbed to all the passing temptations and having overcome them all on the way, finds himself face to face with Nature, Spirit ruined in his contemplation. We remember that the saint completes his torture with his nose in the grass, aglow with sensations, dazzled with little perceptions, dissolved in dust: "To be matter!"[10]

But we also recall that one of Saint Anthony's last temptations was the apparition of an animal so stupid that it devoured its own paws.[11] No one on earth could lift its pinkish eyelids and meet its gaze without dying on the spot; and the saint came very close to succumbing, so strong was the attraction of thankless stupidity, stupidity strong enough to eat its own paws. It is the same with treacherous thought, which eats up logic. And if God could later, under Bataille's pen, be a whore, if the figure of Madame Edwarda is not far distant from the unending jouissance of the absolute Idea, the philosopher himself is not far distant from the monstrous Catoblepas and his seductive stupidity.

The beast Catoblepas, the baby being rocked, the god who, by himself, is in ecstasy, at the end of the breathless dialectic . . . There is something childlike there. And what if the perfect image of the brother and the sister, this essence without mixture, this pause—what if it were nothing but the reflection of the sister rocking the brother? It is not only the "brother-sister" relationship that belongs to the "unmixed." There is also thought: "The self of the mind, pure of all admixture, is thought." One could say that right at the bottom of Hegel's philosophical activity sighs a happy rocking, soothed at last.

Young children's logical mechanisms are astonishingly similar to Hegelian dialectical logic. It is as if the logical universe developing in the child, confronted with the real world and learning to distinguish between itself and the world, reproduced the most sophisticated philosophical thinking of the West. Admittedly, Melanie Klein, in whose work one finds these mental landscapes, made her deductions as an adult based on difficult observations. Admittedly, the constructions that she mapped out are no doubt partly imaginary. For all that, let us see: for Melanie Klein describes a violent effort to master the immensity of a chaotic, inordinately large universe.

The Hungarian psychoanalyst, confronted with very young children, engaged in an astonishing reconstruction of a mental universe, about which the least one can say is that it does not give itself up easily. They are superb philosophical constructions that help one to guess, if not to understand, the violence of a world often still without language, profoundly unfinished. Now, look for example at this description of the interior world of a child:

> For to the introjection of external objects corresponds at every step the projection of internal figures on to the external world, and this interaction underlies the relation to the actual parents as well as the development of the super-ego. In consequence of this interaction, which implies an orientation outwards and inwards, there is a *constant fluctuation between internal and external objects and situations*. (emphasis added)[12]

Curiously enough, it is the same movement as that of Hegel's great logic. *Repulsion-attraction, projection-introjection.* The Child—an entity that must be accepted when reading Melanie Klein—expels and pushes away its bad objects when projecting; when introjecting, it reintegrates them. One finds here the same reciprocal whirling, the same endless oscillation defined by an identical distinction, which separates the interior and the exterior. Between the two, the *objects* come and go, equivalent to what is, for Hegel, *thought*: glints of an aggression or a seduction, anamorphoses of a repulsion or an attraction that cannot stop. The phase known as pre-Oedipal, as Melanie

Klein describes it, only ends with the succession of the "Oedipal" structure: we emerge from the two and find ourselves in the three, father, mother, baby; something is at rest, even if it is on a tripod. We emerge from the "loves me, loves me not" that gave Serge Gainsbourg the modern formulation of passionate love.

Hegel says little about love. Just barely, at the end of the *Encyclopedia of the Philosophical Sciences in Outline*, at the moment when Absolute Spirit prepares to push away religion in order to yield to the attraction of philosophy, at that boundary between pantheism and philosophy, the philosopher just barely agrees to the Sufi abandon, and cites the "excellent" Djalâl ul-Dîn Rumi, of whom it is known that, going also under the name of "Mawlana," he was the founder of the movement of spinning dervishes. That is where love lodges: a spiritual unity elevated above "the final and the vulgar"; to describe Hindu polytheism Hegel used the same word, "vulgar." It goes without saying that this is not a question either of copulation or of fondness. It concerns only mysticism, and the immediate fusion of the Spirit with the One. One more turn of the waltz will suffice—the one we read of just now—and the Spirit will be at rest. It is as if to say that the love Hegel speaks of is not that of lovers: it is the solitary love of the man united with and deeply rooted in his god. If it is not the huge and diffuse Asia on whose brink Hölderlin stood, it is close to it; if it is not yet the absolute dissolution of the individual that we will see in the work of Hindu thought, it is the Sufi interaction, appropriate for a geographical zone whose name also suits the philosophical enterprise: the Middle East. Not the whole East, but its middle; not Asia, but the areas around Turkey where Sufism originated. If Hegel speaks of love, he only knows how to speak of a love in which the man-woman interaction has no place.

One can have the strange feeling, however, that without knowing it Hegel really is describing love. Even if he does not think so, his words evoke it. Those who push away and attract each other are concepts, not lovers, but they embrace. Those who switch from hate to love are not living bodies but movements of thought. Before dialectic rigidifies into the stupor of ecstatic Reason, it resembles "Dame Minne," the deadly German goddess whose function, if one listens to Isolde in Wagner's opera, consists in making man and woman move from hate to love, from repulsion to attraction.

Loves me, loves me not. And One pushes away what is not yet its Other, but a heap of Ones, its Multiple, which it then attracts in order to ingest it better. And Isolde pushes away Tristan, who is not yet her Other, but who represents to the eyes of the princess, who is full of hatred, heaps of other multiple men—King Mark to whom Tristan is taking her, the men of Cornwall, and even her own murdered fiancé, Morholt who disappeared. At the moment of being struck by love, repulsion changes signs; Isolde reintegrates Tristan, and the void is filled. Loves me, loves me not.

At the heart of the gray night where the owl's yellow eye persists in explaining the world in detail, the double shadow of the lovers projects its appropriate oscillation: loves me, loves me not. And the owl, who should miss nothing, will have once again seen nothing of its own ulterior motives.

Hegel, Faster than Music

There is chiaroscuro in dialectic mastery. There is no doubt about it: mastering time is the goal of dialectic. Wanting to be "the age at its best," wanting with such superb megalomania simply to "conceive what is," is to affirm a will for control through thought that demands, in the Cartesian manner, an avoidance of all precipitation. This metaphysical athleticism is not performed without slowness; and the narrow depressive transition will not be forgotten, the "nocturnal point where his whole being contracts," which preceded the dialectical expansion. That must also be avoided in future: the contraction, the point, the instantaneous. But there is no doubt; without a permanent dialectical speeding-up, thought risks foundering in a kind of logical dereliction: losing the thread of the concept—that is the danger. There is slowness, and there is speed. Slowness inhabits the Hegelian project, but speed fills the act of its dialectic.

The same chiaroscuro is found again between delay and anticipation. Delay is not in question: Minerva's bird only appears as a metaphor for philosophy because it rises at dusk, and is behindhand. That is how the philosopher is: always busy running after a sign of life, and always already too late. That is called reflection—according to Hegel, at least—for whoever wants to understand first what has happened, refusing to go and look in the direction of what could happen. Dialectic's beginning is retroactive, before anything. What comes after the "before anything" will necessarily be a temporal shift back to the origin.

But anticipation is no more uncertain than delay. Let us return for a moment to the dialectic of repulsion and attraction: when the "Ones" are expelled from the single One, they are laid out "in advance." Otherwise the system could stop dead, with the One unified, and without any other form of process for its wandering emanations, the "Ones." Once anticipated, the movement begins anew; it would almost have stopped, but would have been carried along by anticipation alone.

Hegel's philosophy decides to start off from being behindhand; but it cannot catch up except by anticipating the movement. From then on, thought starts off quickly, like a pair of waltzers who start turning, and whom gravity leads in a faster and faster whirlwind. Moreover, the waltz cannot be stopped without an imperceptible movement of the pendulum between two beats, which almost always prompts a kind of fascinated amazement. And it is precisely in this motionless astonishment that the movement of the Absolute Spirit ends, suddenly deprived of Logic, finding no recourse except in the pendulum of a divine jouissance.

From delay to anticipation, that is the very movement of musical syncope. *Delay*: the note is prolonged beyond its beat. *Anticipation*: this prolonged note is ahead of the sequence of the beats. This game exists in Hegel's work: watchful philosophy actually prolongs something of the day—its memory, its echo, the dullness that ends in dullness, he said. And dialectic anticipation is actually ahead of the sequence of beats.

And yet it is *not* syncope. Syncope *creates* delay and accentuates it by prolonging time. Hegel wants to *catch up* with time: always control, always mastery. Hegel does not create delay, he endures it and suffers from it. Hegel does not wish to accentuate discord or profit from it; on the contrary he seeks to direct it, in fine, in order to—despite everything—reduce it. That is not syncope, it is the fear that it might begin again, and the resentment about that. The dialectical contradiction in Hegelianism is not discord: even at the strongest point of tension, there is no forgetfulness of time from which dissonance could emerge.

Hegel talks well about music. He drags in a fine character at the end of the section of the *Aesthetics* devoted to music.

This character is a guitar virtuoso, a poor, dull-witted fellow, says the philosopher disdainfully. He has no taste, and he does not know how to compose anything but war music; by trade he is a weaver, and anyway, the guitar is a completely insignificant instrument. In short, Hegel does not spoil the guitarist. And yet, "when he started to play, you forgot the tastelessness of the composition, *just as he forgot himself* and produced marvelous effects . . ." (emphasis added). Marvelous indeed: the interior freedom of the oafish musician allows him, says Hegel, "interruptions," "fancies," the "caprice of the moment," the "topmost peak of musical vitality" that passes "like a flash of lightning." Yes, Hegel talks well about music, about the "'oohs' and 'aahs' of the soul."[13] At these moving signs one understands that he expended an unusual philosophical energy in order to map out, with the same virtuosity as the small-minded guitarist, a marvelous defense system against the rapture of syncope. Actually, a way *to forget oneself*.

After him, said François Châtelet, one is tempted to play dictionary: "*Philosophy*—noun. fem. Cultural genre, founded in Athens in 387 in the gardens of the Academy and came to an end in Berlin in 1816, with the publication of the *Science of Logic*."[14] After him, the avoidance of syncope ceases.

There are some philosophers who face up to him; they will also face the Hegelian system and combat it, violently. Bataille says it simply: Hegel founds truth on completion, and he, Bataille, sees it founded on incompletion. Hegel finishes truth by plunging it, like an iron reddened in the fire, into the slack water of theology. Bataille, on the contrary, wants, he says, "a torn-apart anthropomorphism." While Hegel "resolves" dialectic by merging things through sleight of hand, Bataille holds the contradiction open and transforms it into definitive discord. That is the directionless contradiction of his God; it is an *acephalous dialectic*. Look at these lines that exclude any resolution:

> Reaching the limit of its development and longing to be "put to death," thought rushes precipitously to the arena of sacrifice. And just as an emotion grows similarly until sobs burst it apart, thought's fullness takes it to the point of being blown down by the wind, and contradiction rages at last.[15]

Thought: directionless, open. The recurrent image of the young girl, dressed, who strips, abruptly displaying an animality in which Bataille recognizes his own.

These are not concepts that arise. They are positions, as indicated by the erotic leitmotif of the Marquis de Sade: "The position is broken." They are positions, *tableaux vivants*, theatrical scenes. Look at this:

> A being can only be touched where it yields. For a woman, this is under her dress; and for a god it's on the throat of the animal being sacrificed.[16]

So anthropology takes over from theology, and where theology offers dazzling visions brushed by mystical wings, anthropology suggests the catalogue with its philosophical entertainments: sacrificial poles through which man reconnects the sun with the sky, torture ceremonies where ecstasy is won, from ancient bull sacrifices to Holy Friday, from brothels to the mythic sensual delights of China. Lacking a philosophical system, one dreams up a theater. After Hegel, philosophers have no choice. The most sensitive know, with a private rhetorical certainty, that the concept will stop up their thought. Kierkegaard, Nietzsche hate whatever is systematic about philosophy; both of them resolutely go beyond the genre of demonstration and substitute at the desired moment the poem, the narrative, the novel for the concept.

It is not a question of dodging. On the contrary: the poem, the narrative, the novel work with the rhythm of writing and break the dialectical thread. Against dialectic, the poem. Against the system, the novel. Against the Everything, punctuation. And against philosophy, "right up against it," as one good joke has it, music.

With the new philosophers, those of syncope and of after-Hegel, music sweeps into philosophy, no longer as a lesser art as Kant decided, or as a major one as Hegel describes it, but as a fully fledged instrument of thought. For the same reasons that make it suspect in Plato's and Kant's eyes, music escapes from the concept. Philosophers can describe its theoretical codes, discern the ideal stakes in the violent conflicts between composers, but the musical effect escapes philosophy as it still escapes the human sciences today. By referring to music, these philosophers are actually new; with music, it is discontinuity they search for, and hatred of the subject's imprisonment in a system of thought. It is a syncope of thought.

Poor dialectic! The power and powerlessness of words: however connected it may be, thought has no other subject matter. Powers and powerlessness of the professor's lesson, made of words carried away by a whirlwind that those who have had more or less to think about in public know intimately. Perhaps one of the problems of thinking is that it cannot stop. On this point, form is crucial. Breaking punctuation, writing philosophy while sprinkling it with poems as do Kierkegaard and Nietzsche, these are operations of thinking: they open up space for silence, for blankness, and they leave a gap for the reader's—or listener's—fantasy to slip in. The Hegelian philosophical owl gives lessons in slowness; but its thought always moves *faster than music*.

For me, theater! And let one of our contemporaries, a dramatic writer, bring me the punctuation that is lacking.

You Who Live in Time, a play by Valère Novarina, presents characters, the Watchman, the Number Woman, Others, the Child of the Ashes, or simply Jean-François . . . They represent absolutely nothing, except humans talking about time.[17] The Watchman's first sentence: "Be Quiet: here it is."

Something was already under way, then, before the beginning of the theater that is called the curtain going up. We do not find out who the Watchman is, since a woman, the Number Woman, comes onstage; she develops some of her own dialectical prosopopeias, as good as anything in Hegel's *Science of Logic*.

> The exterior is outside of the interior. The interior is outside of nothing. The interior is outside of the interior. The exterior is not outside of him. The interior is not inside the exterior.[18]

That, naturally, continues.

Until the moment where she suddenly interrupts herself and cries, "Let's go!"

"Where to?" asks the Watchman.

"To precede that which follows," she says.[19]

There is something of both the Watchman and the Number Woman in Hegel.

Of the one who asks for silence and raises the curtain; and of the one who only knows how to talk, carried away by the mad logic of anticipation.

6

Of Young Girls as Thought: Kierkegaard the Seducer

In the beginning, there is a young girl. Her name is not important: she has been called Zerlina, Cordelia, Mary, Elvira, Marguerite; once she was Antigone. In Kierkegaard's real life, we know, she was a real person, and was called Regina Olsen, the philosopher's fiancée; later, alas, she married Friedrich Schlegel. But in Kierkegaard's philosophy, her name is first and foremost "thought."

See what he does with her:

> Thought was calm, rested happy in its knowledge; then I went to it and begged it to bestir itself once more, to venture the ultimate.[1]

You read correctly. The philosopher Kierkegaard is thought's suitor; it is clear that thought is a little lazy, liking nothing so much as peaceful rest in the snug nest of understanding. Now, look how the philosopher wakes her up and sets her in motion. Thought knows very well, continues the philosopher, that it is "futile"; since she is rather a good girl, however, she does not refuse to shake a leg. "It [thought] labored in vain; egged on by me, it was continually going beyond itself and continually collapsing back into itself. It was continually looking for a foothold and finding none. It was continually trying to find bottom, but could neither swim nor wade."[2] Poor mad thought, unable to float. "It was both a laughing and a crying matter. Therefore I did both and was very grateful that it had not denied me this service. And although I now know perfectly well that it is useless, it could still very well occur to me to ask thought to play once again the game that to me is inexhaustible material for enjoyment."[3]

That is one of the philosopher Kierkegaard's innumerable seduction scenes; this one, which resembles an eclogue, is also a kindly way of putting old Hegel in his place, that old professor who never succeeded with thought—the old hypochondriac who did not even make her laugh or cry. And that is child's play.

There are innumerable seduction scenes in which Kierkegaard puts himself in the place of the seducer, Cherubino, Papageno, Don Juan, himself finally, or one of his multiple pseudonymous doubles. The attempts to make the young girl *fall* are innumerable, with the secret hope that this time, no, she will not fall, she will not search vainly inside herself for support, she will succeed, she will resist. What happens when the game is over, after the young girl's defeat, we will soon see. But at the moment let us watch the seduction carefully, for in it the philosopher's desired *raptus* is concealed.

The Seducer's Diary, transplanted right into the middle of the collection *Either/Or*, tells a tiny, unique story. It is in the genre of the epistolary novel; the plot would be breathtakingly banal if it were not for a touch of strangeness due to the philosophical tone that enchants this passing fancy and perfumes it with heliotrope.[4] A seducer falls in love with a young girl in a green coat; he approaches her, makes her love him, asks for her hand in marriage, they become engaged. From then on our seducer has only one desire: to break the contract, seize her, and carry her off. She is his; immediately, he loses interest in her.

This plot line for a bad film includes two peculiarities. The first is that the seducer is passionately concerned with *persuading* the young girl: she will share the desire for the rupture, the abduction, the erotic night—for everything except the desertion. The second peculiarity is the philosophical element itself: Kierkegaard tells us the story of a *rupture*. He achieves through an interpolated fiction the thing that, in his eyes, Hegel did not succeed in doing to thought. Thought is awakened, it wriggles in vain, outstrips itself without surpassing itself, laughs and cries . . . It will be made to go through a lot. Thought refuses to make an effort: the philosopher will compel her to *break off, and will then sleep with her*. At this level of clear-headedness, it would be vain to wonder who decides what, the biographical and the fictive, the real and the philosophical; Kierkegaard's cunning game leaves no one the trouble of asking these questions, and he asks them himself, of himself, with plenty of brilliance.

With fine rigor, Kierkegaard shows us Johannes, the seducer, attracted by a little leap, a step so mundane that one hardly pays attention to it. The young girl gets out of a carriage, and her foot stays in the air. That is all: "the decisive step," murmurs Kierkegaard already.[5] Of course, it will be explained that the attention that shakes our philosopher's desire is a fetishistic one. But the emphasis—as furtive as the desire of the fetishist for the boot—is placed on the leap, this little leap of nothing at all. We quickly understand that Cordelia's leap, when she steps down from the carriage, symbolizes something completely different. Leave aside some amorous episodes, time spent in anticipation with heart palpitating, successive repulsions and other usual attractions; soon Johannes wants to teach infinity to his young conquest.

He cannot wait for this infinity. Only a young girl is capable of it; only a virgin chained to the rocks, waiting to be devoured by the monster, can attach a thin string to the docile neck of the dragon; this is a matter of virginity. But that is not the most important thing. The important thing is the leap. Suddenly, another philosophy is born.

Man, born to work, does not know how to leap; he prepares himself for a long time, calculates the distance, reflects, takes a running start . . . and falls into the hole that he had hoped to jump over. Man's leap is always ludicrous, continues Kierkegaard, because it is *deliberate*. The young girl leaps so well that the untraversable gulfs between two towering mountain peaks are called "the Maiden's Leap." It is characteristic of young girls that they do not need a running start. Indeed, a running start would go against the grain of the young girl's leap: "That is, a running start has in itself the dialectical, which is contrary to woman's nature." The same goes for Hegel: using the young girl as a stand-in, Kierkegaard indicates clearly that Hegel's dialectic is rather heavy.

The young girl, the ageless Diotima on the edge of the abyss:

> Her leap is a gliding. And once she has reached the other side, she stands there again, not exhausted by the effort, but more beautiful, more soulful than ever; she throws a kiss over to us who stand on this side. Young, newborn, . . . she swings out over the abyss so that everything almost goes black before our eyes.[6]

One feels how this young woman carries myth and dream with her; one feels also that she is the philosophical virgin who will confront the dialectical monster contrived by Hegel, and will put around its neck the halter of infinity; the same infinity in which, a few lines further down, she is invited to "frolic."

It is with the same metaphysical lightness that the young girl Cordelia, after her engagement, indulges in an odd game with "her" Johannes. The engaged couple have already exchanged their rings. The serious burghers around them comment on the symbol of the exchange with such heaviness that suddenly the young man takes the rings, slips them onto a stick, and tosses them into the air, carelessly. At the same moment the young girl understands what Kierkegaard calls by an odd name: the pause. The pause: rings thrown as if launched into flight, by chance and completely freely. Quickly, she in turn seizes the rings and throws them, but so high that no one can catch them anymore:

> There is a story of a French soldier who had been in the Russian campaign and had to have his leg amputated because of gangrene. The very moment the ago-

> nizing operation was over, he seized the leg by the sole of the foot, tossed it up into the air, and shouted: *Vive l'empereur* [Long live the emperor]. With a look such as that, she, even more beautiful than ever before, tossed both rings up into the air and said to herself: "Long live erotic love."[7]

That is the moment, the irreparable moment. We have been there since the initial leap; since the abyss between the two rocks, and the Maiden's Leap. We are approaching the breach that is unbridgeable and yet crossed, a ghastly amputation that is consented to, however valiantly, only through the philosopher's virtue and in order to flout dialectic. Kierkegaard knows the breach by heart; he decided it like Johannes, he broke off his engagement and does not want to reinstate it. It is a matter of breaking and jumping; of breaking off and leaping; of shattering and reuniting. That is what the seducer is going to devote himself to by abducting the young girl the moment she is no longer his fiancée. Horses, carriage, clandestine night; a syncope in bourgeois life, a syncope in morality, and the first glimpses of metaphysical syncope:

> The bond has broken—full of longing, strong, bold, divine, she flies like a bird that now for the first time is allowed to spread its wings. Fly, bird, fly![8]

A quarter of an hour before midnight, the seducer abducts the young girl. "Everything sleeps in peace, but not erotic love."

At dawn: "But now it is finished, and I never want to see her again. When a girl has given everything away, she is weak, she has lost everything. . . . I do not want to be reminded of my relationship with her; she has lost her fragrance, and the times are past when a girl agonizing over her faithless lover is changed into a heliotrope. . . . If I were a god, I would do for her what Neptune did for a nymph: transform her into a man."[9]

There it is then, the true breach: here the seducer appears in his essence. Kierkegaard's scenario is otherwise more complicated than that of a simple Don Juan, even if he were the immortal prototype himself. For two breaches follow one on the other: that of the engagement—a break in bourgeois life and in marriage—and that one, the latter, the true one. Having risked everything—the young girl, or thought—she has lost everything. The philosopher only has to find another young girl, gentle and fresh, to beg her to put herself in motion, and to play the game of throwing rings once again.

But the seducer regrets the "one never knows." He wants the young deflowered girl to be a heliotrope, the flower turned passionately toward the sun—at the time, it wasn't known that this mythical flower is endowed with an autonomous rhythm that owes nothing to the sun. He wanted her to be a man, above all, like the nymph Kainis whom Poseidon turned into Kaineus, and who along with Narcissus is the other model for the Hermaphrodite, endowed with so prodigious a power that it took a whole mountain to bury him and finish him off. Did Kierkegaard know that Kainis, abandoned and transformed into a man, became *immortal* at the same time?[10]

Perhaps not; but in the moment of deflowering—the very moment of breaches, of hymen and love, of membranes and desire—the immortality that always haunts syncope slips in. This immoderate leap that suspends man's weight has the very lightness of fainting away: the magical grace of human time as it passes, of thought as it stops. At this precise moment the myth of immortality begins.

That is called a fall; Cordelia "fell," and the syncopated body collapses heavily. One does not escape from Newton any more than from the seducer. What fascinates the philosopher is the perilous moment of the young girl.

It is a shared danger. The dizzying grace of the young girl is dangerous for whoever is caught up in it. No one knows whether Johannes suffers from having abandoned the deflowered Cordelia; but we will see later on that anguish catches the philosopher by his heels, and causes him to make other sacrifices than a beauty's virginity.

Other young girls, who resemble Cordelia like two peas in a pod, bring about strange schisms: look at Charlotte, across from Werther, and across from Sigmund Freud, Dora.

Poor Werther is not an active seducer, but completely the opposite—he will die for having approached the chosen young lady a little too closely. It is a courtly love scene; from the outset Charlotte has been promised to a certain Albert, and even before meeting her Werther knows all this. On one and the same day, however, he sees her cutting a loaf of brown bread that she hands out to a flock of children, he goes off to the ball with her, and the die is cast. Leaving aside the rosy Charlotte's appearance in a motherly role, and her pronounced unavailability as a young girl engaged to another man, let us see what connects the two lovers from the beginning.

Charlotte has a passion, which she confesses: dancing. "If anything worries me, I go to my old squeaky piano, drum out a quadrille, and everything is well again." The instrument's being out-of-tune matters little to the artless girl; she is carried away as she strikes the keys, and that soothes her worries. The ball begins; they pass each other in the minuets—that is not dangerous. Then come the allemandes, which go on until the waltz, in which, contrary to custom, the couple stays together. "The dancers whirled around each other like planets in the sky . . . " remembers Werther, who writes to his friend Wilhelm:

"I vowed at that moment that a girl whom I loved, or for whom I felt the slightest attachment, should never waltz with another, even if it should be my end! You will understand." We do not know whether his friend Wilhelm has understood, but we understand that Werther will end up dying of having seen Charlotte waltzing with her husband. However, Werther and Charlotte continue to waltz—"flying with her like the wind, till I lost sight of everything else"[11]—to the point where a woman shakes a threatening finger at Charlotte and utters the name of her husband-to-be. Only then does Werther discover what he already knew, which gives him his death blow.

Up until now it has only been one of those deadly, sparkling waltzes that we are beginning to recognize. But the day is not yet over; the storm bursts, and the thunder puts an end to the dancing. Then the young girl invents a game to pass the time and reassure the company. It is called playing "*at counting.*" She sets herself to going around the circle, arm outstretched; as the beautiful girl's finger passes, each person must say the number that falls to his lot. Whoever is silent, hesitates, or makes a mistake gets a slap. "She went round the circle with upraised arm. 'One' said the first; 'two,' the second; 'three,' the third; and so on, till Charlotte went faster and faster. One man made a mistake—instantly a box on the ear; and amid the laughter that ensued, another box; and so on, faster and faster. I myself came in for two. I imagined," said Werther, "that they were harder than the rest, but felt quite delighted." Nobody doubts that Werther—although he does not say—jealously makes sure to miss his count. We do not have to wait long for the result of this magic sequence: the slicing of the bread, the waltz, the storm, and the slap have made Werther a lost man. "And since that time sun, moon, and stars may pursue their course: I know not whether it is day or night; the whole world about me has ceased to be."[12]

That young girl does not leap over chasms, she does not lean over the edge of the abyss of Asia; no, she is more mundane. With a knife, by whirling, and with a slap she makes a split, with her finger pointing and a smile on her lips. Dangerous Charlotte, the engaged woman, who whirls and extricates herself, then slips away: God knows, however, that she does not have the manner of a *femme fatale*. But if she is certainly not that, she is simply a young girl, one of those about whom Søren Kierkegaard made the metaphor about thought. She who cuts, waltzes, and slaps.

With Dora the nineteenth century is over, and from now on the slap is called a smack.

In 1935, the year in which Chekhov died, the great Soviet director Meyerhold staged a performance in his honor. Its title is stunning: *33 Swoonings*.[13] Meyerhold, in three little farces by Chekhov, counted no fewer than thirty-three swoonings. Chekhov, the playwright, knew what he was doing: the swoon is one of those theatrical jokes borrowed from vaudeville. Meyerhold's title is his argument in a nutshell, showing—syncope after syncope—"petit-bourgeois daily life in all its loathsome diversity."[14] The swoon is a weapon in the social game; it is an evasion, a mockery, or a wedding procession. This is the same world that will produce psychoanalysis: a vaudevillian universe in which the joke of fainting will at last be taken seriously.

Freud approaches young girls as Kierkegaard does: as strange birds, capable of converting their most secret shameful acts into odd spasmodic phenomena. Strange white geese who read erotic books in secret, allow themselves to be caressed by an uncle, a father, a governess, or by a woman who is a friend of the family. And they are dangerous for thought, to the point where Freud will hesitate for a long time before deciding: either they are speaking the truth, and all the fathers are vile; or they are liars, and the paternal honor is safe. Who is telling the truth? The young girl who in terror describes her father above her adolescent bed, uncovering a shameless and erect member, or the father who, of course, does not even suspect that his daughter is accusing him? Freud invents an expression for the category of young girls, an expression that already debunks the philosophical idea of every beginning: the hysteric's "first lie," "proton pseudos."[15] *In the beginning was the lying young girl*; but that was, and always will be, the decision of a circumspect and cautious Freud. Does one ever know? He too found himself the romantic prey of one of them; and his friend Breuer impregnated—with a hysterical pregnancy—one of his patients. Freud was warned about "one never knows."

So, Dora was a hysterical young girl.[16] Dyspnea, convulsions, asthma, coughs, nothing was lacking from the panoply of the perfect *fin de siècle* syncope. This case history, much written about, took place in a bourgeois universe, and the case of Dora could without much effort look like an Offenbach operetta. There is an adulterous father, a deceived mother: these are the young girl's parents. Then there is an ambiguous couple, willingly seductive: a certain Herr K. who pays court to little Dora, while his ravishing wife is not averse to caressing her too. Add in the fact that Frau K. is the mistress of Dora's father, and there you have a bourgeois comedy.

As for Dora, she will have nothing to do with all this song and dance; no doubt she is the only one to sense, in a confused way, that real drama can arise from these light comedies, as in Jean Renoir's *The Rules of the Game*. Her refusal is not an open revolt; it is spoken in syncopated troubles, it expresses itself when she coughs, when she chokes. That is why she is sent to Freud's couch. The good doctor quickly renders an opinion: Dora is in love—which is true. She loves Herr K.—that is false.

When the said Herr K. declares his passion to the little one, he is imprudently precise: "My wife means nothing to me," he says, and receives a sound smack. Not the gentle slap that the young girl Charlotte gives to her beloved Werther, but a real smack. Freud strives to demonstrate to Dora that this smack is still love. "Tough love," but love all the same; Freud still thinks he is in *Werther*. So, finding that what Freud tells her "is not very important," Dora leaves Freud, out of the blue. Dora's true love was not Herr K., but Frau K., with the ravishing body that the young girl's father was able to enjoy. Things had changed, and Freud was behind the times. The smack was a smack aimed at all the men in the case, including Freud.

But young girls are dangerous, and drama is not far off. A little later, Herr K., crossing the street in Vienna, catches sight of the young girl Dora.

He becomes flustered, hesitates, loses his balance . . . and is run over by a car.

There was a real Dora, a real Freud, also a real cough. There was a real Charlotte; a real Werther whose name was Goethe; I do not know if he danced with her, but they shelled beans together. There was a real Cordelia, whose name was Regina; and Søren Kierkegaard never stopped signing himself Johannes, the first name of the seducer in the *Journal*, as automatically as one makes a sign of the cross. All that is as true as the dancing and the hysteria; as true as I tell it to you. In order to stymie the philosophical system, to smash the wheel of dialectical thought, nothing is as effective as a young girl's smack, or her first lie.

Toward Anguish

That virgins are dangerous is nothing new. When a virgin is deflowered, what is inside her bites you; at the back of her cavity she has sturdy teeth hidden, made for tearing your member to shreds. The young girl Athena, Greek virgin and goddess of philosophy, does not set one's mind at rest; she is a virgin on the offensive, an impassive warrior, often cruel. As for the young girl Artemis, goddess of the hunt and of chastity, she is quite capable of giving her suitors to the dogs to be eaten. That is to say that the young girl does not always fall before the seducer's blows. If Freud loves young girls so much, it is because they also resist.

The resistance is what fascinates Freud and seduces Kierkegaard. Once deflowered, the young girl becomes an ordinary woman; once analyzed, she also becomes that. But with the hysterics Freud analyzed, there is no danger: they escape him, change symptoms, disappear—they are capricious—and change. From syncope or from the analyst, it makes no difference: they flee.

As for Kierkegaard, while writing the *Seducer's Diary* he goes to the very limits of his thought. With a mixture of repulsion and sadness, he abandons the young girl who did not know how to resist. One part of his philosophy circumvents the eternal young girl: Regina, Cordelia, Antigone . . . Another part of himself goes to look in more highly spiced thoughts for other leaps than the Maiden's. When the philosopher-seducer has finished with the young girl, he is busy with anguish.

Anguish is an old man. An old man from whom God has demanded his son as sacrifice. It is a dreadful, violent scene. Divine Law is savage, and man is crushed.

Make no mistake, however: anguish haunts the first seduction. Kierkegaard has told us often enough that anguish is at the end of the amorous chase; the Commander invites Don Giovanni to the last supper of his life. But what is true of the seducer is not true of the young girl: leaping and supernatural, and as long as she has not fallen, she escapes anguish. The old man Abraham will not escape it, nor yet the seducer Kierkegaard.

To read Kierkegaard is to progress from one syncope to the next; it is impossible to avoid the leap. After the maiden's leap, there is the "knight of faith's" leaping in place: after the young girl, the old man. To read Kierkegaard is to understand the suspended moment; it is to fall in love, to wait for a meeting with heart pounding, to break off an affair, to flee in the night with the beloved . . .

It is also to retire at dawn, disappointed, and to find oneself suddenly, without warning, on a mule path with a little donkey, and at one's side one's only son, whose throat God has demanded that you slit on top of the mountain.

7

Abraham, and a Roasted Lamb's Head

Five lines from the Old Testament, as swift as the swing of an ax: "The time came when God put Abraham to the test. 'Abraham,' he called, and Abraham replied, 'Here I am.' God said, 'Take your son Isaac, your only son, whom you love, and go to the land of Moriah. There you shall offer him as a sacrifice on one of the hills which I will show you.'" The rest of the biblical text does not give the slightest indication, in Abraham's actions, of his state of mind. "So Abraham rose early in the morning and saddled his ass, and he took with him two of his men and his son Isaac." And off they went.[1]

Kierkegaard begins *Fear and Trembling* with four successive versions of Abraham's state of mind on the way to Moriah. This is Abraham as imagined by a Kierkegaard who does not want to be a philosopher, but wants to remain "*poetice et eleganter* [in a poetic and refined way], a supplementary clerk who neither writes the system nor gives *promises* of the system."[2] At the end of each of the versions, in which the dreamer's imagination brings us to the moment of sacrifice, there are four conclusions on the theme, repeated each time, of the *weaning of the child*.[3] For Abraham the sacrifice will cut the thread of a life, that of his son; but for the mother, Sarah, it will separate the nursing infant from the breast where he had nestled. That is to say that the heart of this philosophical poem concerns the essence of separation, at the heart of the suspended moment.

At first light, in the first version, Sarah watches Abraham leave home; in the morning of the second version, Abraham kisses Sarah, "the fiancée of his old age"; in the third version, Sarah has become the "young mother"; finally, for the last dawn, Sarah is merely the woman of whom Abraham takes leave. Sarah is not indifferent in this matter; she laughed when Yahweh told her she would have a child, despite her being ninety years old. Sarah laughed uproariously[4]—and then gave birth. So she became a "young" mother; and even if she had lost the lilt of youth, she nonetheless retained it while laughing, a glimmer of innocence that made the ancient adolescent in her recognizable, the eternal young girl with spontaneous grace.

There is not a word in the Bible about Sarah's behavior at the moment when Abraham sets off to sacrifice their only son. There is also almost nothing on this in *Fear and Trembling*, except for the theme of weaning. For God is also taking her son from Sarah, a brutal and radical separation that would be demanded again only of the Virgin Mary. There are, in *Fear and Trembling*, four ways of weaning. First method: the mother blackens her breast, and the child thinks that his mother has changed. Second method: the mother modestly conceals her breast, and the child no longer has any mother at all. Third method: the mother and the child grieve together. Fourth method: the mother finds food for her child that is stronger than her own milk. Underneath the meditation of a philosopher on Abraham's states of mind, a filigree of strange studies on the grief of weaning is outlined: on the initial sadness of the separation from the mother; on the "stronger sustenance," the life of replacement that can never replace the mother's milk. And while the mother despairs at her window, Abraham plods toward the mountain of Moriah.

The first time, gentle and tormented, he explains to his son why he is going to have to cut his throat; then, as the child laments, Abraham pretends that he is acting on his own accord, so that Isaac calls on Yahweh to help him. Thus Isaac will have lost faith in his father but not in God. Abraham blackened his breast.

The second time, Abraham is silent right until the end, and remains gloomy until his death. Isaac, saved at the last moment, grows up. But Abraham bears a grudge against God; he no longer has a father.

The third time, Abraham thinks about the woman he had slept with, Hagar, and whom he chased away because Sarah demanded it. And he thinks only of this other woman and of this child whom he has lost, he who is trudging off to kill the last son of his old age with his own hands. Then—but this is later—he goes back to the mountain of Moriah and blames himself before God; yes, he is the one who wanted to sacrifice Isaac, he is the unworthy father. But despite his remorse, Abraham finds no peace, for he has sinned. And Abraham's sadness before God is like that of the mother before her weaned child.

The last time, Abraham and Isaac both know why they are trudging toward Moriah. But Isaac can see very well the despair of his father's left hand at the moment he pulls out the knife to slit his throat. So Isaac loses faith, saying nothing of it to his father, who also does not talk about it.

And who then, of the father, the mother, or the child, has lost faith in the other?

On the path up to the mountain, three figures move toward anguish. The father, Abraham, the mother, Sarah, and the child, Isaac, the whole family the prey of a useless sacrifice. For each of Kierkegaard's imagined versions is affected by an irremediable loss: what is lost can be called trust in one's father, faith in God, it is all the same, and it is always-already-lost. The irremediable occurs the moment Yahweh orders the departure for Moriah. And not a word is said about what constitutes the essence of this biblical episode.

Not a word about what happens when Abraham has drawn the knife. There, on an altar of branches, with Isaac bound, the father's arm rises. "Then," continues the biblical Word,

> the angel of the Lord called to him from Heaven, "Abraham, Abraham." He answered, "Here I am." The angel of the Lord said, "Do not raise your hand against the boy; do not touch him. Now I know that you are a godfearing man. You have not withheld from me your son, your only son."[5]

In Kierkegaard's imagined version, nothing comes to replace the sacrificed son. No ram, no angel with a human voice. Nothing is left but God's barbarity—unsaid and unsayable, restrained with great difficulty by fear and trembling. The savage and irremediable barbarity that demands absolute terror to test its power.

When Sikhism, which had succeeded in reforming Hinduism, began to be persecuted by a Mogul emperor who was a strict fundamentalist, the ninth of the Sikh masters was beheaded in public, and the watching people were asked if one of them would dare to declare himself a Sikh. Silence. This silence cried out so loudly that the tenth master, son of the ninth, heard it.

One day in April, in the middle of a celebration, he set up his tent and appeared at dawn, two-edged sword in hand. Then, as in the scene from the Bible, he asked who would come and sacrifice themselves for the cause. The Sikh master called twice without any response; the third time, an Untouchable came forward, entered the tent, and the sword was heard whistling; blood was seen streaming outside. The master came out; his sword was bloodied, and still he asked again. A hairdresser, a cook, a washer, a water carrier came forward;[6] four times the blood flowed. People ran to fetch the tenth Sikh master's mother to warn her that her son was mad.

Then the master opened the tent and there were the five Sikhs, alive; and at their feet were sheep with their throats slit. From that day on, every Sikh is baptized with the sharp blade of a sword; each of them retains graven on his heart the founding scene of men who went into a tent to have their throats cut in honor of their god.

The scene of sacrifice demanded, with the substitution of an animal as its key, is one of the models of the test. Whether it is Yahweh, the tenth Sikh master, or those who offer their children the keys of Paradise, whether one pulls a knife on Isaac, on an Untouchable, or on an army of teenagers who have been offered a kamikaze plane to die in, with a submachine gun or little plastic imitations around their necks, God's barbarity, whatever it is called, is always the same. And the suspended instant when Abraham's arm comes up is identical: it is the instant where one can say "yes" or "no"; the moment where faith, in God or in man, is always lost; the instant, in a word, where beliefs are obliterated as the virgin's hymen yields during defloration. It is the instant of Antigone's "patriotic reversal."

At the end of the test, separation will have occurred; faith is definitively separated from naive and innocent adherence. Weaning, in all its heroic banality, will have occurred. Obviously, it is not only the weaning of the child from his mother's breast; it is the weaning of the believer who clasps the breast of his god. After this falsely bloody episode, all that will exist are "replacement foods": ram, sheep, philosophy, *poetice et eleganter*. "How fortunate the one," says Kierkegaard, "who has this stronger sustenance at hand!"

Fear and Trembling is that stronger sustenance. A real sword against the blindness of the believer who sets off, saddling his ass, to slit the throat of his only son on the instructions of the Supreme Being. A radical and definitive loss of belief results from this brutal weaning; to believe, Kierkegaard tells us, to believe is to know the loss, and its cause.

This is one of the possible meanings of an enigmatic part of the ritual of the whirling dervishes. If an object, or some money, falls out of the bag as the dervish is spinning, he is forbidden to pick it up. That is God's share. Kierkegaard tells us that belief in God includes this radical loss. To believe is to lose. That is Pascal's wager, but betting in the other direction. One is no longer seeking to win; one will always already have lost.

This man, whose name was Abraham and who was a hundred years old, doubted that his son Isaac would be born, and yet he was. This man, who experienced the confrontation with raw anguish, will later in Kierkegaard's text be called the "knight of faith." That is an incomprehensible paradox, a paradox that repulses the logical mind and remains impenetrable. What did Abraham believe? That God would not demand Isaac, or that he would give him other sons? Was he in "infinite resignation," or did he go as far as that leap in thought that Kierkegaard called the "absurd"? "He had faith by virtue of the absurd, for all human calculation ceased long ago."[7] Abraham's "yes" is that of a *metaphysical leaper*.

It is not I who say it, but Kierkegaard who has not forgotten, between the young girl and the old man, the allegory of the leap. Now, among the masses of men, there are some who have access to the infinite: these are not yet the "knights of faith" but the "knights of infinity." They too leap—you understand, in the movement of thought. They also throw their thought in the air and catch it, dialectical acrobats or poets. "They make the upward movement and come down again, and this, too, is not an unhappy diversion and is not unlovely to see."[8] However, when they come back down, they wobble; it is a slight, a very slight hesitation. By that one recognizes the man who has not yet truly passed through the fire of anguish.

Let us see how, on the contrary, the "knight of faith" comes forward (a knight who, by the way, does not exist: except for the imaginary and mythic Abraham, the author of *Fear and Trembling* admits that he has never met one on his way). But he imagines one, in his armor, and, like Italo Calvino's nonexistent knight, who has no body under his armor, he seeks the impossible incarnation of this fanatical believer who believes in God without believing, absurdly. And, impossibility of impossibilities, Kierkegaard disguises his knight of anguish as a solid burgher.

This improbable hero looks just like a tax collector; he goes to church; one would suppose him a pen-pusher. He goes off on walks in the woods and is not even a poet. He has money, he smokes a pipe; he lives "with the freedom from care of a reckless good-for-nothing," watching with interest the rats in the gutter and the children playing. And yet he has gone through anguish, no one knows how or when, and he ceaselessly executes the real movement of infinity. That is, he leaps—but so quickly and so well that he always falls back in the same place, and no one can see this marvelous leap, which is even more prodigious for being completely, totally imperceptible. "But to be able to come down in such a way that instantaneously one seems to stand and to walk, to change the leap of life into walking, absolutely to express the sublime in the pedestrian—only that knight can do it, and this is the one and only marvel."[9]

We should not be fooled by Kierkegaard's notorious irony. This leap in place is a premeditated absurdity, an absurdity designed to wring time's neck, to insinuate the worm of despair into the bourgeois fruit. It is completely the opposite of tragedy, Kierkegaard tells us; in it, the Individual appears deprived of any sign of royalty or grandeur. The modern Abraham, who like the wandering Jew never stops resenting the lost god whom he affirms, is absurd. And he performs the movement of infinity while contemplating the roasted lamb's head that his wife, one never knows, has perhaps prepared for his return home. From the imposing Bible scene, drawn with the drypoint of revelation, to the final image of the knight of faith Kierkegaard imagined, only one thing remains: the roasted ram's head, with vegetables.[10]

The scene, despite the roasting, is not far removed from courtly love—less, no doubt, in the seduction of the archetypal young girl than in the impossible relationship with the lost god; for the seducer approaches and deflowers the young girl. God, on the other hand, holds the position of the inaccessible, the divine law that castrates, separates, and nonetheless demands.

The unbearable test that God demanded of Abraham, the complete absence of explanations, the lack of reason, is seen at work in the commandments that the lady gives her lover; we run across it as soon as the inaccessible joins in. The absurd roasted lamb's head—with vegetables—is a bourgeois counterpoint to the despair of the knight wandering on the spot, jumping without moving; instead of going on the road to Moriah to confront the most terrible of tests for an inaccessible God, he comes back home, and his wife is waiting for him. This knightly and courtly despair must adapt to modern life's slippers. And instead of the sacred mountain, instead of the garden of love where the lady would await him, all the knight of faith finds is the intimacy of his home.

But he has, as one says, his secret garden. He cultivates a variety of anguish there that has neither the grandeur of the tragic nor the elegance of sadness; it is the bourgeois version, it is sorrow.

Look at what Kierkegaard says about sorrow:

> By withdrawing inward in this way, it [sorrow] finally finds an inclosure, an innermost retreat, where it thinks it can remain, and now it begins its uniform movement. . . . At last there is a kind of balance; the need to give vent to the grief, insofar as it may ever have asserted itself at all, ceases; the exterior is calm and quiet; and deep within, in its little nook, grief lives like a well-guarded prisoner in an underground prison, who lives on year after year in his uniform movement, walking to and fro in his cubbyhole, never weary of traveling the long and short road of sorrow.[11]

A metaphysical prison where liberty is played out in the movement of the pendulum, dull to the point of equilibrium; dizziness comes, then soon sleep, defined as "sensual geniality." The supreme moment has already passed; and the knight of faith is locked into an apparent continuity. Even more luminous, with the somber and sad lighting of a Dreyer, look at this fragment of *Diapsalmata*:

> My sorrow is my baronial castle, which lies like an eagle's nest high up on the mountain peak among the clouds. No one can take it by storm. From it I swoop down into actuality and snatch my prey, but I do not stay down there. I bring my booty home, and this booty is a picture I weave into the tapestries at my castle. There I live as one already dead. Everything I have experienced I immerse in a baptism of oblivion unto an eternity of recollection. Everything temporal and fortuitous is forgotten and blotted out. Then I sit like an old gray-haired man, pensive, and explain the pictures in a soft voice, almost whispering, and beside me sits a child, listening, although he remembers everything before I tell it.[12]

That is what the abandoned young girl is like, too: endlessly, tearfully whispering her regrets. And also the young girl Antigone, the main character in *Either/Or*.

Kierkegaard devotes a lecture to her, which he was to have presented before a strange audience: the *sunparanekromenoi*, which means, in Greek, the fellowship of the dead, the companions of death reunited in a fraternal gathering. It is in this charming imaginary company that Kierkegaard talks about Antigone, his creation, his work, his property—in short, he says, his favorite girl. This young girl Antigone has always known that she was the offspring of an incestuous relationship, even before Oedipus realized it:

> In the same way, our Antigone carries her secret in her heart like an arrow that life has continually plunged deeper and deeper, without depriving her of her life, for as long as it is in her heart she can live, but the instant it is taken out, she must die.[13]

The young girl, like the knight, kept the secret and will always keep it, carefully locked up in the prison of sorrow or in the baronial castle of pain. In this fortified enclosure, the rules of logic are no longer applicable. There, everything has been forgotten and everything is remembered; one lives, but in death; one is old, yet one is a child. Time destroys itself; and metaphysical syncope is part of the structure.

Kierkegaard's cry is recognizable: "Why did I not die as a baby?"[14]

The philosophy of a stillborn child. By conferring before the company of the dead, by imagining himself posthumous, Kierkegaard sites his thought in a short circuit between life and death. A lifetime is too long; it is an immense useless parenthesis that the philosopher will fill up with the leap of young girls, with the leap of anguish and of faith.

Syncope of the Believer, Syncope of the Shaman: Kierkegaard and Nietzsche

They share little, these two philosophical heroes, suffering figures that the existentialism of the postwar era immediately recognized as its masters. Kierkegaard and Nietzsche have little in common: enough, however, that they responded in advance to the upheavals of the Second World War even though they both spoke in terms of the Individual, and only of the Individual. Despairing amid the ruins.

What they share is a hatred—the hatred of systems and the hatred of philosophers who erect[15] them. Kierkegaard and Nietzsche loathe the "infinite resignation" that often conceals either religion or sickness. Nietzsche's hatred of Christianity is certainly striking; but in Kierkegaard's violence and in the absurdity of the "knight of faith" it is easy to discern more than a simple ambivalence, a sort of fascinated horror. They also share two things, as we will see, that are closely related to syncope: the *idea of sickness* and the *taste for returning*.

We run into sickness at every turn. Nausea, hysterical symptoms, Hegel's hypochondria, Hölderlin's madness . . . nothing is more logical: the physiological syncope, in Kierkegaard's time and then in Nietzsche's, has emerged from the domain of the sacred and entered into that of medicine. Kierkegaard and Nietzsche turn the idea of sickness upside down and treat it as what syncope is: a symptom of the soul. They treat it with humor; one could say that they poke fun at it. They both find the cure in a return to the self, insolent and anti-establishment.

Kierkegaard: despair is a sickness, a *sickness unto death*. One "catches" despair like tuberculosis; but it cannot be cured. Like every other sickness, the philosopher asserts with assurance, one catches despair through carelessness: one single lapse is enough, for which one is entirely responsible. But then! Then it is a sickness that, unlike somatic sicknesses, is caught at every moment. Each time it is a new attack, a new bout. A bout of what, may I ask? questions the doctor. A bout of time.

Look at the symptoms. A "sickness unto death" does not mean that one dies of it; on the contrary. The characteristic of despair, the sickness of the mind, is precisely that one is sick unto death without being able to die of it:

> It is in this last sense that despair is the sickness unto death, this tormenting contradiction, this sickness of the self, perpetually to be dying, to die and yet not die, to die death. For to die signifies that it is all over, but to die death

> means to experience dying, and if this is experienced for one single moment, one thereby experiences it forever.[16]

Other voices sing the "I die of not dying," like the first harvest, the offering for the arrival of a god; what Kierkegaard says is similar to this, but stops exactly at that place where ecstasy could begin—in the dangerous and seductive "between-the-two": between life and death, at the join where consciousness is lost while pushed to its limit. Access to eternity is part of the despairing person's blueprint, certainly; but what an eternity! Pinned to the Self as the Other was on his cross.

The symptom is, then, a brutal and repetitive bout of time, a paludism of the consciousness. Kierkegaard describes its signs: "It is always the present tense; in relation to the actuality there is no pastness of the past: in every actual moment of despair the person in despair bears all the past as a present in possibility."[17] It is a fever of regret that makes it impossible to experience the present otherwise than as if one had been deported into a past where nothing happened. Every joy is impossible, every jouissance suppressed. The possible, that is the poison. It is precisely like fainting away, says Kierkegaard. Faced with syncope one cries: Water! Water!, and for the person in despair, one cries: The possible! The possible! But possibility is rejected in the past. It is a fine thing to revive a despairing man with a possibility that is always already lost and regretted.

A self without despair could be the cure. "Turning toward himself, and wanting to be himself, the self throws itself, through its own transparency, into the power that sets it up." Without time lag. Without regretting the possible. In an ecstatic present. In a syncope from which one does not return. In order to have access to it one must turn back toward oneself, go back with full force.

Nietzsche: "I am neither mind nor body, but a third thing. I suffer for all and everywhere."[18] Confronted day after day by the "little fusillade of his sufferings,"[19] with this image Nietzsche puts himself in the position of the condemned man in front of an eternal execution post. "For other German philosophers," says Stefan Zweig, "existence flows by with epic tranquillity; their philosophy consists in smoothly and in some ways mechanically spinning out a thread once it has been untangled. They philosophize in their armchairs, with their limbs spread out, and it would be hard to notice any increase in their blood pressure or any fevers in their future while they think." Nietzsche is very different, one of the first to have involved his body in his thought, and he got nothing for his trouble. "With Nietzsche, for the first time the black flag of the corsair and the pirate is seen on the seas of German philosophy: another species of man, of another race, a philosophy that no longer appears in the guise of a professor or a scientist, but wearing breastplates and armed for combat."[20] The philosopher in his suffering is cured.

It is the others who are sick. Nietzsche's suspicions about other philosophers are wonderful: What happens to their thinking when they "fall" ill? The same thing that happens to everyone except Nietzsche: they let themselves go, into a decline that is known to be the secondary effect of sickness. That is not all, however. From the sickness "something" is going to emerge and will take the mind "in flagrante delicto": in a state of weakness. Thus are born sequences of ideas, theories about theories: "Any philosophy that places peace above war, any ethics that conceives happiness negatively, any metaphysics, any physics that foresees any final, definitive state, any aspiration—especially an aesthetic or religious one—toward a next-to, a beyond, an outside-of, or an above, allows one to wonder whether it was not sickness that inspired that philosopher." Systematic philosophers are sickly, secretly tempted by "benches to rest on," the "sunny corners." As for the philosopher Nietzsche, he is "cured": he attains "full health."

He reaches it as a shaman does. Like a shaman, he is a former invalid; the shamanistic test consists of curing oneself, and if not by oneself, at least with one's own powers caught up in the pattern of a ritual. No outside intervention: no doctor, no potions, no rest, no siesta, no relaxation for the shaman, none for the philosopher. Everything lies in the test, everything is in the pain that one must go through in order to cure. Nietzsche's exercise of thought conforms absolutely to the shamanistic scenario. From journey to journey, from burn to burn, confronted with the flames, with narcosis, with the most savage dismemberment, the traditional shaman returns at last, resuscitated by himself, "dead" and remade as new. The freeing of the mind by the "great suspicion" of "great pain" is *Sehnsucht*; it is also laughter, the "morning song, so airy and sunny that it succeeds in *not* chasing away dark thoughts"; *it is still and always Amor Fati*, at the fateful hour of noon—"every lake, every noontime, time without purpose."[21] Nietzsche's shamanism.

And as the shaman "returns" from his horrifying initiatory voyage, Nietzsche also returns; the idea of the eternal return is born. All the roads are blocked toward the ever-suspect beyond, wherever it may be. It is *right in the middle of time* that the curing happens: a time without goal, all game, pure game. The movement is not so different from the transparent plunge into the "himself of me" where Kierkegaard sees the dissolution of despair. The same *nostos* inhabits both, the same taste for return. That would be called nostalgia, if it were not for the fact that it is no longer a question of suffering from homesickness: it is purely and simply a matter of going back without shilly-shallying. It is like an odyssey that one knows only too well exists but that one must violently short-circuit. Kierkegaard and Nietzsche also share a syncopal precision, the affirmation of the "on-the-spot": the "knight of faith" leaps on the spot, Zarathustra appears on the spot at the end of the poem "Sils-Maria." Farewell to progress, farewell to the conscientious progression of intellectual odysseys: the cure, or the despair, is here, suddenly, with or without the present.

They love scandal, reject sentimentalism. Kierkegaard finds that just as one legislates the amount of salmon to be used by domestic servants in Scotland when too much of it has been caught, one would have to restrain by decree the consumption of feelings.[22] The other, Nietzsche: to be a philosopher, one must be "dry, clear, without illusion." Dry, like the shaman with an iron skeleton: no dampness, and no more tears. For Kierkegaard, a scandal involving the individual; a scandal involving the new philosopher, a messenger so unbearable for humanity that he will end up, like Zarathustra, assassinated by a woman. Scandal! And please do not pluck out, as the Gospel wishes, the offending eye, or cut off the guilty hand: one must, on the contrary, corrupt everything in order to pass beyond the body and come close to the eternal return.

There is a figure in Kierkegaard who calls Nietzsche's shamanism to mind: it is demonic despair. And do you know what it is?

A misprint in the text, a slip of the pen. Endowed with consciousness, in revolt against its author, whom it forbids to correct it. "No, I refuse to be erased; I will stand as a witness against you, a witness that you are a second-rate author."[23]

There is no better way of saying to one's progenitor or to the creator of the world that one will be, forever, *incorrigible*. So both Kierkegaard and Nietzsche are incorrigible. One has the nature of a ragamuffin, the other of a mad child; both play with knucklebones, the spinning top, the rhombus, and the mirror. Knucklebones to represent a taste for testing one's luck and for seductive adventure; a top to ensure the subject's dizziness, his fainting; a rhombus for music; and a mirror, to break it in the end.

We will not avoid Dionysus, nor the women around him. The knucklebones, the spinning top, the rhombus, and the mirror are the objects that the Titans used to lure the child Dionysus, in order to dismember him and roast him. We will not avoid returning to Dionysus, for he is the master of syncope. To tell the truth, he has been roaming, using proxy bacchantes, since the beginning. Once one has raised the topic of Nietzsche, it is definitely not possible to ignore him any longer. The price is well known: either one devours or one is devoured. With Nietzsche, the god of orgies and of dismemberment, of lost consciousness and Roman emperors, the god of women and of intoxication, stages a return worthy of himself.

8

The Great Attack

A herdsman recounts how he surprised the bacchantes at daybreak, after they had spent the entire night in orgies.[1] The herdsman comes to tell the story to his king, Pentheus, who dislikes the stranger Dionysus.

At first, there are only women sleeping a quiet and normal slumber, the opposite of a drunken slumber. They are simply tired, and are lying down on the leaves, or sitting peacefully against the trunks of pine trees. Until, suddenly, one of them hears the lowing of the flocks. That is the signal for them to awaken.

Still calm, they bathe, fix their hair, adjust their belts and the serpents that adorn their arms. They retie their tunics made of fawn or goat skin. They are ready, and the first magical and inhuman activity of the bacchantes begins.

They breast-feed, not babies but fawns and wolf cubs. Barely awake, in the natural continuity of animality, appears a woman with a wolf at her breast. And this is not all: crowned with oak and sarsaparilla, they miraculously command water or wine to spring from the rocks. On their thyrsus, a stick covered with vines, drops of honey shine. The scene is supernatural, like that of the breast-fed animal; the bacchantes are in direct contact with the forces of the earth, far from the lengthy procedure employed by man to gather honey or make wine.

These woman are undistilled Nature. The herdsman is already mesmerized and under the influence of their seduction. The bacchanal has not yet begun; there is order in this immense confusion between nature and culture, there are finishing touches to be made in the orgiastic ceremonies. The hour has come. Songs resound, sounds of "evohe! eh!" and ululations are heard:

> And the whole mountain danced with them, the wild animals danced, nothing remained unmoved by the rush of women.

Until now, only the cries of the women have been heard.[2]

But King Pentheus had instructed his herdsmen to watch the bacchantes and to chase them from the mountain. Suddenly the bacchantes' leader, Agave, notices the men hiding in the thickets. This is the signal for the first attack. She then calls upon her companions, her "nimble she-dogs," and soon they have taken off in pursuit of the herdsmen, who barely escape the horde—animal or divine, it amounts to the same thing. Having caught no men, the bacchantes tear the flocks apart, hanging bloody baby lambs from tree branches; bellowing bulls and cows are slaughtered, "overcome by innumerable girlish hands."

In ancient Greece, the transformation of a young girl into a bacchante was only a doe's leap away. But as bourgeois as the ancient figure of the believer in Bacchus had become in Kierkegaard, one can still distinguish, inside Cordelia's delicate stocking, the foot of the maenad striking the ground. And in the game of the rings, the risk of a Dionysian orgy can still be seen. The young girl, definitely.

Yet it is not enough. "Lifted on their speed like birds," they stream out of the mountains and spread out onto the plains. Invulnerable, they pillage; fire does not burn them, bronze and iron do not wound them, no weapon touches them. They make men's bodies bleed, however, with the points of their thyrsi. When they have finished pillaging, they return to the mountains and bathe themselves in the stream. The serpents twisted around their arms lick off the men's last drops of blood.

Charge, bacchantes, charge . . . They only need to hear the call of their god—Eh! Oh! Hear it, hear my voice! Eh! Oh! bacchantes—for them to set out on a bounding race. These women run like no one else; breast-feed newborn animals like no one else; and destroy like no one else. Charge, bacchantes . . . it is time for the great attack.

Scholars of ancient Greece have long recognized the similarity of symptoms between the great hysterical attack and the superhuman strength of the bacchantes. We discovered long ago—since Michelet, who was inspired by the figure of the witch—that the trace of bacchism was not lost after the demise of the god's cult. But it is now the hysterics themselves who are subject to attack, and it is now in their very bodies that is effectuated, via the tautness of a body bent back like a bow, the laceration of a lost consciousness. It is only by mentioning an exceptional news item that the great attack can be conjured up with such lightning speed. In a sleepy little town, among a stingy bourgeoisie, is an ordinary house, inhabited by a mother and a daughter and a father who is a bit too self-effacing. There are two servants, two silent sisters working for them . . . The event takes place in France at the beginning of the twentieth century in the city of Le Mans, far from the Cithaeron mountains where the original bacchantes washed themselves. And yet . . .

After a power failure on an otherwise uneventful evening, the house is left without electricity. The ladies of the house return home and scold the servants. Charge, bacchantes, charge! The two sisters fling themselves on their employers, one of them on each of the women, plucking out their eyes, carving and smashing their thighs and faces with a knife, a hammer, and a lead pitcher. The blood of one of the victims is smudged on the sexual organs of the other. Finally, Christine and Léa Papin, twenty-eight and twenty-one years old, respectively, wash the instruments of their crime, bathe themselves and go to bed, saying to each other, "What a clean job!" This stupefying murder paralyzed and horrified all of France. Lacan, in an article entitled "Crime paranoïaque" (Paranoid crime), ends up with the following comments: "It is sacrilegious curiosity that has caused man anguish from the beginning of time and that motivates them [these women] when they desire their victims, when they track down in their victim's gaping wounds what Christine would later innocently call 'the mystery of life.'"[3]

For if the mountain, milk, honey, and wine have disappeared, if nothing is left of nature nor of the thyrsus, nor of the fawn or wolf cub, the essential remains: the unknown call of a rejected god; the massacre and tearing apart of ritual victims; final ablutions, purification and the last word, "clean," that sounds like a legitimation from another world. A short circuit: suddenly, an electrical failure; suddenly, the attack . . . suddenly, there is chaos and destruction. Suddenly, consciousness disappears; syncope comes to life. The two sisters are condemned to be beheaded.

But let us return to Pentheus. Actually, this king who would have nothing to do with Dionysus had a taste for argument and considerable curiosity. Pentheus disliked this foreign god. His origin was uncertain, he was a comforter of the weak and of women; a god of immigration. In the royal mansion, Dionysus had already corrupted the king's mother, Agave, his two aunts, his grandfather, Cadmus. Even the old soothsayer Tiresias, trembling on his ancient legs, crowned himself with ivy and brandished the thyrsus, one never knows. It is too much for a conservative king to bear: down with the foreigner, death to the immigrant god! And what does he say?

> . . . But if I
> get hold of him inside my palace here
> I'll stop his pounding the thyrsus and tossing
> those tresses high—by cutting off his head
> clean from the shoulders.[4]

Here are King Pentheus's plans: to capture the stranger and behead him. But here is the god, who politely let himself be tied up by the king's herdsmen; his blond hair floats down to his shoulders, and he is smiling. Pentheus tries to extort his secret from him, or a mystery, perhaps the mystery that only the initiate knows. The mystery of life. And since the stranger responds divinely, that is to say, with enigmas, suddenly King Pentheus explodes: "First, I'll cut off those ringlets that you wear."[5]

But once his hair has been cut, what does one see? Pentheus has come around, disguised as his own mother: dress, thyrsus, fawn skin, no detail is missing. And it is he, the king, who anxiously asks the god whether he looks enough like his mother to surprise her. Dionysus offhandedly puts one of Pentheus's curls back into place.

We know what happens next. Pentheus climbs a pine tree to satisfy his curiosity as a frustrated son. Dionysus bends the tree with a movement of his hand, causing the king to fall from it like a ripe fruit. Charge, bacchantes . . . Agave leads the hunt, and this time, the human prey will not escape. You might, says the bacchante to her father before opening her eyes to reality, want to invite your friends to dinner, to share with them this young catch with the lovely mane:

> Soon—how soon?—in the night-long dances
> will I step with white, with white bare feet,
> ecstatic, turning my throat high up to greet
> the dew-drenched air, as a light fawn prances
> in the greenest pleasures of pasture . . . [6]

Metamorphosis of woman: the bacchante makes the transition from sleep to an animal state without hesitating. Everything is important, and will be found again in the other scenes: the mountain, the dew-drenched air, the ravine, the rhythm, the lowing of the cattle, and the head thrown back like that of a fawn.

The bacchantes are not the only ones who massacre an overcurious man. King Battos of Cyrene lost his virility for having wanted to watch the Thesmophoria, a ritual strictly reserved for women. The "choking" priestesses in their white robes allowed him to watch to his heart's content, then all of a sudden attacked him. When Orpheus began to devote himself a little too exclusively to the god Apollo, calling him the "greatest of the gods," Dionysus called the Bassares women, who tore Orpheus to pieces, leaving only his head intact. Even Dionysus himself was the victim of a cruel attack as a child.

Cut into seven pieces by the Titans, boiled, roasted, and perhaps even eaten: the son of Zeus and Selene, who was struck by Zeus in the form of lightning, Dionysus had a childhood that went from anguish to the most extreme dismemberment. In other versions, we see that before being attacked by the Titans, the child-god was attacked by a wolf-man. Lycurgus madly chases the child and his nurses into the crest of the waves, into which they throw themselves; the little god's fear is so severe that he was overcome by an incurable trembling. This is how he got his name: the loud and trembling one. Dionysus is the god of trembling and of fits, who stimulates the weak to render them invincible. In the massacres surrounding him, whether he is their victim or their cause, there is no association: it is the Titans alone, the priestesses of Thesmophoria alone, the Bassares women alone, and the bacchantes alone who indulge in this savage dismemberment. One entire sex united against a single god, against a single king, against a single visionary.

Something always remains of these massacres. Divided into seven pieces by the Titans, the body of Dionysus is piously collected by Apollo, his opposite and "other."[7] Aside from the heart, which was spared in the cooking and is still beating—that is seized by the young Athena. King Battos's sexual organ remains in the hands of the priestesses. Pentheus's head stays in the hands of Agave; as for that of Orpheus, it does not stop singing on its route down the river from Mount Pangeus, until it reaches its final destination on the shores of the island of Lesbos.

Arrived on solid ground, the head begins to dictate, with its eyes fixed on the scribe who collects the glorious tales of the genesis of the gods, and of the epic birth of Dionysus, son of Zeus and his daughter, an incestuous relation complicated by "in vitro" fertilization. According to Orphic tradition, Dionysus is none other than the first-born of the gods, reclaimed by Zeus and enclosed in his stomach, as if to allow him to escape the woman-cycle. Dionysus's birth gives rise to two distinct genealogies: in the first, he is the son of the mortal Selene, in the other, he is the son of one of Zeus's daughters. In both cases, he is not born of a female womb; he only passes through it. He has not experienced uterine waters and the long process of labor. He is son of a male, the god of uncontrollable women, and a protector of their secrets.[8]

These bloody dismemberings, these primitive scenes where a man seeks to discover the secrets of women; these beheadings, this bloodying of sexual organs, this stewing of a child . . .

The distance that Nietzsche had from this kind of woman is not far from that which Plato ascribes in *The Republic* to Orpheus, who, when he must choose a new life in the Underworld, prefers to be reborn as a swan and to come out of an egg rather than being born of a woman's womb.

In Dionysus's genealogy, as in Orpheus's refusal, a more radical refusal is inscribed: that of not being subjected to the slow natural germination of a mother's womb. In the curiosity of the Papin sisters, which was so cruelly transformed into a great attack, as in the curiosity of King Pentheus, disguised in his mother Agave's clothing, the same kind of revolt is expressed. The "mystery of life" is denied and desired; it is the cause of extreme squeamishness. It is a denial of reproduction.

This is why Nietzsche prefers the eternal return, and the abolition of time. Rather than choosing only Dionysus, he chooses Orpheus: Orpheus between Apollo and Dionysus, at the exact point at which their paths join. He resembles this "renouncing" Orpheus, who has vowed eternal chastity, who avoids women and meat, who saves his sperm to protect the "greater health" of his spirit, just as Hindu holy men do. Loving Dionysus, Nietzsche goes off toward Orpheus; he participates in the severed head that sings as it floats down the river.

And in electing Zarathustra to the rank of prophet, Nietzsche does not avoid the theme of dismemberment. The Parsi religion, of which the original Zarathustra is the legendary founder, dictates that cadavers may taint neither the air nor the ground. Even today in Bombay, the bodies of the Parsi dead are left on the tops of towers between earth and sky, exposed as prey to the vultures, who devour their flesh. But before delivering the carrion to the birds, the final dismemberment contains a "primal" return: the dead body is bent into a fetal position, then, finally, will be straightened and laid out. Thus sang the head of Orpheus, thus spake Zarathustra.

If you look upon these women bathing on the mountain, you will be dismembered; protect yourself and flee from them, and the same thing will occur. This short poem by Friedrich Nietzsche is entitled "Lost His Head":

> Why is she clever now and so refined?
> On her account a man's out of his mind,
> His head was good before he took this whirl:
> He lost his wits—to the aforesaid girl.[9]

In contrast, look at Kierkegaard's subtle view of things. He touches and unveils women, rubs up against them, and comes close to seduction; he does not flee them. The experiences of a love that ended and of a broken engagement seem to have given him philosophical wings. Among the personifications of despair in *The Sickness Unto Death*, Kierkegaard introduces a male figure, a female figure, and the figure of a child, and points out in a footnote that it is possible for a woman to have a "male" type of despair, and that the inverse is also true regarding a man and the "female" type. When one looks at a child, it only appears to experience anger; despair is not associated with children as they have no sense of eternity, which only affects adults. One cannot demand despair of a child: its only power is in an act that suddenly breaks and smashes, in an unconscious rage. Women can be expected to have the first form of despair: that despair in which one "does not will to be oneself."[10] Men can be expected to have the second form, that in which one "wills to be oneself." Kierkegaard calls the first of these forms "despair in weakness" and the second, "despair in defiance."[11] It is within this latter form of despair, which is marked with the seal of the infinite, that rebellion and abandon occur; the demoniacal negation of the Subject in the form of a shell filled with self-disgust. But it is in discussing feminine despair that Kierkegaard discerns the essential elements of attachment and abandonment. The abandonment is so radical that all individuality is lost:

> Woman, with genuine femininity, abandons herself, throws her self into that to which she devotes herself. Take this devotion away, then her self is also gone, and her despair is: not to will to be oneself.[12]

Abandoned women, unexplained terms. Which is the abandon being discussed by the philosopher? Is it erotic abandon, the immediate swallowing up of the lover into love itself? Or is it the abandon produced by breaking up, which leaves the abandoned lover in the desert, in a state of double abandonment? In precipitating the maiden's leap, the seducer gives rise to a total metaphysical suspension where the young girl is transformed into pure weakness; even more than the *Seducer's Diary*, *The Concept of Dread* (another name for *The Sickness Unto Death*) demonstrates the radical fecundity of a true morality of syncope: to cut, to break, like the abandoned stillborn infant. To cut, to separate, to suspend, and thus to provoke, by a sort of vaccine, the only moral sickness where faith can take root, without proof.

This is where Kierkegaard, by means of a simple love story, begins to resemble the character of the bacchante. The bacchantes are abandoned—abandoned to sleep, to their emancipated strength, to a god who leads them, and to the hungers that guide them to the raw animal, ready to be torn to pieces. To say the bacchantes in action throw their "selves" into abandon is not to say much; their essence is a demonstration of the very surrender of identity. Their essence is also a proof of the extreme strength of the weakest: their physical capacities are superhuman, as befits abandoned women. Attackers and attacked. With resolute abandonment.

As for the god himself, he shares the ambiguity of the women, who follow him and perform his commands, just as a musical score is performed. Attacked early in childhood, endlessly pursued by the eternal faction of national identity, the foreigner hated and hunted—he does not defend himself. Torn into seven pieces, he dies and is reborn; and when Pentheus's herdsmen capture him, he smiles. A passive god with feminine languor, who willingly wears dresses and long curly hair, Dionysus the Trembling shares the apparent weakness of woman, to whom, with male virility, he grants an uncommon measure of strength.

He has traveled extensively; come from somewhere in the Far East, he has perhaps lived in India for two or three years, or perhaps even farther away, for he must truly be foreign:

> The banks of the Ganges heard how the god of joy
> Was hailed when conquering all from far Indus came
> The youthful Bacchus, and with holy
> Wine from their drowsiness woke the peoples[13]

wrote Hölderlin, at the time that Romantic Germany dreamed of India.

Several centuries went by; the Roman emperors borrowed the notion of the eternity of Dionysus's resurrection, and called themselves "Neos Dionysus," the new Dionysus. One never knows.

At the time that Rome was overturning the Republic for the Empire, one of the most likely candidates for first emperor lost his Roman selfhood first and then his life: there is the example of Anthony, seduced by Cleopatra as Aphrodite in the middle of the Nile; she crowned him with ivy, introduced him to the East that would be his downfall. Recall Anthony's drunkenness, his penchant for dancing and the theater, his bacchic impulses and his untidy appearance. Anthony wanted to found an empire uniting Roman might with that of the Dionysian East; there was always an Octavian or a Pentheus to protest in favor of national identity. Nor did Anthony defend himself; he was not a god; he bid his sword kill him by leaning on it. Cleopatra had only one characteristic of the bacchante: the asp at her breast like the fawn or the wolf.

In order to rediscover the lost taste of honey sparkling on the vine, we will have to wait for Freud who, little by little in chiaroscuro, began to understand that feminine weakness concealed "prehistoric" powers.[14] And since that time, the picture has become clearer. Woman abandoned, in the throes of the hysterical "great attack," neck bent back, arms flailing, hair in disarray, palpitates against the doctor's chest; the woman, upon waking up, having barely readjusted, pounces on the doctor to give him a brutal kiss, a tender and surprising attack. It is Charcot at La Salpêtrière, a hypnotizer and tamer of insane women; it is Freud, a prey to the weak, searching by hook or by crook for the key to psychoanalysis.

The scene where syncope is superbly displayed as a major symptom is that of the bacchantes in chains. Charcot, after hypnotizing his paralytic patients, bids them stand and walk; he unties them, unchains them. Then he dehypnotizes the patient, who awakens and becomes paralyzed again. By stopping "real" time and inducing the "other" time of hypnosis, Charcot, a therapist in spite of himself, notes an enigmatic emancipation that he cannot understand: there is something of a "genital thing" in it, he says; that's all. It is Freud who takes the important step, takes the first Dionysian leap: not only in substituting the spoken word for hypnosis but more significantly by practicing the first therapy in the history of psychoanalysis on himself. Beginning as a "patient," like Nietzsche, he becomes a "healer" by healing himself; like Dionysus put back together from the seven pieces and finding strength in his dismembered weakness. That is what all therapists do when they resolve to abandon their "selves" in order to formulate therapeutic guidelines; we know that this is also how shamanism works. It is one of the possible interpretations that can be given to the strange text by Plato in which he distinguishes between positive and negative dementia: there are people whose delirium is "left-brained" and who never heal; but there are people whose delirium is "right-brained" and who, once they have healed themselves, are able to heal others as well. Dionysus, or Christ, with whom the Asian god sometimes became assimilated, are old-fashioned therapists, classic shamans, miracle workers, raising the dead, which is common with divine beings; they inspire sects, or even religions. Freud's leap resembles this ancient movement.

It is indeed a cured illness, a corrected abandonment; it is Dionysus made all the stronger for being defenseless. No longer rooted in dismemberment, but passing through, as passing through darkness, or getting over an ordeal. Not leaving the subject in the abandon of an inescapable shattering; but knowing this truth, the shattering at the core of the Self, the bacchante at the heart of the world, and the great attack at the gates of the city. Only the person who has passed through the fire of syncope knows the power to be found in the untying of arms and legs, of confused tongues, and of genitals dripping with milk; from this religious belief, Freud developed another story. Freud's passage through syncope in general, the hysterical attack, the spasm or the slap, is a holdover from shamanistic tradition, but it has changed. In Freud's world, as in Nietzsche's, faith is no longer applicable. Not even secretly in the depths of a secret garden; not even whispered.

This is the basis for his new humanism, often desperate, weakness and provocation at the same time; a humanism where syncope has sovereign rule, closely monitoring abandonments and attacks in a world without gods.

Mother, Little Mother, Dear Little Mother

The young girl has gone mad; the virgin has tilted into a savage hysterical state. The writers of Romanticism and the philosopher Kierkegaard were not the only ones to recognize it; during this period, "the age at its best," the greatest characterization of the mad virgin is found.

On the operatic stage she displays herself all the more shamelessly, since music of the Romantic period provides the mad virgin with arias of admirable purity. The more they are subject to syncope, the more beautifully they vocalize. The more they swoon, the more they sing, so high on the scale of sounds that their notes could break. Their character is fragile, devastated; their singing goes to inaccessible heights, their breathing constrained, the voice put to an extreme test, which is not visible or audible to the audience. Only an unreal lightness, intrinsic to syncope, grasps their hearts. Take Lucia di Lammermoor, for example.[15] She is a young woman married off against her will, who is in love with another man. On her wedding night, while she is being deflowered, she kills her husband with the well-placed stab of a knife, the act of a bacchante. Then, still wearing her bloodstained nightgown, she descends the monumental staircase that leads to the reception rooms of the castle where the story takes place. The crowd of society guests assembled there stares at her: she is mad. And she sings, a nostalgic waltz addressed to her lost fiancé, she hallucinates, with faltering vocalizations, at the edge of a precipice from which only the music holds her back like a handrail, for the time remaining: it stops suddenly. The young woman falls into a faint.

It is only a small leap from the heroine of Romantic opera to the paralytic abandoned before Charcot's eyes and a still smaller leap[16] to the young women who are terrified, petrified by the sudden appearance in their doorway of an uncle or a father, who has come there with the intention of raping them. This is the young woman who has become hysterical, and syncope has become the spectacle that she offers the public as she did to the hypnotizing therapist.

The animal in her is not far away, just behind the curtain.

To touch on the subject of hypnosis, if only with the edge of a thought, is to open the door to another animalistic world. As soon as the clear conscience, the pure and undaunted conscience of the philosophers vanishes, the Beast is capable of rising up again. The bacchantes with the animal at their breast, the witches kissing the behind of the large billy goat, are only metaphors of regression, supposedly belonging to an earlier period in human history; with these women, natural prehistoric tendencies return full force. Also returning are the bloody sacrifice and the beliefs of the primitive horde surrounding the body of the offering: goat, bull, ox, calf, heifer, or ram, chicken, horse, humans as well, more often than not, homing pigeons and messengers of humanity.

One of the most ancient sacrifices of Vedic India[17] describes a white stallion, allowed by the king to run free for an entire year but guarded by an army of young men, who protect his roamings and prevent him from having any encounter with a mare. The chaste stallion does not know that the extent of his wanderings will determine the boundaries of the kingdom. A year to roam, a year without female contact. At the end of the period, the young men capture the stallion and bring him back to the palace where, with great ceremony, he is asphyxiated.

The dead horse lies in the king's court. The eldest of the queens goes to lie at his side, under a blanket, and mimics a bestial coupling with the asphyxiated stallion. Into the ear of the lover-animal, she whispers sweet and mysterious ritual words: "Mother, little mother, dear little mother . . . " The king, his other three queens, and his courtesans tell dirty jokes. Then, when the imaginary mating is over, the dead stallion is cut to pieces. When this sacrifice is deemed insufficient, and if the kingdom is being threatened, it is a dead Brahman that the eldest of the queens makes love to under a blanket.

We will meet up again with this strange mother who inhabits the cadaver of a sacred animal. The eldest of the women is given the dangerous honor of kissing the animal: it is unthinkable to go to bed with the mother, even if she is dead. Moreover, it is better to cover this spectacle; left uncovered, it would be unbearable.

Unbearable. The spectacle of syncope can only be unbearable; it transfixes the beholder. Unbearable: that is what Freud had in mind when he introduced the idea of the "primal scene," the spectacle that is forbidden to the child and is heavily laden with an obsessive animalistic fear. It is what is commonly referred to as the "beast with two backs." As is often the case, the vulgarity is ingenious; to make love is to become a double beast. The Western child discussed by Freud, who is raised according to customs that avoid the spectacles of nature, is terribly frightened by the strange animal that is moving beneath its parents' sheets. What are they doing under there, and who is it that is moving around like an animal? Curiosity is piqued, like that of Pentheus who wants to see his mother behave like a bacchante. And if she were to make love? What if the beast with two backs should finally appear naked on the prairie grass? The primal scene is the observation of the beast with two backs. To watch lovemaking. To see the origin of reproduction. To see where one has come from, and more particularly, how.

Sexual union pulsates with this haunting obsession, which is illusory and is filled with prehistoric jouissances. In hypnosis, obsessive animalistic fear is present, alive and untamed. Freud put it admirably when he said that hypnosis is "sexual abandon without the sex."

In the case of hypnotherapy, each is lost in the other: the hypnotized subject in the brilliance of the eye or in the luminous ball, the hypnotizer in the tension of the gaze fixed on the patient. One controls the other, in the margins of consciousness. Between this double gaze in which nothing else is exchanged and that of lovers there is only a slight difference; in love as in hypnosis, the fluctuation of the gaze has nowhere to escape to; it is so cut off from the world that it no longer wishes to see. It can barely discern the gaze of the other, which dissolves into a blur, imperceptible, lost in the infinite. Animality is not far off.

It was long believed that a simple chalk line caused an animal on its back—a cat or a chicken, for example—to enter a rigid catatonic state. Then it became understood that the chalk line served no purpose. It was even simpler: the very turning over of an animal on its back provoked immediate catatonic rigidity. It has been said that a child will follow anyone in a crowd; in that, it is not different from a fawn that follows a larger being, whether animal or human, whom it takes to be its mother, even if not of the same species. It could be imagined that the Pied Piper of Hamelin caused children to follow him by the sound of his flute, but not at all—he himself was enough. The catatonia induced by being turned over, the effects of a brilliant gaze, and the "followism" seen in both humans and animals are the bases for sexual abandon, as they are at the root of the loss of consciousness and of ego orgasm.

What is necessary is to seize the moment. To satisfy one's curiosity. To open the door, lift the sheet, to stop the film at a particular image and to blow up the negative. *Blow Up*. To linger in the moment of syncope. At the precise moment when separation occurs—but from whom?—and when the double-backed beast begins, there is union—but with what? At the precise moment where the only sound of the sacrifice is heard: "Mother, little mother, dear little mother . . . "

9

The Birth of Identity and the Syncope of the Imago: Lacan

The philosopher and the psychoanalyst process subjective experiences: that at least they have in common. But unlike the philosopher, who in order to study experience usually shuts himself up alone in his room, with every thought marshaled, the psychoanalyst always confronts the other: the other laid out before him, the other across from him, the other in his suffering that is mute or cried out, sobbed out or smothered, sometimes also spoken. Whatever form it is expressed in, the psychoanalyst is always faced with suffering, without which there is no true analytic cure. What the psychoanalyst makes of it later will be definitively affected by it, and the subjective experience will be radically changed. It is not that the psychoanalyst cannot isolate himself in his turn; but the multiple echo of what Freud so appropriately called psychic misery haunts him enough to make him think otherwise.

Look at Jacques Lacan, for example. The extreme theoretical sophistication and refinement of his thought do not detract at all from his capacity for observing reality. As early as 1936, he glimpsed one of the essential moments in the subject's development in which syncope plays a role: the mirror stage or, as he later prefers to call it, the mirror phase.[1] This moment, which decides a person's identity, is paradoxically exempt from all suffering. On the contrary, it is a kernel of happiness, an interval that comes together in laughter—a funny moment.

The staging of this momentary scene is a classic patriarchal family, simplified: father, mother, child. A family, then, and within it, a six-month-old child, just come into the world. At that age, the child does not speak. The mirror phase, if one succeeds in observing it, can take place on no other plane than that of the *infans*, which in Latin means one who cannot yet speak. He may be crawling on all fours, even beginning to stand, or walking: some children, slower to develop, pass through the mirror phase at eighteen months.

This is the moment: the *infans* catches sight of his reflection in the mirror, turns to the adult who stands close to him, and manifests signs of intense exultation. He already knows how to laugh, and that is what he does. He laughs, in a delighted preoccupation that contributes to the successful exploit. Nothing else happens except for this image in the mirror, this pause, and this sudden rapture. It is a fleeting and precise moment.

At that age, still, the chimpanzee is far more skillful with its hands; it already knows how to do everything. Compare the chimpanzee and the baby: the latter seems handicapped, and he is—unable to walk alone, handicapped to the point of depending entirely on those around him. But in front of the mirror everything changes: for the chimpanzee walks around the mirror to find his double, and he does not recognize his reflection. The baby may certainly do the same thing for a moment; but quickly, he grasps it. He grasps that the reversed image is his own. And yet he can neither walk nor talk.

Jacques Lacan's reasoning is entirely based in the time lag between the baby's lack of organic development and this moment that is characteristic of all human beings, and which the family structure at least allows us to observe. Alone among all creatures, our species is born prematurely: we are born without teeth, without hair, without motor coordination, with a pyramidal nervous system that is not yet developed. Everything is potentially ready, but few elements truly function. Lacan is not the first to have stressed the specific prematurity of birth in human beings. He is, however, the first to have drawn a philosophical argument from it.

For the mirror phase allows the baby to make a major leap. He recognizes himself simultaneously as a unique individual and as part of this "all" into which he has been born, the world of people. Even before the sudden appearance of language, here is the step of the "imago," the image of self, the first form of the subject. Suddenly what exists there is an independent movement, "a drama," says Lacan, "whose internal thrust is precipitated from *insufficiency* to *anticipation*" (emphasis added).[2]

Something is precipitated and greatly anticipates the completed figure of the subject as he will be, later, ideally, adult, endowed with words and thought. For the moment, he is nothing but a failed chimpanzee, naked and disabled, but who is able to laugh at his reflection; this alone distinguishes him from animals and prefigures his human identity.

Here the imago has the effect of a syncope. Remember the definition of syncope in music: a note lags behind and anticipates the rest of the movement. That is the dynamic of the imago: caught in the mirror, "captured" in the organic gaze, it is prolonged and anticipates the human figure of the animal who thinks. Everything matches: the original clash "between the ego and the being," the twisting that is created by leaning on a delay, and the leaping ahead, the projection toward a future that is as yet unthinkable.

Even better: syncope in music prompts, from delay to anticipation, *dissonance* and then its *resolution*. This last point appears in Lacan's thinking, though it is very distant from the study of musical rhythm in itself. But he uses an obscure musical metaphor to explain the effect of resolution understood in the mirror phase: "first vibration of this stationary wave of renouncings that is going to scan the history of psychic development," the imago glimpsed in the mirror will be "the keynote that will resound in an entire harmonic scale through the phases of psychic history whose function will be to resolve it by developing it."[3] Here once again is the acoustics of the soul that Novalis predicted at the moment of Romanticism.

The psychic history of man is such that it is necessary to "pass" through each stage of life with difficulty. This difficulty of crossing from one body to the next, from one stage to the next, and from life to death, will always be a test: initiations, love at first sight, depressions, syncopes are used to resolve this. But each dissonance carries its resolution within it, every syncope anticipates its limit and its subsidence; that means that the *result of syncope* counts as much as the episode itself. At the conclusion of syncope in music there is harmony; at the conclusion of the crisis there is calm; at the conclusion of the initiation, a brand-new outfit for the new man; and at the conclusion of the mirror, an imago, the first embryonic shape of the *cogito* to come.

The imago, like a single note, engenders infinite harmonics. Lacan goes as far as naming the imago "the psychic causality itself," that of identification. Above I said "identity," since the recognition in the mirror affects what will later be enacted as a civil and juridical identity. But that is not all; the imago also signifies membership in the human race, "this indefinable form in the spatio-temporal complex of the imaginary whose function is to fulfill the resolvable identification of a psychic phase; in other words, a metamorphosis in the relations between the individual and his fellow."[4]

By "individual" and by "fellow," Lacan does not mean only the human race. Far from it: Lacan does not avoid the question of the animal imago.[5] Pigeons, which ovulate when put in front of a mirror, have an imago. So do grasshoppers, whose solitude changes to gregariousness when they are shown the image of a wandering grasshopper. It may only be a grasshopper, but it is transformed into part of its species when it sees itself in the mirror. The difference between this and the mirror phase in the human species, as we have seen, is that the baby recognizes itself as a unique self, eternally distinct from any other. But that does not prevent it from identifying itself at the same time as a part of its own species, and a member of the community of human beings. Nor does that prevent it from being able to become sociable, and falling hypnotically in love. The mirror phase does not completely dissociate the baby from the animal; it detaches it from the animal by the anticipation of the ego, but it stays attached to it by the feeling of belonging to the species, which for the baby appears under the characteristics of the "adult." The adult is at the baby's side in front of the mirror, but the baby can also turn around and identify it, different from itself and similar to itself.

We are moving straight toward a paradox: the imago seems always to be the sign of the species, for the grasshopper as for humans. We are well and truly placed in the space/time of syncope, that mysterious place "between expectation and relaxation": a place in which fusion and separation, animal and human, individual and collectivity, are indefinitely reversible.

The rest of the history of the Subject is going to depend, then, on this first success. Once the feat has been achieved—the feat that distinguishes it from the chimpanzee and the wandering grasshopper—only then can the baby distinguish itself from another baby and acquire language. The autistic child, closed in on itself, does not laugh at its reflection in the mirror. The primordial syncope of the subject in childhood, from specific delay to anticipation, influences all the other transitions, without exception.

These transitions are not without compensation, since psychic history is made up of tests; there will be a reward. Up until then, before human identity, the baby lives in the parceled-out space that connects it to its mother's body: a body at once vast and minuscule, scattered and intrusive, deprived of a proper form. Suddenly, like a chemical precipitation, a proper form, its own form, coagulates, which Lacan likes to call *orthopedic*: absolute, potentially complete, at last autonomous, this form will help the subject to "walk" psychically. Farewell to the mother's arms, the hypnotic gaze, and the tenderness within bodily range, farewell to the food coming straight from the body, farewell to the milky paradise and the excrement released without punishment, farewell mama. The imago thus formed brings about another alienation; the specific alienation of the subject as it is in itself.

He wasn't yet "him," he was his-mother-and-him. He becomes him, in a moment of syncope, and will leave himself with difficulty. This phase is that of "primary narcissism," a buttress that it is dangerous to cross back over in the other direction, a barricade against numerous prohibitions. Some little thing may happen in the course of life's path, a psychic accident—an encounter, the sudden absence of a law, a bereavement, a stumbling in the ordering of the world—and the barricade of the imago gives way, leaving room for broken-up fragments, bits of scattered body, *membra disjecta*, piercing from the inside or piercing the exterior, knives and guillotines, fiercely attacking what is no longer the individual nor his outside but one and the other at the same time mixed up in the "terrible heap / of bones and mangled flesh rolled in the mire" that Athalie dreamed of when she was threatened by her own remorse. There is no doubt that the bacchanalia belongs in the category of the imago's disintegration: the scene of *sparagmos*—the body torn apart, man, priest, or god—expresses in all its dread the scope of the danger. No one will forget that the danger can, in the blink of an eye, move into reality and slit living flesh; no one will forget the various bloody, newsworthy occurrences embedded in forgotten rituals. The alienation of the imago and its effect of syncope are also what lead the subject to comply with the law of the community; if the other then intervenes in his life, it is on a level that will quickly be called *love-hate*; a level on which one devours, or one swoons, or one kills.

The formation of the "I," says Lacan, resembles the construction of a fortified camp. The subject makes itself into an architect; on the outside, on the perimeter, rubble and swamps, shreds of feelings and scattered resentments; on the inside, inaccessible according to the psychoanalytic dogma, the *id*, "the lofty, remote inner castle,"[6] an impregnable fortress. Think of Kierkegaard: "My sorrow is my baronial castle . . . No one can take it by storm."[7] And "I" swoop like an eagle on an unknown prey: "this . . . is a picture I weave into the tapestries at my castle." Thus "I" whisper, old man and baby at the same time, a forgotten story, unknown, without a future or a past, in an immemorial present. Kierkegaard's lugubrious and secret lament, the "sickness unto death," this despair that is indefinable because it never takes place except in the moment, takes place at the furthest point of the imago, where the barricade could give way.

If one sets off to look for the castle and wants to force its portals, one exposes oneself, whether one is a philosopher or Kafka's hero, the surveyor: one step further, and it is aggression—against oneself, or against the other. One step further, and there is the crime of the philosopher who has become a murderer. It is better, like Kierkegaard's knight of faith, to swallow one's tears. The mirror phase protects and alienates; if the mirror cracks because of another round of syncope, one could just as easily not come back, and remain the other that one has become. One can go mad from it.

During the fifties, while European philosophy found itself confronted with the unthinkable aftermath of war, Lacan saw coming from the United States a psychoanalysis that was completely occupied with "strengthening" the ego. This psychoanalysis wanted to dislodge the id, the drive-related, and to give the ego the means with which to defend itself from it—a solid Cold War psychoanalysis. Lacan vigorously protested this orientation, which, under cover of the strengthening of the individual, only managed to isolate it even further:

> It is clear that the promotion of the ego today culminates, in conformity with the utilitarian conception of man that reinforces it, in an ever more advanced realization of man as individual, that is to say, in an isolation of the soul ever more akin to its original dereliction.[8]

At each step Lacan goes back over the loss of ritual in modern society. He does not appear to touch on it but always, insistently and quietly, he addresses himself to the "ahistoricism of culture" that he imputes to the United States.

Modernity is the "increasing absence of all those saturations of the superego and ego ideal that are realized in all kinds of organic forms in traditional societies, forms that extend from the rituals of everyday intimacy to the periodical festivals in which the community manifests itself."[9] In the hollow spaces, emptied of lost rituals, the idea of the individual takes shape as a desaturated, indeed disorganized, collective; one that is thus vulnerable to the caving in of the barricade of the imago, vulnerable to a syncope that is capable of nullifying, through subsidence, the foundational syncope of subjective identity. And it is understood that Bataille sought, in an atheological attitude, through an "inner experience," to found, between debauchery and illumination, a genuine ritual for modern times, singular, lofty, at the outer limits of the transmissible.

Lacan does not conceal it: the suffering gathered by the psychoanalyst when he listens to a patient is a legacy of modern humanism's "*emancipation*."

That is why Lacan speaks of entire communities threatened by the sufferings of neurosis and psychosis. That is why he does not cease denouncing, tirelessly, the secret resilience of altruistic feeling. For American-style psychoanalysis, righter of wrongs and of the unconscious, is motivated—as the Cold War is, by the way—by good protective intentions. But the philanthropist, the idealist, the educator, and the reformer are all liable, despite their goodwill (or because of it), to want to attack the imago, the barrier, the refuge, the fortified camp.[10] As for politics, it is worse; whenever it blames the social fabric and undertakes the construction of the best of worlds, it becomes a terror; real fortresses rise from the earth, and real camps.

What can the psychoanalyst do for those whom Lacan calls "pitiful victims," these "escaped, irresponsible outlaws"?

Practically nothing; a hint of life, a sigh, a simple suspension. A reserved activity. It is a question of making a *reservation* possible; this word must be understood in the way it is used by those who carve out, for ahistorical peoples, reserves of space in the heart of industrial societies.

The words to describe this are difficult; they are out of sync with every society. "*Preserving the subject's recourse to the subject*," says Lacan, for example, without educational or therapeutic interference. And this: defining psychoanalysis as "*a prophylactics of dependence*"—losing one's fondness for imaginary enslavements, abandoning servitude. One can see that it is always a matter of *undoing*, or *untying*: the psychoanalyst can only act indirectly, through derivation, preserving, reserving, adjudicating, but never laying down the law.

There is no ideal city, no psychoanalyst at the command post; and not even any foundations on which to build a world. There is only a "discreet brotherhood," without a manifesto and without a political agenda of direct intervention. On the other hand, on the grounds of dependence and enslavements, the psychoanalyst is in his element.

Let us return to the metaphor of Indian reservations: when Freud began to listen to the speech of hysterics, abandoning the heavy methods of hypnosis, it was *savagery* that sprang up energetically, coming up from an undefined past that he called "prehistoric" because it seemed to come up from the depths of the ages. Freud opened up the reserved space. And so, at the very heart of modernization, its opposite can be inscribed: a secret rite, out of sync with the modern. That is why the psychoanalyst is compelled to feign or to establish his own kind of ritual in the session, a ritual necessary to the preservation of the psychic space in its humanist form, as Western philosophers bequeathed it to Europe.

However one looks at it, the undertaking of psychoanalysis can only be situated "out of sync." It is true for the technique of *anamnesis* (recollection of the past), which brings the ancient disappeared patterns back into the present, into language. It is true for its social inspiration, which is placed deliberately on the margins of society. And finally it is true for its ultimate goal, the cure; for by working on the symptom the psychoanalyst simply makes it a part of the past—he preserves the present in which suffering has buried itself, obtuse and misunderstood. That is how he is able to cure.

Out of sync, then. No futurist prophesying; no prescriptions for the future; no immediate social utility; no promotion of the ego. Out of sync, against the grain of all philosophy, of every social convention. This is the price for preserving the precarious connection that, from delay to anticipation, has held in place since childhood the effect of syncope in which the subject is formed.

The tense of psychoanalysis is always the *it will have been*. The future anterior, a collusion between the past and the future, syncopates time and short-circuits it by excluding the present, which keeps slipping between its fingers. Each advance in the psychoanalytic course of treatment brings to light an obscure concretion that has settled in the present; in order for it to be dissolved, it has to be seen for what it was originally: an event, a point in the past that had not been resolved and that weighed on the future with all the heaviness of repression. One day, this heart murmur, this stubborn cough, these blushes, these faintings, this distress, *will have been* nothing but recollections. As soon as they are mentioned, in that same remarkable moment they simultaneously happen and are swallowed up; indeed, if all goes well, they are no sooner said than forgotten. Still and always out of sync, psychoanalysis—even in its most paradoxical aspects—attempts to be forgotten: that is the law of life, which forbids an excess of memory and demands its own obliteration.

If psychoanalysis arose out of the spectacle of the hysterical syncope, it has also kept that spirit. This begins as soon as the psychoanalyst indicates the rules of the game: what Freud contradictorily called free association, although he knew it to be enslaved. But however much of a prisoner it may be, association roams in discontinuity, in what it suits us, within the social framework, to call *incoherence*. Broken words, sobs held back or gasped out, empty or pregnant silences, laughter or tears, sweating or choking are the materials gathered by the psychoanalyst, like the unknown music of a mysterious tribe. It takes a long time to hear and recognize the rhythms. Lacan advanced in this field to the point of defining all treatment practices as exercises in punctuation. It is, he said, up to the psychoanalyst to interrupt the session at the exact moment when a break would be most effective; that could be during a silence, right in the middle of a word, or at the logical end of a sentence; a good listener must use his talents to find the caesura that will bring about shock and illumination. The best way to put it would be to say that the psychoanalyst's job is to look for an effect of syncope during every session. This is where "syncope" is used in its most colloquial sense, that of radical surprise: one remains syncopated. People often argued with Lacan about this practice, which earned him considerable anathema and a striking ostracism; it was only a matter, however, of protecting the *element of surprise* in the subject's recourse to the subject. In short, it was only a matter of reproducing, by using the poor means of the session structure, the effect of the primordial syncope in which the subject is formed: by suddenly precipitating it into its own language.

The same is true for Lacan's reading of Descartes. Lacan practices punctuation by surprise; he changes a comma, the innocuous comma that separates "I think" from "I am." Let us take the best-known formulation, that of the *Discourse on Method*: "I think, therefore I am." Lacan falters: "I think: 'Therefore I am.'" Instead of the comma there is the colon, signaling a statement of a different nature. "I am the one who thinks: 'Therefore I am.'" There is no more equivalence between the subject of the thinking and the subject of existence; instead there is a gap: is this really the same person, the one who makes the statement and the one between quotation marks? Who guarantees the coincidence between the two? For Descartes, it is God, and can only be God; our philosopher was aware of the crack in time that stretches[11] from one subject to the other. For Lacan the game is reversed, and the crack itself is what is at stake in the demonstration. Finally, he will say exactly the opposite of the *cogito*, and formulate a back-to-front *cogito*: "I think where I am not, therefore I am where I do not think."[12]

All divine guarantees disappear; there is no more transcendental authority to assure the continuity that, from the moment in which *I* think, extends me into the moment where *I* am, by leaping the brief passageway of the comma. From that moment on, "I" am nothing but a syncope, a fault line between thinking and being, a subject that is suspended, "shifted," fainting.

Lacan, with the weapons of poetics, perfected the work that Freud had begun of undermining the guarantees of consciousness. And here is the Dethroned Subject; capital letters to back it up, hypostases of an epoch that idolized its own philosophical failure.

For this dethroning of the thinking subject has had in turn worshipers and iconoclasts. The image of a Faltering Subject has been revered as if it were a substitute divinity; like a mutilated Atys, it has been wept over by legions of eunuch priests under the authority of the Great Goddess. Lacan's theories are the object of a modern cult that is like the *arbor intrat* of the journeymen of medieval cities. A huge pine tree is chopped down and carried ceremonially into town by the journeymen: it is the symbol of the cut-down hero, whose loss must be commemorated in the middle of agony. *Arbor intrat.*

That was the Dethroned Subject.

Personally, I prefer the young Lacan of the years just after the war, busy looking for ways in which the psychoanalyst could have an effect on the world. He knew how to weigh misery; he analyzed ways of remedying it. I have spoken of "poor means," as one speaks of "minimalist art." Poor means, such as speaking and silence; such as the punctuation of a session and the effects of syncope in language. Deprivation, for the early Lacan, is automatic. Does he not say that the psychoanalyst must *be unaware of what he knows*? For it is in weakness that he is able to intervene: weak and powerless himself, he takes action in the very moment of human weakness, the moment in which weakness is paradoxically rooted and from which it takes its power.

It is on this shifting ground that the first image of the individual is constructed, in a mirror, in a brief moment of happy laughter.

Going through Customs

The effects of war.

During dreadful collective upheavals, suicide rates drop dramatically; depressives are cured at the same time. It is afterward that the "elsewhere" of syncope violently reclaims its rights.

After the Napoleonic wars, the Romantic wave gave rise to breakaway groups who imagined themselves as Asian and turned against individuals and against the very notion of the subject. Look at Hölderlin's madness; look at Kleist, haunted by his sleepwalking characters, and so in love with syncope that he chose to kill himself; look at *Werther*, less for the sublimation Goethe achieved than for the epidemic of suicides for which this novel was the mysterious vector. Listen to the muffled vibration that shakes them like a faraway echo of a seismic upheaval, which breaks and cracks the earth long after the first tremors. Better to be elsewhere than here, better to have ecstasy than life, better the final moment of the lightning that sets things on fire.

The path is traced and it is almost always the same; suicidal aggression against oneself, by a subject suddenly deprived of a bearable imago. After the Second World War, better to have nauseous existence than to slowly learn to live without war again. See how Matthieu, in the middle of the war in Jean-Paul Sartre's *Chemins de la liberté* (Paths of freedom) fires for a long quarter of an hour on the German enemy:

> He fired, the laws flew into the air: thou shalt love thy neighbor as thyself—bam! right in the idiot's face—thou shalt not kill—bam! at the creep opposite him. He fired on man, on Virtue, on the world. . . . He was pure, he was all-powerful, he was free.

There is no recovery from these states on the brink of death, from these warlike syncopes. Afterward, one collapses and loses the taste for life.

When the Vietnam War shook up the United States a little too much, the first followers of a new, nonexistent religion flooded into Asia: *Flower Power*.

Asia was no longer a dream but the destination of an actual journey. The impulse remained the same: a spiritual quest in need of syncope.

Western philosophers have long avoided this journey, imaginary or real. Socrates' allergy to nature, Immanuel Kant's famous little regular stroll—just to the end of town but certainly no farther—and Descartes's death, exiled in a cold and far-off country, are just so many small signs of the repression of syncope. Bataille, who understood, wrote about Hegel's life:

> Hegel, loathing the way of the ecstatic (as the only true resolution of anguish) had to take refuge in an attempt—sometimes successful (when he was writing or speaking), but which was vain in the end—at balance and harmony with the existing, active, and official world.[13]

Either harmony with the world, detour by means of the official teaching philosophy, or disagreement. Either one stays at home, or one leaves on a journey: it is just as true of thinking as it is of the thinker.

A highly skilled traveler was one of the first to describe the devastating effects of travel on thinking. Claude Lévi-Strauss speaks of the return of the ethnographer as of a veritable Lazarus, coming back from the dead, suffering from no longer being able to share with his compatriots, in his mother country, what he had come to understand abroad. Wandering between the native imago and the transitory identification with other patterns of thought, the ethnologist walks around like a ghost upon returning home; we know the effects—sometimes suicidal—that this Western profession of reversed shaman has managed to produce.[14]

From a journey, just as from depression; from syncope, just as from love; no one returns the same as when he left: he will not come back as he was at the beginning, he will never be the same. He will be "dis-similar," deprived of similarity with his own people. This is the flaw of identification that shakes identity; it is not the test of the other, it is the impossible return to the same.

This return is even more impossible because in our society the patterns of ritual that saturate the ego have almost disappeared. In societies that have rites of initiation, the same individual, *without moving from his place*, goes on a journey, is transformed, and comes back to his people who welcome him: the same individual can come back to the same individual, having passed through the other. In our Western society, each person has to find in solitude the means of leaving himself. Often, that translates into mass appeals to the "genuine" journey; sometimes, passionate love takes on the burden of the exercise; depression, let us repeat, is part of these misunderstood rites. We are still lucky enough to have rock and roll, love at first sight, and depression; but they try so hard to cure us that soon there will be nowhere for us to test disharmony; nothing for us to know how to "pass," in the sense that we understand "to die."

So let us pass. Let us take the leap, jump into the abyss of Asia. We will never be able to make a tabula rasa of the orientalist impulses that, since the Greeks, have imposed forgotten images on us, which we call so accurately in our language "clichés." A Greek cliché, passed on from Herodotus to Flaubert: the image of the naked wise man, the gymnosophist, motionless and silent in front of the pyre on which he is impassively going to throw himself. An Anglo-Saxon cliché: the Beatles' long stay in an ashram in Rishikesh, in the Himalayas. An exclusively British cliché: Kipling, you will become a man, my son, or how to transform the wolf-child Mowgli into a park ranger for the Empress of the Indies.[15] A German cliché: the swastika, changing from cosmic symbol into the emblem of horror. A French cliché: poverty-stricken Calcutta, the world's dying ground.[16] And when we have despoiled it of all the pearls and jewels, the pyres and their dead, amulets and fetishes, artificialities and rubbish, when we have exhausted the imaginaries that Europe has projected onto India, we will not shy away from the power of the "infinite East," oddly inscribed in the time zones.

Modern Indians hate these impulses. "Westernized" (*ouestifié*) is the scornful insult that an Indian hurls at another Indian whom he suspects of betraying his nationalism. The "Western world" means a lack of cultivation: they speak of our Europe as Lacan spoke of the United States. India reserves a pitiless treatment for those who desire her. She swallows their thought, and sweeps them along with lowered head toward what she has always known how to do: dissolve the subject, unfasten the ego, nullify it. Deprived of reference points, the Westerner who wants emptiness is unceremoniously abandoned. Modern Indians laugh at our confusion; they've known for a long time how to seduce the West. And like Johannes the seducer, they abandon the seduced one, the deflowered subject, who has literally been led astray. Having seen this straying hundreds of times, and seen it result in a restorative repatriation, having heard certain Indian masters recount their exploits, and explain the seduction of the imago of which they had made themselves capable, I know what rejection this country, India, can produce. And it is with reason.

India knows plenty about syncope. Its infinite music never stops playing. The erudite song of the Dhrupad, born in the depths of the belly, slowly raises itself to the highest melody, full of quivering jolts; the dancers all know how to stop time with the anklets of little bells that encircle and transform their feet into a living dialectic. And India's philosophies burn with a violent desire for syncope, so passionate that it will go as far as the abolition of the soul. Let us move on.

It is understood that we are Westerners; we have shown our papers; they are in order, apparently. One never knows . . . It is understood that we will remain on our guard. But who knows whether we will not, upon returning, find the echoes of Indian syncopes even in our own homes.

Let us, however, move on. I promise that it will be a matter of love; I promise that we will find syncope. But love will never be reciprocal, between a man and a woman; and syncope will be the effect of such a perfect technique that at the end of the journey there will no longer exist either a subject or death. That is when we will have to come back. For that is where we will lose our heads.

10

"Inter faeces et urinas": Tantrism Between Feces and Urine

First, let us go to extremes.

For it is in the context of asceticism that they meet up with one another. And we already recoil: the body is naked and thin, the ribs visible, the beard bushy, the gaze feverish; ashes cover the body and a haircloth covers the loins. What are we to make of this type of folklore? It has put off many a soul. Bataille, for example, was suspicious of it: "That an anemic, taciturn particle of life showing reluctance before the excesses of joy, *lacking freedom*, should attain—or should have attained—the extreme limit, is an illusion. One attains the extreme limit in the fullness of mass: it demands fulfilled beings, ignoring no audacity. My principle against asceticism[1] is that the extreme limit is accessible through excess, not through want."[2] And he held India and her yogis on the edge of the mind, with tongs and prudent curiosity. Bataille confusedly expected India to reach these extremes by means of excess. But he was actually far off target.

Let us set off.

There is a city on the banks of a river. For the past three thousand years, people have come here to bathe, to pray; people also come here to die, to deliver themselves from the body's weight and from time, which inhabits it. For the past three thousand years there has existed in the world a city whose metaphysical commerce is that of a happy death. Travelers from the West know it as Benares, but all of India calls it Kashi. Or the Forest of Beatitude. Or the City of Light; also known as She Who Will Never Be Abandoned. Also called, finally (and this is its last name) the Great Field of Cremation.

Let us draw near.

Here is the site of the incineration of the dead, whom men carry cheerfully on their shoulders. Wrapped in white-and-red cloth and placed on a bamboo stretcher, the bodies wait with their feet in the water until a site is available. The ceremony goes quickly and is performed simply; the gestures are sober; too strong a display of mourning is deemed harmful to the deceased. Finally the funeral pyre is lit by the eldest son. The flame flourishes for nearly three hours. This is the origin of asceticism.

It is on the cremation field that some of the most enigmatic rituals are performed. Skull bones are collected to form a bowl that will remind every mouth of the insignificance of every mouthful; the ashes are slept in; the cremators are allowed to remove the liver and heart of the corpse, at the request of a well-known ascetic, who then devoutly devours them. The cremators—who are called "doms"—are a dreaded caste: theirs is the infernal work of the pyres, the tending of the wood fire, the sprinkling of the ashes on the river; also theirs are taxes, wealth, and a palace on the Ganges. It is from these dregs of the land, from these Untouchables of Hindu society's lowest rung, that the ascetics often ask for shelter, in order to have a closer contact with death. This asceticism is spoken of with an air of mystery, for it touches on every extreme: death, orgasm, feces, urine, ecstasy.

Tantrism has long been the subject of gossip in India. Popular gossip: What are they up to on the cremation fields at night, by the light of the funeral pyres? The practitioners of Tantrism go through an extreme initiation, which is known as "left-handed." Hinduism reserves the right hand for purity and the left for waste; eating is done with the right hand, the left hand is used for wiping oneself. To use only the left hand is already to choose to engulf the self in a syncope of values.

And nonetheless Tantrism is a rigorous philosophy. Appearing early among the ancient rituals, it became organized toward the eleventh century, and blossomed in almost all of the major sects that are outcroppings of Brahmanism, such as Buddhism and Jainism; it became embellished to the point where it is considered to be the pinnacle of philosophy and of therapy by Indian intellectuals of today. It has not, however, lost any of its air of mystery; there is something of Eleusis in this affair.

A letter from a disciple to his Tantric master.[3] The disciple wanted to learn the secrets of the occult. It was necessary to call on a female demon, she who "tells in the ear"; the test is so formidable that the master warned his student.

The letter from the Tantric apprentice to his master after the test:

"You had told me that this *sadhana* [invocation]," he wrote, "needs three days. It can be begun in any month three days before the new moon, and a further ten days of rituals to be performed after the *sadhana* is over.

"According to your instructions, I stopped bathing on the third day of [the month of] Posh. For ten days, I cleaned neither my teeth nor scraped my tongue nor changed my clothes. . . . I stopped saying my daily prayers. I did not go to a temple. . . . For ten days I did not make my bed. After eating, I did not wash my plate and used the same dirty plate for every meal."

This is the left hand: filth, the brutal cessation of normal everyday hygiene. The abrogation of the pure.

"According to instructions, on the thirteenth day after full moon, I took some of my own feces from the chamber pot and ate it. Although I felt thoroughly disgusted, I wanted to complete the *sadhana* in the left-handed way. In the three days of the *sadhana*, when I felt hungry I ate my feces and whenever I felt thirsty I drank my own urine.

"That same night, I locked the doors of my house from inside and lit eleven big lamps in my room. . . . I sat down facing south. . . . I took the rest of my excrement and smeared it on my body, I rubbed a little into my hair. . . . I had prepared two rosaries of bones. . . . The bones had been dug up from the cremation ground at night. I wore one string of bones around my neck and held the other in my hand."

The left hand: autophagy—eating one's excrement, drinking one's urine. Such a strong reversion to nature that the funereal remains, the unearthed bones, have no trouble fitting in. Isolation and solitude: Descartes's admonition, all doors closed, and all alterity banished.

"I then started reciting the mantra of the female demon [Karna Pishachini]. . . . You told me to do the *japa* [recitation] for a hundred and fifty strings. If there is need to urinate during the *japa*, you had said, then I should urinate while seated, if there is a need to defecate it should be done wherever I am sitting. Without breaking the rhythm of the *japa*, the urine should be sprinkled and the feces rubbed all over the body. That night I urinated and defecated many times. I was amazed, as this had never happened earlier. The room was stinking. It was difficult even to breathe but I managed to complete a hundred and fifty strings of *japa*. . . .

"As instructed, I lay down on the floor to sleep. . . . Tears came to my eyes. I wished that I had listened to you, and had not undertaken this *sadhana*. . . . My Brahmanhood was lost and I lay in that room like a degraded being—a *pishacha* [disciple of the demon]."

The left hand: a systematic lowering, the enraptured harmony of chaos, an orderly outburst of disorder. The Brahman, whose very definition is of purity, sacrifices his essence and is destroyed. The adult becomes an immobile fetus again, whose only actions are intestinal and urinary excretions. The only human qualities remaining are the prayers and the counting of the beads of the rosary, a rosary of human bones.

"In the afternoon, while I was lying down I felt the door open. Although the room was locked I felt that someone had come in. I even pinched myself to be sure that I was awake. I saw an attractive woman, twenty-five to thirty years old, completely naked, standing next to me. She lay down without saying a word. I was frightened and tried to get up but she forced me to lie down beside her and started to stroke my penis. . . . I could not even bear to look at her while she shamelessly continued to stroke my penis and incite me to 'the act.' There was no intercourse though, and around five in the evening she disappeared. I felt utterly drained and almost decided to discontinue the *sadhana*. But you had told me that who leaves the *sadhana* unfinished is certain to be slain by the Pishachini."

Hallucinatory apparition. This can only occur if one destroys something of the imago. Something of one's own essence, of who one is—the Brahman subject—must be lost, in order to leave room for the total projection of the naked female demon.

"I woke up in the evening, my head splitting from the stink inside the room. At eleven in the night I once again lighted the lamps and started the *japa*. After about an hour, the woman of the afternoon appeared and sat down next to me. Her teeth were protruding. She had short, closely cropped hair and wore a necklace of bones. Otherwise, she was naked. She seemed to be in good spirits and constantly fondled my penis. Sometimes she stroked it, sometimes she kissed it. . . . I was sweating with fear but did not interrupt my *japa*. I urinated and defecated five to six times. Each time, the woman smeared both our bodies with urine and feces. She sat with me till five in the morning and went away as soon as the *japa* was over. . . ."

"On the third, new moon day, the woman again came and lay next to me. . . . [She] forced me to lie with her. She again played with my body and incited me to intercourse. Around three in the afternoon she finally succeeded and left as soon as the act was over. I went on lying there, miserable and full of fear, shame, and remorse."

The left hand: to go to bed with death, with the mother, to return to the precise instant of birth, between urine and excrement, "inter faeces et urinas," according to Saint Augustine's painful expression. The left hand: to turn gusto into disgust.

"When I started the *japa* at night, the woman appeared instantly and sat down on my lap. I went on chanting the mantra while she urinated and defecated all over me and smeared my body with her urine and feces. At five in the morning she got up from my lap and said, 'I am your lover now and I'll stay with you all your life. I'll do all your work but if you ever think of leaving me, I shall kill you.' Then, like a newlywed bride, she exchanged her necklace of bones for mine. I was silent but she said: 'Don't be shy, you have obtained me and I shall stay with you. Whenever I want intercourse I'll come to you and you will have to satisfy my desire. Whenever you ask a question, I'll whisper the answer in your ear. But do not tell anyone about me or I'll strangle you.' After saying this, she kissed my penis and disappeared."

The disciple remained "in mental agony," writes the Indian psychoanalyst Sudhir Kakar, who quotes this testimony. The disciple could no longer practice the rituals of Brahmanism, nor adore a god. But he made a fortune as an astrologer.

Sudhir Kakar, a psychoanalyst in New Delhi,[4] is a strict Freudian: his goal is not, as he clarifies, to study the philosophical system that opens the door to such phantasmagoria; rather he collects testimony that allows him to see—beyond a complex repression made up of Hindu symbolism and the leaden layers of successive colonial empires[5]—the prehistoric fantasies that are characteristic of the Indian imagination. The scene of the disciple making love to the naked female demon amid urine and excrement cannot be understood otherwise. It is pure fantasy, reduced to its essence; and through it occurs the ruthless attack on the imago and on physical causality. The apprentice sorcerer finds himself with new powers of divination that his demonic lover will whisper in his ear; but he pays a high price, that of an absolute, radical, and irreversible psychic degradation that forever transforms him into a possessed man. The "mental agony" is far from over; it is not unlike what is known in our part of the world as psychotic delirium and exhibits, in the midst of the primitive and tainted embrace, an exploded body, deprived of integrity, amputated of its identity.

But in order to have fantasy, one must have a stage structure, as in the theater. Tantrism, if it opens its windows onto a place where this type of popular fantasy can be staged, provides the philosophical framework. For it must be understood where, for thousands of people, the collective authorization to "break" the imago of the body originates. It is in the Shivaism of Kashmir, the least well-known of all of the Tantric sects, that the basis for the fantasy is found. It is important to mention the philosopher Abhivanagupta, who in the tenth century developed a synthesis of hundreds of scattered Tantric sects and who, in his travels throughout India, chipped away at the solid block of Hinduism.[6]

The Shivaism of Kashmir is best known by the name "trika." In the consciously polysemous Indian view, there are numerous possible interpretations of the "three" contained in the term "trika." Let us consider the first and most important: "trika," a group of three headed by the god Shiva, his wife, and the individual soul. It is a kind of holy trinity.

The imagery of Shiva, familiar to anyone living in India, is not that which has crossed borders and been seen in the West; but one need only visit Benares to see it triumph everywhere. Kashi, the holy city, is his city; Shiva loves Benares more than his own wife and, when far away from it, he expresses suffering comparable to that of a troubadour far from his princess. "If the breeze from Kashi would only embrace me, the fire which devours me would go out, but not otherwise, not even if I dive into water. . . . O sweet Kashi, when will I again experience union with your body, thanks to which my own divine body will become instantly refreshed."[7]

Dance and life, fire and love, destruction and death . . . Both virile and androgynous, the god Shiva, like the unconscious described by Freud, is contradictory, scandalous, violent, cosmic. In Benares he is seen depicted on walls in the position of a dancer, with one leg raised high over the other and his arms opened wide, forming with his extremities the suggestion of a swastika that, before its meaning was debased, was the Indian symbol for the wheel of the cosmos. He is also seen in his simple and primitive form: his phallus ballooning into his vulva, covered by garlands of flowers and doused with sacred butter. His sperm is so hot that it destroys as it gushes forth; his gaze is so torrid that in one second he charred the god of love, Kama, the counterpart of Eros, armed with flowering arrows, and of whom nothing remains except a nostalgic memory; and it is the god Shiva that whispers into the ear of the person who is about to die on the banks of Kashi a magic formula, which will allow him or her to escape the cycle of reincarnation. Primeval, generated from one of the most ancient Hindu models, dating back to when he was a mountain god, Shiva retains a barbaric air from his pre-Aryan origins that is well suited to the practice of the most extreme regression: this is also because he is the god of asceticism and of meditation. In his most popular image he is seated in the lotus position on the snowy peak of a mountain, with a serpent around his neck and the goddess Ganga imprisoned in his topknot. The god of solitude, however, is not alone.

Spouse or emanation, born of a foreign father or materialized from his own side, a feminine figure is the double of the god Shiva. Her generic name is Shakti. Men and women in India today have inexhaustible commentaries on who or what Shakti is: feminine energy par excellence, untameable, rebellious, an irresistible force, capable of administering life or death instinctively, Shakti is radically uncontrollable.

One of the best-known representations is the double image of the feminine emanation of the god Shiva: called Durga when she is beneficial and Kali when she is driven by fury. Therefore in the folk imagery of Bengal, the place that most values the double goddess, appears the ambivalent figure whom all Bengalis, without having read Freud, call by her real name, "the Mother." Armed from head to toe, the double goddess holds in each of her outstretched hands an instrument of death, ax, club, sword, or cutlass. Only her expression changes at the same time as her name: when she is smiling she is Durga; when she is Kali, she sticks out her horrible red tongue, and her protruding teeth are like that of the female demon. Around her short, bovine neck is hung a necklace of freshly severed heads. The Mother is smiling or hateful, is love or destruction, tenderness or fury: in one instant, goodness becomes violence, in one impalpable instant. In both cases, she is Shakti.

Shiva and his consort Shakti interpenetrate each other. The point at which Shiva appropriates feminine imagery is one that he incorporates into the very act of copulating: thus Shiva the androgyne is born, more radical than our hermaphrodite, and divided vertically, from his topknot to his toes, into two very different halves, male and female from top to bottom. Shiva and Shakti copulate. The third element in the Tantric trinity is the individual soul, observing the copulating couple. And this is where we meet up again with syncope, repeated to the point of ecstasy, based on a *philosophy of the orgasm.*

But have patience.

Or consciousness. "Granted an inner resonance that never deteriorates and which is called the Supreme Great Heart,"[8] consciousness is a vibration that is like ocean waves: either calm or turbulently effervescent. In the Tantric view, there is no consciousness without this vibrating oscillation, which is called either the Great Heart, the Supreme Word, or the Absolute I. It is clear that the infinite beating of a heart is akin to the resonance of a word, which also has no end. The hidden key to this process is that both pulsation and resonance coincide with an absolute subject. It is vibratory resonance that indicates the path: it is that of orgasm, and of a particular treatment of time.

The god Shiva therefore couples with himself. His other half, his divine and female double, may be called Kali. Tantric philosophy plays with these words: *Kali*, like *Kala*, meaning time.[9] The dark goddess with her tongue hanging out could also be called the "temporal" goddess, whose mood alternates and changes, going from calm sea to turbulent storm. Between time and this woman there is an established complicity; the mastery of time comes only by means of the woman. How could one better juggle the flux of life as it goes by than by making love to the temporal goddess? The couple formed by the god embracing his other half in an indefinite coupling is that of consciousness making love with time: it is the seizing of the instant of orgasm, and its prolongation.

In this suspended moment, differences are abolished. First of all sexual difference: it is no longer Shiva and Shakti, no longer a male god and a female goddess; they merge at the very moment of orgasm, interpenetrating each other until sexual identity vanishes. It is no longer the "I" of "I love you," nor the "You" of "You are good for me," it is the coming together in one of those who used to be two. It is no longer Tristan and Isolde, it is not even the eternal, mythical couple, "Tristan-and-Isolde," still divided by the terrible little "and" of amorous conjunction. No, it is, literally, "between-the-two." As for the individual soul, the third term of the trinity, it is confronted with the incarnation of this permanent love-at-first-sight between masculine and feminine, between I and Thou.

If any philosophical doctrine has sought to discover what the interior of an orgasm was, this is the one; if something of syncope is desired, at the limits of consciousness and up to its loss in jouissance, it is here that one must search.

At the same instant, the difference between the inside and the outside of the body disappears. This is what orgasm is: "an inner stirring whose essence is the tumultuous release of the entirety of one's energy."[10]

Think of Isolde's death scene, and of the waves rising, catapulted by the words and music—consciousness equivalent to the turbulence of jouissance. But this "inner stirring" moves from one to the other so suddenly that the duality of the partners disappears, leaving intact—for the philosopher well practiced in Tantrism—a speck of consciousness: the most vibrant, the most painful, and the most excitable.

It is no longer possible to speak of "feminine" and "masculine": one is transformed into the other, and the body no longer has limits. This is so true that there is a point in the practice of Tantrism where the suspended orgasm may be achieved either with a woman of flesh and blood or with the idea of woman, also very real; it can also be practiced by "interiorizing" the image of a woman who is elsewhere, or can even be realized in a void. Furthermore, in order to attain his goal, the Tantric practitioner may go to bed with his mother or his sister. Or he can fantasize about them when he is alone, inside. Along with difference, other solid taboos also collapse; all human limitations fade away.

"The Other," writes Michel Hulin on this point, "is no longer the wall of indifference that he is and must be—for we would be disconcerted if he were not—in everyday life. It is my project even in literally 'becoming flesh' in exteriority, my flesh turned inside out like the finger of a glove, enveloped in itself, pulsating against itself: a paradoxical space where top and bottom, front and back, right side up and upside down, near and far, are constantly shifting from one to the other."[11]

Orgasm is therefore the foremost means of attaining the dissolution of the individual subject, who thereby becomes the Absolute I, the Immense Heart, or a Forbidden Word.[12] This notion of favoring the moment of syncope is pushed to its extreme consequences; it is true that afterward nothing of value remains. Not sex, nor death, incest, excrement, urine, or even God: it's all the same, or rather, it's All One. For our purposes, we will retain the notion that syncope thus radicalized signifies a transgression and a breakthrough.

So much for orgasm. And then? Then, in the physical world, the paradoxical moment of sexual syncope ends with the final emission. All Tantric exercises contain the idea of control, this one especially. The preeminent exercise, the most difficult, will be to concentrate all of consciousness on the moment of jouissance. Not one's own (whether man or woman) but that of the Other. What is most surprising in a doctrine that is so perfectly free in its transsexual movements is that it always views woman as Other: the precise moment to be watched for, therefore, is the one when the woman cries out with pleasure.

"At the end of sexual intercourse," says the Tantric philosopher in his treatise, "there is a sound that occurs in the form of a spontaneous resonance springing forth involuntarily from the throat of the female beloved: this is an endless and indistinct sound that requires no meditation, no concentration. If one fixes one's thoughts on it, one can become master of the universe."[13] An indistinct sound, far from that of the song; an unending sound, the imaginary font of all engendering, of all germination. This cry is not only the woman's. Metamorphosed, it resounds in the space between-the-two sexes; it is the *medium*. No word could better describe the cry of jouissance than this ambiguous word where the between-the-two of syncope is swallowed up: *medium*, between father and mother, heaven and earth, index and ring fingers.

To arrive at a mastery of the universe, and to fix in one's mind the absolute instant of the cry, one must "do" time. The first exercise consists of bringing perception to the void between two instants. "So that the mind, leaving one thought," says the Tantric philosopher, "becomes blocked and does not become interested in something else. Then, thanks to what is found in between these instants, Realization flourishes in all of its intensity."[14] A propaedeutic lesson in the consciousness of the orgasm: to learn to halt the march of time, to let go of the reins, to make room for the void. Not to unite or bind; rather to separate and untie, allowing the gap to remain free. In the exercises proposed in Descartes's *Metaphysical Meditations*, it is necessary to hold on to time: "All the time I am thinking, I am." I think, therefore I am: I am only if I think. In the practice of Tantrism, on the other hand, it is necessary to prefer the emptiness of the comma, and to choose the gap. I am if I do not think. This is very close to Lacan's interpretation of Descartes: I am present there where I am not thinking, I am thinking there where I am not present. Soon it will be difficult to determine whether the exercise consists in having the subject disappear into the void or enlarge it and fill it with everything. Empty or full? Absolute subject, or unconscious subject?

Let us follow the sequence of the exercises. When the moment arises unexpectedly, it must be seized, immobilized, and utilized: to take stupor on its other side, to catch the bounding of the surprised heart, and to turn it into a garden swing. Tantric philosophy enumerates these sovereign moments: when a forgotten task is suddenly remembered—My God, that's right!—upon hearing good news, or when afraid, when something unexpected happens, when curiosity peaks, when one ejaculates, during a recitation . . . But also when hanging over a precipice like Diotima, when fleeing a battlefield, like Fabrice at Waterloo, when hunger strikes . . .

When you sneeze.[15]

In the sequence of exercises of this moral pedagogy for acts of violence, Tantrism pays a lot of attention to the *sneeze*, even considering it as one of the major means of access to ecstatic liberation. It is actually a crisis on a small scale, a minuscule war that abolishes everything. But as small an event as it may be, it symbolizes the totality of potential crises the apprentice must learn to internalize to gain consciousness of—to "embody," as we say—the instant. It is necessary to catch the sneeze "in flight," necessary that its substantial marrow be extracted, that peppery instant of the explosion of time. It should be noted that ejaculation is present here only as one of a series of crises; it is, in any case, less important than the moments that precede it. Less profitable than the vigilance that, a second earlier, was "ready and waiting" for the cry of the Other; less essential than the great yogic myth of the "awakening of the serpent,"[16] the royal cobra that is coiled in the hollow of the loins and that must be raised through the spinal cord all the way to the top of the brain, until consciousness completely disappears. One must understand consciousness as sexuality. The female organ seeks the rush of jouissance, and the male organ on the way to mystic erection, crosses every vertebra in the spine.

Again in this way, the exercise of pain provokes its abolition as displeasure and its fusion with pleasure. It is the same for the contemplation of beauty, a reality crisis, a true orgasm of the gaze. The syncopal crisis is a perfect example; the mind must take possession of it resolutely in order for it to end.

At the end of this asceticism through excess, consciousness will have devoured the external world, as if it had been aspirated through a minuscule hole. But once the "devouring" is over, consciousness, like a living organ, will not be able to end there; obeying the turbulence of the ocean, it "vomits" the reality it just ingested.[17] A beating of the internal and external heart, pulsation of a thought conceived of like a living being capable of absorbing and rejecting reality as the heart does with blood, as the mouth does with food, and as the fetus does with maternal fluids: a radical philosophy of the "One-inside-the-Other." A lesson on exploding in ecstasy.

Doubtless the perfect model of the divine coupling of Shiva and Shakti gives way only to the most archaic of fantasies; there is no doubt that this systematic interweaving attacks the imago, the body itself, pure primal narcissism. The model for orgasmic syncope, indefinitely prolonged, is that of *limitlessness*, which voluntarily deprives the subject of a sense of belonging and goads it into "conquering" reality by letting go of its own unique individuality.

Then there is a vigorous return to the imagery of dismemberment, which Jacques Lacan calls "aggressive disintegration" and of which he cites Hieronymus Bosch as the foremost Western example. The subject is exploded; narcissism, off kilter; the body simultaneously reduced to abjection and raised to fusional union: the mastery of the instant in Tantric philosophy can only be attained at this high price.

Nothing is closer to the *inner experience* formulated by Georges Bataille, who, however, did not go so far as to take the leap that separated him from the abyss called Asia. Bataille's scenario, a plea in favor of immediacy and a refusal of all transcendence, a reflection on laughter—for which Indian yogis have a well-established daily practice—the perception of philosophy as "lightning in the night, the language of a brief instant," appears to be a spontaneous Tantrism, just as there are spontaneous ecstasies or orgasms. This delicate point is not perhaps as shaky as it seems: based on the experience of the orgasm, not overlooking this most magnificent and everyday of human syncopes, Bataille encounters by himself the paths that compel our minds to follow the same turns and detours. For example:

> I can only be this complete man by letting go. I cannot become it by force of will: my will, of course, wants to be there. But if misfortune (or luck) wants me to let go, then I will know that *I am* a complete man, *who bows to no one*. . . . In order to be the whole universe, man would have to let go of his principle: to accept nothing of what he is, unless he stretches beyond what he is. This being that I am is the revolt of being, and infinite *desire*: for him God was only a stage and he has grown from this excessive experience, comically perched on a stake.[18]

This search for "letting go" and for the infinite perpetuation of desire is an echoed response to Lacan's observations on the destruction of narcissism. What happens if the "passion of being a man" is suspended, what transpires if the narcissism of the imago is menaced?

"When man searching the emptiness of his thought moves forward into the unshadowed light of the imaginary space without even waiting to see what arises from it, a lusterless mirror shows him a surface where nothing is reflected,"[19] wrote Lacan.

To return from this instant of the mirror, to fuse with Shakti, to plunge into the place from where we come, from where we were born, *inter faeces et urinas*, this is what we call madness. We must remember that there exists a world in which this same inverted passage is the object of a philosophical method that is rigorous in every sense of the word, a world where syncope is the object of fierce domestication, of constant and obstinate effort.

But it's one or the other: either the control of syncope or the autonomy of the subject. History has imposed a split between the world where the subject is "strong," free, and conscious of its own identity, and the world where the "weakened" subject surrenders itself, through copulation, to the cry of the Other and reality. Perhaps Lévi-Strauss, returning from Asia, was correct in daring to view Islam as being responsible for this split:

> If the West traces its internal tensions back to their source, it will see that Islam, by coming between Buddhism and Christianity, Islamized us at the time when the West, by taking part in the crusades, was involved in opposing it and therefore came to resemble it, instead of undergoing—had Islam never come into being—a slow process of osmosis with Buddhism, which would have Christianized us still further, and would have made us all the more Christian in that we would have gone back beyond Christianity itself. It was then that the West lost the opportunity of remaining female.[20]

Public Enemy

We would be wrong to deny that these ideas, and the fantasies attached to them, determine the most mundane aspects of everyday life in India. It would be wrong to conceal the blood that is shed, the flesh mutilated, the death that ensues; this is the other side of those releases, those walls demolished and those people embracing. Ideas have a difficult and long life; they persist as do myths, which as we know travel along silently for centuries to emerge suddenly anew; the unconscious proceeds in much the same way. In the India of today, the contradiction between the philosophies that have risen out of Hinduism and the democratic status of this immense nation is manifest every day;

the existence of an autonomous subject borrowed from the West is not automatic; the continuance of daily life and the threat of death depend on it every step of the way. And the great spiritual body of Hinduism actively oversees the unconscious of seven hundred million citizens.[21]

Or more.

Jawaharlal Nehru, a Hindu of the highest caste—that of the Brahmans—from one of the most erudite regions—Kashmir—personified at the time of Indian independence an astonishing synthesis of these two worlds. Influenced by the West, where he gained the tools to lead the ideological struggle for the independence of his country, he was a radical materialist and an atheist. But he was nevertheless profoundly Indian, beyond Hinduism, beyond the seven great religions that share India and too often tear it apart.[22] All his life, as so many Anglo-Indians do today, he tried to discover what India was for Indians. Sudhir Kakar, divided like Nehru between East and West, insists on the "emotional" character of this interminable search.

The word sounds strange to us. The English or French translation scarcely does justice to the Hindu concept of *bhakti*, which is ingrained in everyone in India, regardless of religion. *Bhakti*: it is "devotion"; it is "self-sacrifice"; it is a specific passion that is situated between the birth of a national identity and the adoration of the Mother. The Mother, as we have seen, is benevolent and murderous. The Mother is India. Every Indian citizen carries her within, at the crossroads of the imaginary and the symbolic, with an intensity from which the Father seems strangely absent: here the Mother rules unconditionally. The devotion to the Mother can only be performed with emotion: the eyes become filled with tears. These tears drop like pearls at concerts if someone mentions the place where you were born, where springtimes are unique, and the buttercups are incomparable, and where, from India's north to south and east to west, you will always be told: only there can the true soul of India be found. Indians always seem ready to gush, like the blood that flows in regional disputes. Nehru's feelings while searching for India, and those of Sudhir Kakar, are an integral part of the great collective myth that little by little is forging a still-stammering national identity.

Whether he be Hindu, Christian, Sikh, Buddhist, Jain, Parsi, or Muslim, or from one of the aboriginal tribes, every Indian can identify with Nehru's words, which speak for an entire people:

> As I grew up and became engaged in activities which promised to lead to India's freedom, I became obsessed with the thought of India. What was this India that possessed me and beckoned to me continually? . . .

> India with all her infinite charm and variety began to grow up on me more and more, and yet the more I saw of her, the more I realized how very difficult it was for me or for anyone to grasp the ideas she had embodied. . . . The unity of India was no longer merely an intellectual conception for me: it was an emotional experience which overpowered me.[23]

"Overpowering": the key word. This overpowering is three thousand years old; it is inscribed in the philosophical history of India; it has to do with structure, it concerns the subject, who is influenced in his totality. If it is difficult for an Indian intellectual of today to undertake a filtering of the waters—those of the Ganges where according to myth, every river in India is born, and those approaching from the Western world—it is no easier for a Western intellectual to cross over to the other side of the world. Because to cross over there, into the abyss called Asia, is to accept the understanding of the absolute, radical, and monstrous dispossession of the subject, its degradation, neglect, and finally its destruction in the name of a higher good: order, fusion, the life cycle. It is so prevalent that Sudhir Kakar has tried to forge for India the concept of the "dividual," strictly opposed to the "individual," which is the product of two thousand years of Western thinking. Above all, there is the *nonsubject*, before, during, and after. A deliberate strategy of syncope will be used to abolish the rejected subjectivity of the individual.

The social and political contradictions that have come from this conceptual confrontation will soon become part of the history of the modern world. Islam continues to pose a geographical and political obstacle to the clear understanding of the Indian question. In the middle of the road, between the pinnacle of collective thought—China—and the jubilant or depressive assumption of the autonomous Western subject, is India: democratic, pluralistic, secular, *and* Asian. Between India and ourselves, there is a family history that has long remained hidden: we were separated from her.

January 1989, Calcutta. Satyajit Ray finishes shooting a film whose action takes place that same month, at the beginning of the year of the bicentennial of the French Revolution. The film is set in a small imaginary Bengali village; the hero is a family doctor who has been schooled in Western medicine. There have been outbreaks of hepatitis and typhoid among his patients. He undertakes an investigation and tests the holy water, which is the ritual drink of thousands of pilgrims who come to the newly constructed temple built by a rich Bengali industrialist. The water is of course polluted: the water mains broke. No one dared to think of the temple water. No one *could* have thought of the temple water; it is taboo. That is where the film begins.

The doctor notifies a leftist newspaper. But his own brother is an associate of the man who built the temple, which attracts enough pilgrims to make it a profitable enterprise for the town. The doctor calls a meeting to warn the town's citizens; but his brother puts before them an unthinkable thought. To believe in medicine is to doubt the temple, and therefore to doubt the gods. No one would dare . . . Except for a group of students who begin a street campaign to warn the Bengalis of Chandipur of the temple water's mortal danger. Will they or won't they drink it?

In this game, everything counts.

First of all, there is the artist, Satyajit Ray, whose family belonged to one of the foremost reform movements of nineteenth-century India, the "Brahmo-Samaj" movement, which was syncretic, modern, progressive, and humanistic.[24] Considering the history of the Brahmo-Samaj movement, of which almost no trace remains, it is easy to understand why it is difficult to be both a Hindu and a humanist in India. Western humanism is in deep contradiction to Indian thought.

Then there is the water. Holy, wherever it is found, no matter what its source, terribly scarce in a country so heavily deforested,[25] necessary to accomplish all rituals, no matter what the religion; water cannot be guilty. To defame water, to accuse it of corruption, is to defame the oceanic maternal feeling; it is a violent interdiction. Between Indians and water, the symbiosis remains *usque ad mortem*, until death finally relinquishes the tattered rag to the river's waters, which it never should have left. Water is a weapon against civic and individual identity.

Then there is the film's title, borrowed from Ibsen. The title is symbolic of a combat that Satyajit Ray has always waged alone. This combat French audiences understand only slightly, enough to render homage to him in beauty's name, a combat that has political stakes: humanism against religion; the individual against Hinduism; the citizen against the pilgrim. The title designates the doctor after he has publicly denounced the pollution of the temple's water.

But the title also refers to the individual subject in Indian philosophy: *Public Enemy*.

Finally, there is theater. Against religion, against the polluted maternal waters, theater as a weapon deployed in the street. In fact, it is by means of street theater that India has begun to practice theatrical ritual: militant theater influenced by classical agit-prop, undoubtedly, but one that contains the first manifestation of tragedy.[26] Through theater consciousness is raised; through theater an element of tragedy is introduced to democracy. Through theater—as was the case with the Greek model—the notion of the subject is born.

11

Thought Burned Alive: Indian Philosophies

There is a universe that, unlike ours, hounds the Subject. With the same stubbornness we expend in defending it, with the same passion that inspires us to protect it from syncope, from absence, and from intrusion, Indian philosophers in their own country track down autonomy and ban independence.[1] The single individual has its place; individualism, on the contrary, seems and has seemed for a long time outside the law. Is this an aversion to the Subject?

The Indian search for an absolute Subject going beyond all individual limits, open to everyone by engrossing the whole universe beyond what we call consciousness, could just as easily be defined as the greatest love. It is so immense that it must consume the fragile subjective defenses that prevent the mind, the soul, or the person from moving toward reunion with the divine. The other side of love, Western modernity tells us, is hate, and its law is ambivalence. The hatred expressed in the Indian love of the absolute subject is closely associated with what we consider most important: consciousness, its free determination, its various states, in short, everything that psychoanalysts have gathered under the rubric of the ego. We must make a long detour in order to understand that their idea of the self and of humanity is not the same as ours. We place importance on man in nature; this idea, although we know its long history, has become spontaneous: it is a philosophical reflex. So we hate whatever diverts us from it.

Indian discourse, unlike ours, is that of a burning love as extensive as the universe itself, beyond the humans who constitute it; it is supported by a social tradition that has barely been worn down by modernization, and that puts everyone in a place in a system in which the nonegalitarian collective is the goal that has priority. Emotion, affect, the great outburst that Pandit Nehru evoked in speaking of India, are the same as those that gather together the family, the village, all the members of a community; and the unitary impulse is so strong that it permeates all Indian communities, of whatever religion. This impassioned origin is responsible for contradictory occurrences: the long and noble struggle for Indian independence is its finest hour, but "sectarianisms," those religious wars that even now continue to rend the fabric of the country, are the hateful obverse of the coin. The day a free India was born, in August 1947, the massacres between Hindu and Muslim, between Hindu and Sikh, began. They continue today. Yet lingering still is the living relationship to a Mother India, worshiped in a temple in Benares, under the strange geopolitical form of a white marble map. It is a question of love for the Mother, backed with hatred, and this hatred stubbornly undermines individual autonomy. The harried Subject is not the idea of an absolute Subject itself; on the contrary, it is the principle. But to achieve this, thought sets about a systematic combustion of what we in the West consider the most precious attributes of the Subject: desire, free will, autonomy; a certain idea of life in which romantic passion is the spice.

This love backed with hate, or this hate backed with love, conspicuously marked with the maternal symbol, fascinates Westerners when, tired of the imperfect image in the mirror, they search for a place where they can flee toward a universe without apparent individualism; a world where, they believe, it will no longer be demanded of them to come to terms with themselves as they are. There, I mean in India, released from the self, the Westerner buys a new life; often, such travelers change their names, willingly doing away with the contemptible identities that made them suffer so much; they tinker with their consciousness and believe that they have access to ecstasy; often, they do not return from this immense syncope that is in proportion to the universal mind. There are no illusions about this story in India today; it repeats—without variations, to the point of caricature—the misunderstanding between India and the West. The fascination with *Mother India* is so powerful that, paradoxically, it provokes the "forgetting of India."[2] The concept of synthesis, thought, the idea of the Subject, and therefore philosophy, belong to Europe; "wisdom" reverts to India, wisdom that is passed on only by contact, intuitively, backed up by oceanic feeling, and when one arrives, syncope.

This impassioned search for an entirely free Subject is inscribed in systems of thought, passed on in established schools, depending on implacable logic, running through the pathways of idealism and materialism, as in the West (and even the paths of the between-the-two). Nothing, except the ease of the diffuse attraction and the rejection of our own individualism, permits us to label the whole body of Indian philosophies as simple wisdom. This is a disturbing matter, and the same people who delightedly analyze the history of Western mystics or the negative theologies of the Hellenistic period are loath to take this step. It is only one step, however, and not a chasm; it is only the

Kierkegaardian leap, Nietzsche's outburst, the *Ichspaltung* on which Freud came to a stop; these are the philosophies to which the history of Western thought has accustomed us. A simple relaxation of the mind, and there you are. Only then do the differences, and the reversed mirror, appear clearly. Then the idea of syncope also becomes clear, syncope pushed to the limit in a series of philosophies that use it as a technique, perfectly mastered, in order to arrive at an idea of the Subject that is different from ours. And if we do not return, it is our fault.

Reading through the systems that have constituted Indian thought, however, one perceives a fragile familiarity. There as elsewhere, the ossification of systems of ideas leads to reformism, and opens up spaces where "something else" quivers. This "something else" can be clearly read in certain aspects of Tantrism: a between-the-two without closure, a split, a syncope from which one returns and which serves as a springboard for the exercise of thinking. From both positions, the idea of the Subject evolves. In the West, it becomes weaker and cracks; in India it appears like a watermark in the between-the-two.

For us the idea of the Subject has lost a little of its arrogance: philosophies, then psychoanalysis, and finally ethnology have progressively impaired its freedom; the unconscious, which is the group of structures that determine what a human being is, inflects subjective autonomy in a lasting way. In India, the independence acquired by turning British law back on itself molded the idea of a fight for freedom; the autonomy of an entire people, *swaraj*, had already become a slogan at the dawn of this century.[3] The advances of this huge democracy may perhaps finish this work, and also mold the idea of individual freedoms for each person. The philosophical India I am speaking of, throughout its vast history, proceeded in a way different from our own; and contemporary Indian philosophers of all Indian religions take pains to demonstrate that India was always right. On certain fundamental points the history of Western democracies could well do them justice.

In the beginning are cosmologies. Philosophies develop from these later, when thinking has extricated itself from myth; this history is just as true in India as it was in Greece.

In the beginning (as is usual in cosmologies) is disorder, or rather, confusion. In the India of the Vedas no one will be surprised to find confusion represented by a primordial androgyne, simultaneously a milk cow and a fine bull. But however plentiful the milk and the semen, the wheel of the world is not yet turning, and the sun is not yet in place. To set the wheel in motion, they have to separate: men from women, night from day, the cow from the bull. From then on the divine cow is milked at daybreak; that is because there is now a daybreak, and with it an interval of passing time. The passing of dawn establishes the coming of the sun.[4]

But with dawn comes dusk, when the sun immediately sinks. All the first thinking concerns the rebirth of the sun, the motivation for the first rituals and the future origin of philosophy. Every night the sun goes down, dissolving; every night it goes back to the embryonic state and, buried within a recurrent germination, prepares to be reborn. The sun, a golden embryo clouded over, sucks the milk and semen of the androgyne in the nurturing shadows, the androgyne that is a nocturnal figure from the dangerous "before." But nothing is more important than the reconstruction of the world when we rise in the morning; it is a long internal work that the West has hurried through for a long time—ask the depressive who no longer succeeds in it, and has chosen to remain inside night. In the India of the Vedas, nothing counts except the sun's reappearance. Man ensures it with sacrifices of Fire; it is thanks to Fire that Man fits into the ordering of the world. Performing all the sacrificial gestures for dawn, one causes the sun to be reborn; one constructs one's own immortality; one does well. The sacrificer builds the universe with every dawn; the humans of the first Indian texts breathe the damp breath of the androgynous cow and manufacture their world with immortal fire; thinking begins in the first hearth of the day.

Then, in the universe of the Brahmana, the inescapable figure of the *scattered god* appears, which must be put back together again. Prajapati, the god who behaves like a man, creates the way a male does, by disseminating, exhausting himself. When he has finished creating the gods, the mortals, and finally death to consume them all, there he is, empty, or rather emptied, begging loudly for his lost unity. So the gods set about reconstituting the creator who has been dispersed among his creatures; in order to do this, he has to be cooked. "They [the gods] throw him into the sacrificial pot like a seed into the womb."[5] Keep in mind the striking picture of the cooking pot into which the beginning of a being is thrown, the outline of a cosmic egg . . . Perhaps thinking is a way of reconstructing an egg that one wants to break again.

To put the scattered back together again, to refasten what had been unfastened, to rejoin what has been unjoined: that is how the construction of the sacrificial altar works. Indian philosophy is germinating in this collection of raw bricks, separated by crumbly soil, containing in its hollow a statue laid on a lotus leaf and a gold plate. The sacrificing Fire takes charge of the reunification of Prajapati; and the sacrificer himself takes charge of gathering, on an altar, the symbolic elements of the reunification in-itself-and-for-itself. The bricks, for example, reunite the water and clay in which humans took shelter, terrified at seeing death created; the gold statue is the image of Prajapati, and also that of man—fundamentally scattered, which one must work to reunite. The lotus leaf is the birthplace of Fire; the round plate is a metaphor for the sun. All that is left is to light the Fire and let it do its work of assembling.[6] Think of the image you have of the dispersal of the ashes of a burned body: scattered over the ocean, blown away by the wind . . . Well, here it is just the opposite: *to burn is to reconnect*. Whence, later, the practice of radically burning thought, which burns right down to its own foundations.

But where thinking is practiced, the work of its opposite is also practiced. And if it is a matter of reuniting and reconnecting, the opposite of reconnection will be found without fail in the organization of the Brahmanic altar—that is, disconnection; the opposite of reuniting—that is, the definitively dislocated. Prajapati, the figure of man, will never be completely reconstituted. Something escapes him.

This story is played out in the glistening eyes of animals. When Prajapati, the divine man, was completely exhausted by creating the world, he wanted the replenishing Fire. But Fire wanted nothing to do with it; he hid among the cattle; he concealed himself in the bull, the goat, the horse, the ram, and also in the body of that new type of animal, man, who had just been born. So Fire was crouched in the animal. But Prajapati, overcome with desire, recognized Fire in the glittering gaze of the goat, in the glistening eye of the horse . . . And then, animals let out a breath, which is surely the smoke from Fire. They drop excrement, which is the equivalent of ashes . . . Yes! Prajapati found Fire. That is why the sacrificed heads of the five animals that became Fire are arranged around the altar. Including man. So Fire, satisfied, agrees to fulfill its duties.[7]

The ritual of the Vedic sacrifice, as contemporary anthropologists describe it, misses nothing of the future philosophical concept of the subject. The bricks, the gold statue, the lotus leaf, and the plate that represents the sun have found their place; Fire fulfills its duties. What is left is the crumbly soil, which was dug out of the ground to hollow out the place where the altar would be built. There it is, removed, and for the moment serving no purpose. This left-over soil that will soon find a use has a strange name, which means at the same time *earth*, *excrement*, and *cattle*.

In India, a profoundly rural society, all the products of the cow are used, even the excrement: the dried dung is used as a fuel for little household hearths; sacred, it is also an ingredient in a culinary hymn to the cow, a purifying beverage made of milk, curds, and urine, into which is mixed a little of the precious fecal matter of the animal. The "excremental" excavated earth is not lost; put between the bricks of the altar and well packed in, it symbolizes the *mortal* aspects of Prajapati. Thus from an animal's eye to cow dung, we arrive at the very first metaphor of the Subject: "The core of a person consists of droppings," as the scientists politely translate it. It is better translated word for word by Charles Malamoud: "The Center of the Self is shit."[8] It absorbs all on its way through, but is especially good for burning.

That is not all. When Prajapati decomposed and moaned, broken into pieces, he begged for his unity, his individuality: "Ah, my *atman*," he cried. *Atman*, the *soul*.[9] But the problems were already beginning: that is not "soul" the way we understand it, it is the assembly that holds together the parts that are now scattered. It is the continuity that defines it. *Atman* is only found again in the sacrifice; by building the altar and conducting the sacrifice, the sacrificer manufactures his own person and makes it nonmortal, thanks to Fire, the only true immortal. At this stage, in order to reconstitute oneself, it is enough to do well, without forgetting anything. It is a difficult operation, threatened on every side by dissension, confusion, the void that its purpose is to fill. The Brahman is the one who guarantees the effectiveness of the operation by an essential activity: sitting to the south of the sacrificial altar, he watches and is silent. The sacrifice depends on his concentration; the reconstitution of Prajapati depends on his silence. Here the philosophical gesture appears very clearly: the activity free of all expenditure, the motionlessness of the attentive thinker. And if he spoke out loud, "the sacrifice would tumble like a one-legged man."[10] When the sacrifice is over, the officiating Brahman launches his weapon against the threat of discontinuity, the weapon of secret syllables that must be whispered, soundlessly, at the limits of speech and of silence. An almost-silence, an almost-speech, already, like a watermark, a between-the-two.

That is the sacrificial action that reconstitutes the unity of acts, without loss, beneath the burning gaze of a man whispering to the south of an altar made of bricks and droppings, devoured by Fire and guaranteed by silence.

The Upanishads, which take up where the Brahmana left off, move toward philosophy. These actions connected to each other only by the attentiveness of the officiating Brahman are no longer sufficient. For if one action follows another, this succession is itself fragile; the action itself, however concentrated and ardent it may be, is no longer enough to guarantee the construction of the world at daybreak. The Upanishads search for a more metaphysical guarantee: the conjunction between the lost assembling of the scattered Prajapati and being itself. The term "Upanishad" marks out the connection: it is made between the self—what some would translate by "person"—and being. And the continuity is no longer found only in the silent attentiveness of the motionless sacrificer: it is in breathing.

The philosophers reinterpret the Vedic ritual of Fire: it is no longer the reconstructive ordering, action by action, that builds a continuity whose end is in itself, it is "the sacrifice of breathing in speech and the sacrifice of speech in breathing."

Silence, an inaudible muttering, an indistinct word, a low voice . . . So many minimal activities miming the limitless, the indeterminate: in the Vedas, the whispering officiant turns into sand that runs out, becomes vital seed, seminal time, a period of time that runs out without ever exhausting itself. That was the Vedic tradition of the sacrificer. But from the moment when breathing becomes the directing principle, *one sacrifices with every breath.* The sacrifice is transported from the brick altar and the manure to the very body of the one who, with every breath, regenerates the world and makes the sun rise. "It is in breathing that the sun rises and in breathing that it sets. The gods made breathing the structure. So it is today, so it will be tomorrow."[11]

Yogis have intervened in the delicate metaphysical reconstruction of Prajapati's great scattered body. All the West knows about those ascetic gymnasts is the easy-to-do positions used by beautiful people who want to get in shape. The philosopher yogis of classical India are completely different figures, who can still be found intact on the stairs of the Ganges quays, or in the Himalayan mountains, as they were two thousand years ago. Who are they? *Practitioners of breathing*: "One must inhale and exhale with the purpose of avoiding the clutches of evil and of death."[12] What does "yoga" mean? Derived from the root *yug*, the word indicates the yoke (it is the same word in French)[13] that joins the oxen in the harness. Yoga means *link.* The essential part of the practice of yoga consists in the mastery of breathing; the connected regimen of bodily positions is only the propaedeutic for concentrating on the path of each breath.

The yogi retains the immobility and the silence of the silent officiant sitting to the south of the altar. A strange athleticism whose sole purpose is the achieving of fusion, *moksha*, the abolition of the borders of the self, its definitive inflammation. A strange athleticism that deviates from a so-called natural respiration—which the West has often allowed to get lost in a confused disorder—it establishes it in a daily rhythm, the better to disrupt it later, in a careful and systematic disordering. Disrupt the breathing? Definitely, for it is a question of *suspending* the breathing—first for sixteen seconds, then for multiples of sixteen without limitation; so it is a matter of obstructing the binary course of the breathing by breaking the alternation of inhaling and exhaling.[14] A respiration that stops, that is suspended . . . From this delay in breathing, ecstasy will later burst forth. There we are again: in the midst of a syncopal exercise. Poles apart from Vedic sacrifice, which conceives only of a causal chain of actions (of which the inaudible monotonous murmur is a perfect model), here is its paradoxical prolongation: the *cogito of the desired swoon*, the yogis' great ecstasy, obtained by holding one's breath.

Fire consumes the self's resistance, but it is water that permeates descriptions of Indian ecstasy. Sudhir Kakar, in his excellent study of the Hindu concept of the world, cites the testimony of a famous philosopher, Ramana Maharishi, who compared ecstasy to a bucket immersed in a well: *it is water with water all around.*[15] When Fire has finished consuming all the subjective flesh, the states of consciousness, affect, passions, and angers, then water floods in, and drowns the self in the limitlessness of the ocean. The metaphor of the ocean runs through all the texts of India; we will soon see that, from East to West, it makes a strange journey all the way to Freud, who paid no attention to it. It is already an indication that the West protects its idea of the Subject so well that even one of its most transgressive thinkers did not want to consider ecstatic dissolution, a little death that is intolerable.

If I come back to the little death, it is because love at first sight is the first sign of this long philosophical syncope. The first lightning bolt of the absolute Subject appears in a moment: "Ah! The cry when it lit up the lightning! Ah! When its eyes blinked!"[16] say the Upanishads enigmatically: the cry, the lightning, the glistening eye, *Augenblick* . . . If I speak of the little death, it is because the color of this lightning is blue. Blue is indeed the first appearance of Indian ecstasy; for us, blue is the color of sadness or of lovers who kill themselves. "One evening shades of rose and mystical blue / We will exchange a single bolt of lightning."[17]

The lightning bolt of ecstasy is blue,[18] the blue of the ocean, the sky, limitlessness, blue as Elsa's gaze in which Aragon read the distress of passionate love, blue as what we call "the blues" without knowing with what fire we are playing. For us nostalgia is blue, and not well loved; over there (I mean in India) blue is the color of the loss of the Subject. For us, it is at the limits of the forbidden, while there, it is the color of what is to come. Ecstasy: a blue cry opening onto the ocean reunited with the sky, with no horizon in between.

No more between-the-two, no more cracks: a complete reunion between subject and reality. Syncope stretched out to infinity.

In the art of Western psychiatric diagnosis, the psychotic is described as being "cut off from reality," closed off in him- or herself. Psychoanalysts have often reversed the terms of the relationship between reality and the subject. It is not true, they say, that psychotics are "cut off from reality": on the contrary, they are invaded by *too much reality*, and no longer know how to distinguish between themselves and the world. It is very clear that psychotic states, especially deliriums with mystical themes, are considered in the West to be part of pathology. This really needs to be explained: in India, it is the other way around. Invasion by reality is the ideal norm.

"The ideal of *moksha*, applicable in principle to every Hindu," remarks Sudhir Kakar, "gives him the possibility of living, even at a preconscious level, a 'mystical' experience. In the West, this particular type of experience is only imaginable for an elite group of artists, poets, or those who are 'crazy about God.' The fact is that in India, the concept of *moksha* does not represent a phenomenon of deviance, but occupies a central position in the culture."[19]

It is true that in the course of daily life in India one becomes used to hearing, as if it were nothing special, Indians from all walks of life recounting in a straightforward manner their ecstasies, their encounters with the divine, and their actual oceanic experience. The gaze that they turn on our concept of individual autonomy is marked by an astonished compassion: what use is autonomy, the source of so much suffering, and why deprive oneself of such delights? You do not know how to live, come . . . That is how India's seduction begins: with the young girl's leap into the blue of mystical ecstasy.

What remains is the ascetic work necessary to achieve it. It is a question, as always, of burning. In Ramana Maharishi's comparison, the bucket of water still maintains a shadow of attachment to the world: the rope. Burned to a cinder, but still a rope: in a state of *moksha*, says Sudhir Kakar, "this ego is without defense; like the skeletal remains of a burned rope, it no longer serves to tie anything up, even though it retains the form."[20] Fire has carried out its duty, and all that remains of the subject is the shape about to fall into ashes, a shadowy body, already consumed by Fire. In the yoga of the Upanishads, the set of ascetic exercises is called *tapas*. *Tapas* has a precise meaning: the attaining of heat.

To breathe is to burn. Knowing how to breathe is knowing how to burn the Subject within. Think of the famous image of a moment in the Buddha's life: seated in the meditation position, his flesh has completely disappeared; all that remains of the body is the bones, and he is a thinking skeleton. It is not the result of a fast, not a real thinness; it is the perfect image of one in whom the fire of asceticism has consumed desire. Asceticism is made for ravaging the self.

There are innumerable ascetic tests. The list differs little from that of the anchorites of the Egyptian desert in later years. The ascetic must be able to immerse himself in freezing water, even if that means breaking the Himalayan ice, and coming back to the bank, he must dry a sheet simply with the heat of his body. He can, needless to say, live naked without suffering from either heat or cold. He can stay for years perched on one foot, seated without moving, or shut up in a cave, without eating or drinking; he must know how to become a tree or a plant and merge into nature. He does not notice pain, and can stay buried in the ground, suppressing his breathing, for twenty-four or forty-eight hours, to the great delight of American neurologists, who have been tracking these phenomena for a century.

In Indian mythology, women are the most gifted ones: hysteria—as we understand it from our side—demands it![21] So Parvati, who wanted to marry the god Shiva, the ascetic god par excellence, undertook to seduce him with asceticism, and perched on one leg without ingesting anything until the god gave in. And also Amba, one of the main characters of the *Mahabharata*, wanted desperately to take revenge on the hero Bishma who did not want to marry her: she spent her long life in atonement until the god gave her a sign to throw herself into the fire. So she lit the pyre on which she disappeared, and immediately she was reborn in the form of a strange (*ambigu*) warrior, Sikhandin, who was appointed to let fly the arrow that would finally kill off Bishma. This is the fate of those unhappy heroines who are called *satis* in India. According to orthodox Hindu rites, these holy widows willingly decide to accompany their dead husband on the funeral pyre; Brahmans must verify the authenticity of this ascetic desire. Then, dressed in their wedding gown, the women voluntarily climb up onto the logs and settle themselves, sitting down; they put the head of their deceased husband on their lap. Finally they give the order to light the fire, and perish, burned alive, a reflection of Indian thought. The ritual is certainly old-fashioned, and there is no doubt that innumerable victims were forced to follow this sinister path by being threatened or drugged. This voluntary sacrifice was forbidden by the English at the request of a Bengali humanist, around 1830.[22] When a young widow of seventeen publicly chose this ghastly fate in September 1987, the whole of India thought it was dreaming, and understood that fundamentalism was making a comeback.[23] The central government passed a decree against the incitement to suicide; that was all it could do. But the fact that this custom had been used, through the years, to forcibly immolate millions of women who wanted to live takes nothing away from the myth itself, this ascetic myth of the satis. Following the example of the female yoginis of classical India, the satis decide to burn up, in a gesture beneficial to the village community from which they come, their useless bodies, their abandoned flesh. They are burning their half—which is not even a half—of a conjugal subject, the other half of which, male and essential, is already on the pyre, and whose death they are vaguely guilty of.

In the West, they do not climb up there voluntarily; the village community burns them by force. In the very middle of the seventeenth century, the century of triumphant reason and humanist philosophy, the West also had its women-torches, who had no choice about the pyre. Often, unlike in India, they were not married; young girls, virgins, or widows, they no longer had a position in the village except when, by burning, the necessary fault was concentrated on them. In the West, we stopped burning witches in the middle of the eighteenth century. But curiously, on the opera stage, we watch the sung conflagration of heroines who voluntarily go to the pyre in order to regenerate the world,[24] and it is rapture for our enchanted eyes and ears. No doubt one day India will turn the ritual of the satis into a spectacle, in order to finish distancing it.

Women are always excessive. But their excess fits into the straight line that connects the individual to the cosmos that she faithfully replicates, and in which she finds a place, at the moment of fusion, that parallels the place she had as a living being. This is achieved by resolutely abolishing what stood in the way of union: autonomy, individuation, and that limiter, consciousness. The *atman* that is then spread out, far from subjective limitations, is from then on beyond attack: no action can affect it anymore, no feeling can soil it. The self has become immutable, and no longer has anything in common with the classic Western concept of the Subject: free will has disappeared, its memory banished. The states of consciousness have been gradually curtailed: "All acts, desires, smells, tastes, encompassing everything that is—this soul, deep within my heart, is silent and indifferent. It is the essence of *brahman*."[25] This utter indifference does not bear defining; there is only one way to say it, a way that is in itself double: by saying what it is not, and by repeating these negations whose method is that of negative theology. God is not this, nor that, nor yet that; the *atman* is not this, nor that, nor yet that. The two modes of this stubborn denial are essential. To *describe* would be to *limit*, and to *repeat* is part of the mystical exercise in its essence.

Elsewhere, under other skies and in other eras, consciousness was put to the test through repetition and apophasis (which proceeds by successive negations). At the limits of speech and of breathing, there are Hesychasts who, in a seated position, bend their bodies over their knees and cut off their breathing, while repeating formulas and prayers, reaching the point of ecstatic intoxication. There, near the strait between Europe and Asia Minor, are the whirling dervishes and the chant of "Sama, sama, sama" that is repeated while dancing to the point at which consciousness is invaded by the lightning bolt.

There are a thousand techniques for cutting off one's breathing; dancing is a method that turns words into body, and throws the flesh overboard, as does the accomplished yogi. In the case of the yogi as with the dancer, a paradox is perceived: the bodies are flawless, well developed, harmonious. *Even more so because that is not the goal of the exercise*: if the yogi enters into his morning gymnastics as one enters a temple—"Enter into the temple of your body"—it is not in order to worship his body there, but to separate himself from it. Any dancer will tell you the same thing, and will practice philosophy in his own way: listen to young dancers today, they will all tell you that they are searching, through choreography, for a vision of the world that is not this one, that is not that one, and which, for lack of another word, they bluntly call "metaphysical." Nothing could be further from the truth than imagining yoga or dancing as a physical accomplishment: it is, and is nothing other than, a mental accomplishment that goes as far as a burning that consumes.

When a great yogi dies—or rather, according to religious belief, when he leaves his body—that body is not burned: that has already been done. For the accomplished yogi will have consumed everything in him that should have been burned. So he is buried upright, or in the lotus position, for only those who have not yet reached the point of fusion need to be burned. Time is a cook: "Time cooks all beings in the great Soul."[26] In the Indian stage of the Upanishads, to think means to cook oneself in Time's metaphysical saucepan, to make all the subject's raw meat disappear—its affects, its actions.

Take a deep breath. Is this suspended breathing our syncope? There is no doubt that it is an interruption. But it is difficult to define what it is that is interrupted. The yogi would not speak of a blackout of consciousness, but on the contrary of a consciousness broadened to the emphatic perception of the whole universe. This is true to the point where Mircea Eliade, for example, having served his spiritual apprenticeship in the holy city of Rishikesh, wanted to replace the word "*ec*stasy" (*extase*), which seemed to him to be too marked with exteriority, with the word "*in*stasy" (*enstase*), which according to him was the only way of indicating the prolonging of consciousness within itself. This technique, however, induces something like a *controlled suffocation*;

badly conducted, it can produce cataleptic states, for example. It is clear that what we call consciousness changes in degree, if not in nature. This is the question that Sudhir Kakar poses more than once:

> Does the recounting of certain experiences in the state of *samadhi* [ecstasy] allow it to be assimilated into the phenomenon that Western psychology calls "depersonalization"; that is to say, an evolution in the course of which the individual loses his sense of relation to his body, feels himself becoming unreal, his subjective notion of time is disturbed, and the external world appears improbable to him? Is not the intense sensation of loving the whole of creation, described by certain Indian sages, similar to the diffuse eroticism of primary narcissism in the young child?[27]

And the Indian psychoanalyst resolves the matter: if it is not precise to translate "ecstasy" by "depersonalization," it is no doubt possible to describe it as primary narcissism. That incandescent point of fusion of the self would then be, in psychoanalytic terms, access to a stage prior to the constitution of identity. So the reunion with diffuse eroticism authorizes a little of everything: polymorphous perversity, which Freud attributed exclusively to the young child, or the "communion with nature" in which the specific values of Western humanism are lost. If "I" no longer exist, one can no longer even say, "I is an Other." For the Other no longer exists either; so it will be possible to treat it as one wishes, since it is no longer *I* and no longer *him*. Pushed to the limit by the physical suspension of breath, the prolonged syncope (a respiratory technique) coincides with the extreme metaphysical obliteration of the limits of the self, and no longer has a basis for creating a philosophy of freedom. The Subject is not free; it is freed. In a paradoxical turn, liberation is here the opposite of freedom.

The musical definition of syncope, which has served us as a guide, is also obliterated. The erudite hierarchy of pitch and that of rhythm cannot be analyzed with the classical rules of Western harmony; pitches decay so subtly that the very notion of dissonance no longer means anything. The notion of syncope disappears too. Even so, one cannot say that holding one's breath actually creates a delay, so long as the retention is prolonged, deliberately and without limiting its duration. Ecstasy is unmeasured; "un-measured," the music of India.

If holding one's breath anticipates something, it can only be death that is anticipated. But this is on condition that it neutralizes its violence: the true hub of that wheel is the imperceptible slide from ecstasy to death, the unverifiable myth that the yogi chooses the moment when he will push the fires to the point at which the heart and brain stop functioning. One does not "die," one "leaves one's body." In the exercise of asceticism, this stroll outside the body is apparently common.[28] "Dying" amounts to a slightly longer stroll than usual: one leaves one's body, and one decides not to return. There is no delay or anticipation; there is nothing more than the cycle of reincarnation, hardly interrupted by death, a slight but unimportant conclusion that in the West is the anticipated object of every syncope, and that terrifies us.

When the Buddha undertook to break the outmoded notions of Brahmanism, ossified by centuries of clerical sclerosis, he undertook to substitute, for the fullness of ecstasy, nothingness; for the *atman* (the golden rule of Brahmanism), the *anatman* (the *non-I*, the unconnected); and for this moral sleep, awakening. But most of all, he challenged the notion of the action: he challenged precisely the irresponsibility created by the Hindu system, which has as its objective full union with the world. Look at the gloomy litanies of Hinduism:

> "A man kills or causes killing. . . . Even so, he does not do evil."
>
> "There is neither a murderer or the instigator of a murder: when a man cleaves another's head in two with his sword, this is not someone who is taking the life of another."
>
> "If the killer believes he is killing, if the dead man believes he has been killed, neither of them has true understanding: the latter has not been killed, the other has not killed."[29]

When the figure of the Buddha emerged, the Indian doxas were moving beyond the *atman* (the "person") and beyond a concept of fate that inscribes personhood on the wheel of the world in a more important position than that elementary gesture of morality, the responsibility for murder. One must not delude oneself: that is indeed the meaning of the Bhagavad-Gita, recited every day by millions of Hindus. The god Krishna speaks to the warrior Arjuna, who refuses to fight: opposite him is the enemy army; he recognizes his childhood cousins, his dear uncle, his fencing master—the people he has loved. The god's function is to convince the man Arjuna that he must fight; the god's function is to ensure, thanks to this massacre, the survival of the earth, which is groaning beneath the excessive weight of an exploding population. Krishna is an ecological god; he spares nothing to persuade Arjuna. If one is Mahatma Gandhi, one will find in this text (which is admirable for all that) the god's love for the universe; if one is his Hindu assassin, one will find Krishna's refrain: "That is why you fight!" For to kill or be killed, none of that holds when confronted with destiny; virtue consists in coinciding with it. To kill or be killed, then and always, arises from the mythology of the sacrifices of an earlier age, which reconstructed the universe in a succession of actions whose only virtue was that they were joined one to another and that none must be forgotten. "I" can only be the totality of these complete actions.

So the encounter with death is among the Buddha's first intuitions—or, to be more precise, the encounter with a sequence that moves toward death and is called "pain": illness, aging, death. Among the illusions the Buddha will literally explode is that of the permanence of the Subject, of the *atman*. And first of all, death exists: "Soon, alas, this body will be lying on the ground, empty, without consciousness, like an abandoned log."[30] Death exists, and with it pain, discomfort. Nothing can stand in its way, not even Prajapati's wise enterprise of reconstruction, even less access to *atman-Brahman* and the fusional coincidence between subject and being. "All constructive energies are impermanent, and everything that is impermanent ends up in torment."[31] Desire arises from "impermanence," quite obviously, as do ecstasy and *atman*, the person. In truth, nothing escapes it; but I am wrong to use the expression "in truth," for truth is of course part of impermanence. A single truth remains: "Everything is impermanent." Nonetheless, action is heavy with consequences.

The astonishing paradox of the Buddha's philosophy goes straight to the heart of the Subject. Is it possible that the Brahmanic enlightenment, this absolute mastery of sacrificial reconstruction through breathing, protects one from old age and death? No. The energy used to build is in vain. And in fact, to demonstrate this, Buddhist philosophy uses syncope: "One cannot claim that the ego is unfragmented, since its intermittent character has shown it to be multiple. It is not found in deep sleep, in drunkenness, in fainting."[32] That is to say that syncope, stretched out in duration by the technique and philosophy of breathing, has not eluded Buddhism, which clearly perceives its seriousness and its eclipse. Instead of wanting, in the Brahmanic philosophical style, to stop up the holes of consciousness—not with the hem of a dressing gown now but with the stoking of breath—Buddhism seizes hold of the blaze of light and deduces its consequences: it would be hard to say whether the Subject exists or not. In truth, the question is not important; it simply is not asked, and remains undecidable. It is radical and iconoclastic. It is not surprising that Buddhist philosophy is interrupted with bursts of laughter: its method is to disconcert; clearing the path, that is what matters. Along the same lines, the question of the existence and the permanence or impermanence of a Subject is burdensome. Let us leave it aside.

The Buddha is disconcerting; he shatters the consensual harmony of Brahmanism, and the Hindu inegalitarianism that constitutes the social bedrock.

Confronted with the impermanence of the subject—and notably with the syncope that affects the subject by temporarily fainting—the Buddha uses a strange and familiar "vehicle": the ferryboat, which crosses the river and moves toward the other bank. The ferryboat, a simple device for crossing, is motionless and in motion at the same time. That is what desires are like, and existential malaise; that is what the water around the ferryboat is like, and finally the river itself, between two banks. When the ferryboat is in the middle of its trip, the Buddhist idea appears: the Middle Path. Neither eternity nor nothingness; neither one bank nor the other. Neither I nor the Other, but the boat in the middle of the Ganges.

This precarious resting place is not the fusional ecstasy that yoga methodically seeks; nor is it the stubborn reconstruction of the scattered Creator. On the contrary, it is a premeditated deconstruction. So while Brahmanism begins with Fire, lights the sacrificial altar, burns to a cinder the dead body that is nothing other than one oblation among others, and sets thought ablaze by the exercise of breathing—sets it ablaze to the point of complete combustion—Buddhism does the opposite.

Nirvana means the extinguishing of breath; it is the limit of the power of Fire. If it is a matter of breathing, it is done by *snuffing out Hinduism's infinite flame*. It is a matter of *letting go*.

Here indeed is a disconcerting thought. Let us examine the troubling term "disconcerting." It signifies the dissonance produced by any musical syncopation, and the delay of the note that lingers and dislocates harmony for a moment. It summons up the accidents in the philosophical history of the idea of the Subject, in both East and West; we have seen it in Kierkegaard's wanderings, in the young girl's leap, in the invisible leap of the knight of faith, in anguish. We found it again in Tantrism, when the intertwined couple captures the exact moment immediately before jouissance and suspends it to infinity. This *disconcertedness* is what caused a scandal when psychoanalysis was born, producing at the time a major dissonance. We can recognize it in the avant-gardes, whatever they may be: their function is to *disconcert* the consensus, and to lean—with the help of provocation—on syncope, which is youth, in the moment that precedes maturity.

This is also true when Buddhism began. The extreme fragility of *disconcertedness* can immediately be perceived. Syncopation in music cannot linger; or then, if it becomes systematic, as has happened in the history of contemporary music, the very idea of dissonance disappears. Psychoanalysis was quickly transformed into dogmatism, psychological or philosophical; either one emerges from disconcertedness to defend a good, solid "ego," or one bases one's concept of the Subject on the cracks in it. Avant-gardes die with the aging of their heralds. As for the original Buddhism, it became a rigid, obsessive, nit-picking religion; the Buddha himself predicted the gradual obliteration of his philosophy as it was. The between-the-two only exists in a specific approach; when the uniqueness of the moment disappears, the paradoxical grasping of the "letting go" disappears at the same time. Syncope is ephemeral; even if it reaches eternity by a sudden dive, it is its opposite.

"Let go of the past," the fledgling Buddhist is advised; "Let go of the past, let go of the future, let go of the between-the-two, pilgrim of becoming!"[33]

But in order not to give in to the comforts of dogma, one needs to be in good philosophical health.

Games, Women, Sleep, and Death

The Buddha, beneath a tree, was enlightened; he spoke, from that moment on, of his awakening.

Sleep is dangerous to thought; this is a constant. One of the first threats from which Descartes protected himself when he shut himself up to arrive at the idea of the *cogito* was sleep, and the illusion of dreams that is its outcome. Philosophy stands watch and stays awake. Yet syncope is never far from sleep, and in the very philosophical strategy that tries to capture the instant of syncope, sleep continues to be a threat. In the Vedic ritual there is a preparation for sacrifice: it consists of avoiding the void, *nirrti*. Three occupations symbolize the danger of the void: the game of dice, women, and sleep.

The game of dice, in love with the glamour of chance, involves a passion for time; worshiped as a sensitive divinity, time offers both the luck of the moment and the long duration of an always possible recuperation; one never knows. Like the scattered Prajapati, the ruined player can always "remake himself." To play is to scatter and remake, to break the egg and rebuild it. Ruin, this risk, is essential: without it, the game cannot breathe. In the *Mahabharata*, the most virtuous hero has only one flaw: playing dice. Thanks to that, he loses successively his horses, his men, his kingdom, all his brothers, himself, and his wife.[34] That he is dealing with a notorious cheat does not change anything: the hero shows his humanity by losing everything at gambling, that is, by confronting his passion for the void. They have always gambled a lot in India; the daily effects of this sacrilege have retained their sharpness. One gambles all the more since the social system stays closed.

Women, as we know, are men's downfall. They themselves are abysses, and they engulf men in love. One could think of the Tantric practice of orgasm as a regulating of female danger: on the edge of the abyss, at the moment of falling in, one holds oneself back, while the woman's cry is the proof that she has already melted into jouissance. By "one," I mean man; for woman is continuous with the abyss; she has metaphysical affinities with this essential void. That is why Diotima stands at the edge of the abyss, in an unstable equilibrium that does not threaten her; that is why the young girl knows how to leap; that is why the Pythoness dozes, and tells the enigma of truth while sleeping. But before consecrating the Vedic sacrifice, one must avoid playing dice; one must not touch a woman; one must not sleep. It is an indispensable filling up of consciousness before the world is reconstructed at daybreak.[35]

There is still sleep, which is already to say, consciousness. The Buddha's awakening does not mean that his body will never sleep again; the preceding sleep indicates the preliminary states of consciousness, agitation, scattering, and the alternation of fullness and emptiness. Reaching the void of the between-the-two is to put an end to this irritating alternative, to this itching of time. It is to leave its grasp. European philosophers, during the Enlightenment, also establish degrees of conscious attention: they range from darkness to light, from light to perception; one extracts oneself with difficulty, step by step, from drowsy confusion. The master philosopher on the subject of consciousness and of sleep is the jubilant Leibniz.

For Leibniz, the void does not exist. *In natura non datur saltus*: "In nature, there is no leap." Where we believe we see discontinuity, it is simply that we do not know how to see properly. For if one looks closely, there is neither discontinuity nor evil: a sharper perception makes the illusion of the void disappear. This is the succession of states of consciousness, from the most "asleep" to the most "awake." First, lethargy, coma, the cataleptic state: consciousness is in labor, completely enveloped. Then sleep, the first development, shot through with stray flashes, which prepare for the awakening of the day; then light, followed by perception. Perception sharpens itself, becomes clearer, bends over backward, to the point of perceiving the detail of every flower, one leaf among a thousand others on a tree, and the drops that make up a wave that rolls in at the edge of the sea. Smaller and smaller, infinitesimal perceptions that can only be calculated by the mind. Such slight perceptions that at the end of the course, when the distinction between each element has been pushed to its limits, the mind moves into an ecstasy as great as the ecstasy of the master yogis of India: this is what happens to the simple priest Theophilus when, led by the goddess Athena through the spheres of the world, he perceived with delight the order of the best of all possible worlds, and the beauty of the universe. So he slipped, imperceptibly, into absolute clarity. Did he faint?[36] The philosopher does not say. But one can imagine that he indeed returned to the first moment of the cycle.

It is amazing to note that, in Leibniz's system as in the philosophical systems of India, reincarnation exists. In Leibniz it is not postulated; it is deduced from the nonexistence of death. According to all logic (and since no leap exists) death does not exist. So Leibniz refers to death by the staggering title of "general sleep." Death is not death, it is not the definitive end of consciousness, it is not the terrifying abyss; it is a return to sleep, with all faculties numbed. One reawakens, no doubt, and starts again, crossing the stages one by one: first one becomes an animal, with lethargic consciousness; then one becomes a man, affected by syncopes and regular sleep; only man, however, is capable of developing the powers (*effets*) of perception that lead to ecstasy.

There is no death in the best of all possible worlds invented by Leibniz, no more than in the Indian world. For in the Leibnizian universe the order of reality is the best, and any break, including death, would inevitably make it fail. Sometimes one sees the term evoking syncope appear in Indian philosophy to refer to the brief moment that separates the life that has just ended from that which is beginning: the between-the-two again, between two successive incarnations. But it is barely a sigh. And if one knows how to breathe properly, one avoids this empty moment, and passes without discontinuity from one life to the next.

Leibniz sees "*evolution*" as everything that moves toward awakening; that is what the Buddha does beneath his tree, to protect himself from sickness, old age, and death. And Leibniz, the Enlightenment philosopher, calls everything that moves toward falling asleep "involution": sleeping is "to 'involute' onto a smaller stage." He has fantastic confidence in the exercise of thought: thought is megalomaniac, and sees itself as all-powerful to the point of mastering the passage of death and making it disappear entirely. "We must awaken in ourselves all the sleeping children," said Leibniz; and this single order suffices to disengage man from his natural lifespan.

It is as if there were two ways of thinking. Either one arms thought in order to conquer the whole field of consciousness, developing the "I" to the point of making it absolute; this way, by yielding to fusion, one loses one's identity as a Subject, and, like Theophilus, becomes completely ecstatic. Or one strips thought of its weapons and makes it as "weak" as possible, taking advantage of its moments of fragility: anguish, shivering, the void, orgasm—syncope; but this way one also takes the risk of a temporary disappearance of identity. The first thought is on the side of fullness and rigidity; the second on the side of the void and of suppleness. The first thought constructs a protected system; the second is on the side of the fragment, of hesitation, of risk. The first thought justifies the world; the second argues with it violently.

These are the extreme hypotheses: in all systematic thinking, we have caught a glimpse of syncope, fleeting, immediately suppressed. And the systematic mind implacably threatens the philosophers of syncope: even Kierkegaard's valor ends by giving way and is relegated to the resolute monotony of ethics.[37] There is nothing like madness—Lacan speaks of the "disconcertedness of psychoses"—to keep weakness intact through the delirious connection to the world, and to keep the opposition radical.

12

Syncope Leaves for the Forest: The Renouncers

As powerful as the order of the world is in the Hindu system, it does have certain escape routes. These escape routes are inscribed within the framework of life, a part of it, as if it were a question of breaking through into social time and enlarging it to the extreme. The same is true for holding the breath between two intervals of respiration. The time of social restraint is called "renunciation."

Renunciation is not for just anyone, however; nor can its moment be chosen. The ancient order[1] foresaw everything: the hierarchy of the castes that are assigned social functions, the categories of pure and impure corresponding to these castes, and the phases of life. A person—or rather, a boy[2]—is born, and in the first phase of life is only a child, living in symbiosis with his mother. At the age of seven the boy becomes "reborn," enters the life of the student, and remains under a teacher's tutelage. He gets married, or rather is married off, according to the rigorous laws of prearranged marriages, and from that point on must fulfill his duties as father and husband: now a master himself, but only master of the house, nothing more. It is only when he has seen the "sons of his sons" born that he has the right, if he wishes, to enter the phase of renunciation. The art of being a grandfather may involve a radical abandonment of the family.

The ritual authorizing a man's entry into the world of renunciation is an arduous one. As in the case of the Carmelites, the renouncer celebrates his own funeral ceremony; he dies to the world, and thereby becomes a veritable living dead man. He rids himself of his possessions, no longer has the right to participate in any ritual, no longer wears the sacred thread of the reborn, has for his only possession a begging bowl, for he must live on alms. And he goes off into the forest to live alone for the rest of his life, which, already over, is only an illusory potentiality. In actuality, a leftover.

The forest. It is not necessarily thick and does not necessarily have the shady tree-filled appearance that we imagine when we hear the magic word "forest." As in our collective imagination, however, it is an untamed and infinite space that allegorically represents the immensity of the void. All that is not a village is forest. The village is a concentration of people, essentially limited. "How else would the limit be determined, if not by the village?"[3] No limits without a village; beyond it is the forest.

Within the village limits, sacrifices are performed, exchanges are made, and the reconstitution of the dispersed god proceeds according to tradition. Wood is burned for the offerings. The forest is the opposite: there are no more rituals and nothing is sacrificed; the only fire remaining is that of the renouncer's asceticism. In the village, the gestures of everyday life are repeated on a daily basis; in the forest, nothing is repeated and the procuring of food takes on an animalistic side that suddenly gives way to a natural ferality. Ascetics can eat from the palms of their hands, or "as animals do," searching for food with their mouths on the ground, as a cow might. The men called *sadhus*, in a strange, animalistic form of renunciation, go to extremes in their behavior: they can jump like monkeys, crawl like boa constrictors toward food, or, as we have seen, imitate the immobility of a plant, of a tree. The ascetic is no longer required to bathe or to cut his hair; he wears his dry bushy hair, which begins to resemble vegetable fibers, in a topknot. The renouncer lives in the natural violence of the wind, Vayu, god of the air, never more at ease than in the mountains or in his forest. As for the supreme god of renunciation, it is again Shiva on a snowy mountaintop, Shiva of the mountains, a holdover of the pre-Aryan era when he was still only a wild god of the mountains and heights, Rudra.

Who then is the renouncer in the midst of the forest? Someone who was a man and who, on the outskirts of society, continues to live within the perimeters of the void. The forest is inhabited by animals and marginals: in the forest live thieves, *dacoits*, and other troublemakers whose daytime activity consists in hiding in the forest and whose nighttime activity consists in robbing travelers of their material goods. The forest was the place of refuge for the five Pandava brothers, the collective heros of the *Mahabharata*, after the eldest of them lost everything in a dice game; it is there that the god Ram, his wife Sita, and his brother Laxman went when they were driven from their royal palace by an evil stepmother. The renouncers are now "nothing," but they take power from their exclusion in order to achieve superhuman strength.

That is where mythological heroes meet gods face to face, disguised as lakes, animals, or warriors; there they make their pacts, naturally, with the monkey people; there they can prepare—if such is their destiny—for a glorious return to the world of men. The authority of the renouncers is extreme;

the respect shown them can be witnessed today on the roads and in the mountains, it can be detected in the images shown in "theologicals," films and television series with religious themes. When such a renouncer appears, dressed in saffron cloth with a disheveled topknot slightly to one side of his head with all its curls protruding, his bowl in his hand, people bow down before him, whether on the screen or in real life. His appearance signifies the presence of the divine. The strength of the void is so great that it protects the limits of the village and guarantees the continuity of the world as it is. This system is not particular to India; the vocation of monastic orders, like that of the Greek ascetics and hermits, is to make a contract with the divine that contains a system of guarantees for the world of men. But nowhere more than in India has the renouncer been provided with the context for an all-encompassing philosophical system.

The forest may indeed be nature, but the renouncer has the right to create a hermitage: a kind of nonexistent, imaginary "village" outside the world. He creates a lifestyle different from that of a village but which, contrary to a village, respects nature to the point of taming it. Hermits must live within the rhythm of the seasons and become acclimated to the ways of nature. In Manu's laws, the following instructions for hermits are found: "In summer, he must sit in the middle of five bonfires; in the rainy season, he must remain outdoors and the clouds shall be his only protection; in winter, he must wear wet garments." He is forbidden to protect himself; if an ascetic does not become one with nature, he is not carrying out the vocation of renunciation. But nonetheless he is allowed to have a hermitage.

Shakuntala,[4] one of the rare amorous heroines in the Indian sphere, lived as an ascetic waiting for the return of her husband whom she met by chance near a pond, and whom she immediately married and immediately lost. Waiting for him, she lives as a charming hermit, among her parakeet friends and tranquil fawns. The procession of renouncers who render homage to the young bride recognize her purity through this rigorous detail: her cohabitation with animals and her familiarity with fawns. It is almost the universe of the bacchantes, and we recognize the same passion for animals that inhabited the women possessed with Dionysus . . . the only difference being that the hermit woman does not breast-feed animals and does not tear them apart with her hands.

For the bacchantes' access to nature is total, including its savagery; the asceticism of the Brahman renouncers has access to the violence in nature but refuses its destructive consequences. Since the subject is a "living-dead," he has no trouble identifying with nature; he does not, however, reproduce its bloodletting capacities. Quite to the contrary: there in the forest the ideal of nonviolence of which Mahatma Gandhi made such brilliant use was born. Nature tests and transforms, but what she transforms into an already dead man looks to us like a "*nonattack of the living.*"

Let us cross through space and centuries. This combination, made up of a consenting marginality and a mimesis of nature, can be found in several types of Western novels. Jean-Jacques Rousseau, for example, wrote *The New Eloise* (*La Nouvelle Héloïse*). A young woman named Julie loved her tutor Saint-Preux so passionately that she went so far as to become pregnant by him, which resulted in a miscarriage. Then she was married off, but didn't hide her first love. Her husband, a humanist, decides to engage in a most peculiar form of therapy and, far from separating his wife from her former lover, invites him to come and live with them, believing that habit will undo the bonds of love. This is how a communal life on the margin of society begins; the lovers are constrained to practice an everyday asceticism. Asceticism and marginality combine to create an ideal hermitage: Julie's garden. As in Shakuntala's garden, the birds are at home there; trees grow in liberty; the place that might have harbored guilty love has the vocation of being that of innocence, where nature reigns, where the exchange of love is chaste. In Julie de Wolmar's garden, not unlike Rousseau's solitary wanderings that produced such strong, spontaneous ecstasies in him,[5] nature undoes the corruption of social ties, along with evil, lies, and passion.

Unfortunately, it does not last. The garden is a misrepresentation; the branches are twisted with care, the birds attracted by imitation nests, and everything is artificial. Julie's passion does not diminish; the heroine dies and leaves behind a letter to her lover in which she expresses such burning passion that it is soon understood that she wanted to die. The form of renunciation imagined by Rousseau was merely a provisional syncope in the social pattern. Love's passion was stronger than the garden.

The scenario of the passionate love that is not successfully corrected by the natural harmony of the hermitage is also found in Balzac's admirable novel *The Lily in the Valley*. Henriette de Mortsauf is already married when an adolescent covers her shoulders with apparently inconsequential kisses. She falls in love with the young man, and allows him to enter the community of her family, on the condition of absolute chastity. Nature, resplendent and peaceful in the valley, guarantees this courtly pact; the harmony is such that neither party can imagine it ending. The young Felix de Vandenesse indeed does not touch his beloved, but the valley offers him enough wild flowers to express his love in the form of daily bouquets, masterpieces of jouissance and of frustration. Henriette de Mortsauf lives a happy love affair between her grouchy old husband and her young flowering lover until the latter falls in love with a hot-blooded Englishwoman. The Lady of the Valley dies of it, but as an ascetic. She fasts; after forty famished days, reduced to the state of an emaciated renouncer, she dies attended by her husband and lover, to whom she leaves, once again, a letter expressing the sensual passion that literally consumed her.

Heroines whose passions are only discovered once they have died, by means of letters they leave to their loved ones. These novels have inherited from courtly love the game of separation between the lady, who is married, and the page, who is younger or a social inferior; they have preserved the flavor of the test, asceticism of proximity, that which is impossible but just a kiss away. But they also participate in the burning passion of the forest, a place of contradiction and repose, where even a forbidden love can live as long as the enclosure of the garden is not broken, as long as the ritual of the bouquet is continued.

Unfortunately, failure is there waiting and watching, and wins in the end. These two heroic women are unable to cure themselves; the fire of their passion is inextinguishable. A shared solitude is not true renunciation, and the eternal trio, capable of engendering tragedy or vaudeville, does not win anything by being closed up in nature's garden, except for a fragile provisional peace where the flames of a thousand burning desires are smoldering.

The fact is that in the West passionate love is dominant; it is found nowhere in the Indian sphere, which is categorized to the extreme, even in its exceptions. If in the West we often encounter the imaginary of renunciation, to which monastic orders as well as mystics adhere, the vocation of courtly love continues to be the most complete expression of the ideal of the subject. In this, Julie de Wolmar and Henriette de Mortsauf are faithful to the mystical commandment of the call of the desert: their fervent passion is desertlike and dries them out, even makes them living mummies, like the unfortunate Lady of the Valley, this lily of purity, this flower burned alive. Desertlike is the "cross of love" that will later be spent in the tuberculosis of the heroine in *La Traviata.* Love at first sight is also desertlike, it is well named in French—that is, "lightning bolt" (*coup de foudre*). It is the primary syncope in the West and will be explored in the early twentieth century in the Surrealist avant-garde; "Mad Love" (*L'Amour fou*), conceived of by André Breton, the hymn to the Mejnoun, and "Elsa's Madman" (*Le Fou d'Elsa*), in the book by Louis Aragon, who goes off proclaiming his love in the desert, are the results of courtly love taken to the extreme in a modern mystical context. Nature in the desert or in the forest has no power over this passionate relationship; what enflames the West is the notion of the impossible couple. That is our idea of shared syncope.

As we know, Hindus often travel to Benares to die: a death on the banks of the sacred river puts an end to the painful cycle of reincarnation. Sometimes it happens that a dying man does not die, but is cured after having drunk water or eaten mud from the river. It is a strange, contradictory destiny: the dying man is not dead, which must mean that our mother Ganga, the Ganges, didn't want him. From then on, if he is not really dead, he is no longer living, either. He is a wanderer between two worlds, between the being of an order into which he no longer fits and the nothingness of the disorder of which he is the incarnation. He will join a community of humans like him who form a kind of caste of compulsory renouncers. He will not be killed, but he no longer belongs to the village; he has, without actually deciding, already joined the forest.

The other scene takes place at the end of the great war epic, the *Mahabharata*. A merciless war, destined to relieve the earth of overpopulation, has taken place; men have killed each other off among cousins, friends, and brothers, in family quarrels. An old man remains, the only one of his generation; he is a blind king who has lost all his sons in the war. When he has finished deploring the war for which he was largely responsible, when he has, on the battlefield, shed all of his tears and fulfilled his duties as a king, he has nothing left to do. So he decides to go off into the forest, accompanied by two old women: his wife Gandhari, the mother of the one hundred Kauravas brothers, and another woman, Kunti, the mother of the five Pandava brothers. It is the end of a parental order, and it is also the end of a world; it is twilight for fathers and mothers. They go off, wearing saffron robes, bowls in their hands. Will nature welcome them?

At the forest's horizon, a fire burns. Having to devour the forest is Fire's destiny. The three elders see the forest burning and the burning mass advancing. So the three exemplary renouncers, understanding the message, walk forward to meet the flames, and are swallowed up by them. It is and is not suicide. There is only nature and the forest, and it just so happens that they are burning. The renouncer must refuse the forest nothing, even if a fire is raging within it. There is normally no return from the forest; it is possible to die, or rather to "pass," immobile like a tree, or charred by the fire.

It is also possible to decide to return from the forest, without renouncing renunciation.

As we have seen, renunciation confers incredible moral authority on the person who has chosen its path. The heroes returning from the forest as warriors will soon triumph; their palace rivals succumb to lethargy and carelessness. And if one is not the hero of a legend, all one has to say upon leaving the forest is that one has discovered the truth and the way: this is how sects, great breaches in the system's rigidity, are founded. Anthropologists have determined that the majority of the innumerable sects in India have been and are still founded by renouncers.[6] The person who is separated from the world, no longer living as a social being, is better able to practice the discipline of thought; he "has the time." When renouncers appeared in the Brahman world, there came a time when they proliferated and shook up all of northern India and the Ganges plain with their intellectual discoveries.[7] From this turmoil, which could be compared to the flowering of Hellenism in Lagides' Egypt, Buddhism—the perfect example of a successful sect—was born. The enlightened renouncer can decide to die totally; the Buddha indeed tried to abandon life. He only restrained himself from dying out of compassion for his contemporaries. After leaving the world and living in the forest, he became enlightened under the tree and decided to abandon asceticism and spread his message to the world. This scenario is repeated over and over today; it is one of the sources of democratization in India.[8]

Buddhism is a sect open to all, regardless of caste. It is based on a general doctrine that reduces the list of deities of its predecessor, and chooses either a god or an idea. The more limited in theory it becomes, the greater its social practice. It is for this precise reason that Dr. Ambedkar, the leader of the Untouchables at the time of India's struggle for independence, gave a political directive to the Untouchables in his movement to convert to Buddhism. In opposition to the practice of Buddhism in the Western world, where it often transgresses democratic gains (especially concerning employment legislation), in India it promotes democratization and abolishes the inequalities of birth.[9]

Buddhism is always critical of the established order. Renouncing the world is not without influence on the philosophy of the world that one has left behind. Renouncing the world produces a *reformed* perspective on the world; one does not return from the forest the same person as when one entered. And if I think again of syncope, which as I said has a power of protest, here is one of the first manifestations. Renunciation in India has conceived of a syncopated staging of social life: suddenly the human world disappears, by means of a death in which the ritual is simulated. At the same time protest becomes possible.

In the history of Western thought Bergson is the philosopher who has most clearly localized the complementary duality of village and forest. From one to the other, there is a "leap," a bursting forth, a branching out of the syncopal order.

The "village" is a society that Bergson describes as closed, comparable to a group of animals. Static and inalterable, the closed society goes about regulating communal life by obeying moral constraints. The "forest," on the other hand, is an "open" society, transformed by the vital impetus, obeying nothing, distracted by newness, and dispersing the group by breaking its social cohesion. These two extremes emanate from a common origin: the strength of belonging and of life in society on one hand; the freedom of the forest, the mystical impetus on the other hand. On one side, time; on the other, rupture.

We know that Bergson saw this duality between "village" and "forest" as depending on a deeper division: that which separates time from duration. In the village, time is homogeneous and divisible, enforcing its laws by means of the contamination of the categories of space. In the forest, duration is heterogeneous and indivisible, is in continuous mutation. The same dichotomy leads to the conception of two selves; one self whose states are clearly defined by, for example, a psychology capable of fabricating as many boundaries as there are states of consciousness, which are labeled and identifiable; and a second fundamental self, initially confused, mobile, and inexpressible. The first self is but a shadow of the second projected onto homogeneity.

In his analysis of the deeper self, or rather what Bergson calls the "open soul," he sounds a bit like the Bhagavad-Gita. What does the "open soul" allow inside?

> Suppose we say that it embraces all humanity: we should not be going too far, we should hardly be going far enough, since its love may extend to animals, to plants, to all nature. And yet no one of these things which would thus fill it would suffice to define the attitude taken by the soul, for it could, strictly speaking, do without all of them. Its form is not dependent on its content. We have just filled it; we could as easily empty it again.[10]

Echoes of Hinduism seem to resound in this passage from *Two Sources of Morality and Religion*: when the god Krishna reveals himself completely to the warrior who doubts his duty, he is love itself, and his divine face contains one thousand animal eyes, one thousand leaves of plants, fish, demons, rivers, and among these rivers is the Ganges. The identification with nature, "full" or "empty," the undecidable alternative, belongs to the impulse of renunciation that moves in the direction of the forest. Its immensity is at the horizon; the dissolution of the Subject, the means and the word. But Bergson promptly seeks less remote examples of emotions capable of convincing his reader. All the examples he chooses belong, more or less, to the realm of syncope.

Romantic passion is the first.

"Perhaps a tragedy lies ahead, a whole life wrecked, wasted, ruined, we know it, we feel it, no matter, we must because we must."[11] But this example is still too extreme. The philosopher gives an example from daily life: music. The banalities that he pronounces about music contain thinly veiled instants of syncope. "Every moment we are what it expresses": suspended; "As passers-by are forced into a street dance": suspended in movement. "When music weeps, all humanity, all nature, weeps with it": suspended in movement, caught up by fusion with the universe. And he immediately, almost simultaneously, describes the emotion mountains inspire in him, and the one inspired by women.[12]

But the journey from one to the other, from the "village" to the "forest," is not made with any continuity. Quite the opposite: it is made by "sudden jumps," as if human history were capable of dreaming only if broken by brutal syncopes and unexpected jolts, and could only be analyzed afterwards. Love for humanity, a message that is repeated at each new disturbance, does not extend from the love for the village to that of the "global village," dear to Margaret Mead. It goes beyond a logical interval, climbing over an intermediate space:

> If one thinks only about the interval and the infinite number of points that have to be traversed one by one, one will be discouraged from leaving, like Zeno's arrows; one will not see anything interesting or attractive over there. But if one enjambs the interval, thinking only of the far side or even looking further, one will easily accomplish a simple action at the same time as arriving at the end of the infinite multiplicity to which this simplicity is equivalent.[13]

One may as well say that the inspiration of the open soul depends on the forgetting of logic, the collapse of a clear perception of reality; the ideal is its reality, thought becomes its obstacle. It is in a kind of unconsciousness that the dynamic vital impetus bursts forth, alone in its ability to foster innovation. This is like the renouncer who returns from the forest after having forgotten the village and fused his thoughts with nonexistence.

The creative impetus is not, however, passed on to everyone. It belongs only to exceptional heroes in whom "absolute morality" is incarnated. It is they who, Bergson says explicitly, form "humanity's elite." This unwittingly brings us back to the opposition between "village" and "forest." In Indian society, which seems to be so accurately depicted in the writings of a French philosopher at the dawn of the twentieth century, the Brahman dominates: the sacrificial reconstruction of the village is his privilege, as is more particularly the adventure of renunciation. The Brahman system, even when later altered, is directed by a strict and pitiless hierarchy, of which the exclusion of those who dared not die next to the river is but an example; only an elite is capable of inspiring the village.[14] It was necessary to wait until our century to see the rise of renouncers of more humble origins, when those excluded from elite spirituality come to the fore: I'm thinking of Ramakrishna, a Brahman but a poor peasant, and of Mohandas Karamchand Gandhi, the son of a merchant.

Even if Bergson attributes the spiritual inclination to all of humanity, the words are there: "humanity's elite."

The "village" is for all. The "forest" is for the elite. It is against this social sclerosis that Buddha rebelled. By limiting the capacity for spiritual syncope to exceptional beings only, Bergson remains within a closed system. But that is the way of philosopher-kings, whom India calls Brahmans, whose function is to think for the world.

Brief Encounters

In our society, anyone can fall in love at first sight. Everyone has the undeniable right to fall in love. This has not always been true and, we will soon see, this banal activity of daily life is the result of a long history, of a slow progression toward equality of opportunity. The opportunity to fall in love at first sight has gained ground at the same rate as democratic progress: it was first reserved to rulers, then extended to others, and finally became immensely common in the general population. This opportunity to fall *in* love is also the opportunity to fall *out* of communal life; it is the possibility of leaving the village and entering a symbolic forest with the beloved. Our concept of love at first sight, that blessed state, holds the position in the West that is reserved for ecstasy in India.

This exceptional moment makes the surrounding world and its harsh laws disappear. It is an exceptional moment of surprise followed by an implacable certitude: it was meant to be; the Other is someone I have always loved. From the first glance, perhaps even before we met, before I was even born, the Other was meant for me, one never knows. If such an adventure should take place in Indian society, in conditions where everything separates men from women, there can be no doubt: if I love this Other who possesses me so totally, it is because we have already loved each other in a former life. The cycle of reincarnation conveniently explains away this inexplicable attraction and desire; there is no longer any reason to be surprised or startled. Everything is in order.

In the West, love at first sight has lost nothing of its surprising freshness. In fact, it has been popularized through the cinema, one of whose principal vocations is to sustain the myth of passionate love in the face of modernity. Indian cinema, which is as we know the most productive in the world,[15] has already taken on the task of polarizing true love at first sight, which is so disturbing and perturbing, which destroys, and which plunges those who become its victims in a shared ecstasy.

Brief Encounter was Vladimir Jankélévitch's favorite film; in it he found the inspiration for interminable and magnificent commentaries on a subject that fascinated him in philosophy: the instant, the "je-ne-sais-quoi," the almost-nothing, of fleeting or fainting duration. The plot is as follows. A married middle-aged man meets a woman who is also married and middle-aged. He is a doctor, she is a housewife. They have never met; a minor incident causes their eyes to meet. It's hardly a small catastrophe.

The first glance is always innocent; in the film, the man and woman meet innocently four weeks in a row in the station where they first met. The second week, they go to the movies; the third, they go rowing on a lake in the park; the fourth, they go for a walk in the country. When evening comes, they return late and both miss their trains, and the moment of reckoning has come. It is the time for confessions, the time to act on their passion . . . Adultery is averted, only barely. On the day of their last meeting, a month has gone by, and the man announces to the woman he loves that he is leaving for South Africa. They will never see each other again.

Stripped of its legendary heroism, spectacular finery, and noble lace, postwar love at first sight takes place in a station and begins in a waiting room. The future lovers have nothing to do; their minds ramble. From this momentary idleness is born their brief encounter. The darkness of the movie theater replaces the mystic night of lovers, and surrounds them with enough shadow to create a passing fusion, a preliminary for the wedding night that will never occur. The lake, despite its numerous inopportune idlers, remains the eternal lake with its watery mirror. The station does the rest, because each of them, the very night of their meeting, takes a train in the opposite direction, and in the end this will separate them forever. There will be no mistakes made switching tracks; reality will have a speedy victory.

Speed is clearly the first and final cause of this story: the meeting in the station is brief, and is as rapid as the train. Time is limited, the affair moves forward quickly, so quickly that it can be synopsized in a few scenes; without trains or stations, it would have taken months or years to develop. The innocence of the first glance, the consciousness of what has happened, the adulterous situation sized up, rejected, and cast aside, with the triumph of bourgeois morality—all of this takes place with the intensity of wanting-to-love, but also with prudence and sublimation. Mourning will only last the length of a return train trip. This appears rather far removed from Tristan and Isolde, years of separation, and of exile in the forest. All the elements are present, however, as if swallowed up by acceleration: there is the forest in the country, empty of its inhabitants; there is night; there is the fatal drink of the first meeting . . . it's a cup of coffee in a station, not a love potion on a boat. But is there really such a difference?

Forty years later, cinematic love at first sight is set in the world of an automobile dealership. He is a car salesman and she is a secretary. They are both married. The situation is so prosaic that it must be manipulated to establish the emotion sufficient for a love at first sight. The director/screenwriter[16] had the idea of depicting an inexplicable love at first sight. The woman loved is rather homely.

Too Beautiful for You (*Trop belle pour toi*) is a film that is different from others. It tells the story of the development of a love at first sight apparently turned around and transformed, but identical in effect. The strangeness of the situation and the choice of the "homely" woman as opposed to the "beautiful" one changes nothing of the essence of love at first sight: two people's eyes meet, and as we have seen, an immediate obsession of unrelenting intensity develops, resulting in fusion. It is soon lost. The lovers do not die; therefore they separate.

As in *Brief Encounter*, death is not the order of the day. That is perhaps one of the only elements that modernity changes in love at first sight: it isn't as fatal as before. In becoming more popular, it has become more reasonable; one can experience it and survive.

The original myth of love at first sight was closer to renunciation. Lovers always find a forest where they can hide their love; but when they leave the forest they are still burning with the fire of ecstasy; they have lost the taste for risk that prompted Julie de Wolmar to jump into the lake, and Henriette de Mortsauf to starve to death. But the alternative between "village" and "forest" remains: the protagonists of *Brief Encounter* find little forests—a lake, a movie theater, a country stroll. Those of *Too Beautiful for You* find the forest in a motel; what happens there is as mysterious as Tristan and Isolde's love song, as powerful as any night of love that creates the forest in an empty lot and turns highway street lights into twinkling stars.

No, it is not ecstasy that changes. Actually, it is the choice of the "village." If in our great love myths there is a hesitation between the conjugal abode—the "village"—and the nomadic wandering of adultery—the "forest"—love at first sight in the past always chose the "forest," renunciation and death. Today we "thesaurusize." We choose a temporary forest and then return to the village: it is no longer renunciation, but a model of courtly love inherited from the *Bildungsroman*. It is no longer life-shaking syncope, but a painful aborted initiative, the kind of education available to all hearts.

13

Educational Love at First Sight: The Lady, the Guru, and the Psychoanalyst

In India, the dominant social and metaphysical system seems tailored for prohibiting love at first sight. At least in Hinduism, and for lovers; for one sees it reappearing elsewhere among other partners.

In the West, love at first sight, a shared ecstasy, is along with depression our main social syncope. One must have an escape route; it is love at first sight. In India, it is renunciation.

Everything about passionate love and solitary renunciation seems opposed. But when one looks carefully at our history of love, one perceives the same plan at work. In the West, passionate love thwarts marriage; in India, renunciation thwarts the caste system, which itself can only survive by strictly observing the laws of matrimonial exchange. Surprisingly, this form of syncope is educational. We will soon see what it teaches.

Look at the mad position of marriage in India.

At the center of social life, swallowing up fortunes in extravagant ceremonies, marriage is the supreme act. Rich and poor expend sums equally proportionate to their income: the poor often end up permanently ruined; it is an old story, the one about the peasant who must face his daughter's marriage and the lack of the monsoon in the same year. It is hard to say which is more deadly, the daughter or the drought; in any case, he goes off to the city where he hopes to find a job. The novels of modern India vie with each other in telling this story of how the slums sprang up.[1]

Marriage in itself has a duty to "blaze"; extravagant, brilliant, it is royal; blatant or reduced to a minimum, it will never be temperate. The sparkling garlands, the sweets, the orchestras are obligatory. For it is not the religious ceremony that is expensive: it is the expenditure in itself and for itself. Whatever the wealth or poverty, it must undermine the financial security of the family; and a man's importance is judged by the manner in which he marries his daughter. If the wedding is only sumptuous as opposed to imperial, a businessman will be subject to venomous articles about his loss of credit with the government in power.

As for the parties concerned, it is not their business; they are there as extras in a ceremony much larger than they. Marriages are still almost always "arranged" ahead of time. Ask an Indian couple who think of themselves as modern about the love-match that they are proud to have entered into: with very few exceptions, one speaks of "love-matches" when the engaged couple met each other alone the day before the wedding, for a brief stroll fraught with progressive transgression.

Accepted tradition demands arranged marriages, and old customs also persist: Hinduism marries girls off young. Child marriage may be prohibited by law—Mahatma Gandhi, who had had the terrible experience of one, argued against them—but even today brides are still fifteen or fourteen years old, sometimes less. Marriage is never a matter of feelings; in fact, this word is not considered relevant to amorous relations between man and woman: it is, as in every kinship structure, a matter of the exchange of women and of material goods. This is so true that the dowry system also still persists, although that has been prohibited in Indian law since 1961; but no law can prohibit the girl's family from bringing as wedding presents such treasures as motor scooters, radios, television sets. Numerous crimes result when the agreements about material goods are not adhered to; the wedding is managed like a business affair, brisk and abrupt. That is, of course, not only true in India; but nowhere better than in India can one notice so clearly the economic essence of marriage and its function as exchanger of wealth. There is no question of love.

The young couple must provide for their desires as they can, and carve out a space for love against which everything seems to be conspiring. Around them, the *joint family*, the extended family, which admittedly has a tendency to break up but which still endures, is determined not to let the young newlyweds have anything but a restricted intimacy, reduced to brief nighttime encounters; those almost clandestine moments are only tolerated for exclusively procreative purposes. Songs tell of the relentlessness of mothers-in-law and sisters-in-law who invariably prevent the bride from going to join her husband at night. Intimacy comes later; there is nothing amorous about it, as Sudhir Kakar testifies, sending us back to our Western paradigms: "I do not claim that conjugal life in India lacks intimacy—that mutual enrichment within the patterns of love determined by the culture, which Westerners generally consider as the criterion of a 'good marriage.' In India, this intimacy develops later in the couple's life, when the spouses become mature adults, responsible for a household. In an ideal conception of marriage, and opposed to the Western vision, the shared responsibility for the education of the children constitutes the basis of intimacy."[2] The term "intimate" refers to "what is introduced"; intimacy therefore is a shared introduction, each one entering into the world of the other. In India, intimacy is obtained systematically, with time; in the West, love at first sight produces intimacy by breaking and entering; it is a violent disorder and a departure from time.

Whatever one's original religion, the love-match still has no place in Indian life. The West experienced an analogous situation. Look at how Georges Duby describes the framework of marriage in Europe during the High Middle Ages: marriage is no less premature, no less arranged; it has the same function of social exchange and preservation of wealth.

But in Europe, the history of love changed course with courtly love. Seeing how India lives, one understands Denis de Rougemont's point: Love is an invention of the West.[3] Whatever profound reservations I may have about his fine book, for the most part the demonstration is striking in its power and truth. And in modern India, where this invention is gaining ground, one could often imagine oneself in a Molière comedy: the middle classes, recently become rich, are experiencing the first rebellions of adolescents in love who, on one hand, balk at arranged marriages, and on the other, reject the important central ritual that is the ceremony of marriage. Nonetheless, it is the Western model that they are using as an alternative solution; badly integrated and in all its aspects contrary to Indian ideology, it does not really "take," and leaves hearts unsatisfied.

Is there a single great myth of adulterous love in Hinduism? Yes—in the adventures of a god. But it does not disturb anything; and if it serves as a model, it is not for lovers.

When the god Krishna was a child, and was about to become an adolescent, he seduced thousands and thousands of shepherdesses in the surrounding neighborhood; and he chose one, the model of the ideal lover, the beautiful Radha. All the shepherdesses were married, Radha as well. And after Krishna was himself ritually married to a well-born girl, he kept the shepherdess of his youth as a lover; there are plenty of anecdotes about the malevolent jealousy of the wife, and the god's fidelity to his mistress.

What is it then that makes this myth incapable of satisfying the imaginary of passionate, adulterous love?

The love affair of Krishna and Radha is essentially on the order of an adolescent game; often, they are surrounded by other shepherdesses, for endless circle dances in the spring nights. One of their favorite accessories is a swing; their love has an essential playfulness that makes Radha's adultery resemble a barely disguised maternal adoration; for Radha is much older than the teenager, and she succeeds in making their rural encounters and nighttime meetings accepted by arguing the tender age of the divine Cherubino.

Krishna is indeed Cherubino, madly in love with every woman who passes by, ready to talk of love to himself if he does not find anyone else in the vicinity; smitten with one beautiful woman but also with all the others, powerfully sexual, with a distracted tenderness—infantile, in a word, and adored by women. Sudhir Kakar claims to be convinced by this:

> Krishna, the legendary god, is the savior of women not so much as an adult male and sensual partner, but as the son indispensable to the consolidation and confirmation of the identity of the Hindu woman around the core of maternal aptitude. The legends of the adolescent Krishna, Radha's lover, alter nothing of the intensity of the affective investment in her son made by the Indian woman, but serve rather to incorporate, simply, elegantly, the phantasmatic satisfaction of her sexual desire for the latter.[4]

Let us, however, keep two or three signs of passionate love; two or three indications of an amorous syncope that is going to take place *elsewhere* in India's system. The *swing*, which is part of a ritual for women: once a year, on hammocks decked with flowers, they have the right to identify with the beautiful Radha. The circle dance, with feet joined, arms oustretched, mad circles carried away to a point between balance and disequilibrium, ecstatic circles in which *the divine joy of play bursts out*; it has such a beautifully misleading name that one cannot resist it, just once, "Lila." And the nights. We have already run across Krishna's circle dances and the nights of his eroticism. Now they will carry us off elsewhere.

Love at first sight exists in India. It is not "amorous"; or rather, even if it corresponds exactly to our mythology of the perfect encounter, it is not in the same place.

"Oh you who are mine, you have come to me . . . How many years I have waited for you!" Who says these words, indefinitely reproduced in an identical scenario? Who speaks like this of love, so strongly? What Isolde is waiting under a tree for her Tristan?

It is not Isolde. It is the master. When at last the darling disciple appears before his dazzled eyes, the master behaves as a lover would. The disciple, who is silent, is overwhelmed with emotion; the master's gaze is always so brilliant that it blinds, his beauty enthralls; time stops, the heart ceases to beat; suddenly, eternity is there. All the signs of Western love at first sight are found together in the first meeting between master and disciple. Gender matters little; the master may perhaps be a woman. Something is brewing there that, through the syncope of the mystic encounter, is ready to pass beyond the split between the sexes. Listen to the story of the meeting between a disciple and a master:

> "Oh you who are mine, you have come to me!" My Master repeated these words several times in Bengali, his voice trembling with joy. "How many years I have waited for you!" We were one in our silent communion; words seemed vulgarly superfluous. Eloquence poured out from the heart of the Master to that of his disciple in a silent song.[5]

Up until that point, this text adheres to the imagery of love, sublimated tenderness. Now it changes tone:

> An irrefutable perception made me feel that my Master knew God and that he would lead me to Him. The obscure elements of this life vanished in the fragile dawn of pre-birth recollections. A dramatic epoch! Past, present, and future constituted the cycles.

The first meeting, the first fusion: the immediate dissolution of one subject in the other, the "silent communion"—none of these symptoms deceive the Indian soul. Only reincarnation explains them, and the syncope that one no longer dares call amorous, since its object has so much changed its meaning, opens wide the doors of the prebirth universe. The master's wait, his joy, his gaze, his silent song stop time and reverse its course:

> The brief Indian twilight had let fall its curtain before the Master spoke again. His eyes expressed an infinite tenderness. "I give you my unconditional love."[6]

The relationship that begins in this stunning encounter has, theoretically, no end. The great mythic epics are full of these love affairs, sometimes harsh, often cruel, between master and disciple; the disciple expects everything from the master, even the tests that he will gladly bear, as, we will see, the Western mystics do for their god. The master is the vector of god, and god himself. So he becomes known by becoming visible: the "demonstration" of a holy master is nothing other than his exhibition. The master appears; the vision that the disciple has of him is enough to satiate his desires. To see him is to absorb him; and the same word, *darshan*, signifies the vision, the contemplation, and the philosophical points of view. That is, emotion is the principal method; the disciple learns and knows through communion, silence, the test. It is enough that he lives by the master's side to take from him what resembles a maternal food that is drawn out day after day.

The initial "love at first sight" of the meeting between master and disciple has the same outcome as passionate love. The time for separation will come; it will be painful, emotional, bathed in tears. This traditional way of transmitting knowledge reminds one of the impassioned love that Socrates inspired in some of his disciples, and the secret beauty hidden under his apparent ugliness.[7] Love at first sight stimulates the thirst for learning: on this point, East meets West. But the eroticism that permeates the master-disciple relationship cannot be compared with that which carries lovers off toward an often fatal fusion; it is entirely nonphysical.

The Indian word for "master" is passed on to the West in current language: whenever a European intellectual gathers fervent devotees around him, he will soon be labeled, ironically, a *guru*. It is not a mistake for the West to recognize the phenomenon of the charismatic syncope as a product of the East, and as a way of transmission that is no longer familiar. In India, that method is the norm; few political leaders can do without it; one needs to know how to move people in order to persuade them, and it took the spiritual power of a Mahatma Gandhi to refuse the ritual of *darshan* to the crowds who innocently demanded it each day.

There is a specific name, which we have already come across, for the style of devotion that is given to the master, and sometimes to the gods: *bhakti*. Again, the master of *bhakti* is the adolescent, rowdy god, our Krishna with the shepherdesses, an incarnation of the most austere values as well as the most passionate outbursts. For Krishna has two faces. The first, the older one, is that of the *Mahabharata*: respected by everyone, perfectly in control, heroic but also cunning and a liar, Krishna took the place of referee in the middle of the great war. The day before the massacre, he revealed himself as what he was: an incarnation—an avatar—of Vishnu, the greatest of the gods. The message of the first Krishna is on the side of order and virtue. Later, the time came when the childlike figure of Krishna got the better of the image of the perfect hero; then his ritual worship became fanatical and disorderly.

No more asceticism; or rather, asceticism of a particular type. The faithful, moved by a haunting music, whirl like the dervishes, while chanting; it is an orgy of mystical and artistic emotions in which the faithful must lose themselves:

> As long as the pores of the body do not overflow with joy, as long as the mind is not dissolved, as long as tears of happiness are not being shed and the mind is not melting into a flood of devotion, until then, there is no possibility of purification for the disciple. He whose voice cracks with emotion, whose dissolved mind flows in a single direction, who without ceasing to cry, bursts out from time to time in noisy laughter, who abandoning shame, starts dancing and

singing with all his strength, that one not only purifies himself but also purifies the whole world.[8]

These ancient prescriptions with their Dionysian or quietist overtones indicate the object of the *bhakti*: amorous devotion to a god. To dissolve the subject: to burst its limits by causing the body to exude—a sweat of joy, tears of happiness, resounding laughter; to smash the sound of the voice, mix laughter and tears, enact stirring contradictions, lose one's head, plunge the devotee into a state of emotional syncope to the point where there is no other solution than to throw oneself at the god's feet in order to, as our language says clearly, lose oneself there.[9]

The belated devotion introduced by the *bhakti* of the god Krishna follows the procedure of sects: it is open to all, according to the procedure of democratic openness. The most famous worshipers of Krishna are women, pious women chanting and dancing, chastely composing endless poems in honor of their divine lover. These handmaidens of love have also suffered an initial love at first sight; as children, they were struck by divine love. The pious Hindu women are poets, tender mystics; they spend their entire life at the feet of their god; and if I emphasize these feet, it is because these beloved feet, whether they belong to the god or to the master, are always described as two lotuses. The lotus is a matricial flower, the image of a cradle: to lose oneself at someone's feet is to love them with the deepest love, a love that returns one to the cradle and comes close to the accursed moment of birth. The beloved, god or master, is also the one through whom one will finally leave this life, perhaps not to be reborn. These devotional loves at first sight aspire to put an end to the syncope of death, to that of birth.

Those who set out on this course are always disengaging themselves from a burdensome life; the poet Mirabai devotes herself to Krishna's feet to escape from the husband she wants nothing to do with, and she refuses, when that husband dies, to become a sati; her love at first sight with the god frees her from the marriage.[10] Other devotees escape their families in this way; but it cannot be said that the renouncer leaves her family with a light heart. In cases of misery, the between-the-two life is preferable to a daily triviality.

In Europe, the history of love changed twice in the twelfth century. Georges Duby, in *Mâle Moyen Age* (The male in the Middle Ages),[11] compares two saintly married heroines to show how, in one century, the model of the victim changed to that of the happy wife. In 1084, the unfortunate Godelive suffered all the adversities in the world: her mother-in-law persecuted her, her husband did not show up on the wedding day, then, when he reappeared, it was to starve her; finally, under the pretext of a test of love and magic rituals, he had her drowned by a witch. One century later, in 1113, Ida de Bourgogne, well married, subservient to her husband, gave birth to two equally famous sons; when she became a widow, she fed the poor and performed miracles. From one to the other, the century changed course; love, which had not existed in marriage, became its ally. Conjugal love was born.

But toward the end of the century, when the Church had restructured the rules of life between men and women and imposed models of conjugal love by force, the great movement of courtly love began.

We know the version that Denis de Rougemont has given us in *Love in the Western World*. A product of the Catharist heresy, courtly love invents amorous passion; it is born in adultery, but between the inaccessible woman and the troubadour scholar an unbridgeable distance makes any carnal encounter impossible. This nonphysical sexual conflagration made a long journey through Eastern mysticism before settling temporarily in southwest France. From the Catharist movement and from the East, courtly love inherits the cult of an ecstasy that is attained through precise techniques, a whole range of tests and of poems. The lady is celebrated all the more because she will never be touched; but without the danger of touching, without the risk of an overflow of physicality, there could be no courtly love. This "little flower" and this flirting are metaphysical; and the Lady is not far from divinity. Georges Duby's version does not contradict this version of the facts, but changes the interpretation remarkably: passionate love may be an invention, but it is also a game between men in which women take the place of the decoy; the role that they are assigned is to educate young men. If one looks closely, each of these versions joins up, through odd paths, with the Indian model of love at first sight between master and disciple, and with chastity and passionate love.

The Catharist heresy, product of ancient Manichaeism, thirsted for purity. Whatever is of the body is impure, whatever is of the mind is pure. The logic of purity consists in radically separating the body from the mind, or from the soul; consists in forced chastity, to begin with. But the Cathar also had permission to stop feeding his body and to let it die, or rather to permit the soul to leave it at last.

If this is not entirely Brahmanic or Hindu, we need only read the daily papers in today's India to discover an absolutely identical practice; it belongs to the Jain religion, a great reformist sect, contemporary with Buddhism, which has survived better than Buddhism in the subcontinent. What exactly does one read? "Mr. X, a Jain, having decided to start a terminal fast, happily left his body after twelve days of fasting, and entered into permanent ecstasy at such and such a time." These are the phrases used in death announcements and news stories; they are very common and shock nobody. In the Catharist heresy so monstrously repressed at Montségur by the Catholic Church, the Dominicans, and Simon de Montfort, mystical suicide through starvation was called *endura*: the ultimate test. In India this test exists, and is found in one of the branches of the logic of ecstatic syncope, the one that consists of pushing it, in its most extreme consequences, to the point of death.

A result of the same logic, the great test of love, *asag*, consists of the lovers spending the night together, naked, in the same bed; that they remain chaste goes without saying. They do not even have the sword that separated Tristan from Queen Iseut when the king found the lovers in the forest; true lovers do not need this metaphor to live a joint ecstasy in which there is no place for bodies.[12] The soul is thought to have absolute power over the body. And that is how courtly love, that stand-in for adultery, can establish itself; the lady allows herself more willingly to be loved by the scholar, troubadour or trouvere, in that she yields her body to her husband and her heart to her lover. Or to God: for the lover, at the beginning of this great affair, is nothing other than a substitute for God, a divine lover, the true possessor of the soul, who has lent the body to the husband for the needs of reproduction of the species and in accordance with "grow and multiply."

The two readings are developed on this common ground. The first emphasizes the emergence of the poetry, that of the women as well as of the young men, and glorifies the birth of passionate love; the second analyzes, through "*fin amor*," "*the adventures of liberty*,"[13] the competition between young men, the education of unmarried men of a lower rank than the lady to whom love gives them access.

But is this so distant from India? The movement of passionate love began in a *sect*; it opened out onto *democratization*; it invented a new type of *devotion*. That is how love at first sight came to occupy, in the West, a pervasive place in everyday eroticism.

It will always be a matter of crossing social divides. But when the scholar worships the lady, it is not she whom he wishes to approach. The lady is married and will remain so; the lord governs, if not in person then through the shadow of his law. The scholar is not in competition with the lord but with the young men, his contemporaries; let the best one win the lady's favors—that is, her attention, and a privileged relationship that is deprived of sex and constrained to undergo a sublimation. The lover and the lady, for lack of kisses, exchange words and speak of love.

Jacques Lacan caused a stir by telling whoever wanted to listen: "There is no such thing as sexual relations."[14] Around this disconcerting assertion drifted a long discourse on courtly love, which Lacan saw as the very principle of what we call "love." "To speak of love is in itself a jouissance," he said, and this chatter is the essential element of courtly activity. Love was invented to fill in the unbridgeable gap, the same one that is at the heart of sexual activity; by criticizing the idea of sexual "relations," by breaking the expression up into its component parts, by showing the meaninglessness of the word "relations" when it has to do with subjects caught in language and gifted with speech, Lacan did not invalidate love but restored to it its letters patent of nobility and its historical moorings. Amorous "chatter" has nothing to do with copulation; the scholars and the ladies found in this everyday sublimation a real jouissance, from which poetry springs.

One of the main figures of poetry goes by the name of "syncope," or—and it is the only field in which one finds this exact term—"*enjambement.*" The poetic spate gushes toward the lady: it "steps over" the order of feudal society, plays at equality, neutralizes reality, the castle, the lord of the manor, and finds its source in the void between the two lovers. The void of the minimal space between the two bodies during the test of *asag*, the void of the social space, the void between the arms that will never close around the beloved body: it is the void of asceticism. Courtly love practices with two partners the asceticism of the hermit in the forest; instead of a severe and complicit god from whom one seeks tenderness and awaits revelation, there is the lady, the substitute for the divine, divine herself and perceived as such. Alive, incarnate, and yet abstract; alive, represented, and yet remote.

The counterpoint, however, was not long in coming. In the novel *Tristan and Iseut* there is a genuine *enjambement*, a splendid metaphor for love poetry. Tristan is asleep in the apartments of his uncle the king; not far from the hero's bed is that of Queen Iseut. And in order to join her in the night, Tristan steps over the gap and leaps onto the Lady's bed.

Courtly love in this era has changed its meaning; Tristan and Iseut have consummated their adultery, and are lovers. A spiteful dwarf, who has suspected the queen for a long time, has sprinkled the space between the beds with a fine layer of white flour. Tristan saw the flour; that explains the *enjambement*. But since their bodies are in an embrace and since the lovers are not chaste, the *enjambement* is not flawless. For Tristan had gashed his leg that very morning, while hunting . . . the exertion of the leap pulled on the bandage and spread the edges; the blood spurted out. On the flour-whitened floor, the court could see the red drops sprinkled like so many confessions of adultery. Tristan, by jumping over to Iseut's bed, crosses over; but the crossing confesses the fault, violates the prohibition, and, bloodied, becomes public. It had not been public before: to conceal from King Mark that his bride was already not a virgin on their wedding night, the servant Brangane had taken her mistress's place. This deceitful substitution was not enough for the legend, which demands both the sin and its impunity. The lovers betrayed themselves; they were almost burned at the stake, but with a completely Indian logic, they escaped and went off, as renouncers of love, to the forest where nature was waiting to take care of them.

When she does not yield, and because she resists, the lady, in courtly love, teaches the young man the art of distance; she is an instructor. It is her job to tame the young man's roughness, to domesticate his ardor; it is her job to teach him good manners.[15] All good manners (see Claude Lévi-Strauss's brilliant analysis in *The Origin of Table Manners*) generate distance. The badly brought-up girl of Amerindian ethnologists[16] is the one who dares to eat the honey straight out of the tree hollow, that is, alone, without sharing it with her people and especially without waiting for the honey to undergo ritual dilution. She will be harshly punished; it will be her turn to be eaten alive by a husband too quickly married and somewhat cannibalistic. Table manners, ways of speaking, ways of loving: the essential thing is always to *delay*. One does not fall on the food: one uses utensils, one waits, and one shares. One does not speak whenever and however one wants: one waits one's turn in speaking and respects the rules of language. Ways of loving: when these do not have to do with marriage, which delays copulation by multiple rituals and numerous exchanges, they make one wait. The amorous rendezvous reproduces the scenario of syncope: the lover will be quivering even more because he has waited longer. Amorous expectation is ahead of schedule; it delays the encounter, and anticipates its outcome. In courtly love, the outcome is resolutely lacking; the instructor has to overcome this obstacle in order to guide the young man to the desired result. Thanks to this sentimental, rhetorical, and social education, the young man will be admitted to the Garden of Love, in the company of his peers.

The lady instead of the master, the lady as mistress: we are not far from the Indian love at first sight between the disciple and the guru who has always been awaiting him. Henriette de Mortsauf proceeds in the same way; out of her hidden passion she constructs a court of love and transforms the young Vandenesse. In the first pages of the novel, he is still a clumsy boy in a tight cornflower-blue suit; when he leaves the attentive hands of his fond and chaste mistress, he is a sophisticated man. From this model, as we know, later springs the *Sentimental Education* and its dreadful nostalgia. The lady appears wizened; she has gray hair; her youth, which the hero had no use for, is gone. Balzac knew how to make the Lily in the Valley wither, and if she dies faded, terrible to look at, at least Henriette de Mortsauf dies in the flower of her youth. Flaubert, who knew a lot about the art of syncope, who lived its torments and made an art of writing about them, sacrifices the myth of love for the ecstasies of Saint Anthony; and the room where he shut himself up alone to write took the place of the forest for him.

The movement of the centuries has swept away what Georges Duby considered the true driving force behind the Court of Love.

If his interpretation is accurate, the lady, this beautiful decoy, is only used to attract young men into a circle that surrounds, pushes against, and protects the sovereign. This system is not without consequences: Duby sees in it the seed of the future French Revolution. The ardor of the young men close to the inaccessible lady would favor the first emergence of the clergy, that is, the third estate; their poems, their love affairs carry with them a secret protest for equality. This protest affects only the elite: for peasants are excluded from the Court of Love in the thirteenth century; they are not even mentioned. They will still be excluded in the gathering of the three estates in 1789:

> In the hall of the Tennis Court [Jeu de Paume], in 1789, three arms were raised for the oath. These were not the arms of workers. Nor were the deputies of the Third Estate—those well-appointed men then busily engaged in the destruction of "feudalism"—peasants, but rather the "plebeians" of the treatise *On Love*. . . . The original rift, accordingly, continued to gape as large as ever—a moat beyond which, as though under guard, the "toiling classes" had been corralled.

Thus writes Georges Duby.[17] In 1978 he added: "I do not see that this moat has even today been entirely filled in."

Are we going to have to reconstruct our courts of love? And does not the power of Bertrand Blier's film *Too Beautiful for You* rest in the *social triviality* of the two partners, struck, finally, as Tristan might have been, as Iseut was? Love at first sight challenges social exclusion; that is a good slogan for dispelling French mediocrity. In India, one is still very far from these amorous and social transgressions; and numerous people remain excluded; today, for example, despite the laws of the Indian Union, the Untouchables are still impure, and the government is obliged to reserve quotas of admission to "noble" occupations for them; without those, they would not be allowed into modern society.

Other traces of exclusion remain, and love at first sight, which brings together socially distant lovers, often causes a scandal. Look at the storybook adventures of love at first sight in literature: it follows the laws of the Courts of Love.

The Red and the Black: The lowly peasant who has become a cleric by chance decides to seduce a married woman; she succumbs, and while he educates the lady's children, she undertakes the education of the young tutor, who will emerge ready to seduce a lady of higher rank. The scandal comes from the discovery of the affair; in one shot, in a church, Julien Sorel brings down the house of cards of love and of society[18] and fulfills his ascetic destiny: to reach the peaks of human ambition and fly to the summit like an eagle, it is better to climb the scaffold and perish at the guillotine than to suffer a social comedown.

Devil in the Flesh: During the Great War, a high school boy seduces a married woman whose husband is at the front: a repeat of what happened during the Crusades. The flame blazes in the forbidden conjugal bedroom, and the adolescent learns to act like a man by refusing a "corked" wine in a restaurant; bed manners, table manners. The love affair ends badly, with the lady, who dies in childbirth, paying the price. And look at Louis Aragon sunk down at the feet of the blue-eyed instructor; look at him, intent on becoming domesticated, in the position of love-crazed man,[19] treating Elsa Triolet as an inaccessible lady at the very moment when he has her in his arms in the middle of the bed . . . The clear message about the imposture of love at first sight, which one sees with Aragon more than anyone else, is that it actually has nothing in common with sexuality.

Georges Duby is right: love at first sight is men's business.[20] Nothing demonstrates this better than the strange figure of the initiatory hero of passionate love: I mean Tristan. For it is he who, all the way through, determines the great myth. Every action of his life precipitates the deadly game of love; in the adventure of passionate love, Tristan is the alpha and the omega, the beginning and the end, the hidden god, the traitor, the victim, and the executioner. A syncope-hero.

The king's nephew, Tristan is the best organizer of the scandalous love-rebellion into which his incestuous love for Queen Iseut leads him. Did he not himself go to look for her, did he not know where to find the only woman with hair of gold, like the blond hair that a bird had placed on the shoulder of his uncle, the king? Apparently loyal and a good nephew, Tristan never ceases to use cunning, to deceive, to lie. Before even meeting Iseut, when she was not yet the king's fiancée, Tristan was mad about disguising himself: as a merchant's son, as a fisherman, later as a madman . . . trickery was his currency. He lies to Iseut, the first lie while he is suffering as she laid her healing hands on him; he lies to his uncle the king when he brings him back the fine bird, who is already his lover; in order to meet with his lover he finds a thousand tricks, shavings of bark in a rivulet by way of a love signal; he disguises himself as a pilgrim, a leper, who knows what else . . .

He even lies to God. Disguised as a leper, he carries Iseut in his arms to help her cross the river; on the island where the false leper puts down Queen Iseut rises the pyre for God's test, the great ordeal. Iseut, summoned by her royal husband, will have to swear: no, no other man has ever taken her in his arms, no other man except the king, and this poor leper who just now helped her get over the river. The lying queen, the lying lovers . . . Iseut takes the red-hot iron; her perjured skin remains white and intact. Tristan's trick frustrates even the vengeful power of a god of truth. Look at the defeat of the men whom Tristan dupes! Look at the fantastic leaps he is capable of!

For Tristan, like the virgin, leaps. Over the river; or even, when he is being dragged to the torture, suddenly into the ocean from a chapel. What *enjambements*! What jumps! And what strange secret solitude is hidden behind the illusion of the lover overcome by his love . . .

A traitor to his king, Tristan becomes a traitor to Iseut when he marries a second Iseut, whom he betrays immediately by leaving her a virgin, in memory of the first. From all these betrayals, death would finally have to follow. The real secret of Tristan's lies, the real source of his antiauthoritarian power, is revealed at the moment of his death. Tied to the memory of Iseut like the rosebush to its stake, and racked for having returned her to her legitimate proprietor, Tristan finally stops using trickery, stops cheating, jumping.

The son of Rivalin and Blancheflor, Tristan got his name from a queen who was an inconsolable widow; she marked him with her deadly sadness. His father, Rivalin, was dead; his mother, Blancheflor, died while giving birth to him. Father dead, mother dying: Tristan was the son of this. It is not surprising that he lived out of sync; it is not surprising that he made a strength of this void. His whole life resembles an endless delay. Only death managed to fulfill the act marked by profound lack that produced him; and it guided him back at last to an identity that had until then been disguised.

Let us contemplate Tristan in his last hour, wounded in battle, by chance. These wounds among knights often exude mysterious poisonings . . . One could say that suddenly the hero decided to end his heroism, and to give himself up to the common death. But Tristan does not want to die without having seen Iseut again; and the other Iseut, his legitimate wife, Iseut of the White Hands, she who has never been touched because he has engraved on his heart the image of the only Iseut, his wife watches at the dying man's bedside, waiting for the arrival of the vessel with the white sails that will announce the beloved's presence. Here is the boat; its sail is white. Tristan's wife lies and says the sail is black; Tristan turns on his side.

"I can hold on to life no longer," he says, and dies.

Could one not say that he had since birth been holding on to life? Could one not believe that he had, for his whole life, been posthumous? From birth on, Tristan inherited only sadness; he also inherited love at first sight. His father, Rivalin, and his mother, Blancheflor, loved each other with an unequaled love. "The true Minne," spirited goddess of Love, had carried Rivalin into another world of love where his senses, says Gottfried von Strassburg, were as if delivered from natural restraints. Blancheflor and Rivalin already loved each other passionately; Rivalin's life, "consumed," was extinguished by accident thanks to a wound; Blancheflor died of it, while bringing Tristan into the world.[21] But is it really day that this mourning woman is giving to her child? It is not day, it is night.

Tristan inherits night. His life is nothing but a long delay in dying. "Love" is the name of this delay; "Iseut" is the name that anticipates death. Tristan is the incarnation of a long, amorous syncope, which ends by the ocean when Iseut is absent.

Tristan, syncope-hero. Hardly a man; a child rather, proceeding—like syncope—by leaps and tricks, disguises, delays, and anticipations. Stubbornly giving up the choice of the forest, refusing the court and its castes for the sake of a shared asceticism, in exchange for the cold, the damp, and endurance, close to the *endura* of the Cathars. A hero "enraptured" several times over, as syncope can become enraptured in its blessed absence. When he is wounded by Morholt and his flesh is decaying, Tristan drifts in a skiff, his first deathbed, with a harp in his hand; the harp starts playing by itself. This music magically draws the deadly boat onto the bank where Iseut lives, and guides the dying man toward the lady; the enchanted music delays the moment of Tristan's death.

Tristan, far from the rest of humanity. Close to the animals whose voices he borrows, changing himself into a nightingale, a warbler, or a lark to make himself recognized; offering a magic dog to his Iseut, a dog whose bells make music that charms the heart forever. Friend of a dog who loves him dearly. Close to the Greek hero and the monstrous superman, an outlaw, a savage overcome by love. Tristan is a stillborn lover; this character *between two deaths* was necessary to incarnate the model of passionate love.

If Denis de Rougemont is right, if passionate love arose from heresy, then the syncopated essence of Tristan is to be a troublemaker. For the myth arises from his confusion, and the myth signifies nothing other than the disorderly impulse of Western love at first sight.

Heresy is always a dogma too late. When it springs up, it arrives just in time to fill a gap that has been created between an institution and its believers; but when it is declared a heresy, it is already too late. Only resistance is possible, which leads to the great funeral pyres of Montségur, or, more in the Eastern style, to the solution of collective suicide chosen by the thousands of True Believers when faced with the modernism of the new czar Peter the Great in the seventeenth century in Russia. Resistance always comes from the past; it calls the sectarians behind the times, and yet in the same move, at the precise moment when dogma declares the delay, the heresy and the resistance prefigure a future and anticipate a future development. Tristan comes from the past; the love at first sight that struck his parents to the heart reproduced in him the model of courtly love; but from the moment when Tristan was born, in this suspended eternity that separates him from his death, he anticipates the whole fate of love in the Western world; he will be the arrow that will puncture the institution of arranged marriage. What Tristan resists is order: social, religious, and conjugal.[22] That is the bounding leap, that is his forest, that, his solitary death. *I can hold on to life no longer.*

When Iseut reaches Tristan, who is already dead, she has no other choice than to let herself die, carried away in her turn by the antique melody out of which Richard Wagner fashioned the musical signifier of the hero of passionate love. It is only fair that nature should be the organizer of the last link that unites the lovers: the stubborn rosebush that bursts out of Tristan's grave to plunge into that of Iseut sides with the lovers against the rules of culture. The strength of love at first sight is supernatural: understand that it supports nature and the sublime in transcending the world of men. In the West, love at first sight brutally arranges the transgression of the existing order. Without this bound, no love at first sight is possible.

In the East, I mean in India, heresy is not as severely punished. The ever-possible founding of sects, the ever-possible appearance of a new master, the choice, always open, of the forest and of renunciation make provision for retreat, even disorder. Order is so strongly inscribed that it can contain, in all senses of the word, its internal disorder like one of its legitimate laws. There is no heresy, no passionate love; instead there is a forest where the subject dissolves in its limitless infinity. There is no *cogito*; syncope is set up as an accepted outcome, never as an uncertain digression. But neither is there any genuine Otherness: the husband does not function for his wife as the place of the soul's intoxication; and the disciple who at last finds his master finds in him the path to solitary dissolution, and the apprenticeship of techniques that lead there. At the end of the path, the ascetic in ecstasy in the forest is without an Other, devoid of all otherness, devoid even of the primary narcissism of his image in the mirror:

> If it is possible for others, for [Easterners] whose imagination does not burn at the names of Theresa, Heloise, Isolde, to abandon themselves to empty infinity with no other desire, we cannot conceive of ultimate collapse in a way other than in love.[23]

Bataille says the necessary words: "imagination," "burn," "desire," "collapse," "love."

For us, imagination, desire, and thus the collapse of love hold out. For the East, the burning fire of thought consumes the detritus of the imaginary, temporary flesh that is desirable and desiring. We have Otherness and passionate love at first sight; India reserves passion for the ascetic apprenticeship and, crossing the mirror of subjective identity, rejects collapse and love. On one hand, the little death of orgasm anticipates the terrifying great death and comes back to life; on the other, the ascetic heat of chastity leads to the dissolution of death itself.

In the West, love at first sight prepares the emergence of the Subject, its metaphysical rebellion, its resistance to the collective order. In the East, love at first sight prepares the defeat of the Subject, its absolute obedience to the collective order. From one world and the other, the same Fire strikes hearts; but for us it destroys while for them it constructs, without respite. It is a matter of dispute, a matter of between-the-two.

A matter of "liberty."

Rich Means and Poor Means: "Insight" in Psychoanalysis

Love at first sight, shared ecstasies: these are intense interior celebrations. But they take place without external splendor, and to be attained require only weak means. A secluded place, a forest; two gazes that meet, a bed perhaps . . . less than nothing. "*It is necessary to reject external means*," asserts Georges Bataille while speaking of inner experience. And abruptly, perceiving the essence of Indian techniques, he moves on in the same breath:

> Hindus have other means, which have in my eyes only one value, to show that poor means (the poorest) have alone the property of effecting rupture (rich means have too much meaning, come between us and the unknown, like objects sought for themselves).[24]

So there are rich means, just as there is rich food. India's means are actually poor, for however spectacular the gymnastic tricks of the ascetic, they are only positions of the body and breathing techniques. The mythology of the forest is poor, a simple and natural image of the void; and if one meets divine monsters there, they disappear before the ascetic's calm. On the other hand, there are all the stagings of the trance: the humming of rhombuses, the beating of drums, fumigations, legendary rags, lights from candles floating in bowls, multiple operas for so many syncopes obtained with the help of scenery and costumes. The catalogue of epileptic symptoms is rich, uniting all the quiverings, all the raptures, all the tremors of the earth.

There are equally rich therapeutic techniques for bringing the inspired one back from his foray outside the world. Electroshock passes lightning into the nervous system, and comes close to a simulation of the electric chair; insulin shock plunges one artificially into a deep sleep close to death; sleep treatment lasts indefinitely. These are simply fabricated syncopes from which the patient is supposed to reemerge like new; one stages one's own death, one will celebrate one's rebirth. No less spectacular is the primal scream, to which is attributed the power of plunging one into the dark passage of birth by repeating the exhalation of air from the lungs. Those are powerful interventions, heavy means; they need equipment, they need electricity, chemistry, or scenery. They are violent therapies, reflecting syncope as Western medicine has isolated it: convulsive, swooning, at the point of death. The appearance of syncope in music and dance brings something else to light: the lightness of syncope, its leaps, its ability to flow—as one says of writing or of a graceful movement that it flows. The suppleness of syncope, its cunning—and when one moves to the East, the infiniteness of its powers. Thus syncope leaves the reign of violence and enters its secret domain, the least known, the most despised: the kingdom of weakness.

The framework of psychoanalysis falls into the category of poor means. Almost nothing, as I have said. The staging has minimal accessories at its disposal: an enclosed space, a bed, a chair, speech, silence, and money. But with very little, psychoanalysis recalls, oddly, courtly heritage and Indian yoga positions.

The psychoanalyst is a "guru": the banality of that remark hides a certain truth. Like the Indian master facing his favorite disciple, the psychoanalyst chooses his patient in order to travel with him the long path of a love affair. Like the Indian master, he does not decide to accept a "client" into analysis until the equivalent of love at first sight has taken place, however minimal; there has to be an initial shock in order for what is known in psychoanalytic jargon as transference to occur: transference—an ugly and modern definition of love. As with the guru or the lady, the distance between the psychoanalyst and the patient is assumed to be unbridgeable; that is the rule. The psychoanalyst and the patient are not supposed to maintain any relationship other than the therapeutic one: no social encounters, no sexual closeness, no complicity outside the enclosed space reserved for psychoanalysis. A garden of love, or a forest: outside, there is the village, where one exchanges words, affects, loves, and material goods. Inside is the forest, secrecy, the space where nothing is exchanged, and where love is going to unfold naked, to the point of definitive liquidation and complete combustion. At the end of the session, only the gesture of paying the psychoanalyst effects the crossing from the forest to the village.

The patient lies on a bed; the therapist sits behind him, within touching distance but not touching him; contact and the gaze have become taboo. A stringent proximity is established, with any drawing together forbidden. It is the equivalent of the *asag*, the great test of courtly love. One loves without touching, one loves absolutely, to the point of disregarding the analyst's gender; whether he is the same sex or the opposite sex makes no difference. One loves, that is all.

The psychoanalyst, Lacan often said, is the "subject-supposed-to-know"—as is the lady in the courtly relationship that the cleric undertakes with her. It is not that she knows a lot, except for the art of putting herself at a distance; it is not that the analyst knows more, nor the guru. But the lady, the guru, and the psychoanalyst are supposed to let themselves be loved; that is the whole of their fragile knowledge. In each of these three cases a choice of education has been decided on which has nothing to do with the style of education common in the West. This knowledge can only be aimed at one person at any one time; it is not compulsory, and it consists of no *corpus*. From the moment that what is passed on undergoes the effects of syncope—whether it is called affect, emotional demonstration, silent communion, adoration, ecstasy, poetry, lovers' rendezvous—syncope inhabits this transmission and renders it, *stricto sensu*, incomparable.

And just as in courtly love the lady finally matters very little, the analyst also should not matter much in the end. Forgetfulness enables one to regain one's right to live; the lady and the psychoanalyst occupy the position of a decoy. This is the cost of the ruptures Bataille was looking for.

In and of itself, recollection in therapy does not belong to syncope; it is simply a construction, piece by piece, of a story that was engulfed and that has to be transformed into conscious memory. *Insights*, as they are called in the jargon, are more sudden, more violent.[25]

Difficult to translate into French, the word "insight" usually indicates perspicacity, penetration, or even, more precisely, *aperçu*—a glimpse or perception. Without warning, in the course of a session, without any reason, strictly unforeseeable, abruptly, a whole slice of life appears. It is an inescapable and sudden linking, unperceived until then. Everything about the phenomenon demands to be related to syncope: the suddenness of its appearance, its clarity, its obviousness; the abolition of time; and the strange submission of the mind that gazes, fascinated, at the string of successive incidents that have made the ego what it is today. It is impossible to escape the feeling of "too much": it is a hypermemory, a hyperconsciousness . . . The "too much" has joined in; it will disappear as it came, an angel's wing.

It is equally impossible to avoid the comparison with ecstasy: there is a wave of peaceful joy, hypnotizing consciousness. A weight has lifted; that is how one understands what the technical vocabulary of psychoanalysis calls the "lifting of repression": as one escapes by jumping over a fence. This panoramic perception is even strange because it is accompanied by the apperception of sober conclusions. Is that all life was? And it was indeed all that? Simplicity itself?

In *Les Paravents* (The screens), Jean Genet dispatches his characters into the next world through paper hoops. On the other side of the torn paper, other dead people calmly await the living. "That's it?" says the newly deceased person. "Yes, that's it," they reply in chorus. "And people make so much fuss about it . . . "

Between life and death, only syncope opens the doors—and immediately closes them again. Psychoanalysis participates in syncope through its capacity, at its best, to open the doors of the between-the-two that separates life and death. With poor means. Marriage is rich, but love is poor.

The same style of poverty affects the system of courtly love: the garden, the bed, the letter, or the poem create a simple decor. Wagner's opera *Tristan und Isolde* presents the director with a difficulty arising from the extreme simplicity of the surroundings: the bridge of a ship, a large tree at night, the seaside. It is in this opera that music comes closest to attaining ecstasy: that is the only plot offered to the audience. Beyond the lightning and the shattering, the scrutiny of syncope's weakness becomes apparent.

That is the road that must now be traveled; we must try our hand at understanding the function of syncope's weakness, and the nature of its secret power.

Overwhelming.

14

Jouissances: Between the Angel and the Placenta

To speak of love is a jouissance in itself. But to speak of jouissance itself is another matter.

The "little death," as it is known in the West, brings to mind images of weakness. The languor experienced at the moment of climax causes us to "fall" with weakness; we "lose" consciousness. Popular slang has found an even better expression: to have an orgasm is known as "to get one's rocks off,"[1] for a man, that is. This is a way of reconnecting with the fallacious and mythical feminine weakness whose nature we saw when the bacchantes tore the fawns apart with their bare hands. No matter, orgasm does bring on a temporary languor, an instantaneous mellowing, a softening of which the diminution of the penis is but a sign.

A noticeable weakness, perhaps, but a sacred one. A prodigious rallying point for the proponents of a new genre.

There was a king named Pandu, meaning "pale"; his mother had in fact gone pale when she first saw the abominable ugliness of the child presented to her as continuer of the royal race. King Pandu had two wives, and he was happy. Alas, one day he went hunting for antelope, and with a well-aimed arrow in a double blow, he shot through a pair of coupling animals.

Unfortunately for King Pandu, one antelope was not actually an antelope but a yogi sage who had spring fever and who had decided to transform himself into an animal. Accomplished yogis have these powers, and are able to return to nature as an animal in heat without breaking their vows of chastity. The dying yogi, pulling out the deadly arrow, addressed the anxious king. I curse you, he said, because you killed a couple in the moment of weakness that all of nature respects. I curse you: you will not be able to couple with a woman without dying at the same instant. Having said these words, the yogi left his body and died. At first King Pandu was worried: Would he have no offspring? And after negotiating this delicate point with several surrogate procreators, all of whom were gods assembled for the occasion, and after several children were born to him by proxy, he could no longer resist. The same springtime that had inspired the yogi seduced him as well; disregarding the objections of the more beautiful of his wives, he made love to her and died immediately, in rapture. His young widow chose to be burned with him on the funeral pyre.[2]

The only difficult point in this episode of the *Mahabharata* lies in the question of engendering; once this matter was solved, the man-king calmly let himself go, because it is preferable to die while making love than to live without jouissance. The yogi coupling with his beautiful antelope had shown him nature's true path.

But the essence of this natural weakness remains, in the strictest sense, ineffable. The Tantric philosopher allows himself a privileged role: he suspends the male orgasm by attuning it to the cry of the Other. This suspension is neither animal nor human; it reaches a superhuman level where the Tantric practitioner reaches ecstasy, therefore the universe, therefore the other side of nature. The Tantric practitioner has nothing to say about the jouissance of the Other.

Lacan calmly affirmed, rather prudently taking as witnesses those he saw in his audience who "appeared to be men," that a woman knows nothing about her own jouissance. She experiences it and is aware of experiencing it, but that is all. In order to escape from feminine muteness on the subject of jouissance, Lacan calls on the mystics for assistance. Because generations of psychiatrists at the end of the nineteenth century wanted to define mystical jouissance as "matters of sperm," Lacan reverses the position: it is not psychiatry that is capable of explaining human jouissance but the mystics. But at the densest point their language remains mute as well: like the woman who experiences an orgasm but cannot explain it, the mystic feels and describes a jouissance of which he knows nothing.[3]

In the West as in the East, when male or female mystics speak of this, they all describe the same ocean. A flood; a torrent of waves; a delicious immersion; a feeling of drowning; arriving in a liquid that rolls, shakes, exhausts, and draws one up. Romain Rolland invented the image of the "oceanic feeling," and tried to confront Freud, who couldn't do anything with it; he was unable to find the slightest hint of this kind of feeling in himself.[4] Freud was willing to admit that the oceanic feeling is often apparent when, for example, despite all evidence, a lover is so impassioned that he declares himself to be "one" with the Other; Freud grudgingly accepted the definition of the oceanic feeling as the "restoration of a narcissism without bounds," but did not concede the point about religion. The origin of religion is an infantile position of abandonment proclaiming misery. This was a total misunderstanding: Rolland was not speaking of religion but of mystical syncope.

But they were both right: Freud to maintain that oceanic feeling had nothing to do with religion; Rolland to affirm its existence and particularity.

Freud had a valid point; the mystic in the process of dissolving himself inside what he calls his god wastes no time but takes the most direct route. This creates a short circuit: what should be done is to "skip" the steps marked out by religion. Joan of Arc, when brought before the Church tribunal, persisted in giving an obstinate answer: yes, she would agree to recognize the "militant" Church, but "I serve my Lord first," or "God is served first." This is the superb stubbornness of a young girl in direct contact with God or his royal incarnation, and rejecting "militancy." Another short circuit: the mystic is of necessity a dissident, cut off from the established circuits. And the dissident must also participate in mysticism, because in order to have direct access to any emotion, whether libertarian, nationalistic, or erotic, the shortest route must be taken, which springs from "boundless narcissism." To project the voice or image of divinity outside the self, or to project a passion for liberty outside the self, is a thought process that presupposes a radical breaking-through of the limits of the self. From this apparent weakness narcissism will later find the power of protest and restoration. But oceanic *in and of itself*?

Romain Rolland had experienced the oceanic feeling[5] as an adolescent, thanks to music, especially that of Beethoven.[6] Having become a historian and writer as an adult, he heard about a person who had described uninhibited mystical jouissance better than anyone else: Ramakrishna, a poor illiterate Brahman from Bengal. Ramakrishna was an amazing ecstatic who allowed himself the luxury of having access to all available gods, those of Hinduism, Islam, and Christianity, to such an extent that Rolland, in the biography he wrote of Ramakrishna, called him the "gods-man." It is from this small, frail man with a large mouth and distorted gaze that Rolland borrowed the notion of oceanic feeling.

This small man had become tired of waiting for ecstasy, so exhausted from this long, fruitless quest; one day in the temple of Kali, the goddess to whom he was devoted, he saw the large sword of the sanctuary. He swiftly made for the weapon; enough of this life!

> And lo! the whole scene, doors, windows, the temple itself vanished. . . . It seemed as if nothing existed any more. Instead I saw an ocean of the Spirit, boundless, dazzling. In whatever direction I turned, great luminous waves were rising. They bore down on me with a loud roar, as if to swallow me up. In an

> instant they were upon me. They broke over me, they engulfed me. I was suffocated. I lost consciousness and I fell.[7]

A classic description, often quoted, and which develops the theme of the ocean that is latent in all Indian texts. This ocean is like the famous statue of St. Theresa's ecstasy: "All you have to do is go to Rome to look at Bernini's statue to see that there is no doubt, she is orgasmic [*elle jouit*]," said Lacan.[8] The same evidence can be applied to the ocean that swallows up the mystic.

Karoline von Günderrode, whom we encountered at the edge of the abyss of Asia shortly before it swallowed her up whole in a voluntary death, magnificently describes the effects of jouissance as an ocean that had nothing to do with god and everything to do with herself:

> Suddenly my heart contracted and was numbed by fog. Soon it vanished: it seemed to me that I was no longer myself, while remaining myself more than ever and if my consciousness had crossed the borders, it was different and larger, nonetheless I felt myself to be within it. I was free from the narrow borders of my self; and ceasing to be an isolated drop, I was returned to the "all" that I possessed in my turn; I thought the "all," I felt the "all": I was a wave in the ocean, a ray in the sunlight, I was gravity with the stars; everywhere I felt myself and in myself I enjoyed [*jouir*] everything.[9]

If the oceanic feeling is well adapted to the core of syncope—this ecstasy—it is because only there is the horizon found, and the infinite movement of waves rolling in and pulling away; there is the sexual drive of the universe.

Rolland's access to the gentle Ramakrishna was carefully regulated by his pious disciples; Ramakrishna himself didn't worry about useless precautions. His divine visions do not distinguish between "raw" words and the expressions skillfully recooked and transcribed by his entourage. One day, he saw excrement, urine, rice, and vegetables:

> Suddenly my soul left my body, and like a flame, touched everything: excrement and urine were tasted. It was revealed to me that everything was one, that there was no difference.[10]

Another day, he saw God in a vagina, then in the coupling of two dogs. And when he experienced the rising up of a serpent coiled up in the depth of his loins and who, vertebra after vertebra, aroused his spinal cord until the ecstasy reached his head, the image was that of a young man who resembled him like a brother and who penetrated his anus with his tongue. When he reported the extent of his visions and sensations, Ramakrishna had no desire to offend; nothing was more hidden, nothing was more natural; the absolute wandering of this syncretic eroticism could just as easily have turned him into a Christian, the Virgin Mary, a Muslim, or a monkey-god . . . It was all the same. He experienced his first ecstasy as a child when he saw a group of white cranes flying across a mass of black monsoon clouds . . . [11] The vision of the Bengali child in the fields was pure and modest. The rest—the dogs, the feces, the urine, or the ocean always susceptible and ready for a typhoon in the Ganges estuary—is commensurable. Simple, sublime, animalistic, and mystical. There is no need to search for interpretation; it would be like the "rich means" spoken of by Georges Bataille, and would create a screen between the mystic spasm and ourselves.

In 1886, Ramakrishna died; religious books in India, as usual, do not speak of his "death" but rather of his "Great Ecstasy." Ten years later, an unknown Parisian female transient was hospitalized at the La Salpêtrière Hospital and lovingly cared for by Pierre Janet, who made her the tragic heroine of his most important book: *De l'angoisse à l'extase* (From anguish to ecstasy). Madeleine, who identified herself to the police as "the Goat,"[12] was in fact the emissary of mystical dementia. The therapist was soon able to discover simple orgasms amid the joys of his patient.

"I have," she told him, "large sweet patches on my lips and on my stomach that throb with truly divine tremors . . . My whole body trembles when God softly places his burning hands on my body and caresses me all over, it is indescribable, and it seems like the jouissance that I feel makes me faint. I feel as if I am being lifted into the air, it seems as if my body is being carried by a thick rope between my legs, and that this rope is pressing on my genitals, pushing them inside. It begins to affect my bladder; a seal is placed on the opening but this difficulty in urinating is not an agony but rather a sensual delight . . . I very often feel the sweetest tremors both on the inside as well as the outside of my body which are so unusual that I cannot describe them."[13]

Pierre Janet's commentary is no more self-conscious than that of his patient: "Let us note here that the appearance of this jouissance is not surprising in the least. When we realize that jouissance exists in all the senses, in all parts of the body, it would be unusual if it were absent from the organs that produce it most easily."[14] Pierre Janet couldn't have said it better, nor could Madeleine.

The passionate curiosity of essayists, novelists, and philosophers about these testimonies resembles that of children. This is the reality of *Hic Rhodus, hic saltus*. This is jouissance, *even without the sexual act*. Here is jouissance: falling, rolling, trembling inside.

But before attaining the syncopated spasm that creates an outpouring of the ocean, before identifying with feces or the copulating dog, the mystic must undergo innumerable tortures; thousands are endured before "uncorking" (like a cork that "jumps" from a bottle of fermented wine) into orgasm. We already know that the techniques of ecstasy sometimes cause accidents: nosebleeds and blood clots in the mouth. Ramakrishna died of throat cancer, which doctors believe to have been caused by a chronic irritation of the respiratory tract, due to the exceptional frequency of his ecstasies. There's the rub: ecstasy has intoxicating effects; as noble as the term "ecstasy" may be, its effect is not very different from that of a drug. Ramakrishna was an ecstasy addict as others are drug addicts. The mystic attains ecstasy by taking in breath (*ingestion*), or restraining digestion, depending on whether he holds his breath while inhaling or exhaling; drug addicts get "high" by injecting a foreign substance. In both cases, the body is a simple accessory, behaving as a tube through which the vast winds of the ineffable pass, and it is undoubtedly not by accident that drug addicts call their substance "shit." The values of ecstasy are considerable but the chaste, light body that floats gently is not without bloody wounds.

It is actually hard work to put oneself in a state of weakness. In order to do so, mystics have no shortage of methods: crosses, crucifixions, stigmata, bones that are broken or that become paralyzed, ulcers that flourish and that become wormy, even leprosy. One scarcely knows who to choose as emblem: Lydwina of Schiedam, Catherine Emmerich, Angela of Foligno, all of whose bodies became blistered, putrefied, bloodied flesh . . . Such is the extensive register of female saints in the West, celebrated by adoring writers who were often infuriated[15] and who appeared to be in need of orgasms. The corporeal landscape of ecstatics in India, even if it does not feature as many purulent secretions, is also affected by terrible sufferings. But they are not of the same kind.

Take blood, for example. In the bodies of Western ecstatics, it flows from the palms, the soles of the feet, from the heart and from the part of the chest where Christ was struck with a lance. Sometimes, it forms a little bloody cross, as on Catherine Emmerich's chest. Blood springs forth spontaneously, always in the places where Christ's body was wounded. In the Indian practice of ecstasy, respiratory techniques, always excessively congestive, cause the blood to give a flushed cast to the skin all over the body, so much so that one should be able to recognize a yogi by his reddish, "burned" complexion. Ramakrishna made a point of verifying the skin tone of a person who claimed to be an ecstatic, checking to see if his chest was the right color: whether like burned bread, crayfish red, or, the sign of supreme talent, golden and radiant, the skin retains forever the fire of ecstasy. Sometimes, but not often, blood trickles through the pores. But never does it favor a particular part of the body. In the West, ecstatic martyrs have Christ's blood springing forth from their bodies; in India, ecstatics voluntarily become "burned."

Where blood does not flow, there are trembling, convulsions, a metal band squeezing the head, a stiffening of the extremities and bodies in revolt. Janet's Madeleine experienced autonomous flight; Saint Theresa of Avila accepted the sensation of levitation without refusing sexual pulsation. The body leaves wetness behind, dries out and bursts into flames, becomes light, and even winged. Saint Theresa of Avila invented the appropriate expression: "violent transport."

The word accurately corresponds to the experiences described by Indian ecstatics when they "leave their bodies" and are temporarily transported elsewhere. Indian tradition, for example, requires that a yogi in ecstasy not be left alone; Ramakrishna's disciples held him up when he fell into a swoon, as seen in a photograph where rapture struck when he was in a standing position, with one arm in the air.

The philosopher Krishnamurti, who died in 1986, asked two female friends to accompany him to his home one evening; behind closed doors he implored them not to be afraid and especially, not to call a doctor. The two women were not to talk to him, nor to bring him to his senses, but to perform an important task: if he completely lost consciousness, they were to close his mouth. Pain swept over his body, his teeth, neck, head, spinal column, and stomach; he sweated profusely. Then, as is often the case in shamanic trances, his voice changed and became that of a child who was complaining. And this child began to call out to him, adding:

> I must go back and find out what had happened on the walk. Something happened and they rushed back. But, I do not know whether I returned? There may be pieces of me on the road.[16]

Western saints or Eastern masters, we know that they, like shamans, "travel." If Krishnamurti's testimony is gripping, it is not so much in its content, which conforms to the great shamanistic doubling or hysterical depersonalization, as in its modern-day freshness. As a child, Krishnamurti was designated World Instructor by the Theosophists; by age eighteen, he had escaped, and peacefully discontinued the school of which he was the president and guarantor; then he went off alone to Big Sur to philosophize, in the company of Greta Garbo and Aldous Huxley. Later he became the master of the prime minister of India, Indira Gandhi, because he was able to teach her to find the necessary tears for the most difficult type of mourning: her son had died in a plane crash.[17] And despite the vital modernity of his words and appearance, despite the discontinuation that reminds us of so many others, he "traveled." Krishnamurti's biography is on the whole typical in every respect of the classic destiny of a "shaman": he had an extraordinary birth—he was born in a room designated for sacrifice and usually prohibited for childbirth, was sickly, subject to convulsions, was a slow learner, and experienced his first trances as an adolescent. That is when the intense struggle that he called his "wheels" began: invisible creatures worked along his spinal column, enlarging his head to bore the hole through which he could easily leave his body. Then, like all shamans, after being tortured, after having had "out-of-body" experiences, he felt the calm, weakness, the collapse and happiness of the body in post-jouissance.

To travel—or "trip"—is key for mystics, shamans, witches, and users of drugs. To travel, the pure fantasy of lovers; if the princess is far away, it is necessary to rescue her from across the seas and return her soul to her before even laying eyes on her. To travel out of the body: rubbing an ointment on one's skin, as sorcerers do; holding one's breath; whirling to the sound of a chorus of drums; using alcohol, drugs, or experiencing love at first sight. To extract from psychological teguments for which no language has a name, something that is neither living or dead, neither body or soul, a bird, they say, no doubt. Leaving the body is not only a practice of Indian ecstatics or European saints; customary in shamanism, a ritual in witchcraft, it is the currency of drug addicts' imaginations—who indeed pay a high price for the experience.

Something leaves the body. There is no jouissance without this departure, without the falling away of an unnameable fragment, undefinable as an object. The geography of jouissance is that of the orifices through which the object can escape; each time, the spasm may pulsate there, a cause of all or part of the oceanic tremors. Feces and urine, anus and urethra, principal locations of mystical debasement—of which Ramakrishna is not the sole practitioner—are the closest places to actual genitalia. Purulence, pus, mucus, and spittle are also subject to saintly devotion: so much so that it is clear that the shudder of disgust, sublimated and overcome, can generate the opposite response. The milk flowing from the nipples turns against the fawns that the bacchantes were breast-feeding; in a painting by Ludovico Gimignani we observe Catherine of Siena kneeling at Jesus' side, offering him her breast to suckle, which will provide either milk or blood, it's one and the same.[18] Vapor, breath, voice, cry, chant . . . the buccal cavity is one of the richest in jouissance; and fairy tales describing princesses who had toads, serpents, or indeed pearls drop from their mouths were inventing nothing. It is through the mouth that breath escapes; it is from there that sighs are exhaled, including the final one—that is where one expires. Tears stream from the slits in the eyelids, an essential rippling; at the end of the adventure comes supreme fulfillment.

The ways in are less fortunate; but they open wide to the doors of ecstasy. It is while breathing in that one's breath can be held, causing the blood rush, encumbering one's vision by filling it with flaming points and luminous circles. Taking in breath forces a rhythm, breaking the breathing cycle into two halves: suddenly, time gets stuck. From this door so suddenly shut, from which breath cannot escape, gushes the beginning of ecstasy. But if it is not air filling the body's pipeline, it is wine. Wine is like suffocation: it swells up one's insides, puts pressure on the joints, weakens the rivets. William James put it admirably:

> Sobriety diminishes, discriminates, and says *no*, drunkenness expands, writes, and says *yes*. It is in fact—the great exciter of the *Yes* function in man. It brings its votary from the chill periphery of things to the radiant core. It makes him for the moment one with truth. Not through mere perversity do men run after it. To the poor and the unlettered it stands in the place of symphony concerts and of literature.[19]

The "time of wine"[20] is also that of all ecstasy: by saying "yes," it annuls the bipolarity between yes and no, refuses all contradiction, positions itself on a single side of reality: in a single bound. Whether Christ is represented as a mother proffering a bloody nipple to suckle, or if he is represented as the "Jesus of the Taverns" who lets the wine of the Wedding at Cana flow into the poor, dilapidated cavity of the human body, he is always the one pouring; the body's bottle does not matter, nor does the nature of the liquid, as long as there is intoxication and as, breathing in God, one becomes one with Him by absorbing Him whole. The mouth becomes enormous, and swallows Him up. Intoxication is like the unconscious as defined by Freud: it ignores contradiction.

What could be more logical? Syncope occurs at the moment when the alternating movement of entering and exiting becomes jammed. The Tantric practitioner, who simultaneously suspends the in-and-out motion of the sex act and of breathing, seeks to grasp the precise moment when "it" can stop. "It," the pulse of life, nourishment swallowed and excreted, breath inhaled and exhaled, life given and taken away, or the ebb and flow of the precious tides that sweep in but eventually cease to surge toward the horizon. Syncope defends its territory by forbidding the ebb-and-flow: "Stay, O moment, thou art fair," it says to the instant as it goes by.[21] *Remain*. From then on, the words "life" and "death" indeed lose their meaning, and we can cry out, like Saint Theresa: "I'm dying of not dying."

The heavy brake of time has such power over the body that in the mystical imagination nature appears ready to violate her own laws. Saints and yogis can fast indefinitely; but they also can fall victim to a frenetic bulimia, like Ramakrishna, and eat thirty days' worth of food in the space of an hour. The texts say that a true yogi, having burned everything through flatulence, no longer excretes. And odors become reversed. Common mortals have repugnant odors; the secretions of the mystics, however, are comparatively more pleasant when compared with the fetidness they would have had in their natural state. The body of Saint Lydwina half-rotten on her bed of tribulations, oozing pus and putrefying, gave off the exotic aroma of quintessentially Indian fragrances: her boils smelled of cinnamon; and when finally, having been seduced by Lydwina's mortifications as Shiva was by those of Parvati, Jesus appears to her, the scent of cinnamon became that of fresh flowers: roses, violets, and lilies. "The saint was a living perfume bottle."[22] When they die, saints give off an even stronger smell, and exude even finer perfumes; sometimes the odor of sanctity is enough for the Catholic church to classify the perfumed cadaver as one of the Blessed. Even in the Liebestod of the beloved Isolde, even in the "mystical jaculations" of Saint Theresa of Avila, there is the vocabulary of perfumed scents.[23]

Man does smell, however, even more so when he begins to fast, and gives off the bad smell that suggests the characteristic smell of certain epileptic fits, that of "boiled turnip." Man's stench is such that Freud was able to imagine, in his representation of prehistoric progress, that the upright stance was adopted as a refusal of excremental and humoral fetidness. It is easy to understand how a desire for purification forced Nature's imagination to suppress its odors; even better, to transform them into their opposites. The saint, the yogi, and the mystic distill their odors: they are living perfume bottles.

It will escape no one's notice that putrefaction thereby slips out through a trap door. The more the body rots while alive, the more perfume it gives off: and so, once again, death disappears.

Sounds penetrating the ear undergo a similar "cooking." This may occur by taking a drug; henbane, for example—which is mixed with belladonna in sorcerer's rituals—suddenly creates the illusion of thousands of little bells ringing in the distance. Bells, large or small—a mystical reverberation, the music of the spheres—but always ringing. The dying, it is sometimes said, hear the sound of a heavy bell tolling; and this tolling could be, when all pulsation has ceased, the ultimate ebb-and-flow, the final palpitation. Musical terminology is obliging to the mind: it offers the term "waves," vibrating like ocean waves. Strike one wisely alloyed cymbal against another, as is done in Tibetan Buddhism: you will easily hear the prolonged vibrations, harmonically discrete and magical. The lone harmony of the vibrating waves predominates, and the last palpitation of life in the silence of syncope seems strangely perpetuated.

There is no longer any dissonance: it was the result of tumult, and existed in the "beforehand." Dissonances are the bad odors of music: in the mythology of ecstasy, they are quickly converted. A pungent odor speaks of a biological cycle; dissonance tells a musical story. Ecstatic syncope consumes everything: it burns the smell, burns the dissonance, burns the subject and its stories. If the center of the self is excrement, then it is this excrement that must be burned. And it is necessary to turn it into fuel, as is done with cow manure, which is lit in the evening in the homes of rural India.

The people known as drug addicts also burn—they burn the candle at both ends. Among one of the strongest motivations is the desire not to grow old, a refusal of time-induced degeneration. How many rock musicians have died young? In traffic accidents or drug overdoses, the means are less important than the *need to die young*. These deaths are not "premature," but rather preapproved; they occur in time to offset any future deterioration. Because of this, "excess" is everywhere, not only in the "too-strong" dose, the overdose. *Over* is the order of the day: too much percussion, too many lights, too much screaming, too many decibels, too many nights, too much jouissance, a deliberate overflow of life, from which the nothingness of sleep and expiration are absent. To absorb. Nothing rang more true, in a recent staging of Mozart's *Don Giovanni*,[24] than the idea of transforming the seducer into a dealer and the women he seduces into addicts, and the champagne aria into a scene where the heroine shoots up. And nothing was more relevant than equating drugs with vocalization, which like the overdose tends toward "excessive" singing. *To absorb*: champagne or cocaine, women or rock; absorb, and to cry out with pleasure, a spasm, "to get off," or to vocalize. Afterward, nothing: a calm, floating harmony after all of the uproar, the calming effect of singing after all of the acrobatics, the end of life after so many follies. A refusal of time, a refusal of corruption, a refusal of "no." But in its place, a "yes" without contradiction and a world outside the self. Something has left the body for which no language has a name; it is neither living nor dead, neither body or mind, perhaps it is a soul, undoubtedly a bird . . . As light as air and, if one likes, it can be named, as Max Ernst did, *Hirondil-Hirondelle*. Or as Lacan did: *Hommelette*.[25] Something that midwives call the "afterbirth." "A large crêpe that moves around like an amoeba, super-flat for sliding under doors, omniscient for being led by the pure instinct of life, immortal so as to be fissiparous. Here is something that it would not be pleasant to feel noiselessly sliding over your face as you sleep, to seal it,"[26] says Lacan, in a Grand-Guignol evocation that situates the libido—because that is the Subject—as it should be: worrisome, viscous, as physical as possible in its nonphysicality. Between the placenta and the angel.

Because, in the distant aftermath of jouissance, after assorted liquids have been released by all of the body's orifices, after the blood has oozed through the minuscule pores of the skin in a thousand ways, and after the boiling inebriety has filled and emptied the imaginary cavity that the body has become, an image of the soul is forged.

But let us return to the origin of syncope. In music, it delays, displaces, breaks, causing dissonance and in the same motion resolution; the rocking motion of the dancer and the use of the poetic technique of *enjambement* provoke the same shiver, that of a dangerous and fleeting irregularity. Jouissance, wherever it is found in the body's geography, whether linked to a real partner or developing in absentia, provokes a similar irregularity. It creates a separation, a shift; limits are pushed aside, the subject faints . . . Ernest Jones, for lack of a better word, used the Greek term *aphanisis*.[27] The subject disappears, the better to "liberate," like an egg at birth, the evil side of jouissance, this indefinable residue that breaks free, the "afterbirth," the natural complement to the child brought into the world. It is impossible to escape birth imagery; there are the first contractions, contradictions, tensing and relaxing the space; the sac breaks and the water is lost, then there is the exit and, finally—following the model of previous syncopes—the cry.

There is the child. And there are the remains of what is no longer the child; a lost object, meant to be thrown away . . . But other mammals eat the placenta, and if human females do not, they nevertheless do not find it disgusting in the least to smear this mixture on their faces later, in order to ward off aging. This first debris of human existence anticipates the tragic fate reserved for all other corporeal debris: normally destined to be disposed of, but potentially suitable for touching or eating, suitable for returning whence they came. To eat the placenta, one's excrement, or one's *Dasein*, to devour the loved one with kisses or to make love with God: these are some of the possible equivalents to the body's debris. The angel is part of it, as is the beast that follows him like a shadow since Pascal united them, one behind the other in an ineluctable procession.

As far as the Beast is concerned, it is easy to see. When Ramakrishna is able to see God in the coupling dog, or when he tastes excrement in order to experience the unity of being, or when the Tantric disciple encloses himself with his own stench, confuting all the rules of basic humanity, it is a return to animality. Our charming European saints are not exempt from actions of this kind. Saint Theresa became so weak that her body almost disappeared; only the soul survived and she had to be carried in a sheet by four nuns; when she came to, she was crawling on all fours. The countenance of martyrs tortured by illness is often transformed; their faces become muzzles or snouts, they lose their humanity. Aside from the fact that when you fall into syncope, you never know in what shape you might return: with wolf's paws, the tail of a serpent, a bark at your lips, a pelt or fur . . . One never knows. During the night, while all are asleep, the beautiful woman crosses the frontier and becomes a serpent; the nobleman or the churl crosses the invisible border of his world and wakes up a wolf. That is the principle behind the wolf-man: lose consciousness, leave your body, and you will return half-man, half-beast.[28] The animal side is always ready to graft itself onto the lovely imago of the "clean" body; always ready to sully it by growing, for example, a tail on its rear, or fleece on its *cogito*. Including Hölderlin the nightingale, who turns himself into Scardanelli. Reason cannot avoid the sleep that makes it "create monsters": in repeating this phrase from Goya, one almost forgets that monsters are inevitable, like excrement, tears, or the soul.

As far as the angel is concerned, he dawdles in the most philosophical heads with an even greater lightness because he is able to hide his animality beneath his feathers. Remember the story of the beautiful Marquise of O. We see her dragged into the courtyard of a castle under siege by enemy troops—who happen to be Russians. A "dreadful rabble," writes Kleist, "lusting dogs" attacking their prey . . . The Marquise is about to succumb, when an officer arrives on the scene: "To the Marquise he seemed an angel sent from Heaven." A brief combat, followed by a courtly scene; the angel offers his arm to the lady and takes her to a wing of the castle. That is when . . . she falls into a dead faint.

The ellipsis is inserted into the text by Kleist. A syncope of punctuation. A few weeks later, the Marquise discovers she is pregnant. That is the way of angels.[29]

Let us seize the angel by the feathers of his most avant-garde contemporaries. Ten years ago in the West, when the great Chinese Cultural Revolution was over, once the Great Leader was shown to be an impostor, two formerly Maoist French philosophers[30] shed all the tears of their beliefs and departed, as they put it, "to the desert." The desert became one of the most sophisticated metaphors to designate the studious retreat that sheltered so many young people from the City. Those who had been enamored of Mao's theories found in their disillusionment and the "desert" the figure of the angel.

He had returned, the same as before, with his smile (the smile of stupidity, according to Lacan), his wings, his fearful darkness, the Romantic and Baroque angel extolled by Victor Hugo, Rainer Maria Rilke, and Walter Benjamin, the angel of the bizarre and of catastrophe.[31] From pure, hard-line Maoism to the symbolism of the angel, there was only a flap of the wing; it was the same Angel that transported hermits living like animals in the desert, the same radical angel who impulsively wants to change man and the world, and who, succeeding only by terror, suddenly falls back in horror, and chastises himself in seclusion. From the philosophical theory of Maoists to the holes carefully plugged up by the dressing gowns of the philosophers who were my schoolmates, to the mysticism of the angel, there was only a flea's leap, or a cleric's step, whichever you prefer.

Jambet and Lardreau, the brilliant authors of *L'Ange* (The angel), were lucid enough not to refuse the Saint Sulpician imagery of their winged inspirer. They described their choice of the angel as follows: "It was necessary to propose a generous figure, one who did not promise salvation from damnation but who has eliminated the accursed share: *the rebel will be beyond sex or will not be at all.*"[32]

The phrase that counts is this last one. For the fundamental principle of the angel is not to have a sex. It is in this way that it rebels against nature, and by another turn of syncope, once again, contributes to changing man.

Now, ten years later, the angel has returned to the imagination of learned astrophysicists, confronted with quandaries regarding the notion of time. I will not risk deciding if theirs is a new myth or actually a part of science, but I can describe their dreams.

The Angel of Astrophysics and Shiva's Phallus

This is the portrait of two astrophysicists of today.[33]

They are solid rationalists: nothing that cannot be measured exists. Without the enormous particle accelerator, they would not have been able to "see" the flood of neutrinos radiating from the explosion of a supernova in 1987, after more than three hundred years of celestial silence. The last astrologers to see the explosion of a star with the naked eye were Tycho Brahe and Kepler. Suddenly, in 1987, another was detected, and with it, because a flow of invisible particles had spanned the earth, the neutrino was discovered.

This is when we see the time-honored angel appear in the vocabulary of astrophysicists, as if it were nothing unusual. The angel is only slightly disguised: "The angels of physics," one of them said:

> Neutrinos are invisible particles that are free and almost impalpable. They do not shine, are not part of any structure; they determine, however, the destiny of the universe. Particle accelerators cause microcataclysms thanks to extremely violent bombardments. Then, because of the transmutations that follow, the "angels" fly away.
>
> They fly away, they never sleep. They are visitors, moving across the earth at the speed of light. They are errant, permanent, immortal. These nomadic angels, immortal and invisible, are not made of the same matter as stars and humans. For the moment, we have postulated their existence, measured them, and recently, captured them. They exist; they signed their birth certificate twenty years ago, after an army of physicists was united to prompt them to appear; and they appeared.[34]

If the rigor of the method resists, the myth retains its rights; and to a greater degree, the imagination yearns for familiar figures. How is it possible to resist the call of the angel with the discovery of particles that are roving, invisible and determining and yet outside the structure? How can one escape from the dream once it has been determined that the particles are the result of violent transmutations and that they are neuter?

Three types have been discovered: "It can also be said, and sometimes we do, that there are three *sexes*. Or even three *savors*. Large particle accelerators are utilized to identify these 'savors.'"[35]

A *neutrino*: a nearly matter free yet whole physical being, one astrophysicist says; nearly perfect, says the other. A triumph of subtlety, says one: "We affectionately call it a neutrino because of its exceptional neutrality." It carries no electric charge and has negligible, if not zero, mass.

Where are our two astrophysicists headed? Their instruments are real, their methods irrefutable: "We can only study matter or the trace of matter—in all of its forms, whether luminous or obscured." But their words do not escape from the poetic association of centuries of imagination, unrelentingly inciting them to search for angel's wings. From this coalition, a combination of concepts and imagery, rebellion is not missing. Listen to the more contemplative of the two:

> The neutrino is a very beautiful physical being. It can be said of photons, for example, that they have a kind of gregarious instinct. They like to line up in rows. Neutrinos, however, like all fermions, are *independent, proud,* and *indifferent.* What never ceases to intrigue me is their characteristic *revolt against symmetry.*[36]

Here is a brutal syncope, a bombardment, that provokes a transmutation—possibly analogous to jouissance—from which the angel escapes, independent, indifferent, irreducible to a sex, and in revolt against symmetry. The sequence is nearly complete: all that is left is to examine the notion of "savor."

"Savor" is the name by which the West tries to translate a concept that is the most foreign to it: the concept of *rasa*, borrowed from India. Vibration, tonality, pleasure, jouissance, color . . . *rasa* is all these things. Emotion, undoubtedly, identification with spectacle and therefore the source of all Indian aesthetics, *rasa* is not far from sympathy: in *rasa*, consciousness expands, spreading itself out like a thousand flower petals, and is found in the state we have already seen it attain by means of the suspended orgasm. There are a contraction and a dilation that "devour" time only to "vomit" it out later, producing two time frames, as well as the essential period of suspension and of the between-the-two. Savor qualifies the jouissance of this fading moment; only savor seems to apply. Is it because it runs through the body, from the mouth to the abdomen, and leaves behind so many small tremors in the esophagus and the stomach? Saint Theresa once dared to ask the Lord what these savors were; she was later ashamed of having asked, as if she had crossed the impassable border beyond authorized limits, even though it was during mystical transport. In assimilating "savor" and "sex," our two astrophysicists are not concerned with decorum. Savor has the taste of syncope; syncope tastes of sex.

Our astrophysicists have therefore assimilated "sex" and "savor"; since they must invent names for new particles, and since these particles are "neuter," we tip over without warning from "gender" into "sex"—which is fine—but from "sex" to "savor" . . . The spontaneous language of contemporary astrophysicists takes a slip into specifically mystical equivalence: the angel tastes of and relishes himself—everything that leaves the body and is ingested. Sublimated, the angel's savor seems to have nothing in common with the savage and brutal savors that we have observed in extreme circumstances; it has changed, like Saint Lydwina's purulence, from serous discharge to cinnamon, from death's putrefaction to the smell of roses.

That particle accelerators are able to distinguish one "savor" or another is less important here than the strange vocabulary used by these new explorers. Like the former Maoists who converted to Christianity, like Walter Benjamin in the depths of despair over Mittel Europa, these astrophysicists dip into mystical vocabulary to find the words they need. It is not easy to invent new words for beings of a new kind; it is clear that our astrophysicists are also in the difficult space between-the-two. For scientists whose research takes them to the extreme edges of the universe, this exercise consists of attempting to stay on the far edge of imagination without falling into the grooves already formed: a nearly impossible task. They are confronted with the same difficulty that

Georges Bataille encountered: the experience of "atheological" limits, a godless mysticism. It is exactly this type of watershed that Jean-Paul Sartre so violently opposed.

Therefore, at the border between scientific discovery and poetry, we see the return of these words revolving around jouissance. Sex, savor, angel. A revolt against symmetry. Liberty. I saw that the thought circuitry of the major philosophical systems of the West put them ill at ease; however, I saw them listen, delighted, to the great mystic myths of the West and East. Neutrinos are like angels: apparitions of jouissance.

In the West, pious images do not mislead: the long streams of light that connect the palms, feet, and sides of mystics in ecstasy before Christ are threads of jouissance. And if it is not directly through light, it is through the Annunciation, and the angel with his golden arrow piercing the heart of the lady. In the East, however, nothing is pierced; there is no wound, the body remains intact. The major link that keeps the world in order is the phallus, whence comes jouissance, Shiva's immense phallus. In continual erection, pillar of the universe, it functions much like the neutrino: it invisibly crosses over the entire world. And after having incubated an egg of his own issuing, he no longer holds himself back, he bursts forth with a flow so strong that it even burns the Fire. The Fire waits in readiness to receive the divine sperm in its mouth, in order to avoid a disaster . . . But it is not possible; it burns too strongly. The Fire stronger than fire brims over and gushes into the banks of the Ganges at Benares, where he impregnates all the wives of the Brahmans who are praying there, unawares. Indeed, this invisible matter that travels like an arrow impregnating bodies is, as the astrophysicists said of the neutrino, "a very beautiful physical body," in revolt against symmetry, independent and proud.

And, of course, immortal: because it is man who "dies" during jouissance, man, like King Pandu. But not what springs forth from his body, which he imagines will live after him.

To have an orgasm, that is, to survive the "little death," is to spare oneself real death by anticipating it.

15

Ego Orgasm and the Indolence of the Subject

Jouir, *jouissance*, *jouissances*: my vocabulary is ambiguous.[1] Sometimes it applies to the jouissance in orgasm, sometimes it tips over into something else, ego orgasm. It is not the same, and yet it is the same. It is not the same: one would have to be stupid or angelic to confuse the jouissance of orgasm with its sublimation in syncope. And yet it is the same: one would have to be naive not to recognize, in ego orgasm, the overt jouissance that inspires it. The human race has the strange privilege of being able to seize the jouissance of sex and transform it into an intimate explosion, diffuse and generalized. Ego orgasm cannot be localized; it invades the body, the skin, the consciousness. It has everything that the other orgasm has, except the coupling.

The expression itself was coined by an English psychoanalyst who worked with children long enough to identify in them a precocious moment, steeped in sexuality and filled with a desire for jouissance that was impossible to satisfy.

D. W. Winnicott patiently observed children at play, drawing all his ideas from that. That is how he observed the most common of experiences: the excitation of play. The normal child (or rather the child that is called "normal") is completely able to get excited while playing, and to feel satisfied with the game, without needing a definite physical outburst. The unstable child, by contrast—"a deprived child with antisocial tendency, or any child with marked manic-defence restlessness"[2]—lets itself get carried away by the stimulation of play. A climax is necessary, says Winnicott; often, it is a spanking, an artificial outburst of violence, administered by the parents, that puts an end to the child's overstimulation and results in the equivalent of a physical orgasm. "A very useful one," adds the English psychoanalyst. So he invents, to designate the fleeting moment in which the subject demands this internal outburst, the "ego orgasm."[3]

In other terms, it is an unfortunate game that gets out of hand.

The list of examples given by Winnicott to illustrate the idea of an "ego orgasm" is closely related to syncope. Consider them: an ecstatic joy that can be felt during a concert or at the theater; the intense experience of friendship; ecstasy. The spanking does not detract from the series: we have met up with the road of ecstasies—of mortification, torture, and flagellation. Friendship permits everyone to murmur sweet nothings to his own sex, and to play at love without the risks of love. Friendship has its emotions, its magical pleasures, its intense involvements. Love at first sight is the beginning of a journey, and that same journey is there in friendship: because it was him, because it was me. There are ecstasies in the true experiences of friendship, the same ones that one feels listening to music at a concert, or going to the theater.[4]

Naturally, the Tantric philosopher Abhivanagupta is inexhaustible on the subject of the Indian aesthetic communion found in the equivalent of the theater:

> In large gatherings, for a performance of singing and dancing for example, joy is visible when every member of the audience, not just a single individual, is in harmony with the performance. Consciousness, which is potentially saturated with happiness in each individual, yields to unity in the presence of the object, the dance, etc., and tastes the fullness of happiness.[5]

The Tantric pursuer of orgasms named this one, too: ego orgasm in the presence of shared beauty.

Winnicott is not satisfied with that. His is the clearest analysis—using terms that appear simplistic but are nonethless effective—of what has confusedly been called bisexuality. We need to digress here before understanding more about ego orgasm.

The assertion that there are male elements in the fantasies of young girls, and *a contrario* of female elements within the male personality, is by now commonplace. Winnicott, while listening to disturbed male adults, locates among some of them an *internal young girl*, well hidden, who never gets any older. That is the makeup of eternal seducers, those who are sexual initiators of the eternal girl—the *giovin debutante* so dear to Da Ponte and Mozart's Don Giovanni. The scenario is reversed, obviously, with the young girl burdened with an interiorized hidden man; a man who can also, by the way, be the fleeing object of an endless seduction. Winnicott calls these secret internal images the "split-off elements."[6]

He then tries to define these elements in a "pure" state. A formidable question: what is the pure masculine, the pure feminine? Before responding, Winnicott defines his terms: it is not a matter of homosexuality, or of transsexuality; it is a matter of a hidden girl or boy that both sexes have in them, split off, which determines desire.

The *masculine* element consists in *actively linking oneself*, or in *being passively linked to*. It does not matter which: the criterion of masculinity is neither passivity nor activity, but the movement that connects the child to the world, and which is in the realm of action. *Act, or agree to being acted upon.*

The feminine element, less dialectical, simpler, and more radical, is the experience of being. *To be* before even the notion of separation; "to be," before a true identity is formed. From the moment when separation occurs (most often in the form of weaning) the movement begins, and with it the necessity of being reconnected to the separated one, simply being. "Little mental structure" is required, says the English psychoanalyst firmly.

The first example chosen by Winnicott is surprising. It is a question—again—of Prince Hamlet of Denmark. More accurately—again— a question of the famous monologue "To be or not to be."

Winnicott hears in that little phrase an unavowed hesitation between the feminine element and the masculine element. "To be": that is the feminine element. "Or": moment of faltering, of syncope. But no; the sad hero will not reach the masculine element. What comes out of his mouth is not "or to do," but "not to be." The rest of the text, according to Winnicott, shows Hamlet giving up the pursuit of the alternative and falling into the muddled turmoil of paths that lead nowhere:

> Whether 'tis nobler in the mind to suffer
> The slings and arrows of outrageous fortune
> Or to take arms against a sea of troubles,
> And by opposing end them?[7]

"Hamlet is depicted at this stage," says Winnicott, "as searching for an alternative to the idea 'To be.'"

Prince Hamlet, it is true, does not make up his mind to "do"; it is true that he punishes, but by mistake; it is true that he kills, that he dies, but without having sought it, powerless to bring out the lost part of his identity, the masculine "to do" that is not expressed in him, but that is concealed beneath the suicidal rags of "not to be."

Winnicott's conclusion cuts through these subtleties. It is there, in his terseness: "After being—doing and being done to. But first, being."[8]

In other words, the "pure" feminine element is a necessary beginning; no less necessary, the "pure" masculine element that follows on it is the motivator for action.

When psychoanalysts consider bisexuality they get tangled up. Sometimes they concern themselves with homosexuality, latent or manifest; sometimes they relentlessly observe transvestites or transsexuals. They rarely follow the path marked out by Freud himself, however, who had quickly discerned in certain crises of hysterical women the coincidence between feminine and masculine gestures: a patient in a trance, feigning an attempted rape, hides her genitals with one hand but tears off her clothes with the other. The discrepancy is obvious once one pays attention to it.

This is as clear for Winnicott as it is for Freud. These pure feminine and masculine elements are inside each of the two sexes, and are constantly in play.

What takes place in the ego orgasm comes under the heading of play:

> Look, inward man, look at your inward maiden,
> her the laboriously won
> from a thousand natures . . .

said Rainer Maria Rilke in a poem entitled "Wendung" (Turning-point).

When the subjective frontiers dissolve, when the Subject melts into syncope, into ecstasy, into jouissance, it crosses, with a leap, the limits of its own sex, and finds itself in the other. This fundamental breakthrough is ego orgasm. Tantric philosophy expresses itself on this subject with the greatest clarity: the sought-after orgasm does indeed pass through coupling and jouissance, but it definitely does not linger there. The physiological orgasm is the way to reach the more important ego orgasm.

Consider carefully the mystics already discussed. In the guise of a beast or an angel, between these two extremes the pure feminine element and the pure masculine element will be found. Hardly disguised. Within sight.

Saint Theresa of Avila and Saint John of the Cross, an inseparable couple, are linked to each other like two parents giving birth to their descendants, their monastic orders; but, oddly, Theresa is called *La padreza*, and John of the Cross *Il madre*. This gender confusion is not new; it is found in the Byzantine era: holy women named Pelagia or Marina are commonly disguised as men. There are also god-crazed men, the "idiots" about whom Evagrius remarks that, in the public baths, "They want to be men with the men and women with the women, and have a part in both sexes without themselves belonging to either." Michel de Certeau, taking an inventory of these gender confusions, remarks that they are done less to transgress than to "abolish difference, and surpass the law of 'one or the other.'"[9] Just as Jesus declared openly that one had to leave one's family for his sake, so an aphorism from the Gospel of

Thomas asserts, "Let the man not be a man, and the woman not be a woman."[10]

It is the same in the East. Ramakrishna, the Bengali mystic, married, according to custom, a very young girl, and immediately hoisted her up onto the pedestal of the Mother so as to be absolutely sure that he would not touch her; he could not bear to brush against anything female at all, and the very sight of a woman troubled his concentration. He carefully advised his disciples to avoid two main enemies, women and gold. He himself, however, lived openly as a woman; he wore women's clothes and professed himself a devotee of Krishna, whose statue he embraced. His ecstasies, the waves that cast him at the feet of the Mother Goddess, were openly experienced as pure female orgasms. Just as he wanted to reach all the gods in the world, he wanted to reach the other sex in order to no longer have one. There is nothing astonishing about the fact that this great mystic, who tasted excrement the better to arrive at the notion of indifference, might also have passed beyond his own sex in the same manner to meet up with the sex that was not his own. That is the price of ego orgasm: the abolition of one's own boundaries.

Jacques Lacan, in his own jargon, said that woman is "not-all." And that the words "man" and "woman" are only signifiers, which only function as part of discourse: underneath, things slip from one sex to the other. It is difficult to understand this matter of the not-all: deprived of something, woman still gains a kind of compensation. Excluded by the nature of words and things—and being a concerned party in the species "man"—woman, being not-all, can have access to the ego orgasm. Does Lacan mean that man, to achieve this, must move over to the female side? Yes, that is exactly what he says:

> One can also put oneself on the side of the not-all. There are men who are also women. That happens. And who are quite comfortable with that. Despite, I do not say their phallus, despite what burdens them under that designation, they glimpse, they experience, the idea that there must be a *jouissance* that goes beyond. They are what is known as mystics.[11]

And in fact, it is easier to find the pure female element among male mystics, enclosed within, like a motivator of ego orgasm, than it is to find the contrary. If we read the accounts of the female ecstatics carefully, we begin to perceive that the holy woman is in the position of wife as well as husband. In her turn, she possesses God, as she is possessed by him. One Pentecost Sunday, Hadewijch d'Anvers had a vision at dawn.

Her heart, her arteries, her limbs shivered with desire; a dreadful tempest! Inspired, she confessed that she wanted to *jouir* fully with her Beloved, "to achieve the perfect fruition of his humanity with mine." Then: "So I desired that *God be mine* in order to be his, and *to satisfy him in my turn.*" The saint goes to the limits of the pure masculine element: no longer only "to be," enraptured by ecstasy, but "to do," to satisfy God. And just as Ramakrishna achieves ego orgasm by passing through a "female who *is*," Hadewijch achieves ecstasy by passing through the "man who *does*." The goal in possessing God is to become God with God himself; to ravish his divine identity from him. When the rapture occurs, the ecstatic attains "union without difference."[12]

Indifference is a key word.

Just as Zeus's eagle came to abduct young Ganymede for his master's love, it is an eagle that announces the hour of her rapture to Hadewijch. The eagle is not there accidentally. It comes from a long line of birds, including vultures and sparrow hawks, that play a role in common myth: they beget themselves, hermaphrodites, like the snail. The paragon of these birds is the phoenix, the legendary bird, the bird of immortality. The phoenix is immortal because it has neither father nor mother; gender is immaterial to it, it is the neuter bird par excellence. Among the accounts that touch on its self-begetting, there is one that is completely successful: the phoenix goes back up the Nile to its source (reversing the course of nature); then, heaving itself up to the top of a pyre of sandalwood, it rubs its wings against each other to produce the spark that will set the logs ablaze. The kindling is ready: it is the phoenix's excrement—that is, cinnamon. The fire blazes up, burning the phoenix, who will be reborn from its ashes, just as indifferent as it was in dying.[13]

This myth, of Hellenistic origin, is permeated with India. Burning in order to achieve immortality, setting ablaze with excrement, feces that smell of cinnamon—a reminder of Saint Lydwina, whose purulence was fragrant with spices. To burn, and by doing this to overcome the difference between the sexes. Achieving ego orgasm always involves to a greater or lesser extent the desire for immortality by passing through the indifference to gender. It involves becoming a phoenix.

The Church did not see it this way, and condemned the women who, like Hadewijch d'Anvers, wanted to become God. Soon they burned the Beguines.[14] The indifference to gender, pushed as far as God, defied the hierarchy.

For beyond indifference, beyond the confusion of gender, there is a social rebellion that causes trouble with the hierarchy, whatever it may be. Michel de Certeau goes as far as saying: "Whatever dissociates itself from the institution is mystical." The hierarchy—whether it be religious, monarchic, or familial—does not like ecstasies, nor god-crazed men, nor even love at first sight.

And ego orgasm, nestled in the slightest of syncopes, throws the world into a panic.

It goes further. Look at the West. According to Michel de Certeau again, the mystics of the sixteenth and seventeenth centuries come from social classes that were impoverished by the wars or by progress.[15] Saint Theresa, like John of the Cross, was a ruined hidalgo who had lost class status; many Spanish mystics were *conversos*, newly converted to Christianity by force, ruined and hunted down, compelled to hide their past. And even Jansenist spirituality is explained by the social origins of its membership, *noblesse de robe* stripped of their prerogatives. This is also true in Germany in the seventeenth century. And it is also true, in the East, of Ramakrishna, Brahman son of a Brahman, but extremely poor.

The ancient past comes back, raging, to attack the present. Through his ecstasies the mystic leaps beyond social distinctions, crosses them with a bound, annihilating them. The fallen nobleman becomes a new hero; the former Jew, converted, invents a new form of Christianity, and in doing so changes the face of his new community. The way of syncope struggles against the religious hierarchy and wins: new orders are founded. And the social order often represses these rebellions of the sublime: syncope always opens up the way to the stake—the phoenix's pyre as well as that of the Inquisition.

That is what awaits the lovers at the bend in the road. Tristan, the bounding Tristan of the medieval novel, crosses several impassable barriers by loving Iseut: kinship, royalty. He was the nephew, he becomes the lover: it is a transgression. He is almost burned at the stake: it is the same logic. The natural and magical rosebush that rises out of his grave to connect it to that of the dead queen tells the truth about the lovers' mystical transgression: erotic rebellion makes the past return to the present, or again, places nature above culture. One could just as well speak of "super-natural" to refer to this transgression of human order.

Let us be attentive. For if it is true that the mystic is always a dissident in the West, then a renewed fervor in the impoverished classes is inevitable in the recently democratized countries of the East. We should see new saints rise up, like Innocent, the false czar Dimitri, martyrs raised from the dead; we should see a rebirth of the supernatural, of the ecstatic, and of changes in sects. The great American democracy has accustomed us to understanding that its other side produced charismatic preachers, witch-hunters, god-crazed men: these syncopes of the social order coincide with disguised rebellions. After a long period of dictatorial order, the syncopes are more rebellious and more violent. Transgression is not an innocent gesture.

When he began to understand the nature of the unconscious, Freud said the same thing. He compared the areas abandoned by memory to "*fueros*":[16] these are areas in Spain where the ancient customary order endures, passed down through history without being affected by it. The *fueros* function in the midst of another order, like a forgotten after-image . . . Then suddenly, violently, "that" returns; the repression yields, the breach is opened, time is suspended, as if it were coagulating physically in a material symptom. The rules of everyday logic rupture, chronology blurs; the past is there in its customary presence and reappears, intact but unrecognizable. Freud was fascinated by these balls of time—time frozen in suffering, knotted flesh. He observed the paralyzed arm, the pimple on the nose, the obsessive gesture; he listened to the cough, and recognized in the paralysis, the swelling, or the choking the pressure of the age-old, surging through the body and forgetful of the order of the world. When did the rupture occur? We do not know; the symptom is always already there. And the genesis of syncope works unseen.

"The world is too complicated; it causes too much deception and suffering; it demands actions that are too enormous, too costly."[17]

Who is speaking here? It is Pierre Janet, the French psychiatrist, faithfully reconstructing his patients' nostalgic refrain.

Here we are on the brink of the twentieth century, in an era when women no longer have the right to be in ecstasy. From this point on they are "delirious women" with a mystic bent. Lovingly, patiently, as honestly as possible, Pierre Janet, hostile to Freud but seduced all the same, follows the path of syncopes. Along with him, we will discover that syncope, starting from the end of the nineteenth century, takes on an air of guilt. It moves into the world that Janet himself calls *psychasthenia*.[18] *Psychasthenia: weakness of the mind.* Morally forbidden—even politically.

The "poor women" Janet was concerned with were often ecstatics, like Madeleine, a beautiful mystic inmate whom we have already met along the way. And the psychiatrist tracks down in their behavior the most absurd, the most Western sign, the one that turns him most sharply away from the values of the East: *the capacity for action.*

Evidently, the action of ecstatics does not obey the criteria of the observer who scrutinizes them according to a properly acting and properly thinking normalcy. Slightly envious, nonetheless: a close reading of Pierre Janet's major book, *De l'Angoisse a l'extase* (*From agony to ecstasy*), convinces us that the psychiatrist often feels frustrated not to be taking part in this extravagant joy that he calls "elation," and that Winnicott calls ego orgasm.

Everything begins, however, with a delirious activity. Janet's patients act suddenly, with lightning speed; they seem gifted with a bacchante's power, but their action is outside the norm. Everything happens as if the determination and the speed for doing were inversely proportional to normalcy. Look, for example, at Sophie, a specialist in "absurd" actions:

> She is absolutely certain that she has to eat fecal matter, and that it has to be done immediately, the moment the idea comes into her mind: "It is sacred, sacred, sacred, like one's mother's milk." She rushes to devour it and says: "No doubt it is bad and repulsive, but I have done well to make this effort, and as soon as I can I will start again." Her tremendous stubbornness lasts for weeks on end, and she resists desperately if anyone tries to stop her actions.[19]

The psychiatrist concentrates on the patient's *effort* rather than on the choice of action—or at least on what appears to him as effort: twenty years earlier, Ramakrishna did the same thing, as we have seen, and in so doing followed one of the most ancient initiatory traditions in the world. Sophie, the patient, says it clearly to her doctor; yet in so doing, she does not do enough: "she still does not do all those unheard of things that she would have to do to recover her soul." No, she must be prevented, until the poor patient topples into shame, and thus into normalcy. If she had been Indian, she would have been recognized as saintly.

An immense and useless effort, excessive fatigue: the joy of elation gives way to an effort "*that no longer has any job*." A beautiful expression: the delirious mystic is as unemployed as can be. The absolute vanity of these orgasmic joys overwhelms the psychiatrist. Certainly, they are found in dreams, and even more often in the famous "euphoria of the dying," or in the revival after a lengthy coma: to put it plainly, in physiological syncopes. Dm., a thirty-one-year-old woman, fell into a syncope while suffering from typhoid fever: "It is such a sweet sensation that it is a pity that it does not last forever." Or Byx., a sixty-three-year-old man, whose digestive problems caused him to swoon: "It is an infinite happiness." Janet explores one syncope after the other: opium, peyote, morphine, epilepsy, hysteria . . . [20] But these absurd joys remain inexplicable.

The languor that follows the fatigue is suspect. When Janet classifies the nature of the "states of bliss," he sets out three factors:

> (1) an almost total suppression of all motor activity and a tendency toward immobility; (2) a rather pronounced mental activity; (3) a great feeling of joy.[21]

Only the first factor counts: the bliss, the calm, the languor, the infinite happiness of syncope are guilty of *immobility*.

The ecstatic is indeed immobile. Every time the psychiatrist argues with Madeleine, she makes a big effort to understand and then boom! off she goes into ecstasy:

> All of a sudden I seem to be floating through the air, and I experience a indescribable well-being; it is so easy to breathe, movements that just a moment ago were so difficult no longer tire me [Janet's commentary: "In fact, they are no longer being done."] and nothing can disturb my happiness anymore.[22]

The female saints recognized by the Church were immobile, just like the mad inmates or the witches hallucinating broomsticks on which they could fly away. Ramakrishna, suddenly frozen upright, was immobile; the Brahman mumbling to the south of the altar, and thereby guaranteeing the appearance of the sun and the construction of the world, was immobile. Descartes, the philosopher shut up in his room, was immobile, as are lovers transfixed with happiness, who make no other move apart from the gaze they direct at each other.

The sleeper Laetitia, who literally staggers Pierre Janet, is immobile. She begins with symptoms that the psychiatrist, in his language, calls "morose inaction"; today one would call them mood disorders, or depression. Then she stayed "immobile, doing nothing, apparently asleep, and it was impossible to wake her."[23] Feeble, incontinent, fed intravenously, she could be woken once in a while for half an hour of "conversation," from which, like Madeleine, she escaped. What she tells the psychiatrist in her waking moments sends "reality" back to the *oubliettes*[24] from which she has decided not to remove it:

> Ask Mother whether I really did it or whether I dreamed it. . . . I myself know absolutely nothing about it, and I don't care. . . . I find nothing real in the past, nor in the present. . . . I have no awareness of ever having lived, I have no past, and if I ever return to life I will be a big baby who has just been born at age twenty-three.

Faced with the astonishing stubbornness of the great sleeper, Janet observes a "sleep delirium"[25] that leaves him, as it must, powerless. It is a violent refusal; it asserts the predominance of syncope over action, and inverts the order of motility.

Even more scandalous is Agatha, who is affected by a "laziness delirium." When she plays the piano, she only plays the left-hand page; when she translates from English to French, she puts the French word where she is supposed to but stubbornly refuses to finish the sentence; she makes no movement that is not expressly demanded of her. She opens her mouth but refuses to put the spoonful of food in it. But Janet notices that one day, as she is being taken to Mass, she is muttering: "They want me to eat by myself, but no! I will not eat by myself, I promise you, my God, I promise." And Janet concludes: "It is not only lazy behavior, it is a system of laziness, a delirium of laziness."[26]

This is still the same style of syncope: *to suspend*—time, human activity, the functioning and the order of the world. To refuse, but by pushing assent to its extreme: the mouth does not refuse the food, it is the gesture that is suspended. It is not sleep that is chosen, but the forgetting of the universe. In the East, this choice still exists; in the West, from this time on, it is ridden with guilt.

The inventor of psychasthenia knows this. He asserted that there was no difference between the ecstasies of his patients and those of the great saints:

> I am sure that Madeleine will remain a pseudo-ecstatic, because she will never receive a certain official imprimatur. These conversations that would have had some importance in the Middle Ages no longer mean anything today. . . . I would even say, at the risk of causing scandal, that the description of Madeleine's symptoms seems to me more exact, within the limit of possible error, than the descriptions based on the ancient writings of traditional mystics.[27]

One can see that Pierre Janet is split between medical science and rebellion: if he were not a psychiatrist, if he could guarantee the status of sainthood for his delirious women, they would live much better! Their ecstasies would be public and revered, their suffering would be rewarded by the Church, and he would not be forced to subject the "poor women" to the constant treatment of doubt and verification. Putting magnifying glasses on Madeleine's feet to observe the formation of stigmata, checking the pulse, the circulation, questioning, weakening the delirium—he has done all that. He has the impassioned lack of belief of someone who confusedly perceives that the value system that requires him to do this overlooks an essential rebellion.

So his vocabulary moralizes. The delirious women are affected by a *shrinking* of the mind; their consciousness operates without any logic . . . and especially, above all, the delirious women are *triumphant*.

This annoys Janet: "Under the normal conditions of real life, the feeling of freedom arises when there is a feeling of personal action, along with a feeling of effort and of success."[28] This is clear, it is modern: *action, effort, reward.* Those blissful people are not making an effort anymore, but they continue to triumph . . . how unfair! A decline of belief in life, he says. A premature triumph. Wasting of strength. No word is strong enough to discredit the ego orgasm that the patients attain so easily, that they seem to have within the range of consciousness while the "ordinary person" has to labor to attain freedom.

A lazy freedom, that is ego orgasm, that is syncope in its moral truth. One must suffer? That does not matter. Another of Janet's patients, to whom he gives the springlike name of Flore, has a genius's stroke of inspiration. "Black" is the moment of distress, "champagne" that of exultation. The effect of syncope is to move from "black" to "champagne"; it begins in blackness and continues in sparkling bubbles that never stop rising. Kierkegaard compares Mozart's character Don Giovanni—the last incarnation of "spontaneous eroticism"—to champagne; like Flore, Kierkegaard moves ceaselessly from the "blackness" of anguish to the "champagne" of seduction.[29] Must one move through "black" to reach "champagne"? That is nothing. Madeleine successively confronts tortures, temptations, terrible "dry spells" before attaining, in a regular cycle, "consolation." These are lost paths, forgotten initiations, buried memories that linger, "fueros," ancient rules that begin by breaking out and end in orgasms of consciousness. In the East, that path has evidently not yet been forgotten. Janet says:

> We have to make an effort to understand that joy does not have the privilege of being always reasonable and correct: there are false joys and pathological ones, and a person does not necessarily have a superior intelligence just because he imagines he understands everything.

But anyone who classifies joy, corrects orgasm, has to "make an effort." The seduction of syncope is not far off: one never knows . . .

Indeed, one never knows. Men of letters often take this path. Janet mentions a book by Leon Chestov on Dostoyevsky and Tolstoy, *Révélations de la mort* (Revelations of death). And there is no doubt that Dostoyevsky, as a connoisseur of the great happiness of the epileptic aura, does not spare sound thinking in *Notes from Underground:*

> The man of character, the man of action, is, in most cases, of limited intelligence. This is my conviction at the age of forty. . . . If only my doing nothing were due to laziness! How I'd respect myself then! . . . And so, in the end, ladies and gentlemen, it's best to do nothing at all! Conscious inertia is the best! A toast to my hole under the floor![30]

Those rebellions—of Pierre Janet's delirious women and of Dostoyevsky—are still current. If *mediocrity* is the characteristic of the man of action, then the society we live in today is deeply, firmly situated under the sign of this mediocrity; it leaves no room for syncope to break out, it acts and wants everyone to act. For rebellion, it maintains the institution of psychoanalysis, enclosed in its function of allowing talk, allowing movement; it remains powerless faced with drug-addicted youth who thumb their nose at it and, like Flore, prefer to move quickly from "black" to "champagne," without growing old.

For syncope is youth. Ego orgasm testifies to the subject's capacity to escape from the world. It is a game, a child's game like those Winnicott observed, which allows itself to manipulate the jigsaw puzzle of reality by exchanging roles or sexes, moving from one heart to the next.

Or rather, moving from doing to being. If we go back to Winnicott's axioms, the desires of Madeleine, Laetitia, Flore, and Agathe are clear: they are in being and refuse to budge from it. Acting—the normal law of the human race—does not suit them; they are completely immersed in the pure female element. The interior girl has overflowed into the social identity of the young girl, of the woman, of the spinster: she remains, immobile in her inherent strength, the eternal young girl on whom these women of the twentieth century have forever settled. No psychiatrist will ever be able to detach them from it: they are inorganic, statues from which only the tears of ecstasy slip out.

A vacation of the soul, a gift of time: ego orgasm deserves a detour through syncope, taken by abandoning for a lightning moment men's law of doing.

Only after this should one *do*. Syncope's usefulness is understood: it lightens this burden.

Dancing: "Virginity, but for the Waltz"

If there were one vanity of action in the world to choose from, and if the practitioners of syncope often choose immobility, it happens that from time to time they prefer dancing, the height of motion. Dancing contains the same vanity, and yet it is nothing but action. It is so engulfed in action that it goes beyond the simple objectives of normality. Beyond the watershed, completely opposed to ecstatic immobility, dancing is the other way to reach the ego orgasm.

"The Vain Dancers" is the title of a poem by Paul Valéry. Vain, they "who are light as flowers came." Valéry, elsewhere, uses a striking metaphor to philosophize about the dance:

> a state of nothing but action, a permanence that is created and consolidated in the middle of an incessant production of work, comparable to the vibrating stasis of a bumblebee or of a sphinx-moth before the calyx of the flowers that it is exploring; the insect remains almost immobile, powered by a motivating force, and held up by the incredibly rapid beating of its wings.[31]

It is easy to recognize the vain work of syncope: the pure energy of the mystic en route to ecstasy, a vanished dream of the woman who is made pregnant by an angel, it is a power that moves while immobile. That is not nothing; it is even the opposite of nothing. It is a simulation of everything: there is no dance that does not come close to the mimetic reproduction of the sky, of the universe, the stars, and the neutrinos. Jean Cocteau compared it to the dance of the planets that David mimed in front of the Ark of the Covenant; this diffuse impression is expressed by evoking the dancers' lightness, their passing beyond weightiness—that is their main quality.

What they themselves say today is always strikingly philosophical. There has been a vigorous revival of new dance in France over the last decade; I do not know if sufficient attention has been paid to the web of words with which choreographers have surrounded their creative work. In unison, they say over and over again that they want to express what cannot be expressed except through dancing; but when it is a question of articulating what that is, we have seen that they give deliberately negative definitions. Above all, we do not want to define, they say; our purpose is not this, nor that, nor yet the reproduction of the world, nor its destruction, nor theater, nor dance, nor words, nor music. They are genuine spontaneous mystics who unconsciously use the processes of Eastern metaphysics, the same ones that the great Indian philosopher Sankara called the "*neti, neti*": the neither . . . nor. They intermingle figures of onomatopoeia, of songs, of words, and of legends; they shatter models, strain the conventions of traditional Western representation as well as those of Asia, which they use as inspiration without neglecting to break them. Jean-Claude Gallotta, for example, invents remarkable true mythologies, depicting true-false legendary heroes, spinning hordes of dancers around an imaginary tribal fire; Daniel Larrieu dances underwater, while philosophizing interminably on his dances' extreme slowness; and I recall having heard a very young choreographer from the company *Roc in Lichen* explaining in disjointed words why she had come up with the idea of having her dancers dance along a wall, vertically: there is no longer any other way to reach the sky, she said, there is no longer any other way to rejoin something like a god. So from now on one can dance by climbing a wall; a metaphor—climbing the walls—is suddenly made literal.

Elisabeth Petit, a Frenchwoman, is a dancer of Bharat-Natyam, the most classical of the five great dances of India. Like most Indian dances, Bharat-Natyam springs from the temples, and is danced in front of the statues of the gods; it is often said that the holy dancers, the Devadasi, served as prostitutes; they were without the shadow of a doubt maintained, like up-and-coming ballerinas in our country, by rich patrons. One sign will not deceive us: they were not allowed to cut their hair, nor to wash it. The proximity of this sacred filth indicates the origin of this dance: it is the same for all the world's dances. The style is diabolically precise, sometimes mimed, sometimes tremendously abstract, punctuated by pure onomatopoeia; the dancer bends and contorts herself, then suddenly, at the tip of the folded limb, there is the gesture, there is the god, caught by the lightning of the dance. A moment of repose passes. Remember the spanking that Winnicott spoke of: an easily excited energy, stimulated; an excessive and unruly game, then suddenly, the spanking, the orgasm, the calm.

She speaks: "What changes when I dance is the perception of time." (She is only repeating what every dancer in the world says.) She says: "Time is slow, drawn out as when one makes love. It is like eating a mango." She says of the abstract phase of Bharat-Natyam: "It is joy, escaping from consciousness. One day, I simply had 'the experience,' a day when my body did not really want to. And yet on that day, I experienced Shiva; I was also a lion with Vishnu, and a tortoise; I was an animal and a god." (This is a young Frenchwoman, very sensible, very up-to-date, not at all affected by the hippie trope.) She continues: "Something came to me that day. I told myself that it was the dance; but it was nothing other than myself." One could not find a better way to express primary narcissism in its creative purity: an arrival of the self at the precise moment when it vanishes. And she says finally: "Dancing is the opposite of modernity; it is the opposite of speed and of virtuosity."[32]

The source of today's reinvigorated dance is doubtless the rejection of the fast pace of modernity. The dancers could adopt this fast pace if they wanted to; but dance has made the choice to reject a world that moves too fast. People who are mad about rock rush ahead, and topple, overwhelmed, into what they reject: quick, too quick; it has to end. Dancers, on the other hand, slow down the pace of life; these are strategies for applying the brakes. And since the liberal world, this world made of gains and losses, loses its head, they choose pure action, which must in its essence be futile. Valéry again: "The person who is dancing closes herself off in some way in a Duration that she herself produces, a Duration made up only of present energy, made up only of what cannot endure."[33] It is the perfect representation of impermanence, the empty heart of Buddhism. Immobility in motion, a controlled instability. Metastabilized equilibrium.

Another dancer, Françoise Adret, speaking of the syncope in dance, said without hesitating for a second: "It is like the salt in food. It is the pebble in your shoe, the obstacle."[34] If, within the moral norms that are imposed on us, it is a matter above all of getting over obstacles and of overcoming resistance, dance on the contrary glorifies and sublimates the obstacle. Spices—little obstacles ground into powder—do the same: they glorify what stings, chokes, burns, attacks, the better to savor: a dish, life. Spices, dancers, mystics, and the East resist history; syncope is their secret weapon, the suspension of time is their only tactic. This is a new kind of battle.

Or rather not. As we will see, the genre is not new; it is the appearance in the West of a perceptible and obvious refusal that is being expressed by contemporary French dancers. One should pay attention to this wave in dance: every time one wave appears, history also expresses itself in a muffled way. There have been epidemics of the strange disease called chorea, more commonly called St. Vitus's dance; there have also been, without going as far as pathology, frenzies of dancing at particular moments and particular places in history.

"Morbid vertigo," "contagious frenzy," "collective epilepsy" are the terms that ethnologists and psychologists found in the 1930s when they were confronted with the already distant testimony of citizen Mercier. It was just after the Terror, during the Directory. Mercier was indignant:

> They are dancing at the Carmelite monastery where the beheadings took place; they are dancing at the Jesuit novitiate; they are dancing in the Carmelite convent in the Marais; they are dancing at the Saint-Sulpice seminary; they are dancing in three ruined churches in my neighborhood, and on all the tombstones that have not been stolen yet: the names of the dead are under the feet of dancers who do not notice them and who forget that it is sepulchers they are trampling. . . . They dance, this sovereign mob, they dance every day. . . . Who, amid all this dancing, would believe that war is pressing on all our borders, on the banks of the Rhine, of the Sambre, of the Meuse, beyond the mountains, and on the sea?[35]

Of course, citizen! Exactly, war; exactly, cemeteries, sepulchers. What better act of sovereignty, what more brilliant dismantling than dancing, after the guillotine? What act could be more futile? It is only life; it approves of itself and refuses the past, the future, reality. Morbid, epileptic, contagious; this is what the era's pundits said about the Jazz Age between 1914 and 1940; they were not much more clear-minded than citizen Mercier. So people dance during periods of great bloodshed. Council of Exeter, 1287: prohibition on dancing in cemeteries; Wurzburg, 1298; Bayeux, Basel, 1435; Soissons, 1456; Narbonne, 1551; Melun, 1579; Cahors, 1604: prohibitions on hoofing, banqueting, and feasting in the cemeteries. Lyon, 1566: "Priests are prohibited, under pain of excommunication, from allowing dances, bacchanals, and other insolences in churches and cemeteries."[36]

With or without the clergy's prohibition, dance is still sacrilegious. Or rather, mystical; struggling against institutions (often, by the way, the institutions of dance itself), tuned into the axis of death. An absolute, vast, and radical denial of death; every dance takes part in the *danse macabre* that merrily leaped over the abyss of the Black Death, and celebrated with intoxication the deep mourning that Europe already had to bear.

In India, where one often has the feeling that everything is explicit, nothing about this matter is hidden. The god of the dance could only be Shiva—called Nataraja, master of the dancers, for this occasion. Remember: before becoming the glittering and baroque god of the Hindu pantheon, he was the god of the mountains, a kind of Dionysus but even more savage, if that is possible. There he is in his representation as a dancer; in his left ear, a pendant earring of a woman, in his right, a pendant of a man. One hand holds a little drum, another is raised, palm erect. Indian gods are overendowed with hands and arms: the third holds a flame, the fourth points to a dead monster on the ground. The god is surrounded with a halo of sparks that circle around him. In his hair are hidden a coiled cobra, the ascetic skull, and the little head of the goddess Ganga, the river, who has foolishly been made prisoner there while trying to flood the earth. A garland of black currant crowns him, as well as a crescent moon. The hands are inverted, the flame spins, death is tucked into the hollow of his hair, the serpent of sexual energy is dozing there, and the god dances the crossing, the crossing from death to life. He dances *shakti*, energy, he dances time, he is beyond neuter itself. And naturally he dances death, good master that he is.

No one will be surprised to see him choose the cremation grounds for dancing; one of his official titles describes him as "Dancer of the burning grounds." Devout Bengalis address to Kali the Dark, his female embodiment, a prayer that would defend the parish priests:

> Because Thou lovest the Burning-ground,
> I have made a Burning-ground of my heart—
> That Thou, Dark One, haunter of the Burning-ground,
> Mayest dance Thy eternal dance.
> Nought else is within my heart, O Mother:
> Day and night blazes the funeral pyre:
> The ashes of the dead, strewn all about,
> I have preserved against thy coming. . . . [37]

Happy death, confronted and averted.

Death won over, freshly beribboned, fêted like a fiancée. If the Indian master of the dance constitutes the most perfect expression of danced orgasms, the costumes of the whirling dervishes are like simulations of gravestones; the circle and the cycle laid out by the whirling dancers dance the same destruction. I will resolutely dance on your graves: that is the dancers' credo.

The Chevalier de Ségur's wonderful phrase echoes this faintly; he said it about an unknown damsel he had glimpsed at a ball: "She is still a virgin, were it not for the waltz."[38]

16

Syncope's Strategies: The Creative Act and the Un-Governing of the World

Weakening, shrinking, exhaustion . . . Pierre Janet saw neurasthenia as an impediment to life; since his job was to bring his patients back through the doors of life into society, he felt obliged to help them leave behind the enchanted world of their syncopes.

He tenderly described the symptoms of Martial, "a young man who was neuropathic, timid, scrupulous, subject to depression."[1] At age nineteen Martial became illuminated by a sparkling glory, and began to write an immense poem, tirelessly and enthusiastically. But once the work was published, the light that he carried within him suddenly went out; people did not turn around and stare at him as he thought they would. A lengthy depression ensued. Martial continued to write works made up of "combinations that were quite creative, ideas from a extra-human world," wrote Janet. The now-patient held on to the memory of his luminescence and of "the incredible sparkle that was mine." Martial had known glory, it still was his; he was sure he'd made a powerful contribution to literature.

Martial was right. His real name glows with a solar glory that will shine forever; Martial's name was Raymond Roussel. Pierre Janet understood the magnitude of this "secular ecstasy," but the dictates of his profession prevented him from taking it seriously. "As it is not necessary for me to discuss the true objectivity of ideas and feelings whose psychological mechanisms I analyze, as I do not have to try to determine whether or not Madeleine was indeed transformed into God . . . I am able to understand the word 'delirium' in the sense of a collection of beliefs accompanied by complete certitude, in opposition to the outward signs that determine the beliefs of most human beings. Ecstasy then boils down to an attack of optimistic and static religious delirium,"[2] he wrote at the end of his observation of Martial. Like other patients, Raymond Roussel also will have suffered a weakening and shrinking of consciousness.

In immobility, in indifference to a world that allowed him to speak of a "shrinking" of consciousness, Janet wasn't wrong. That was in fact the spectacle presented by the ailing writer. But the more intelligent psychoanalysts have understood that weakness must be reversed to its opposite. Anton Ehrenzweig has devoted a masterwork, *The Hidden Order of Art*,[3] to the free flow of creative thought. The phenomena he describes seem to be the same from the outside, but the conclusions he makes are exactly the opposite: *there can be no creative act without an expansion of the field of consciousness*.

Ehrenzweig goes over to the other side of the mirror; he doesn't stop at objective fact. He does not employ criteria of daily normalcy, nor does he take into consideration the capacity for adaptation to life. It is quite the opposite: the creative process is described as a temporary, obligatory psychosis. That the artist is considered to be "crazy" is not an accident: it is a necessity. Usually, the author is only passing through this state, but sometimes does remain there. But the artist's reality demands crossing through an essential syncope, a veritable mental collapse, resulting in new work. In fact, from this chaos only something new can emerge. This eclipse that fractures consciousness is the very prerequisite for the creative act.

Syncope is resistance, rebellion, rejection of the world and dissolution of the subject; we have explored all the avenues. But we must go further in order to understand why no creation is possible without the syncope of the subject. From then on signs—clearly apparent—of a remarkable return of the past in the present begin to change meaning and appearance.

How does one widen the edges of consciousness? By fragmenting the attention span. Something begins to leave the precision of the wakened state, and suddenly goes astray. Artists such as Paul Klee acknowledge this passage into the void that induces them to suddenly abandon normal perception. Klee comes very close to this moment, which Bataille called "sovereign," of attention to music: he calls it "multidimensional" or "polyphonic" attention. Focus has disappeared; limits are abolished. Ehrenzweig speaks of an unconscious "scanning": the term "scanning" comes from the verb "to scan," which first meant scanning lines in poetry, or scanning a measure, and later, to sweep. The act of dissolution that begins creative perception borrows from both meanings: it is both an incessant sweeping and the pulsating of duration.

This activity of a kind that is not far from criteria generally classified as "passive" seems empty; if perception is undifferentiated, however, it participates ideally in the little perceptions dear to the philosopher Leibniz. A detail is not perceived consciously as such, but is part of an overflowing ensemble in which each of the elements interacts with the whole. The artist finds himself in a position comparable to that of the hero of the *Theodicy*, the priest Theodore whom we see moving ceaselessly from discomposed but perfect perceptions to brutal, ecstatic syncope. The act of unconscious "scanning" is situated at the frontier of disorder; an imperceptible order, uncontrollable and uncontrolled, is created both gently and with great violence. Chaos and order equally menace the artist's perception.

In the eyes of societies that make a wholesale condemnation of depression, rapture, ecstasy, and laziness, the creative act is part of psychasthenia. Weakness, malediction, fragility, drugs, and passing to the act form the long cavalcade of complaints that encompass the artist's mythology: in the best cases, a circle of affectionate followers surrounds the artist, who is pushed a little further along the road toward syncope. Nevertheless, the artist is still the object of veneration; the fear of that veneration remains one of the very ways by which syncope regains the dignity that in fact it never lost. One never knows . . . From this pot of roses that smells of alcohol to drug-induced sweats or overt madness, perhaps a caution will be born that is today as yet unknown. Our society, which is bent on healing all ills, even the pangs of love when they convert into depression, has burned its witches and formed a tabula rasa of its potential shamans. All that is left are artists and their syncopes; all that is left is a hint of internal dissidence that it would be wise to avoid domesticating. The Church no longer creates saints, but the body of society still engenders resisters; in Mittel Europa they have successfully played their role as rebels and innovators; and if they become presidents of newfound democracies, if so many artists are answering the call of politics, it is undoubtedly because their *capacity for detachment* is indistinctly perceived. It would be wise not to let them fall into the trap of reality, not to abandon them to the syncopated between-the-two that, if they are true creators, will catch up with them wherever they find themselves.

Ehrenzweig speaks of the creative act the way we speak of an unusual person: the individual who will later be designated by the name of artist has been effaced. The creative process can be broken down into three phases, to which Ehrenzweig assigns clinical categories that are not much better than those of Janet; in fact, all clinical labeling by category gives rise to uneasy misinterpretation, systems of vocabulary being as arbitrary and transitional as they are. Let us consider them provisionally. The first stage is called "schizoid": these are the premises of disorder, the appearance of diverse elements, "accidental, fragmented, undesirable and persecutory." If we think of the *Nevermore* that haunted Edgar Allan Poe like a second-rate refrain, we will have an idea of the first effects of the creative act. There is something resembling the aura of epileptics in this: "it" is recognizable, "it" is, however, unknown, "it" never happens, and "it" is always incongruous. Premonition, obsession, idea, fantasy, air, breath, the wings of an angel going by: the premises of the creative act are contrary to habit, even that of thought. It is the pebble on the road spoken of by the dancer; it is the bad object, still unrecognizable, shapeless and slimy, a nightmarish figure. Tranquillity gives way; disintegration begins.

The second phase begins, without intimating, to construct. Without intimating: the action is as yet invisible, its genesis is produced slyly, and it begins to function when the mind becomes blank and the unconscious begins its "scanning" process. Ehrenzweig calls this syncopated, rich moment "dedifferentiation";[4] it is a rather unpleasant word, but it goes beyond the simple term "indifference," which although similar has the opposite meaning. Indifference: a key word, I should venture. The artist, in fact, like the ecstatic or fainting subject, seems indifferent to the world: that is to say, "unfeeling." And it is true, because artists are no longer a part of the world's routine; they are outsiders, between-the-two, inaccessible, invulnerable to daily concerns. In the midst of the continuing order of things, the artist is a *casualty of time*. And we must return again to Leibniz, who does not admit indifference, never, under any circumstances; there are no two things alike in nature, and indifference is but an illusion of our numbed senses. This is the artist's mindset: indifferent to the eyes of the world, but highly sensitive to all differences in his interior world that gives rise to a new apparition. The "dedifferentiation" described by Ehrenzweig refers to an eradication of limits between the subject and the universe: exactly like the moment of ecstasy described by the mystics.

Ehrenzweig calls it the "manic-oceanic" period.

Recall Virginia Woolf being swallowed up by the waves:

> I will pick flowers; I will bind flowers in one garland and clasp them and present them—Oh! to whom? There is a check in the flow of my being; a deep stream presses on some obstacle; it jerks; it tugs; some knot in the center resists. Oh, this is pain, this is anguish! I faint, I fail. Now my body thaws; I am unsealed, I am incandescent. Now the stream pours in a deep tide fertilizing, opening the shut, forcing the tight-folded flooding free. To whom shall I give all that now flows through me, from my warm, my porous body. I will gather my flowers and present them—Oh! to whom?[5]

Here is the oceanic essence, and the violent drive of the sea; the body is light and permeable, the orifices are open. And here is the manic: gathering flowers, weaving them into garlands, hugging them, and giving them away. Only the despondent search that finds no one to whom the flowers may be given signals the disappearance of reality. Perhaps there still exists someone to whom the garland may be given; perhaps. The mysterious break that held back the interior ocean is about to give way: it gives way. To whom, indeed, could this poet give her flowers?

> Creative differentiation tends towards a "manic" oceanic limit where all differentiation ceases. The inside and outside world begin to merge and even the differentiation between ego and superego becomes attenuated. In this "manic" stage all accidents seem to come right; all fragmentation is resolved.[6]

Let us go beyond the insufferable jargon of psychoanalysis and try to decipher it. We have seen the oceanic in the exaltation of the Bengali Ramakrishna. For Ehrenzweig, it is the same blinding wave that swallows up the subject giving way to an Indian-style disintegration. The "manic," however, totally belongs to the artist. In the terms of psychiatric classification, mania is defined as a state of animated excitement, combined with obsession and hyperactivity. But we should not forget that the very word "mania" comes from ancient Greek, and refers to the madness that is always infused by a god, is always divine possession. The artist's subjectivity has "melted" under the invisible pressure of oceanic waves; it is still at work, however, like an active and invisible ant, unconsciously working away at the very mass of chaos. "It" begins by a stone on the road, "it" continues as a blinding tempest. But the Subject, in the classical Western sense, is not always in attendance.

It is during the third stage that it reappears. Consciousness returns to the artist; and with it the imperfection of the work of art, the accidental, and the dreadful portion of the chaos from which the new work was born. It is a depressive phase, to which the term self-criticism does not apply, for the level of rejection of what has been created is much more intense. Ehrenzweig puts it aptly: "Part of the creative capacity is the strength to resist an almost anal disgust that would make us sweep the whole mess into the wastepaper basket."[7] But the harm—or the good—has been done; *the new work is there, born of syncope*. The artist's return to self resembles the postorgasmic state, with the customary sadness that a well-known proverb associates with the animal kingdom—*post coitum animal triste*; there is a dejection and a lucidity of vision, but there is also calm and repose.

This is when the mystics say: God has departed, God has abandoned me. Lovers feel similarly: they miss the other. The young girl has gone beyond the abyss, no longer is there the wonderment of syncope aside from fatigue, hardly the memory of a memory, the shadow of a shadow. *For the creator alone*, the *remainder* of syncope is present before his eyes, unfinished but possible. Then the cycle begins anew, analogous to that of drug addiction; the artist falls into the schizoid phase again, then sinks into the agitated ocean of the busied ant, finally returning to the self disheartened. The West has always called artistic dejection, oceanic and manic, "inspiration."

But the artist stays within view of his work. It seems that there is always one too many: either the work or the artist. If the work is not thrown in the garbage, which is possible, often the artist totally destroys himself.

Later in his argument, Ehrenzweig adds a strange sequence that he aggressively applies to society, and in particular to the Jewish people, affected, so he believes, with an "anal phantasy of voluntarily casting oneself out."[8]

I will leave to Ehrenzweig the responsibility for his analysis of the Jewish question, hastily and carelessly thought out. The notion of a voluntary casting out, however, is indeed part of the syncope game. The artist is a "renouncer."

It is something from which the "syncope-people" that we have encountered along the way cannot escape. Those who practice inspiration as a profession, be they artists, mystics, prophets, philosophers, or dancers on a crowded dance floor, go back and forth between the world of the banal and that of the extraordinary. By entering the blessed syncope of supreme moments, by temporarily losing the secured identity that constitutes them as a single member of the social body, they escape its confines: they are free, with an unreal and extraordinary sense of emancipation. Pierre Janet, as we have seen, had a difficult time accepting the freedom of his patients, which was obtained effortlessly and without a sense of obligation to anyone. When they "return" to themselves, these "syncope-people" lose their angels' wings. It is indeed a form of exile, which will be eternal, interspliced with excursions between the orgasmic state and the banal, between the absence and presence of the Subject. Their vision of the world is inverted: *it is the Subject that is left over*, and who throws himself onto the road, into intoxication, into creation, into a passionate love affair, or into the trash.

Or, like Virginia Woolf, into the very real waters of a river.

When they depart onto the roads of exile, human beings suffer the nostalgia of their lost country. It is this very experience that will make them become, in a foreign land, sort of artists of daily life. The foreigner naturally lives his exile as a misfortune; he is often persecuted. But this displacement, which little by little disappears in the new country, provides a particular strength, an energy that belongs only to him; sometimes he is listened to as a purveyor of the truth. If he remains completely in the world that has been left behind, and if he continues to affirm his distinct origins by jealously preserving them, he will remain in the equivalent of the "schizoid" stage alluded to by Ehrenzweig; if he takes root immediately in the new country, the same phenomenon will occur. But if he is truly the stranger, he will experience moments of disintegration, agitation, devastation, and disgust in which the essence of the creative act can be discerned. It will then be possible, like the storyteller who told Socrates the tale of the old people who did not grow older, to tell stories from elsewhere that are destined, like Virginia Woolf's garlands, to everyone, to no one, to ourselves.

The same is true for the major events that break up our lives; the first of these is mourning, the experience of loss. No need to be "inspired" in order to experience its effects; they are comparable to the effects of creation and give way to a new era, for better or for worse. Each of us goes through the experience of mourning, which underscores certain moments of our lives; each of us can recognize a schizoid period—death is an unforeseen accident, a stone on the road, fragmentary and obsessional as well as a persecutor; each of us can identify at the beginning of mourning the second period of the act of creation—a painful blend of diffuse suffering and inexplicable euphoria, a lightheartedness alien to a world entirely molded by grief, a dispossession of reality. Finally, everyone knows that the third stage will be the hardest: the brusque return to reality—the funeral, and all that ensues on a day-to-day basis—the slow reconstruction in which the dead person who has been lost is interiorized, and enters a hiding place from which he can no longer trouble the mourner.

The Tantric philosopher Abhivanagupta, when enumerating the moments that must be seized to attain the ecstatic between-the-two, does not neglect mourning: "We tell ourselves: 'They will never return,' and such is the reality of the suffering, a certain astonishment where one is in the empire of despair."[9] And just as the Tantric practitioner must yield to jouissance when it arises, he must not resist pain but must abandon himself to it, in order to seize the moment at which suffering and astonishment are fused into another logic. It is not surprising subsequently to find instructions of a "masochistic" type that mystics know by heart: "After having pierced some part of one's body with some sharp instrument or other, if one's mind is able to concentrate on this particular point, a striking progression will occur."[10] Masochistic "abasement" has no other source but this: to force an outcome.

Exile, pain, migration. Jewish mysticism, more than any other, has refined its myths over the centuries. The lost being, country, ground, city, or earth becomes the feminine principle that is in God, the Sekina.[11] At once the productive receptacle, the community of the faithful, and the road open to return, the Sekina is described by kabbalists as a radiating light, a rose circled by thorns, the source of joy and of destruction: here astonishment merges with suffering, a blend that is not contradictory or illogical, a result of exile. Mother, spouse, sometimes daughter, Zion and Jerusalem, the Sekina stands alongside the "to be" with which Winnicott identified the principle of pure femininity. Because even the God of the Jews cannot escape the hold of life: the Sekina is its feminine interior, its repose, the time before and after history. And the long history of Jewish mysticism includes, at the heart of the Law and its absolute commandments, its nomadic wanderings, the whirling dances of the Hasidim, their illuminations and even the orgies of the false Sabbath's Messiah. It is not easy to leave God to himself; it is uncomfortable to situate one's self eternally in action, eternally in the being acted upon, in obedience, and without revolt.

The fields of syncope open up onto an astonishing secret activity, and an astonishing immobile energy; they make use—as we have seen—of an abundant jamboree of defiant inventions. But they have one more wager, one last bluff.

"Sovereignty is revolt," wrote Bataille. "It is not an exercise of power. True sovereignty refuses . . . "[12]

"Syncope-people" have no desire for power. They guard themselves against it obstinately, often astoundingly. These are precise strategies, as opposed to political power's use of force. Or rather, these are other means of attaining the political; specific means, finding strength within syncope itself. These people were clearly identified by Bergson; according to him, they participate in the vital impulse. The techniques used must be looked at closely: impoverishment of means, perfect intuition for staging, playing with the accidents of time. Impoverishment of means: words. Radical staging: miracles. Games with time: disappearing, reappearing, resurrection.

Luckily, one such man is enough of a contemporary for us to know almost all of his techniques. He was an Indian, but sufficiently familiar with the West to have perfected his game. He was traditional, but modern enough to know how to use the very sources of modernity that today, as in his day, are capable of starting revolutions. Through his action, he championed an energetic resistance, almost a nonaction: *nonviolence*. It is easy to recognize this man as Mahatma Gandhi.

Gandhi was not a mystic. He became angry when he was credited with ecstasies that, he said, he had never experienced. And he hated to be treated as a guru; he refused to be adored in the Indian way, with devouring gazes. His status as "syncope-person" is found elsewhere.

First of all, in his body, which he subjected to an asceticism of his own invention. From the Indian tradition, he inherited the choice of a renouncer's chastity; he has described at length the insatiable sexual excesses, always unfulfilled, that he imposed on his thirteen-year-old bride, in order to explain the difficulty he had in taking this vow. The people of India did not believe him and spread horrible rumors about him involving his sexual exploits with young girls, his nieces—walking canes and young flesh: the rumors were untrue, but these calumnies focused on the object of his renunciation. The old man indeed suffered from his chastity; an infinite and cruel task, which always had to be begun anew. As a man of truth, he never hid anything, even the erections he had when beautiful female journalists came to see him in his prison. He punished himself for them by fasting. Rumors circulated about his difficulty with chastity. Chaste, therefore, as the great mystics were, but without ecstasy. Reducing his daily intake of food to a draconian diet: a few fruits and nuts. His thinness was extreme, as if he too were burning with the ascetic fire of the yogi that he was not. And as some yogis are, he was athletic, vigorous, capable of walking for long hours, and had an incredible, calculated resistance. His calculation was of the nutritional type; his diet was established with scientific criteria. It was tradition—the ancient past—and modernity.

When he had chosen the path of sexual renunciation, he became a mother, a role he asserted with vehemence. And if he was a bad father to his oldest son, who died shortly after his illustrious father—poverty-stricken, alcoholic, and a drifter—the Mahatma was full of a universal tenderness for his numerous adopted children, the Untouchable and the poor, even adopting Madeleine, the daughter of an English admiral, with whom he traveled to London; photographs show us Gandhi flanked by his English daughter, to whom he had given an Indian identity, along with his favorite goat. Nothing about him seems paternal; by rejecting sex, he abandoned the rigor of giving orders and the epic rages he had been famous for when encountering resistance.

Ascetic, maternally feminine, he suffered from many violent symptoms: frequent dysentery, asphyxiation, fainting, disorders for which he had a single treatment: *to do nothing*. This refusal, more obvious that the refusal of sex, food, and the law of the father, often put his life in danger. He refused to take medicine; he refused outside intervention on his body. Once, only once, he agreed to be operated on for appendicitis by some English surgeons, because he was in prison and did not want to overwhelm his captors by making them responsible for his death.

Against illness and English power, Gandhi used the same weapon: fasting. Arrest. The suspension of the act of nourishment.

And what fasting! It was perfectly staged. When he wanted to denounce an injustice, when he wanted to put an end to fighting between communities, *he issued a press release*. From that moment, the headlines in the newspapers and on the radio were only interested in one thing: his blood pressure, his vital signs. The announcement was brief: "Gandhi has decided to fast until death." Everyone knew that the stakes were genuine. It was in South Africa that the young lawyer first became aware of the oppression exercised on the Indian community by the English and where he became conscious of the modern technique of using the press. He kept journalists informed, he offered to meet with them; he himself published newspapers. The fast until death became a ritual of mass communication; a ritual both astonishingly archaic and astonishingly modern.

To fast until death is an extreme exercise that cannot be compared to typical hunger strikes; Gandhi was old and refused all wiles; he nearly did die. But by putting his life on the line, he succeeded; the most reluctant of his adversaries were obliged to capitulate, at the foot of his deathbed—and under his vigilant eyes were obliged to sign the peace accord that he wanted.

He also fasted for pleasure, and recommended it to others. You must fast, he wrote, if you are constipated, feverish, queasy, if you have a migraine, if you have rheumatism or gout. If you are tormented or angry. If you are depressed. And most extraordinary of all: *you must fast if you are excessively happy*.[13]

To suspend the life cycle, to suppress the biological, to disengage oneself from the process, and to use it as a weapon to blame the other. Also a weapon used against the self, in order to escape. Gandhi's fasting was his main syncope.

The remainder of his choices are borrowed from Indian philosophy. Nonviolence exists in Buddhism, and even more so in the tradition of the Jain religion, which is so nonviolent that it is forbidden to kill the slightest living thing. The Jains wear a square mask of white cloth over their mouths to avoid swallowing a microbe; they sweep the ground as they walk with a small broom in order to avoid stepping on an insect. Gandhi's family was Hindu, of the merchant caste; the future Mahatma's father, however, was friendly with Jains, who had a determining influence on the young boy. From his earliest childhood, he was familiar with the philosophy of nonviolence; and his family, which was strict in its dietary prohibitions, also taught him tolerance long before he learned its necessity. Later Gandhi discovered India's violent side; it is everywhere in Hinduism; he fought as hard against the cruelty of his own people as against that of foreign occupiers. But nonviolence as a political instrument still had to be invented, for in Buddhism or Jainism it exists strictly on an individual level. We have seen his fasting; Gandhi also invented *hartals* and marches.

The hartal resembles our strike; it is a cessation of work. But it is part of a broader resistance, which Gandhi defined in the negative: *noncooperation*. In order to be free, India had to cease participation in the economic system of the empire of which it was a part: it first had to separate itself through refusal. Refusal is also a refusal of signs. Gandhi would gather together entire crowds who would undress on the spot; he lit a bonfire in which were burned India's clothes, made of cotton harvested by the empire, and which returned as cloth to its country of origin with large profits being made by merchants. Lawyers such as Nehru refused to exercise their duties, and were punished by the English justice system; dignitaries resigned. Following Gandhi's example they retired, either to ashrams or to jail. Gandhi lived in ascetic communities that can easily be seen as the Indian forest of renunciation; when he wasn't on his ashram with his children and his goats, he was in prison, an ideal retreat where, he readily admitted, he could finally detach himself from his activities and think. Gandhi, who did not give orders but inspired by his example, ignited a veritable fever of imprisonment in the hearts of his militant followers; and it is not rare, even today, to hear a "freedom fighter" evoke memories of his youth with nostalgic pride. Without having spent twelve years in prison, says one man, you can't say you've been part of a liberation struggle. Alas, says a woman, I couldn't go to prison; I fell ill . . .

As for the marches, one could think of them as practical exercises of the Middle Path in Buddhism. The march that served as the real signal of the decline of the British Empire was the object of a knowing surprise.

1931. Silent ruminations, anguish: at that time the Mahatma no longer knew what action to take against the British. But he had committed himself to action. All of India looked to him for an answer; and the Mahatma remained silent, in a schizoid phase of unconscious "scanning." Suddenly, he published a notice in his small newspaper that an action will begin in nine days. No one knew where, or why; the notice was addressed to the people of India and to the Viceroy, who was courteously informed that he would probably have to jail Gandhi again.

Nine days later, he left his retreat and took to the road with a hundred of his militant supporters. They walked for twenty-four days; finally they stopped; he was surrounded by thousands of people, at the seaside. Gandhi found the right gesture, a poor and simple gesture: he bent down and picked up a handful of salt. That was all. But militants in India understood that they had to boycott the British tax on salt; people feverishly begin to collect the salt water, from which they would obtain salt. Each would process their own Indian salt on the shore of their own ocean; the British Empire was short-circuited. A peaceful army of nonviolent militants stormed a salt factory; the Imperial

Police were waiting for them. The demonstrators, dressed in white, were unarmed, empty-handed; as they advanced, the police beat them with iron-reinforced clubs. Off to the side, a makeshift infirmary cared for the wounded and evacuated the dead. The others went off to prison to join Gandhi, who was the first person arrested. That had been the plan. The Western press, invited by Gandhi for the occasion, attested to the fact that the police beat people gathering salt at the seashore; the Empire wavered. The negotiations that would result in Indian independence would soon be under way; Gandhi was released from prison and went to visit the Viceroy in his palace in Delhi. Churchill understood immediately and disparagingly called Gandhi "a seditious Middle Temple lawyer, now posing as a fakir of a type well-known in the East, striding half-naked up the steps of the Viceregal Palace." After that, there was nothing more to be said.

Churchill had seen the nudity, the weakness, the scandal; he had seen the incongruity of the scene; an antihero, a poor man, goes to discuss independence for his country face to face. Churchill, who dreamed of Gandhi's death and who later tried to facilitate it, was a strong man. And it is possible that he later remembered the lessons of the aged Mahatma.

Lessons of weakness, they were courtly lessons, lessons of chivalry. The militants close to Gandhi often despaired: when they were about to win, when they were at the edge of victory, suddenly Gandhi would halt an action, spoiling everything. Either the movement had accidentally given way to bloodshed, or the adversary was simply in a position of weakness for reasons external to India; Gandhi could not bear to see his enemy at a disadvantage. His attitude was that of a knight: he was always prepared to fight, but stopped the battle if his opponent lost his weapons. This strange metaphor of combat chivalry is all the more surprising in that it is being used in discussing the most pacifist of heroes; these are imaginary simulacra and successful sublimations. When the first blood was drawn, Gandhi suspended the action. And he waited, with a peaceful certitude, for his own to flow in turn.

In February 1949, Gandhi had been dead for more than a year, assassinated by a Hindu extremist who disapproved of his excessive tenderness toward Muslims. Georges Bataille, reflecting on the exercise of power, wrote:

> A paradox.
>
> If one wants to govern the world, one must renounce governing: the ungoverning of the world
>
> . . . Pragmatic program:
>
> —Local unions and an umbrella union

—Extension of the principle of striking (Gandhism, noncooperation, nonviolence)

—A negative universal coalition considered as a country, something to belong to

—Related to an understanding of the limits of government.[14]

What Gandhi accomplished is nothing other than a *un-governing of the world*: to undo, untie, liberate. When Indian independence was declared in 1947, Gandhi, who had long refused to become president of the Congress Party, refused all honors, and spent his first day in liberated India in Calcutta, praying and fasting; he allowed himself one glass of fruit juice.

For the syncope-person whose struggle consisted in abstaining from food, sex, and fighting, for this man who remained silent one day a week, this new country for whom he was the birth mother was still too fraught with ethnic violence; no affiliation or fellowship, not even with India, could justify bloodshed. Not to be Indian became a virtue for him: India was a universal negative coalition considered as a country.

Nationalism and patriotism do not enter the mindset of this type of person; spontaneously holding back from life, on the verge of holding back from death, they are spontaneously syncretic, spontaneously without a country. Gandhi walked through the Indian countryside always carrying three books: the Bhagavad Gita, the Koran, and the Bible. Nothing further was required to be brutally massacred.

It would undoubtedly be wrong to believe that only India could produce this contemporary variety of syncope-person. Naturally, India was a determining factor for Gandhi, but the West was enough a part of him to provoke feelings of embarrassment and discomfort in his British adversary. This discomfort was not only a product of India; it had to find a crossroads, it needed a pathway from one world to the other. I did research to find a French equivalent to Gandhi. I found one that was as French as Gandhi was Indian, as little interested in national affiliation, as courageous, as emaciated and as mirthful. And I believe that it is his laughter that led me to discern in Voltaire the equivalent of Gandhi.

At first glance, perhaps all they have in common is laughter. Voltaire's appears to be ironic, but that is not necessarily the case; all laughter retains something of childhood innocence, all true laughter is a mockery of the father. That was Voltaire's case; it was Gandhi's case: he laughed often, so often and so heartily that modern India prefers to forget this trait of its hero, whom it pompously called "the Father of the Nation" when in fact he was the mother of the people. Perhaps the laughter that shatters conventions and creates affinities is the flight of the arrow that connects one to the other. Beyond laughter, however, I saw something else.

Voltaire also used poor means: the pamphlet, the spoken and written word, nothing more. Voltaire was also imprisoned, harassed, fleeing from one end of Europe to the other in defiance of national affiliations. Voltaire was also constantly ill, always at death's door, even putting his fingers down his throat to induce vomiting; perpetually in agony, perpetually in a swoon. Voltaire also argued with the religious hierarchy in favor of an abstract God, and wanted to destroy that disgrace, the institution of religion, always guilty of the same crimes of bloody intolerance. Whether it be Calas, Lally-Tollendal and the Chevalier de la Barre, or the Muslim/Hindu massacres on either side of the invisible frontier between the chador and Shiva's trident, it is the same battle, using the same means. Poor means.

There is no other resemblance: Voltaire was as French, frivolous, impertinent, pathetic, and libertine as Gandhi was Indian, serious, emphatic, solemn, and chaste. For if it is possible to cross one's own borders, to go beyond one's own identity, if it is possible to access the ego orgasm, one cannot escape the timeless traditions within which one is born, that determine the mundane side of life. These two men, who have nothing in common except perhaps the trembling and heroic image of two emaciated old men with toothless smiles, perhaps represent the seed of universality, this "universal negative coalition" of which Bataille had a fleeting intuition, and which is barely recognized today.

Freud can be used to oppose these strategies of syncope. For strangely enough, this man who was constantly confronted with the syncopal symptoms of hysterics, and who vainly struggled to clarify their mystery, rejected, throughout his life, what syncope brings.

As we have said, Freud refused to recognize the existence of the oceanic feeling: it was not part of his theory. His correspondence with Romain Rolland, expediter of Hindu ecstasies, was, however, courteous and interested. The day he received Rolland's two masterful books on India, a biography of Ramakrishna and another on his disciple Vivekananda, Freud politely wrote to him:

> With you as my guide, I am now trying to penetrate the Hindu jungle which had eluded me until now due to a certain mix of the Greek love of limits—*sophrosunè*, Jewish moderation and philistine anxiety.[15]

Could Freud have known? In India, the jungle begins where the village ends; the jungle is already the forest. And Freud was not in the least a renouncer; his family is his niche, he was, as Lacan said, uxorious and conjugal, and he totally defined himself in terms of the search for limits, moderation, and anxiety. It does not matter that the Greeks spoke more often of limitless tragedy than of prudent limits; it does not matter that Jewish mysticism leaned toward the kabbalistic excesses of Safed, who danced on the graves of cemeteries and spoke the language of the insects. Entrenched in his rut of moderation, Freud avoided the massive transference of his female patients by keeping himself at a distance, neither too close nor too far, behind them: no more hugs. He dismissed ecstatic tendencies; Jung and his collective subconscious; Jung and crudely defined bisexuality; Ferenczi and the wailing waters of a return to the oceanic maternal. Only psychoanalysts of the "village" remain in the communal home; the others have already left for the "forest" where Freud does not follow them. Trapped in a city he did not care for, Freud saw himself as an "unfaithful Jew": something of a Zionist, but not overly so; a radical atheist, but respectful of the universe into which he was born. And if he thought of the liberating exploits of others, if his thoughts were able to follow the swerving mystical delirium of Dr. Schreber, it was not from close up, but from afar.

He knew of syncope's powers in a confused way. His letter to Romain Rolland does not end there:

> I should really have ventured there [into the Hindu jungle] earlier, as the products of this land should not remain foreign to me; I even reached a certain level of inquiry delving into its roots. But it is not easy to rise above one's own limitations.[16]

There is an alternative exploration that will move us further forward. Freud said that three things were impossible: to govern, to educate, and to psychoanalyze.

Syncope-people such as Voltaire and the Mahatma had no doubt that they could change the world. In this they were akin to avant-garde movements, whose primary function is to incarnate this belief even to excess, absurdity, and a terrible naiveté, without which they could not exist. Freud did not want to go beyond his own limits; he was, apparently, rather content with them. And it was impossible for him to change.

After getting over his depressive hypochondria, Hegel leaves behind avant-garde thought and decides he no longer wants to change the world:

> And since I find that it would be an utterly ungrateful task to set an example to people here and it is certain that St. Anthony of Padua had greater success preaching to the fish than I would achieve by such a life here, I have resolved

> after lengthy meditation to make no attempt to improve these people but instead to follow the crowd.[17]

It is the end of a reformer's youth; the end of a nocturnal point, of syncopes and their poetic richness; Hegel's access to them has only been a parenthesis before his sheltered expedition into the system of dialectics. The birth of an owl. There is something of the owl in Freud.

But above all, and Freud made no secret of it, he had no feeling for music. And it is music that opens wide the doors to syncope.

Conclusion

Deceiving Death and Embracing God

Suddenly, time has tipped over into revolt, an abrupt and fragile immortality. From the slightest swoon to the most extreme sexual techniques, from being out of breath to suffocating, all means are used to escape. Escape from time? Futile. Through this same futility, the Subject in search of syncope does not want to escape from time, but from a part of itself that denies it access to intimacy. And if it is, no doubt, futile to try to find what I am escaping from, or what I want to have access to—since there you will find gods and demons, angels and beasts, infinitely turned back on themselves, inextricably mixed together—you will guess, as I do, what man in the grip of syncope is rebelling against.

There is no rebellion that is not up against a wall. The wall that fortifies the Subject is its collective share, its psychic habitat, the stronghold of its membership in the social body. The expression "social body" defines the shackles that must be destroyed: an enormous flesh made up of constraints and customs, of conventional gestures and paths taken, an invisible and everyday network—the socius, citizenship, relations, are suddenly unbearable. It is nothing other than identity: it is I, standing, in a photograph, in a picture stuck on a card that has to be produced before the authorities; it is I, with my distinguishing marks, my left eye slightly smaller, my size and profession, my children and forefathers, my spouses and collateral, my ins and outs. I, with my definitions: an unbearable collection of *belongings to.*

It is "my" imago, fascinated like the bull by the matador's cape. Against self, I have no refuge but the let-out of syncope. Syncope will always make a fuss: it cannot be discreet, it demands to be seen; and even if the only viewer is the statue of a goddess, syncope is a spectacle—gaudy, it shows off, exposes itself, smashes, breaks, interrupts the daily course of other people's lives, people at whom the *raptus* is aimed. I disappear, I am no longer there, I am elsewhere—where, you will not know; you will only have of this "me" the unimportant remains that you will hasten to revive. As for my self, I am, precisely, gone from there; it is from my self that I have escaped, I wanted to displace self, I wanted to dissolve self. Belonging no longer exists; access is absolute, it accedes to nothing, since the "to" is no longer there. I am access, that is all there is to it. Do not look for me "elsewhere"; you will find nothing but monsters.

I will end up coming back to myself, as you say. This unpleasant return will happen painfully; for a long time, my legs and hands will not be completely mine; you will tell me that I am still trembling, I will be cold, hot. The head will turn; you will tell me that it is "my" head that turns, but I will not know much about it. At the end of the waltz the torn-down walls will still be turning like kites in the middle of a clear sky. Coming out of the concert the ground will falter underfoot; after pleasure, we will drift without knowing who is what. One must, it is true, stand up; life . . . It is then that you will start to ask questions. What happened? How did that begin? How was it, what was it? Was it painful, was it good? You will not rest until you get a reply, you say. What a business! And how to reply to you, since there was no longer anyone, neither self nor you, no questions or replies?

And yet I am burning to talk about it. Perhaps it is just as well that it is not to you I want to talk, perhaps it is to my self I want to talk about the game in which self no longer exists. I only have words to describe it; I will tell you that they are inadequate, I will try to convince you that wherever access is, it can do without words. You will not believe me, of course; you will be right, probably, one never knows! So I will use substitutes, fragments, scraps of syncope. Delicious, ineffable, adorable . . . I will evoke dizzying falls, oceans, chasms; hearts turned inside out, dazzlement, gale-force winds. You will shake your head, not satisfied.

And then there will be something else to do; you will turn your head away, another dance, another dancing partner, the alarm clock goes off, the milk is on the stove . . . you will forget. I will too, I may add; for I will be self again, and I will do as you do, I will go off to live. The vacation of or from the self will be over.

There are one or two things that you do not know. Once one has gained access without paths or doors to this country that is not a country, one can go there easily. It is strange work, and I use this word deliberately to cloud the issue for you; for, you have understood, the syncope that disconnects, unfastens, unties, and abolishes defends itself against the very idea of work. Nonetheless I will persist: syncope is lazy work, passive activity, a sly disaffection from those who surround me. The smallest thing is enough: a surprise, a little fright, a burst of sunshine,[1] or you coming toward me around a bend in the road. But this smallest thing insists on being seized; this smallest thing demands all one's attention. If you do not watch out, it will catch you one fine day, without warning; you will no longer want anything but this smallest thing; you will be completely shaken up, you will no longer have a taste for life.

Whatever you do, do not be afraid. Abandon your reservations; let yourself go, as they say. Straddle your horse, and embrace the foam on the waves. You laugh, you look angry: you say it looks like breathing lessons for a woman in labor, a fiancée longing for her wedding night, or someone at death's door.

Exactly. Syncope is the spice of dancing; it is the very taste for existence, its exquisite savor. And if birth and death terrify you, then turn to music, which provides syncope for each and everyone. Turn to music, which is the assumption of syncope.

And when we are there, you will understand how one has to return from it, and why one never can completely. In your turn, you will tell me that that is so much the better. So maybe we will be able to discuss death calmly again.

Do not imagine that in music we will discover a secret that has always been hidden: you know that music escapes on all sides; when one analyzes it, one forsakes it; and if one calls it to mind, one makes poetry, because that is the only act of language that resembles it closely enough not to deflower it.

It escapes; everyone who has tried their hand at it ends up saying this. Claude Lévi-Strauss, having thought about it, as far as he was able, in its relationship to myth understood it as the emotion hidden within the musical moment, the emotion whose function is not to be grasped at the moment when it appears. Jankélévitch spent his whole life writing about the music he adored, in a sparkling verbal vertigo around what he called the "Ineffable." One must resign oneself: the syncope function of music is also that of escape.

And if I speak of "deflowering," it is to return to the waltz, which in itself understands the taking of a young woman's virginity. If the young girl loses her virginity by waltzing, what does this have to do with music? And what could be more boring than what has been written about laughter? Fortunately, it escapes us. I prefer to appeal to the style of Noh theater that the Japanese critic Zeami calls "*the style of the marvelous flower.*" This style, which is the product of complete technical mastery, is only attained when the artist is mature; it consists above all of reaching nonconsciousness, nontechnique, and *noninterpretation*. If there is a trace of art for art's sake, or art as skill, even as genius, the flower disappears. "The marvelous is the ineffable," says Zeami. "It is the point at which the thought process is destroyed."[2] You can understand that any analysis of music makes the flower disappear, or produces postcoital sadness. And yet music epitomizes syncope.

Let us go back to the Western model of syncope in music, as, for example, Jean-Jacques Rousseau formulates it excellently in the *Dictionary of Music*. "*Syncope*: prolongation on the strong [beat] of a sound begun on the weak [beat]; wherefore, every syncopated note is in counter time, and every collection of syncopated notes is a movement in counter time."[3] These are the effects of syncope that we have come across along the way. Depression prolongs night into day, and overwhelms daily activity; the initiation of Dionysus prolongs the supernatural rage of the weak bacchantes into the city's strength, blinding the women; the passion of love for love prolongs a hypnotic oblivion into what we call humdrum routine, putting a spoke in its wheel.[4] The yogis holding their breath prolong the moment of exhalation unduly, to the point of destroying and burning what we call consciousness; the erudite ritual preparation for the Tantric coupling prolongs the flash of orgasm and holds it back, transforming supreme weakness into supreme ecstasy; and the ecstatics prolong a violent, absolute desire for immobility and inertia into holy laziness. Everywhere, we have run across the pebble in the road, the obstacle, the chasm that has to be leaped. And we have glimpsed weak people suddenly endowed with enough prodigious, metaphysical strength to cross over, in a single bound: the weak Tristan, a posthumous infant; the weak Ramakrishna, eater of turds; the weak Hölderlin, preyed on by the divine discordance of his out-of-tune spinet; Kierkegaard, a stillborn child; Nietzsche, with his imploded head; Dionysus, the dismembered child; Prajapati, the scattered god—all struck with the same weakness. Everywhere we have recognized the angel's wing, the game of the child intent on constructing his space by scattering, and finally the young girl imagined by Kierkegaard, or Hölderlin's beloved Antigone. The internal young girl that men and women carry within them and who, long ago, was called the *pupilla*, the pupil, in the center of the eye, this corner of gleaming self where an unknown image is reflected, appearing and disappearing . . .

But when Rousseau abstractly breaks down syncope into different moments—weak beat, prolongation into strong beat—he does it as Lacan will later do when he is trying to break down the sudden appearance of subjective identity. The mirror phase, if you recall, reproduces the scenario of musical syncope detail by detail. Weak beat: the baby is born prematurely, affected by the defect characteristic of the human race, the incompletion of the nervous system, which results in the inability to stand upright and to walk, and which makes of man's young a monstrous and moving imperfect animal. Strong beat:

it is in the depths of this weakness, when he is not yet speaking, that the child is captivated by himself in the mirror, anticipates the complete figure of what he will be later, and prefigures his completion by recognizing himself as Subject, he, me, I, an identity not to be confused with the other. The anticipation is prolonged for his whole life; so that subjective identity can be defined as an emanation of weakness, overcome in the blink of an eye, and from then on cannot be crossed.

Cannot be crossed? Indeed. For precisely when man is tired of the regularity of his life, he grants himself the crossing of his identity. He prolongs unduly the smallest accident found in his path, and pays for the detour with weakness.

"Pay for" is not too strong a word, for the price is high. The subject has to be left as security, identity has to be abandoned, left at the pawnbroker's, and one hopes to be able to come back and get it one day when one has finished with temporary youthful follies. Those who are reluctant to offer themselves the extremes of ecstasy, those who are legitimately afraid of passionate love, those who are as wary of love at first sight as they are of drugs, those people turn to music. It is just a little crossing, a crossing without major risk; a bearable syncope. A syncope despite itself.

Of all syncopes, those that music provides are the most directly "natural." We have seen nature, or rather its image, haunting the content of syncope: return to the cosmos, to animal life, suckling fawns or metamorphosis into a werewolf; Saint Theresa walks on all fours and Ramakrishna licks his excrement. The "naturalness" of music is more simply vibratory. And the ears are not the sole port of entry for music: it is received through the whole expanse of skin, through the whole body. When the trance accompanied by music begins, those who are struck by it often put their hands over their ears as if they wanted to stop up the orifice through which syncope is entering. But it is not to close it; it is in order better to take in the flux of vibrations, to savor the hearing. In India, singers keep one hand on their ears to accompany their internal inspiration; the other, placed on the lap, beats time, with the palm turned up. From time to time the hand leaves the ear and moves toward another invisible hand: toward you, or toward it, one never knows.

Sometimes, when a high-pitched sound is produced by rubbing a damp finger around the edge of a crystal glass, if the sound is too pure, the glass shatters. Music's natural vibrations are powerful enough to make bridges collapse when regiments march across them with a "too" regular rhythm; and so they are compelled—the army's dishonor, the music's strength—to break ranks, to cross the bridge in disorder . . .

That is what music does: shatters crystal, makes bridges collapse, suppresses time—always by surprise. The development of music does not coincide at all with biological rhythm: not with the heartbeat, nor the rhythm of breathing, one-two. Musical rhythm goes beyond these regularities, nibbles at them, devours them; it is ahead of them, behind them, syncopated. But the crystal that the sound breaks is not broken in vain; it is elsewhere that syncope crystallizes, as love at first sight does to lovers, and as happens in salt mines in tunnels that are abandoned and then found later covered with sparkling stones. Music shatters the crystal of a glass; but it is the self that it envelops with another crystal, invisible: the salt of thought.

By forcing the limits of the self, music follows the rhythm of the creative act as Anton Ehrenzweig understood it so well. It contradicts the visceral rhythms, penetrates subjectivity, disperses identity from there by submerging subjectivity with emotions: it is the "schizoid" phase in which one is separated from the world, not without feeling a subtle and familiar aggression. However *pianissimo* a piece of music may begin, it compels one to leave without moving from the spot where one is, and to come back to oneself where one already knows that one will no longer find oneself. Once this moment has passed, one has crossed over the disharmony with reality, and one has found, with music, fundamental harmony. From then on the equivalents of unconscious "scanning" come into play, along with a sovereign invasion in which music is queen, absolute queen.

A shudder. The shudder produced by music is, more than any other, an ego orgasm. It springs from surprise, from the erudite musical work that long ago, in the history of Western music, was named syncopation. And if we hardly have any more official ecstatics, we no longer count the spontaneous ecstatics, the people who are crazy about music, who search for the erotic shudder that a voice can produce: they are ready and waiting. Of course, music can be dangerous; tyrants willingly use musical accompaniment in their group celebrations; but in truth, it is not music that brings about tyrants. Music is content to open the way to inner orgasm to everyone. It is each person's business to make good use of it when he comes back to himself.

The final moment is arriving. The return to measured time. The music stops. A brief encounter; life starts again. But it is no longer altogether the same; more than any other syncope, music, which creates such rich ones, knows how to soothe. The violent emotion, the ego orgasm have passed; but the echo lingers, imperceptible, happy, reconciled.

Syncope always provokes this sensation of reunion. It is the moment of calm, which seems endless although one guesses that it is tenuous. You return to yourself; it is a "disheartening," but you find yourself again. Does one find *oneself* again? No. The reunion that was the object of syncope is of another sort.

Lost homeland, nourishing earth, paradise, light, ocean, odyssey, flash, celestial city, the worlds one has gone to are not on the order of the self. One must come back to the imaginary return to nature that inhabits syncope.

Nothing, however, seems natural in the practice of syncope; on the contrary, the signs overflow with excesses against nature. It is not natural to stop breathing, to twist the body into catalepsy, it is not natural to lead the singer's voice into singing exercises that are unbearable for the body and sublime in their beauty. It is not natural to dance the waltz, the Bharat-Natyam, or to whirl around, "Sama, sama, sama."[5] Nothing in all that is natural, and contortion is de rigueur. And if it is natural for human beings to couple, it is not natural truly to "make" love. When man is in action, he wards off his animal side, even if it means meeting it again in his dreams. That is what the word "ecstasy" means: a displacement, a deviation. In this sense, *we are all deviants*.[6]

The West and the East have different conceptions of this radical deviation. In the West the Subject prevails, "master and possessor of Nature," as Descartes said when he founded the *cogito* as an authority to be referred to. From then on nature is treated with respect; by overriding it, one does not damage it, one exercises over it the sovereign power of the human race over animal and vegetable species, by virtue of a general right within which human rights are included. Escapes from the Subject always have the appearance of an adolescent absconding. These are escapades, sudden changes of mood. They are infractions of a tacit rule for which Western philosophers, until a rather late date, as we have seen, made themselves spontaneous town criers. Prohibiting syncope, shutting it up in a sort of reservation for savages—that is an integral part of philosophical practice, a barrier between the Subject and nature; it is prohibited to "go native," prohibited to syncopate philosophically: make way for the absolute sovereignty of the Subject. Only ethnologists and psychoanalysts can divorce themselves from this consensus.

In India, this consensus about the human race is reversed. We must place a restraining order on the individual Subject, which must burn its emotions and desires to a cinder in order to meet up again with Nature, of which the human race is a part—but without rights or privileges. The cycle of reincarnation may have made you a bird before it made you a human: it can precipitate you into another animal destiny at any moment. Humanity, as we understand it in the West, is and is only in passage from one cycle to another: merely a stage. The worship of cows in India, which for us is unthinkable, is accompanied by a respect for all living things; and ecology in India, in its modern form, is inscribed in the ancient metaphysics of a world that never made man the owner of nature. Of course, there as in the West, industrial pollution and deforestation wreak their havoc, deprive the peasants of water, and ruin the health of urban dwellers. But the conversion to practicing ecology is made effortlessly; it flows from the source, it goes without saying. The renouncers begin to fast to protect valleys threatened by the building of dams. The logic of India demands the right for syncope to be established: permitted, incited, respected, it remains an always possible solution. There is no barrier between nature and the subject: please melt into the universe. Only the *Westernized*, those who have been contaminated by the West, divorce themselves from this consensus.

Claude Lévi-Strauss, asked in 1977 to formulate proposals for a new bill of human rights, engaged in a violent critique of the human race in the name of all the destruction it has been guilty of throughout time.[7] This idea became accepted. On the other hand, no one has yet thought, as he did then, of the new *cogito* capable of defining man within nature. For if he is thought of as merely a species and no longer as the sovereign king, how does he find his place? And what formula could come to replace the founding master-subject on which the whole of Europe still depends?

Three times in the history of philosophy, according to Lévi-Strauss, systems of thought appeared that achieved this. The Stoics—of whom it was said that they were now slaves, now emperors, as if detached from mastery of the universe for the sake of mastery of the self—first conceived of the cosmos, that great animal, and man in the cosmos. The "savage mind,"[8] wherever it still exists, allows us to recognize an equivalent concern for integrating man into an equilibrium that he has no right to undermine. In the particular case of aboriginal peoples, the species are protected on pain of death; it is a question of biological survival. The final example is Indian thought. In these three examples, Lévi-Strauss decided on a new definition of man: no longer as a thinking being but as a *living being*. That affirms at the same stroke the inviolable rights of other species; we have all begun to understand today that on the scale of planet Earth this demand has become, as it is for oral societies, a matter of collective survival.

In its short and sudden excess, syncope performs precisely this turnaround. It is not a matter of "returning" to real nature, by eating roots and drinking only goat's milk, as Gandhi did. If there is a return it is on the order of myth, whose primary function is to regulate. But finally, that is where the question arises: by escaping for a lightning moment from the city's laws, by plunging into becoming angel, becoming beast, becoming light, becoming two sexes at the same time, man clearly simulates the return to a nature confusedly threatened by the order of its own subjects. The paradox is that the return arrives there against time, against the demands of the body, against all "reason." That is how the contortions of syncope unveil the vast powers of nature, and restore them to an important position. This process of extreme twisting is sleight of hand: I overstep nature, but by doing so I overstep the human race and find nature again. This produces the sensation of reconciled calm that follows syncope; later, it also produces the discomfort of reentering one's body, covered again with worldly clothes.

But under the clothes—even if on one's return they have become too tight—a restoration has taken place. We have lost a lot of the feeling of internal restoration: the mystic is treated, the depressive is sedated, syncope is taken in hand by the ambulance, the hospital, or the psychoanalyst. We struggle tooth and nail against the most scandalous deviations; soon it will be demonstrated that love at first sight is dangerous for our health. One democratic expedient remains: the marvelous deviation of music; there are poetry and dance, free of all salutary restraints, protected from the desire to be cured. The forgotten therapeutic traditions, however, demonstrate the restorative uses of syncope, with music as support.

Music is an accompanist: when one must go through syncope, it is always there. The yogis hear it in their ears, the song of the lover to his beloved steals into love at first sight, and trances demand it. It is not that music determines syncope; but it is the initiating signal of the mysterious gap between visceral rhythm and the rhythm that I would like to call *supernatural*, on the condition that this word is taken literally. Beyond nature, but not without it.

In southern Italy—this is almost the last story—in the heart of the Puglia region, a syncopal and restorative musical ritual still existed until recently. It was said that tarantulas, those poisonous spiders, stung human beings; in truth, usually women and young men. The attack was syncopal and violent. To cure it, a little orchestra was called together and played for hours for those who had been stung. They danced like spiders, flat on their stomachs, on all fours, simulating the animal that had to be exorcised. Sometimes, the "tarantulized" people were hung from trees at the end of a rope, like spiders. And they swayed. When the music had had its beneficial effect on this particular trance, the "tarantulized" people stood up again; they were cured. For a while: on a yearly rhythm the spider's attack began again, and with it, the musical ritual.

The spiders were hardly ever real; the stings were almost all imaginary, as you already might have guessed.

A team of scholars from all disciplines, including historians, studied this phenomenon, which is very well known today. The historians recalled that this region of Italy was where the cult of Dionysus and the ritual of the bacchantes had been introduced, centuries earlier. Their syncopes had not disappeared; no more had the image of the young girl on the swing. Syncope cannot be gotten rid of so easily; it cannot be so easily "medicalized."[9]

It makes people temporarily afraid—certainly those who are close by: syncope, through which man escapes, is created to disturb the world. Whoever falls into syncope is afflicted with harrowing torments that are the beginning of free play inside the self. But however terrifying it may be, it is cured, or rather, it cures. If the example of the "tarantulized" people's musical trances is linked to the most common musical ecstasy, it is just an excessive extrapolation, nothing more. Jean-Jacques Rousseau, in the *Essay on the Origin of Languages*, spoke of the "tarantulized" people of Puglia, explaining the therapeutic nature of music through its commemorative side: "It is not the case that absolute sounds or the same songs are the indicated cure for everyone who has been stung by that insect; rather, each one requires tunes with a melody he knows and lyrics he can understand." Even better known is the famous example in the *Dictionary of Music* of the cowherds' song: "This tune was so generally beloved among the Swiss, that it was forbidden to be played in their troops under pain of death, because it made them burst into tears, desert, or die, whoever heard it; so great a desire did it excite in them of returning to their country."[10] Music, the art of syncope, always brings with it, even if it surprises or attacks, a long-standing familiarity, and a burning desire to see one's place of birth again, whatever country that may be, *and especially if it does not exist*. It is a fine thing that a tune used by the military was forbidden because it encouraged soldiers to desert, but in truth, syncope always makes the world desert: that is why it is useful.

That is how the Sufis proceeded; if they rend their clothes when they are in a state of music and dance, they have the solemn duty to gather up the pieces of torn coat and sew them back together.

So one has to return from it; and one will be compensated for that. But by escaping the self man also escapes something else, which nonetheless he simulates.

Syncope deceives death. In all ways. By delaying the weak beat, excessively prolonging time, and by making it disappear subjectively, it pretends to delay progress toward the biological conclusion. By crossing the limits of consciousness, it anticipates immortality. I leave the world, and then I return to it. I die, but I do not die. I am placed between the two, between life and death, exactly in the between-the-two, refusing one and the other. And that is how I dupe not only death but the difficult exercise of *the end of life*.

For from little death to little death, the truth of aging that naturally leads up to death is overshadowed. That is why syncope is youth, striking and unchanging. Dying young like rock stars; avoiding the swift wrinkle, the shortened breath, ruination, collapse, and above all the dying. It is not for nothing that hagiography turns sickly stench into the smell of roses, and excrement into cinnamon: that is precisely what syncope avoids and resolves.

To delay, to anticipate, to provoke dissonance, and to resolve it. Syncope is an act of rebellion against the natural deterioration of the aged body, against the living decomposition that alters the imago of one's own body as real time moves on. Better to melt into nature before one's time, better to dissolve, better to topple intentionally into a weakness agreed to in advance . . . better to die than to die.

But often, syncope addicts, religious fanatics, and the ascetics of love at first sight have a hard life. No doubt syncope, by dint of leaping into the afterlife and returning restored, permits a laziness of being, a pause in thought, and an absence to the world that are so many savings on life. It is to the credit of this fantastic expenditure of energy that it is futile. Illogical. Absurd, like the dot on an *i*. At least one can, precisely, by escaping, save time on Time.

Once there was a mad poet. He had gone mad and become a poet at the same time, the day he had been separated from the woman he loved, and from that time on he began singing as he roamed the desert. She got married; he died mad, singing her name. The Mejnun, which means the madman, loved Leila until the day he died.[11]

Once there was another poet, who knew that poetry—like syncope—can protect one from madness, as long as one knows how to make use of it. He decided to love a woman; he extolled her without respite to the jeers of the crowd. He went as far as reproducing the mad poems of Mejnun, as far as calling himself Mejnun, the madman. He dared to change Leila's name to Elsa. And since he was not really mad, but merely a poet, he wanted to reverse the course of the myth of Mejnun. The lovers were not separated at all, and soon, oh horror!, the poet realized that they would grow old together.

So he made the best of a bad thing:

> *To grow old* . . . remember what this word meant to you in the disdainful vertigo of your strength (your strength, Love!) and the abstract idea that it already was in your childish mouth, when you were young . . . to grow old, to grow

> old . . . but what do people say? What was at the end of this verb—another little word—the word that gave it its musical flair, that made it shine, that gave it its dazzling finish, *to grow old* . . . bitterly, ah you said of those who loved each other: *they will grow old together.*[12]

But he was not mad enough to believe what he said. He knew the truth about poetic art; the truth about love at first sight; the truth about syncope and life's multiple twists. And he addressed this poet of the "growing old together"—who was none other than himself—adding: "And you, when you are at the point of death, *alone absolutely uselessly naked* . . . "[13]

Alone. Naked. And to thwart all syncope's guile, the poet faces the final moment:

> Oh death Oh God by whatever name you call yourself
> You can keep for yourself your fear your paradise
> . . . oh impious man
> You will not take the name of the Lord thy God in vain
> because he does not exist.[14]

After which, nothing.

Notes

Foreword: East Meets West

1. Claude Lévi-Strauss, *Tristes Tropiques* (Paris: Plon, 1955), 40–41 (translation mine).

2. Gilles Deleuze, *L'Image-Mouvement* (Paris: Minuit, 1983) and *L'Image-Temps* (Paris: Minuit, 1985). Translated by Hugh Tomlison and Barbara Habberjam as *Image-Movement* and by Tomlison and Robert Galeta as *Time-Movement* (Minneapolis: University of Minnesota Press, 1986 and 1988).

3. For a similar problematization, see, for example, the films of Jean-Luc Godard, especially *Prénom Carmen*, and Wim Wenders's *Himmel über Berlin*.

4. Claude Lévi-Strauss, *Le Regard éloigné* (Paris: Plon, 1983).

5. A similar position has recently been taken by Michel Serres in *Le Contrat naturel* (Paris: François Bourin, 1990). See also Luc Ferry's rather supercilious *Le Nouvel Ordre écologique* (Paris: Grasset, 1992).

6. Lévi-Strauss's pronouncements are developed through a history of heredity in François Jacob, *La Logique du vivant* (Paris: Gallimard, 1971). Translated by Betty G. Spillman as *The Logic of the Living* (New York: Pantheon, 1974).

7. Michel de Certeau, *La Fable mystique* (Paris: Gallimard, 1982).

8. Clément borrows the expression from an Indian psychoanalyst and writer, Sudhir Kakar, whom she quotes repeatedly and who is at last coming to be known in the West. The same concept appears in Gilles Deleuze, in a discussion of free indirect discourse in cinema in *L'Image-Mouvement*, 107 (in *The Movement-Image*, 63).

9. Félix Guattari, *Les Trois Écologies* (Paris: Minuit, 1990). Basing his conclusions on earlier assertions by Gregory Bateson, Guattari distinguishes between a mental, a social, and an environmental ecology.

Introduction: Where Am I?

1. Selection from "La Syncope," doctoral dissertation for the medical degree, written by Oswald Hermabessière (Librairie Lac, 1931).

2. *The Marquise of* O, by Heinrich von Kleist, tells the following story: A widow who enjoyed an excellent reputation placed an ad in the local newspaper asking for the father of the child she is carrying to identify himself; that she would then marry him. In the course of a battle that was taking place in the citadel where she had taken refuge, a few months earlier, she was rescued by a courteous Russian officer, then fell into a deep faint. She remembered nothing and woke up, as one might say, pregnant. The officer had taken advantage of the situation. Having long refused to believe that this officer was the father of her child, and the propagator of the rape, the marquise finally marries him, and they are happy together. In a moment of happiness, her husband asks her why she hadn't recognized him when he appeared before her, confessing his crime. "Throwing her

arms around his neck, she answered that she would not have seen a devil in him then if she had not seen an angel in him at their first meeting" (p. 112). This is the final sentence in the story. (Trans. David Luke and Nigel Reeves [Harmondsworth: Penguin, 1978].)

3. [Trans.: The French word *syncope* means both "loss of consciousness" or "fainting" and "musical syncopation."]

4. The Bharat-Natyam is the most important of the styles of classical dance in India; the dance is made up of abstract moments, others mimed with coded gestures (called *mudras*) that generally tell the story of the fervent waiting of a female devotee and the appearing of a given god. The god in this dance is Shiva, who will be discussed often and at length; but the erotic adventures of the god Krishna constitute the finest hours of Bharat-Natyam. A solo female dancer (there are few male dancers) dances all the roles, alone on stage, accompanied by an orchestra of musicians and singers, some indicating the rhythm while others sing the narrative. The dancer's fingers are often reddened (traditionally with henna) up to the second knuckle, as are the toes and the soles of the feet; the dancer dances barefoot. On her ankles she wears bells. The colors of her costume and her makeup, as well as her head jewelry, create a vibrant and intense image, far from the pale white image of the romantic style of dancer in European ballet.

5. This book was already finished when two excellent books on the tango and the waltz appeared in France. The book on the tango is *Le Tango* by Horacio Salas (Paris: Actes Sud, 1989). The book on the waltz is *La Valse* by Rémi Hess (Arles: A. M. Métailié, 1989). See also *Le Tango de Buenos Aires* by Claude Fléouter (Paris: Lattès, 1979).

6. The passage on the "Sama" is not by Hegel; it is by Djalâl ul-Dîn, Rumi himself, quoted under the name of "Mawlana" by Michel Random in his very fine book, *Le Soufisme et la danse* (Tunis: Sud Edition, 1980); also of note are his *Odes mystiques*, trans. by Eva de Vitray-Meyerovitch and Mohammad Mokri (Paris: Klincksieck, 1973).

As far as the passage by Hegel is concerned, it is in a note in the third section of "Philosophy of Spirit," the section "Absolute Spirit," in *Encyclopedia of the Philosophical Sciences in Outline*, trans. Steven A. Taubeneck (New York: Continuum, 1990). [Trans.: The poem does not appear in this English edition; Clément is using Gibelin's French translation (Paris: Vrin, 1952), pp. 312–13.] Later we will return to the passage by Rumi and the use made of it by Hegel in his dialectic of the Absolute Spirit.

7. Entry on "syncope," *A Complete Dictionary of Music*, trans. William Waring (New York: AMS Press, 1779, rpt. 1975), pp. 390–91.

8. "Eventail de Mademoiselle Mallarmé" (Mademoiselle Mallarmé's fan) by Stéphane Mallarmé.

9. [Trans.: Mallarmé's original line reads, "Stagnants sur les soirs d'or, ce l'est"; we have amended the Caws' translation, "Stagnant on golden eves, is" in order to retain the notion of East—Orient—that is so important in Clément's reading.]

10. Quote from the second issue of the review *L'Ordinaire du psychanalyste*, p. 61. The idea behind this wonderfully refreshing review was that the texts were presented with the strictest anonymity (Paris: Editions des Mains libres, 1973). In April 1978, with its twelfth issue, the review ceased to exist.

11. See G. Bataille, "The Torment," in *Inner Experience*, trans. Leslie Anne Boldt (Albany: SUNY Press, 1988), p. 34. Also *Oeuvres complètes*, vol. 5, *La Somme athéologique* (Summa atheologica) (Paris: Gallimard, 1973); also pp. 83, 106–14, and especially 355: "The laughing fit or ecstasy brings us to the edge of the abyss, it is a 'putting into question' of all possibilities. It is the point of rupture, of letting go completely, the anticipation of death." The passage quoted here is found in "Notes. La Limite de l'utile" ("Notes. The limits of usefulness"), in *Oeuvres complètes*, vol. 7, p. 527.

12. Paul Valéry in *The Graveyard by the Sea* (*Le Cimetière marin*), trans. Graham Dunstan Martin (Edinburgh: University of Edinburgh Press, 1971).

13. *Travaux du Laboratoire de Psychologie de la Salpêtrière* (Paris: Librairie Félix Alcan, vol. 1, 1926; vol. 2, 1928).

14. Raymond Queneau, *The Skin of Dreams* (*Loin de rueil*), trans. H. J. Kaplan (New York: Howard Fertig, 1979), pp. 11–12.

15. François-Bernard Michel, *Le Souffle coupé: Respirer et écrire* (Stifled breath: breathing and writing) (Paris: Gallimard, 1986). Read the especially interesting introduction, and the chapter on Queneau, "L'Anti-Rousseau, un asthme ontalgique" (Anti-Rousseau: An ontalgic asthma). In fact, the entire book is a masterpiece.

16. Louis Aragon, *Le Fou d'Elsa: Poème* (Elsa's madman) (Paris: Gallimard, 1983), p. 309.

17. In G. Bataille, *Le Dossier de l'oeil pinéal*, "Le Sacrifice du gibbon." Translated as "The Sacrifice of the Gibbon," by Alan Stoekl with Carl Lovitt and Donald M. Leslie, Jr., in *Visions of Excess: Selected Writings 1927–1939* (Minneapolis: University of Minnesota Press, 1985).

18. In Marchand and Ajuriaguerra (Desclée de Brouwer, 1948), especially the chapters on convulsive epilepsy; see also Gaston Ferdière's *Conduite du traitement de l'état de mal* (Course of treatment for an epileptic state) (G. Doin, 1942); and Temkin's *The Falling Sickness* (Baltimore: Johns Hopkins University Press, 1945), on the history of epilepsy in its anthropological context as a sacred malady.

19. [Trans.: *Je change de coeur*, literally, "I'm changing heart."]

20. Ajuriaguerra, p. 14 (on state of dejection), pp. 30–31 (Dostoyevsky's testimony) and "Je change de coeur." Dostoyevsky also alludes to Mohammed's air of rapture: "All of you healthy people have no idea of the happiness that we epileptics experience in the moment before a fit. Mohammed, in the Koran, affirms that he saw Heaven during an epileptic fit (for he, too, was afflicted as I am). I do not know whether this blessed state lasts for seconds, hours or months, but believe me, I wouldn't give it up for anything in the world."

21. [Trans.: *Louche* means "cross-eyed," but also "suspicious," as in "a suspicious character."]

22. Aragon, *Le Fou d'Elsa*, p. 45.

23. See Georges Lapassade, *Les Etats modifiés de conscience* (Modified States of Consciousness) (Paris: PUF, 1987); and *Extase et sports de l'extrême* (Ecstasy and sports of the extreme) (Paris: Albin Michel, 1988).

24. G. Bataille, preface to *Madame Edwarda*, trans. Austryn Wainhouse (London and New York: Marion Boyars, 1989), p. 143.

25. G. Bataille, *Oeuvres complètes*, *Le Coupable*, vol. 5, p. 296. Trans. Bruce Boone, *Guilty* (Venice, Calif.: Lapis, 1988), p. 57.

26. Bataille, "The Sacrifice of the Gibbon," p. 86.

27. Bataille, *Madame Edwarda*, pp. 157–58.

28. [Trans. *Jouissance* can be translated as "ecstasy," "orgasm," or "enjoyment, pleasure, delight"; in other words, it can be physical, intellectual, or spiritual. We use the French word throughout to retain levels of meaning.]

29. [Trans.: *Flamber* as in *flambeur*, "big-time gambler"; the literal meaning of *flamber* is "to burn."]

30. [Trans.: *Coup de foudre*, literally "struck by lightning." Depending on context, we sometimes translate this as "love-struck."]

31. *Iseut* when referring to the medieval novel; *Isolde* when referring to Wagner's opera, *Tristan und Isolde*.

32. Unpublished script of the film *Trop belle pour toi* (Too beautiful for you), which the writer-director Bertrand Blier consented to lend me in its original handwritten version.

33. Quoted by Pierre Fédida in a very enlightening article, "Hypnose, transfert et suggestion" (Hypnosis, transference, and suggestion), in *Résurgence de l'hypnose* (Resurgence of hypnosis), a collective work edited by Léon Chertok (Desclée de Brouwer, 1984), pp. 49–74. In this article,

Fédida discusses the effects of hypnosis on transference during therapy, and raises the possibility of a metapsychology of transference.

34. André Breton, "Second Manifesto of Surrealism," in *Manifestos of Surrealism*, trans. Richard Seaver and Helen R. Lane (Ann Arbor: University of Michigan Press, 1969), p. 39.

35. [Trans.: *Dépaysement* is literally an "out-of-country" experience.]

36. Urdu is the language, largely based on Persian, that is spoken in India by a hundred million Muslims who have chosen to remain despite the partition between United India and Pakistan.

1. Choosing Night

1. Title of the play by Thomas Bernhard.

2. [Trans.: *Nuits blanches*: "white nights," as in "sleepless."]

3. [Trans.: *Retraite*, indicating both "retirement" and "retreat."]

4. See the excellent article by Guy Rosolato, "L'Axe narcissique des dépressions" (The narcissistic axis of depressions), in *Figures du vide* (Figures of emptiness), *Nouvelle Revue de Psychanalyse* 2 (Paris: Gallimard, Spring 1975). "In depression, the desire to return to the protective womb dominates, as much through isolation, the breaking off of social ties, as through the demand made on a single person for a privileged relationship of dependency and mothering, whether this be a parent or psychotherapist, who is forced to take on the role of 'holder' or 'container'" (p. 19). Rosolato also mentions the devastating effects of the disappearance of rites of passage: "Instead of rites of initiation, passage, or sacrifice, a simple catabolism is substituted, a breakdown to the state of debris, an incineration. The irrecuperable person, the deviant or member of a minority, is still useful to society, but, according to its rules, only as a scapegoat" (p. 33). This is true, but Rosolato, in mentioning incineration, is undoubtedly thinking about our European crematoriums; in other parts of the world, where these rituals still exist and where the ego has not been "desaturated" as we will see it described by Jacques Lacan, the dead are nonetheless burned, which does not mean that they are reduced to the state of "simple debris." Perhaps it is important to point out which is the real debris that is eliminated by the rite itself.

5. See Myriam Kerhof's *L'Univers du sommeil* (The universe of sleep) (Brussels: Editions de l'Université de Bruxelles, 1987), and especially D. Sezchtel and C. Poirel's *Chronobiologie et psychiatrie* (Chronobiology and psychiatry) (Paris: Masson, 1985).

6. [Trans.: *Décalage horaire*, literally "time lag."]

7. Notes to *Etre Oreste* (Being Orestes), p. 533, G. Bataille, *Oeuvres complètes*, vol. 3 (Paris: Gallimard, 1971). In this passage Bataille comments on Orestes' feelings upon hearing of Hermione's suicide. Here is the decisive quote: "But in the midst of the night, desire lies and thus ceases to appear to be its object. The existence of the self led 'into the night' resembles that of the lover upon learning of the death of the beloved, of Orestes learning of Hermione's suicide. It becomes impossible to find, in this particular kind of night, 'what was hoped for'"(p. 223).

8. [Trans.: *Ecoeurement*, literally "de-heartening" or "dis-heartening."]

9. Jules Laforgue, who is the subject of a chapter in the book by François-Bernard Michel, *Le Souffle coupé*, is this tubercular poet who saw himself as hypertrophic. *Complainte du temps et de sa commère l'espace*, *Oeuvres complètes* (Paris: Editions l'Age d'homme, 1986), pp. 607–8. The poem is translated by Peter Dale as "Complaint of Time and Her Crony Space," in *Poems of Jules Laforgue* (London: Anvil Press, 1986).

10. See Clémence Ramnoux's *La Nuit et les enfants de la nuit dans la tradition greque* (Night and children of the night in the Greek tradition), an essay on Greek cosmologies; Ramnoux's work is the source for my analysis of the bacchantean state's return to public consciousness since Euripides (Paris: Flammarion, 1959), pp. 25–26.

11. Descartes was thinking of Elisabeth, Princess of Bavaria, while writing *Le Traité des passions* (The treatise on the passions). Article 30: "That the soul is united to all the portions of the

body conjointly." *The Philosophical Works of Descartes*, vol. 1, trans. Elizabeth Haldane and G. R. T. Ross (Cambridge: Cambridge University Press, 1967).

12. Ibid., article 31: "But, in examining the matter with care, it seems as though I had clearly ascertained that the part of the body in which the soul exercises its functions is in nowise the heart, nor the whole of the brain, but merely the most inward of its parts, to wit, a certain very small gland which is situated in the middle of its substance and so suspended above the duct whereby the animal spirits in its anterior cavities have communication with those in the posterior, that the slightest movements which take place in it may alter very greatly the course of those spirits; and reciprocally that the smallest changes which occur in the course of the spirits may do much to change the movement of this gland" (pp. 345–46).

13. Ibid., article 10: "How the animal spirits are produced in the brain."

14. Ibid., article 47. "In what the strife consists which we imagine to exist between the lower and higher part of the soul," article 21.

15. Ibid., article 21.

16. *La Vie de monsieur Pascal, écrite par madame Périer, sa soeur, femme de monsieur Périer, conseiller à la cour des aides de* Clermont (Life of M. Pascal, written by Mme. Perier, his sister, wife of M. Périer, counsellor at the Court of Assistance of Clermont).

17. Ibid., p. 18, *Oeuvres complètes*, *L'Intégrale* (Paris: Seuil, 1975).

18. Périer, *La Vie de monsieur Pascal*, p. 21. "The doctors believed that in order for him to be cured he must renounce all mental activities of any importance and that he must try as often as he could to find ways to divert his mind with something that would occupy him and which he enjoyed, in other words, with ordinary daily conversation; because there were no other diversions that were suitable to my brother."

19. Ibid., p. 23.

20. Ibid.

21. Ibid., p. 618.

22. Ibid., p. 307, paragraph 286.

23. [Trans.: His *assiette*, literally "his plate."]

24. Michel Serres devotes an important part of his book on Leibniz, *Le Système de Leibniz et ses modèles mathémathiques* (Leibniz's system and his mathematical models), to Pascal; in particular, "Le Paradigme pascalien" (The Pascalian paradigm), pp. 648–712. Serres discusses, with the rigor and mastery that he is known for in philosophy and in the history of science, the Pascalian obsession of searching for the fixed point. See chapter D, "Jésus-Christ et le reversement des lois" (Jesus Christ and the reversal of laws), p. 702, for the exact quotation (Paris: Epiméthée, PUF, 1982).

25. See also: "Our senses perceive nothing too extreme, a noise that is too loud deafens us, too much light blinds us, too great a distance or too great a proximity prevent us from seeing. Too long or too short a speech makes it obscure, too much truth astonishes us . . . If one is too young or too old, the mind cannot function; as with too much or too little education." Pascal, *Oeuvres complètes*, p. 527.

26. Ibid., p. 528.

27. G. Bataille, *Le Coupable*, "Rire et tremblement," trans. Bruce Boone as *Guilty*, p. 108.

28. [Trans.: We have translated Clément's *désaccord* and *accord* as "being at odds" and "being in agreement"; in French the terms also have musical resonance, "being in or out of tune," a concept on which Clément will expand in chapter 4.]

29. J.-P. Sartre, "Un Nouveau Mystique," *Cahiers du Sud*, nos. 260–62 (October-December 1943). Bataille's answer is rigorously honest: "Thought is produced in me by means of uncoordinated illuminations that withdraw endlessly from the term that facilitated its approach. I do not know whether I am describing a generalized human incapacity—or one that is particular to me. . . . I don't know, but I have little hope of attaining this goal, even in a way that appears sat-

isfactory from the outside. But isn't there an advantage to doing philosophy my way: the illumination in the night, the language of a brief instant?"

30. Blanchot's oeuvre, like the work of Roger Laporte, is located in a mode of inquiry that is strictly atheistic and strictly swooning. Blanchot is quoted by Bataille in *L'Expérience intérieure* (Inner experience), a work attacked by Sartre. These are the syncopes associated with writing, or with writing that is anchored in a syncope that refuses to return to the realm of daily life. Of particular note is the book by Roger Laporte, *Une Vie*, which gathers together an ensemble of texts and drafts an entirely interiorized biography, contrary in every way to the biography based on events.

2. Philosophers and Their Daemons

1. This happens for the first time in the *Phaedrus*, and for the second time at the end of the *Phaedo*.

2. Phaedrus, the disciple, addressed the following words to Socrates: "Anyone would take you, as you say, for a stranger being shown the country by a guide instead of a native—never leaving town to cross the frontier nor even, I believe, so much as setting foot outside the walls." And Socrates responds: "You must forgive me, dear friend; I'm a lover of learning, and trees and open country won't teach me anything, whereas men in the town do. Yet you seem to have discovered a recipe for getting me out." This recipe is not the charm of nature but the discourse that Phaedrus has waved under Socrates' nose, and which has enabled him to bring Socrates outside the city walls at last (*Phaedrus*, section 230d-e, trans. R. Hackforth. In *The Collected Dialogues of Plato*, ed. Edith Hamilton and Huntington Cairns [Princeton: Princeton University Press, 1961]).

3. Ibid., section 242c.

4. Ibid., section 254e.

5. The definition of "counterlove": "the image of love." The test: "So when they lie side by side, the wanton horse of the lover's soul would have a word with the charioteer, claiming a little guerdon for all his trouble. The like steed in the soul of the beloved has no word to say, but, swelling with desire for he knows not what, embraces and kisses the lover, in grateful acknowledgment of all his kindness. And when they lie by one another, he is minded not to refuse to do his part in gratifying his lover's entreaties; yet his yokefellow in turn, *being moved by reverence and heedfulness*, joins with the driver in resisting." Ibid., section 256a. Emphasis added.

6. Ibid., section 238d.

7. *Phaedo*, section 61b. In *The Collected Dialogues of Plato*, ed. Hamilton and Cairns. "I thought it would be safer not to take my departure before I had cleared my conscience by writing poetry and so obeying the dream."

8. [Trans.: For "complied," Clément uses *s'exécuter*, which makes a pun on Socrates' imminent execution.]

9. Crito to Socrates: "But surely, Socrates, said Crito, the sun is still upon the mountains; it has not gone down yet. Besides, I know that in other cases people have dinner and enjoy their wine, and sometimes the company of those whom they love, long after they receive the warning, and only drink the poison quite late at night. No need to hurry. There is still plenty of time." To which Socrates responds, "It is natural that these people whom you speak of should act in that way, Crito, because they think that they gain by it. And it is also natural that I should not, because I believe that I should gain nothing by drinking the poison a little later—I should only make myself ridiculous in my own eyes if I clung to life and hugged it when it has no more to offer. Come, do as I say and don't make difficulties." Ibid., section 117.

10. Ibid., section 118.

11. The myth of the cicadas is found in the *Phaedrus*: in the middle of the day the cicadas are "singing after their wont in the hot sun and conversing with one another," but Socrates insists that he is resistant to their song. If one gives in to them, they laugh; "If, however, they see us con-

versing and steering clear of their bewitching Siren song, they might feel respect for us and grant us that boon which heaven permits them to confer upon mortals" (section 259a). Phaedrus, naturally, knows nothing of the privilege nor of the myth surrounding it; Socrates makes it his duty to instruct him and tells the story of the cicada people. The privilege granted by the cicadas is to make known to philosophers and "those who cultivate Music" their two patron Muses, Calliope and Urania. We shall see that this is not just any music.

12. *Discourse on Method*, in *The Philosophical Works of Descartes*, trans. Elizabeth S. Haldane (Cambridge: Cambridge University Press, 1967), vol. 1, p. 92.

13. Ibid., p. 91.

14. It is in the opening passages of the *Meditations on First Philosophy* that this warning against youth is found; Descartes insists on it in *Discourse on Method*. "Age" is necessary to reject opinions and to find one's own direction. First Meditation, "Of the things which may be brought within the sphere of the doubtful" (p. 144).

15. Ibid., p. 148.

16. Ibid., p. 150.

17. Ibid., p. 154.

18. G. Bataille, *Inner Experience*.

19. Ibid.

20. Descartes, *Discourse on Method*.

21. *Lettre à la princesse Elizabeth*, May 1646, in *Oeuvres Complètes* (Paris: Bibliothèque de la Pléiade, Gallimard, 1949), p. 992.

22. Ibid., p. 1004.

23. According to the "Baillet account," after all of the gossip surrounding Descartes's death had been played out (saying that he had become tired out by putting his papers in order, that he had been poisoned by rivals in the Swedish court, or that Queen Christina had not paid enough attention to his lessons), this explanation is put forward: "The real and only cause of M. Descartes' illness was the division of his time between the Queen and the ailing Ambassador, in the midst of a season that was an enemy to his constitution. It is easy to understand the disruption when he was obliged to change the routine he had established for himself, since he had immediately decided to treat his health on his own."

24. Immanuel Kant, *Critique of Judgment*, trans. Werner S. Pluhar (Indianapolis: Hackett, 1987), p. 130.

25. Ibid., pp. 7–8.

26. Ibid., p. 37.

27. Ibid., p. 115.

28. Ibid., p. 98.

29. Ibid., p. 130.

30. Ibid., p. 198.

31. All these judgments on music are from ibid., pp. 198–99.

32. Remark 54, *Critique of Judgment*, p. 202.

33. Ibid., p. 205.

34. Claude Lévi-Strauss, Introduction, *The Raw and the Cooked* (Chicago: University of Chicago Press, 1964), p. 18: "But since music is a language with some meaning at least for the immense majority of mankind, although only a tiny minority of people are capable of formulating a meaning in it, and since it is the only language with the contradictory attributes of being at once both intelligible and untranslatable, the musical creator is a being comparable to the gods, and music itself the supreme mystery of the science of man, a mystery that all the various disciplines come up against and which holds the key to their progress."

35. Kant, *Critique of Judgment*, p. 203.

36. Ibid., p. 127.

3. Depriving the City of Spices: Plato Purges the Republic

1. The Stranger, who came from Elea and was a faithful follower of the philosophers Parmenides and Zeno, makes his entry in the *Theaetetus* and continues to intervene in the *Statesman* (trans. J. B. Skemp, in *The Collected Dialogues of Plato*, ed. Edith Hamilton and Huntington Cairns [Princeton: Princeton University Press, 1961]).

2. *The Statesman*, section 271c.

3. Ibid., section 269c.

4. Ibid., section 272e.

5. In a dialogue with Adimantus, *The Republic*, II, sections 376, 377 (trans. Paul Shorey, in *The Collected Dialogues of Plato*).

6. Ibid., section 379a.

7. Ibid., III, section 387c. Here are a few examples of censored quotes: "Forth from his limbs unwilling his spirit flitted to Hades / wailing its doom and its lustihood lost and the May of its manhood" (section 386d); or, again: "Under the earth like a vapor vanished the gibbering soul" (section 387a).

8. Other examples of censorship: "Quenchless then was the laughter that rose from the blessed immortals / When they beheld Hephaestus officiously puffing and panting" (*The Republic*, section 389a). Plato attacks here one of the most famous episodes of the mythology of his culture: Zeus quarrels so loudly with his wife Hera that he is on the verge of beating her; the limping god gets up and pretends to play the butler, and his appearance is so grimacing that the gods burst out laughing. Perhaps the enormity of the censorship doesn't escape Adimantus, who hesitates, for once, in agreeing with his interlocutor.

9. Ibid., III, section 395 and following.

10. Ibid., III, section 395, p. 951. Adimantus's answer: "We certainly should do that *if it rested with us*" (section 398b; emphasis added).

11. The gymnasts' regimen: no fish or meat stews, nor spices, Attic pastries, or Corinthian girls. This regimen is not so different from the one followed by gymnasts throughout time; it is unusual in that Plato compares it to the regimen that must be imposed on music.

12. *The Republic*, III, section 399e.

13. Ibid., VI, section 484b.

14. [Trans.: There is no way in English to get the structure of the original: *du bout de la pensée*, as one says *du bout des lèvres*, on "the tip of the tongue."]

15. Georges Bataille, vol. 8, pp. 69–70. "We are ashamed of the life of corruption, etc." is the title of the second section of chapter 3, "Death"; "We have no greater phobia than that of this matter that is pulullating, fetid, lukewarm, where life ferments in a revolting fashion. This matter in which eggs, sprouts, and worms swarm does not simply make us flinch, but actually makes our stomachs turn. One day this living world, etc." (p. 70).

16. At least according to tradition; she may decide to survive her husband and not die with him on the funeral pyre. See below. White is beginning to be worn in India with a festive or fashionable connotation, no longer relating to mourning; however, it is still rare.

17. *The Republic*, X, sections 616–18.

18. Ibid., X, section 614. Er had remained on the battlefield for twelve days; he was thought to be dead, although his body, unlike that of the other cadavers, had not begun to decompose. In order to avoid future misadventures of this type, Plato elsewhere suggests a three-day waiting period before funerals to be sure that the death is not just a prolonged syncope.

19. See *La Source noir* (The dark source) by Patrice Van Eersel (Grasset, 1986). This book, which is courageous, idealistic, delirious, and perfectly reasonable at the same time, is a long reportage that began as a discussion of the modern-day techniques of accompanying the dying, which has began to develop in France, inspired by the work of Elisabeth Kübler-Ross. Then the reporter from *Actuel* collects the testimonies of patients who have "risen again" after resuscitation,

and analyzes and interprets them. He returns to the myth of Er before taking off, with Elisabeth Kübler-Ross, on a long imaginary and theoretical trip to India, where the mystical techniques of reincarnation make their remarkable apparition near the end of this rather mad but fundamental book.

20. [Trans.: *Part maudite*, which is also the title of one of Bataille's books, translated into English as *The Accursed Share*.]

21. *The Republic*, IX, section 571.

22. See the wonderful book by Daniel Wilhem, "Les Romantiques allemands" (Ecrivains de Toujours, Seuil, 1980); also, by Marcel Brion, *L'Allemagne romantique: Le Voyage initiatique*, vol. 3 (Paris: Albin Michel, 1976); and by Michel Le Bris, *Le Journal du romantisme* (Geneva: Skira, 1981).

23. Quoted by Geneviève Bianquis, "Femmes romantiques," in *Le Romantisme allemand* (Paris: Editions 10/18, 1966), based on a work published in 1947 that was taken from a collective work published in 1937.

24. Ibid., quoted by Charles du Bos in *La Notion de 'Stimmung': Fragments sur Novalis*, note 13, p. 186, Fragment 365, Ed. Minor, vol. 2, p. 224.

25. Ibid., quoted by Pierre Moisy, *Paysagistes romantiques allemands: Runge, Friedrich, Carus*, p. 53.

26. Ibid., Albert Béguin, "Préface," *Lettres*, ed. Gilbert Guisan (Paris: Bibliothèque des Arts, 1976). In 1952, Béguin went to India; he wrote to Marcel Raymond: "The excitement of its spectacle, colors, faces, the admirable depth of the centuries, in this country, the horrific presence of human suffering . . . " Later he published *Les Indes, l'Inde* (Paris: La Bâconnière, 1953).

27. Quoted by Georg Lukács in *The Young Hegel*, trans. Rodney Livingstone (Cambridge, Mass.: MIT Press, 1975). At the time when he was studying history in Berne, Hegel was interested in trying to characterize life in antiquity, and to describe the relationship, in the city, between public and private life. According to Hegel, the principle of antiquity was this return to ordinary life; Christianity, however, gave rise to witchcraft, "the advance from isolated outbreaks of madness to a thoroughgoing and permanent derangement of the mind" (p. 50). As we see, Hegel's thoughts on witchcraft anticipate the modern psychiatric movement.

4. The Owl and the Nightingale: Hegel and Hölderlin

1. Quoted in Lukács, *The Young Hegel*, trans. Rodney Livingstone (Cambridge, Mass.: MIT Press, 1975), p. 102.

2. *The Phenomenology of Mind*, trans. J. B. Baillie (New York: Harper and Row, 1967); "The Conflict of Self-Consciousness in Self-Opposition" followed by "Lord and Bondsman" [Trans.: more commonly translated as "Master and Slave"], pp. 230 ff.; "The Ethical Relation of Man and Woman as Brother and Sister," pp. 477 ff.

3. Lukács, *Young Hegel*, p. 105.

4. I am thinking of the night watchman who, at the end of a particularly boisterous Saint John's night celebration in Wagner's opera *Der Meistersinger*, forces everyone to go home in a hurry; all he does is appear and blow into his horn, giving the call that will send each person back to the bed from which they never should have strayed.

5. [Trans.: We changed "familiar *from* Scripture" to the more accurate "with."]

6. "The Vatican," trans. Richard Siebirth in *Friedrich Hölderlin: Hymns and Fragments* (Princeton: Princeton University Press, 1984). The birds that are "guardians of the senses," that the poet discovers while traveling, are the sea gull, the eagle, the crane, and the owl, a hoarse-voiced woman.

7. In Hölderlin, *Oeuvres complètes* (Paris: Pléiade, 1989), "Documents," pp. 1109 ff. This is what the carpenter who is caring for him says: "Actually he is no longer mad, or what we call mad. His body is quite healthy, his appetite is quite good and he drinks his mug of wine every day in

good time. He sleeps well, except in the heat of summer when he roams the staircase all night. He is an agreeable house-mate. . . . It is not mental deficiency that drove him mad. It is all his knowledge [*science*], believe me. When the jar is too full, and closed, it can only burst. . . . It is his obsession with paganism that clouded his thoughts. He stopped thinking at a certain point, and since then has kept going over that same point. His thoughts are like a flock of doves flying around a weathervane on a rooftop. They circle [it] together until they collapse, exhausted." One day when Kühne was visiting, the carpenter told the bogus spinet tuner, just before Hölderlin came in, that the mad poet was in a bad mood that day. "He has declared that the font of knowledge is poisoned today, that the fruits of knowledge are empty nutshells, a sham." Hölderlin had found this "debris" of ideas in the plum tree he had been climbing in (p. 1110).

8. [Trans.: *Désaccord*, literally, "in discord."]

9. Hölderlin, *Hyperion, or the Hermit in Greece*, trans. Willard Trask (New York: Frederick Ungar, 1965). These are almost the last words in the text.

10. Hölderlin, *Oeuvres complètes*, p. 1112.

11. Hölderlin, "Remarks on *Oedipus*," in *Friedrich Hölderlin: Essays and Letters on Theory*, trans. Thomas Pfau (Albany: SUNY Press, 1988), p. 107.

12. Ibid., p. 108.

13. Hegel, *Phenomenology of Mind*, "Religion" and "Religion in the Form of Art," pp. 709–49.

14. Again, a statement from the carpenter Zimmer, in Hölderlin, *Oeuvres complètes*, p. 1110.

15. [Trans.: Clément's original says "*retournement natal*"; in French, the word *natal* could connote either "primal" or "patriotic." The translation we have used prefers "patriotic" in the English context, but to keep the sense of Clément's argument, we have sometimes used "primal."]

16. Hölderlin, "Remarks on *Antigone*," in *Friedrich Hölderlin*, trans. Pfau, p. 114.

17. Hegel, *Phenomenology of Mind*, p. 475.

18. Ibid., p. 477.

19. Ibid.

20. See Hegel, "The Philosophy of Nature," section 3, "Organic Physics," article 287.

21. Hegel, *The Philosophy of Right*, trans. T. M. Knox (Oxford: Clarendon Press, 1952). Part II, "Ethical Life," article 166, notes: "For this reason family piety is expounded in Sophocles' *Antigone*—one of the most sublime presentations of this virtue—as principally the law of woman, and as the law of a substantiality at once subjective and on the plane of feeling, the law of the inward life, a life which has not yet attained its full actualization; as the law of the ancient gods, 'the gods of the underworld'; as 'an everlasting law, and no man knows at what time it was first put forth.' This law is there displayed as a law opposed to public law, to the law of the land. This is the supreme opposition in ethics and therefore in tragedy; and it is individualized in the same play in the opposing natures of man and woman."

22. In Lacan, Seminar 7, *L'Ethique de la psychanalyse* (The ethics of psychoanalysis) (Paris: Seuil, 1986). "The wind was blowing hard and everyone was covering their head," comments Lacan, "when Antigone appeared next to the body making little plaintive cries. This is the nightingale as defined in Euripides, as an image in which the human being seems to change on the level of this lament" (p. 307).

23. Philemon and Baucis are rewarded for a love that continues into old age; Adonis was killed by a boar; Daphne resisted the god Apollo; Arachne dared to challenge the skill of Athena, the goddess of weavers; Niobe cried so hard after the death of her children that the gods took pity on her and turned her to stone.

24. Hölderlin, *Hyperion*, p. 67.

25. *Patmos*, trans. E. S. Schaffer, in *"Kubla Khan" and "The Fall of Jerusalem": The Mythological School in Biblical Criticism and Secular Literature 1779–1880* (Cambridge: Cambridge University Press, 1975).

Secret-laden
In a golden haze infolded
On the steps of the sun up-shooting
Full-blown
A thousand towers of fragrance
Asia I saw: dazzled. (lines 27–32)

[Trans.: We altered the translation, as Clément uses it in the text itself, to remain closer to the point she is making.]

26. "In Lovely Blueness," in *Friedrich Hölderlin: Poems and Fragments*, trans. Michael Hamburger (Cambridge: Cambridge University Press, 1980).

27. Quoted by Marcel Brion in *L'Allemagne romantique*, p. 10.

28. Not far from the Ganges' source is Rishikesh, the first holy city, traditionally devoted to meditation; religious retreats (ashrams) abound there; Westerners as well. Sometimes they are seen naked in the nearby forests. At the other end of the Ganges—which in the meantime will have traversed the holy cities of Haridwar, Allahabad, and Benares—is Calcutta, and the exquisite madness of the festivals honoring Durga and Kali, to which many Europeans have expressed an aversion.

29. See the biography of him by Romain Rolland: *La Vie de Ramakrishna* (Paris: Stock, 1978).

30. Mira Alfassa, called "the Mother," who died in 1974, is the founder of the ashram of Pondicherry and the future city of Auroville, a few kilometers away.

31. It would be a mistake to neglect the financial aspect of the ashrams, which play a role similar to that of the monasteries in Europe during the Middle Ages; in Pondicherry, the ashram of Aurobindo and the Mother owns nearly half the stores in town, a hotel, a printing press, and several small factories.

32. Hegel, *The Philosophy of History*, trans. J. M. Sibree (New York: Willey, 1900), pp. 103 ff.

33. Ibid., p. 140.

34. Ibid., p. 141.

5. Loves Me, Loves Me Not; or, The Love of Dialectic

1. G. W. F. Hegel, *The Science of Logic*, trans. A. V. Miller (London: Allen and Unwin; New York: Humanities Press, 1969). Book 1, section 1, "Determinateness (Quality)"; Chapter 3, "The One and the Many," p. 168.

2. Ibid., p. 175.

3. Ibid., pp. 176–77.

4. Ibid. Book II, section 3, "The Idea"; chapter 3, "The Absolute Idea," p. 835.

5. Ibid.

6. Hegel, *The Philosophy of Right*, Introduction, p. 11: "To comprehend what is, this is the task of philosophy, because what is, is reason. Whatever happens, every individual is a child of his time; so philosophy too is its own time apprehended in thoughts." The text I quote follows these well-known phrases.

And now, his text on the rose and the cross, no less famous: "To recognize reason as the rose in the cross of the present, and thereby to enjoy the present, this is the rational insight which reconciles us to the actual, the reconciliation which philosophy affords to those in whom there has once arisen an inner voice bidding them to comprehend, not only to dwell in what is substantive while still retaining subjective freedom, but also to possess subjective freedom while standing not in anything particular and accidental but in what exists absolutely" (p. 12).

7. Hegel, *Encyclopedia of the Philosophical Sciences in Outline*, trans. Steven Taubeneck (New York: Continuum, 1990), p. 257.

8. Ibid., paragraph 475, p. 263. This is the complete text: "This initial appearance is formed by the syllogism, which has logic basically as its starting point, with nature for the middle term,

and is linked ultimately to spirit. Logic becomes nature, and nature becomes spirit. Nature, which stands between the spirit and its essence, divides itself, though not to the extremes of finite abstraction. For the syllogism is in the idea and nature is essentially determined as a transition point and negative moment. But the mediation of the concept has the external form of transition, and science takes the form of being." Paragraph 476: "In the second syllogism this appearance is suspended, for the spirit is the mediating factor. This is a syllogism which is already the standpoint of the spirit itself, presupposes nature and joins it with logic. It is the syllogism of reflection on the idea; science appears as subjective cognition." Paragraph 477: "These appearances are suspended in the idea of philosophy, which has self-knowing reason, the absolutely general, for its middle term: a middle which divides itself into spirit and nature, with the former as its presupposition, and the latter as its general extreme. Thus immediate nature is only a posited entity, as spirit is in itself, not a presupposition, but rather totality returning into itself. In this way the middle term, the self-knowing concept, has as its reality primarily conceptual moments and exists in its determinacy as general knowledge, persisting immediately by itself."

9. Ibid.

10. The last words spoken by Anthony at the end of Flaubert's book *La Tentation de Saint Antoine* (The temptation of Saint Anthony).

11. The Beast, borrowed from Pliny, is called Catoblepas.

12. Melanie Klein, "The Oedipus Complex in the Light of Early Anxieties," in *The Oedipus Complex Today: Clinical Implications*, ed. John Steiner (London: Karnac Books, 1989), p. 67. Before this phase of "polymorphous" thought, the child does not possess the conceptual means to differentiate; for example, a child shows a picture depicting a bulldog next to a dead chicken and says: "I know, they are all the same, the chicken, the ice, the glass, and the crabs." Melanie Klein asks him what the *ratio* of this relationship is, and gets the answer: "Because they are all brown, and broken, and dead"; in "Contribution to the Theory of Intellectual Inhibition" (1931). Logical thought is achieved by means of rapid oscillations that move from inside to outside and from the self to reality; often, as Melanie Klein has noted, "The archaic and symbolic forms of representation which the child employs in its play are associated with another primitive mechanism. In its play, the child acts out instead of speaking. It puts actions—which originally took the place of thoughts—in the place of words." In *The Psychoanalysis of Children*, trans. Alix Strachey (New York: Delacorte Press, 1975), p. 9.

13. *The Aesthetics: Lectures on Fine Art*, trans. T. M. Knox (Oxford: Clarendon Press, 1975), vol 2, p. 957. See also the return of the "theme" of the being's contraction: "For it is precisely this sphere of inner sensibility, abstract self-comprehension, which music takes for its own and therefore brings movement into the seat of inner changes, into the heart and mind as *this simple concentrated centre of the whole of human life*" (vol. 2, p. 905; emphasis added).

14. In François Châtelet's fine book, *Hegel* (Paris: Seuil, Collection Écrivains de Toujours, 1968), p. 64.

15. G. Bataille, *Guilty* (Venice, Calif.: Lapis Press, 1988), p. 26.

16. Ibid.

17. *Vous qui habitez le temps* (You who live in time) by Valère Novarina (Paris: Editions P.O.I., 1989), p. 9. Presented at the Avignon festival the same year.

18. Ibid.

19. Ibid., p. 10.

6. Of Young Girls as Thought: Kierkegaard the Seducer

1. Søren Kierkegaard, *Either/Or*, trans. Howard V. Hong and Edna H. Hong, vol. 3 of *Collected Writings of Kierkegaard* (Princeton: Princeton University Press, 1987). "The Immediate Erotic Stages, Insignificant Introduction," p. 58.

2. Ibid.

3. Ibid.

4. The return of the heliotrope plays an important symbolic role in *The Seducer's Diary*—but one must wait for the seduction to have taken place.

5. *The Seducer's Diary*, pp. 313–14: "Take care, my beautiful stranger! Take care! To step out of a carriage is not such a simple matter; at times it is a decisive step. . . . There! How firmly this tiny foot is standing now. I have noticed that girls with tiny feet usually stand more firmly than the more pedestrian big-footed ones."

6. Ibid., pp. 433–34. See also p. 391: "Everywhere, wherever she turns, a young girl has the infinite around her, and the transition is a leap, but, please note, a feminine, not a masculine leap. Why are men ordinarily so clumsy? When they are going to leap, they have to take a running start, make many preparations, measure the distance with the eyes, make several runs—shy away and turn back. Finally they leap and fall in. A young girl leaps in a different way."

7. Ibid., pp. 433–34.

8. Ibid., p. 438. The rest of the text is as follows: "Truly, if this regal flight were a retreat from me, it would pain me very deeply. For me it would be the same as if Pygmalion's beloved were changed to stone again. Light have I made her, light as a thought, and should then this thought of mine not belong to me! It would be enough to despair over. A moment before, it would not have occupied me; a moment later, it will not concern me, but now—now—this now that is an eternity for me" (p. 438).

9. Ibid., p. 445.

10. See Ovid, *The Metamorphoses*, Book 12. Caenis or Kainis, a virgin from Thessaly, was surprised at the edge of the sea by Neptune; the god found her attractive and raped her. Then, with the exquisite politeness that is characteristic of the Greek gods when they have raped a beautiful woman, Neptune asked her what she wanted. Without hesitating, Caenis asked to be immediately transformed into a man in order never again to undergo a similar outrage. Her voice changed; she also became immortal, as is often the case with bisexual characters. Under the name of Caeneus—or Kaineus—she warded off whole tree trunks. From the mountain of trees that eventually buried her alive flew a "bird with dark feathers."

11. Goethe, *The Sorrows of Young Werther*, trans. Victor Lange (New York: Rinehart, 1949), p. 21.

12. Ibid., pp. 23, 25.

13. In *Écrits sur le théâtre* by Vsevolod Meyerhold, vol. 3, 1930–36 (Paris: L'Age d'homme, 1980).

14. Ibid., p. 190, regarding the presentation of *33 Swoonings* in 1935. Meyerhold chose to present *Le Jubilé*, *L'Ours*, and *La Demande en mariage*. In *Le Jubilé*, there are 14 swoonings; in *L'Ours* and *La Demande en mariage*, 19 swoonings. "In other words, *33 Swoonings* is without hyperbole." He was nevertheless attacked for his penchant for hyperbole.

15. See *The Birth of Psychoanalysis: Outline of a Scientific Psychology*, Part II, "The Psychopathology of Hysteria," sections 4 and 5. Section 5, The determinants of "Proton Pseudos," the first hysterical lie: "Although it is quite rare for a memory to excite in the psyche an emotion that no actual incident justifies, that is however what is produced in the ordinary course of things in the sexual level—precisely because of the delay of puberty. This delay constitutes a general character of the organization. Every adolescent harbors some mnemonic traces that only become comprehensible after the appearance of sexual sensations. Each must therefore carry inside himself the seed of hysteria. . . . Analysis demonstrates that it is the affective discharge that constitutes, when there is a sexual trauma, the disturbing element. Also, experience teaches us that hysterics are people whose sexuality has been precociously awakened, thanks to mechanical and emotional stimulation (masturbation), and we would say of them sometimes that they are predisposed to precocious sexual discharges."

16. *Dora: Fragment of an Analysis of Hysteria*.

7. Abraham, and a Roasted Lamb's Head

1. Genesis 22. *The New English Bible*, Oxford Study Edition (New York: Oxford University Press, 1976).

2. Søren Kierkegaard, *Fear and Trembling*, trans. Howard V. Hong and Edna H. Hong; vol. 6 of *Collected Writings of Kierkegaard* (Princeton: Princeton University Press, 1983), p. 7. Kierkegaard's text on the sacrifice of Isaac demanded of Abraham by Yahweh is called "Atmosphere."

3. [Trans.: *Sevrage*, "weaning," or literally "separation" (from the mother).]

4. [Trans.: *Rit de toutes ses vielles dents*: literally, "she laughed with all her old teeth." Unfortunately, the expression cannot be caught in English.]

5. Genesis 22:12.

6. They are the Untouchables who, in the Hindu caste system, perform "impure" tasks. As a reminder, here are the levels of the caste system that reform groups—including the Sikhs—have opposed. At the top, there are the Brahmans, intellectuals and priests; then the Kshatriyas, warriors and rulers of society; then there are the merchants, the Vaisyas; and the Sudras, the peasants and laborers. The Untouchables are at the bottom of the scale. From its inception, the Sikh religion was one in which every man had the power to make war. See Khushwant Singh, *A History of the Sikhs*, in two volumes (Princeton: Princeton University Press, 1963 and 1966; second ed., 1984).

7. Kierkegaard, *Fear and Trembling*, p. 36.

8. Ibid., p. 41.

9. Ibid. "I honestly confess," says Kierkegaard ironically, "that in my experience I have not found a single authentic instance, although I do not deny that every second person may be such an instance" (p. 38). Kierkegaard imagines this man; here he is. At first glance he has the air of a tax collector. "I move a little closer to him, watch his slightest movement to see if it reveals a bit of heterogeneous optical telegraphy from the infinite, a glance, a facial expression, a gesture, a sadness, a smile that would betray the infinite in its heterogeneity with the finite. No! I examine his figure from top to toe to see if there may not be a crack through which the infinite would peek. No! He is solid all the way through" (p. 39). Later, when the philosopher meets him in the street, "one would take him for a mercantile soul enjoying himself. He finds pleasure in this way, for he is not a poet, and I have tried in vain to lure the poetic incommensurability out of him. Toward evening, he goes home, and his gait is as steady as a postman's. On the way, he thinks that his wife will surely have a special hot meal for him when he comes home—for example, roast lamb's head with vegetables" (p. 39). An echo—no doubt innocent—of the knight of faith's culinary tastes can be found in Georges Bataille, in a strange text in *Inner Experience*: "Laughter, dream, and, in sleep, the rooftops fall in a rain of gravel . . . to know nothing, to this point (not of ecstasy but of sleep): to strangle myself thus, unsolvable puzzle, to accept sleep, the starry universe my tomb, glorified, glory constellated with deaf stars, unintelligible and further than death, terrifying (*nonsense: the taste of garlic which the roasted lamb had*)" (p. 61; emphasis added).

10. Ibid., p. 39.

11. Kierkegaard, *Either/Or*, "Silhouettes," pp. 170–71.

12. Ibid., p. 42.

13. Ibid., "The Tragic in Ancient Drama Reflected in the Tragic in Modern Drama," p. 164.

14. In *Diapsalmata*, a text dedicated "ad se ipsum," to himself. The rest of the fragment is: "Then my father would himself have laid me in a little casket, taken me under his arm, carried me out to the grave on a Sunday morning, would himself have cast the earth on it and in a low voice said a few words understandable only to himself. Only in the happy days of yore could people have the idea of babies weeping in Elysium because they died so prematurely" (p. 40). In *The Point of View for My Work as an Author*, trans. Walter Lowrie (London: Oxford University Press, 1939), Kierkegaard writes this: "The thought goes very far back in my recollection that in every genera-

tion there are two or three who can be sacrificed for the others, are led by frightful sufferings to discover what redounds to the good of others. So it was that in my melancholy I understood myself as singled out for such a fate" (p. 79).

15. [Trans.: The word Clément uses here is *sécrètent*, literally "to secrete."]

16. *The Sickness Unto Death*, trans. Howard V. Hong and Edna H. Hong, vol. 19 of *Collected Writings of Kierkegaard* (Princeton: Princeton University Press, 1980), p. 18.

17. Ibid., p. 17.

18. Quoted by Stefan Zweig in *Le Combat contre le démon* (The fight against the demon) (Paris: Stock, 1978; rpt. Laffont, 1983).

19. Stefan Zweig: "No diabolical suffering is missing from this horrible pandemonium of sickness: headaches; pounding, numbing headaches that consign the unfortunate, delirious invalid to the couch or bed for days on end, in a daze; stomach cramps, including the vomiting of blood, migraines, loss of appetite, hemorrhoids, intestinal distress, feverish chills, night sweats—it is a terrible cycle" (ibid., p. 209).

20. Ibid., pp. 226–27.

21. "Sils Maria"

Here I sat, waiting—not for anything—
Beyond Good and Evil, fancying

Now light, now shadow, all a game,
All lake, all noon, all time without aim.

Then, suddenly, friend, one turned into two—
And Zarathustra walked into my view.

Trans. Walter Kaufmann, *The Gay Science* (New York: Random House, 1974), p. 371.

22. *Diapsalmata*, p. 42: "Salmon is in itself very delicious eating, but too much of it is bad for the health, inasmuch as it is a heavy food. For this reason, once when there was a great catch of salmon, the police in Hamburg ordered each master of a household to give his servants salmon not more than once a week. Would that there might be a similar police notice with regard to sentimentality."

23. Kierkegaard, *Sickness Unto Death*, p. 74.

8. The Great Attack

1. This entire chapter is inspired by the tragedy by Euripides, *The Bacchae*; the herdsman's tale, lines 677–774.

2. One, taking a thyrsus, struck it against a rock,
from which a stream of pure cold water sprang.
Another drove her shaft into the ground
and there the god sent up a spring of wine.
And those who had a longing for white drink,
brushing the ground off with their fingertips,
had milk welling up in abundance. From their wands
with ivy trimmed sweet honey dripped in streams.
. . . Shouting with all their mouths the jubilant cry:
Iacchos!—calling the roaring child of Zeus.
And the whole mountain danced with them, the wild
animals danced, nothing remained unmoved
by the rush of the women.

Ibid., trans. Donald Sutherland (Lincoln: University of Nebraska Press, 1968), lines 702–11, 724–28.

3. Jacques Lacan, *Motifs du crime paranoïaque: Le Crime des soeurs Papin* (Motives of para-

noiac crime: The case of the Papin sisters), p. 397 in *Premiers Écrits sur la paranoïa*, based on the dissertation he wrote for his medical degree, entitled *De la psychose paranoïaque dans ses rapports avec la personnalité* (On paranoiac psychosis and its connections with personality) (Paris: Seuil, Collection Champ Freudien, 1975).

4. *The Bacchae*, line 233.

5. Ibid., line 493.

6. Ibid., line 862.

7. See the recent book by Marcel Detienne, *L'Ecriture d'Orphée: Orphée récrivant les dieux de la Cité* (Writings of Orpheus: Orpheus rewriting the gods of the city), especially the pages where Dionysus and Apollo appear as complementary, rather than in opposition (Paris: Gallimard, Collection L'Infini, 1989), pp. 117–32.

8. "The Orphic gods," writes Detienne, "are bizarre. Beginning with the First Born, First Father and First Mother, called Phanes-Metis, or Protogonos in the book by Derveni and also Erikepaios, with his repeated insults as to the shape of the human body: two pairs of eyes, golden wings, the voice of a lion and tiger, and two sexes, one of which decorates the place above its buttocks. But there is also Zeus of the fifth reign, who will give his power over to his son and who, instead of being the eternal sovereign over the gods, places the First Born inside his stomach, on the advice of Night, thus becoming a matrix, the shell of an egg whose dimensions are All. The same god, in fact, worsens his situation by becoming his mother's husband and by impregnating his married daughter who becomes his mother again: a double incest. There are five reigns from Phanes to Zeus, going through Night, so close to Phanes, Uranus and Gaea, Kronos and Rhea; and finally Zeus, born of Rhea-Demeter, marrying Demeter 'the Second' before becoming again the husband of Demeter 'the Third,' Demeter-Kore who will give birth to the child Dionysus. A Dionysus already present in the First Born and who inaugurates the sixth and last generation of the gods" (ibid., p. 123).

9. Nietzsche, *The Gay Science* (New York: Random House, 1974), p. 63.

10. Søren Kierkegaard, *The Sickness Unto Death*, trans. Howard V. Hong and Edna H. Hong, vol. 19 of *Collected Writings of Kierkegaard* (Princeton: Princeton University Press, 1980).

11. Ibid., p. 49.

12. Ibid., pp. 49–50n.

13. Hölderlin, "The Poet's Vocation," in *Friedrich Hölderlin: Poems and Fragments*, trans. Michael Hamburger (Cambridge: Cambridge University Press, 1980).

14. This is the word used by Freud several times in his letters to Fliess and in the manuscripts collected under the title *The Origins of Psychoanalysis*.

15. The opera by Gaetano Donizetti, with a libretto by Salvator Cammarano, 1835.

16. [Trans.: The French is *un saut de puce*, literally "a flea's leap," but also a play on Kierkegaard's *saut de pucelle*, "a maiden's leap."]

17. See, based on P. E. Dumont, *L'Asvamedha, description du sacrifice solennel du cheval dans le culte védique* (Paris, 1927). Mircea Eliade, *Histoire des croyances et des idées religieuses*, vol. 1, p. 231, paragraph 72. And especially the comments by Madeleine Biardeau in *Extraits du Mahabharata* (Paris: Flammarion, 1985), p. 66. Translated from the Sanskrit by J. M. Peterfalvi. *Asvamadha*, the sacrifice of a horse, *purusamedha*, sacrifice of a man, from *purusa*, figure of a man, which we will see below.

9. The Birth of Identity and the Syncope of the Imago: Lacan

1. See, in Lacan, *Écrits*, "The Mirror Stage as Formative of the Function of the I" (July 1949) and "Aggressivity in Psychoanalysis" (1948), trans. Alan Sheridan in *Écrits: A Selection* (New York: Norton, 1977); and "Propos sur la causalité psychique" (1946), in *Écrits* (Paris: Editions du Seuil, 1966).

2. In Lacan, *Écrits*. Here is the entire passage: "This development is experienced as a tempo-

ral dialectic that decisively projects the formation of the individual into history. The *mirror stage* is a drama whose internal thrust is precipitated from insufficiency to anticipation—and which manufactures for the subject, caught up in the lure of spatial identification, the succession of phantasies that extends from a fragmented body-image to a form of its totality that I shall call orthopaedic—and, lastly, to the assumption of the armour of an alienating identity, which will mark with its rigid structure the subject's entire mental development. Thus, to break out of the circle of the *Innenwelt* into the *Umwelt* generates the inexhaustible quadrature of the ego's verifications" (English version, p. 4).

3. Ibid., French version, p. 187.

4. Ibid., French version, p. 188.

5. Here are the examples given by Lacan in *Propos sur la causalité psychique*: referring to Harrisson's work of 1939: "Harrisson's experiments show that ovulation is determined by the specific form of the fellow creature, to the exclusion of all other forms of sensory perception, and without it necessarily being a male that is seen.

"When placed in the same room with individuals of both sexes, but inside cages that are made in such a way that the subjects cannot see each other but are easily able to perceive each other's cries and odors, the females do not ovulate. Conversely, when two subjects are able to see each other, even through a plate of glass which is sufficient to prevent setting the game of courtship into motion, and even if the separated couple is composed of two females, ovulation occurs in a period varying from 12 days for a male and female separated by glass, to two months for two females.

"But even more astonishing: an animal catching sight of its own image in the mirror is enough to induce ovulation in two and a half months.

"Another researcher has noted that the secretion of milk in the male's crop, which is normally produced when eggs are laid, is not produced if he cannot watch the female as she lays them."

He continues by citing the examples used by Chavun concerning the wandering grasshopper, and the process of sociability created through the recognition of the imago of the species.

6. "Correlatively, the formation of the *I* is symbolized in dreams by a fortress, or a stadium—its inner arena and enclosure, surrounded by marshes and rubbish-tips, dividing it into two opposed fields of contest where the subject flounders *in quest of the lofty, remote inner castle* whose form (sometimes juxtaposed in the same scenario) symbolizes the id in a quite startling way" (Lacan, "The Mirror Stage," *Écrits*, English version, p. 5). Emphasis added.

7. Kierkegaard, *Diapsalmata*, p. 42.

8. Lacan, "Aggressivity in Psychoanalysis," *Écrits*, English version, p. 27.

9. Ibid., p. 26.

10. "At this junction of nature and culture, so persistently examined by modern anthropology, psychoanalysis alone recognizes this knot of imaginary servitude that love must always undo again, or sever.

"For such a task, we place no trust in altruistic feeling, we who lay bare the aggressivity that underlies the activity of the philanthropist, the idealist, the pedagogue, and even the reformer" (Lacan, "The Mirror Stage," *Écrits*, English version, p. 7).

11. [Trans.: *Lézarder* has the word *lézarde*, "lizard," in it, and so suggests a slithering motion rather than just a "stretch."]

12. This is undoubtedly the best time to acknowledge my debt to Alain Badiou's work. I am speaking of all of his work, beginning with his novel *Almagestes* through his *Manifeste pour la philosophie* (Manifesto for philosophy), including *L'Etre et l'Evénement* (Being and event) and *Théorie du Sujet* (Theory of the subject), without forgetting his important "opera-novel," *L'Echarpe rouge* (The red scarf), set to music by Georges Aperghis and directed by Antoine Vitez. Novelist, musician—flutist, if my memory is correct—and philosopher, a lover of poets who struggles side by side with them, searching for a rigorous contemporary philosophy that would be nei-

ther caught up with lyricism (that is what he will undoubtedly say of this book) nor alienated by Anglo-Saxon positivism, nor obsessed by psychoanalytic practice, but making the best use of psychoanalytic thought. In my opinion, Alain Badiou is one of the greatest contemporary French philosophers. As far as Descartes and Lacan are concerned, see *L'Etre et l'Evénement* (Paris: Seuil), p. 471, "Meditation Thirty-Seven," entitled "Descartes/Lacan." Based on the reversal made by Lacan during one of his seminars (at which we were both present), Badiou announces the following program: "(a) It is possible to rethink the entire history of philosophy, beginning with its Greek origins, on the hypothesis of a mathematical ordering of the ontological question. We would then see the design of both a continuity and a rather different periodicity than those used by Heidegger. In particular, the genealogy of the doctrine of truth will allow us to pinpoint, by means of unusual interpretations, how categories of event [*événement*] and imperceptibility, without being named, are at work throughout the metaphysical text. I believe I have given several examples. (b) A close analysis of logico-mathematical procedures since Cantor and Frege would allow us to think that this intellectual revolution, a blind return of ontology to its own essence, conditions contemporary rationality. This work will allow us to undo, in substance, the monopoly of Anglo-Saxon positivism.

"(c) *Regarding the doctrine of the subject*, the individual examination of each of the generic procedures will give way to an aesthetic, a theory of science, a political philosophy and finally, to the mysteries of love, to a hybridization without fusion with psychoanalysis. All of modern art, all scientific uncertainties, everything that ruined Marxism demands in militant action, and finally, everything that the name Lacan stands for, shall be encountered, rearranged, and gone over by a philosophy brought up to date by clarified categories. And we will be able to say, in the course of this voyage—if at least we do not lose our memory of that which only event allows—that being, what is called being, founds the finite place of a deciding subject: Nothingness having departed, the castle of purity remains" [emphasis added].

Syncope is an event that is not one; it happens and it does not happen. Even if I do not feel concerned (or capable of being so) by points (a) and (b) of this philosophical program, I totally recognize myself in point (c); this book—in its way—seeks, if not a philosophy of science, at least the mysteries of love and a certain political philosophy; aesthetics comes first, without any effort of its own.

13. Georges Bataille, vol. 5, p. 129.

14. Alfred Métraux and Lucien Sebag, for example.

15. The story of Mowgli as narrated by Kipling is told in three parts. During the first part, the child is stolen from his mother by a tiger and saved at the last minute by a pack of wolves, is ransomed by the leader of the pack, and is raised in the jungle (that is, outside the village, which is the real meaning of the word "jungle"). In the second part, Mowgli has grown up and takes revenge on the tiger, with the help of the serpent, the bear, and the panther, as well as "minor" species like cattle and kites. The third part is less well known: Mowgli must return to the world of humans. He lives on the edge of the jungle, near the village, exactly between the two, and goes from one to the other. During the course of one of these trips, he meets a woman—a Muslim—who will become his wife. Finally he accepts employment from His Gracious Majesty as a forest ranger, a job that will allow him to remain between-the-two; he has become a man (see "Mowgli's Last Appearance").

16. [Trans.: *Mouroir*, a place where people go to die; an old people's home.]

10. "Inter faeces et urinas": Tantrism Between Feces and Urine

1. [Trans.: The original "ascesis" was changed to conform with Clément's style.]

2. G. Bataille, *Inner Experience*, trans. L. Boldt (Albany: SUNY Press, 1988), p. 21. Throughout this chapter, "Principles of a Method and a Community," Bataille searches for but is unable to find the Hindu "inner experience." Often he uncovers something of interest; about yoga, for

example: "This mastery of our innermost movements, which in the long run we can acquire, is well known: it is *yoga*. But *yoga* is given in the form of coarse recipes, embellished with pedantism and with bizarre statements. And *yoga*, practiced for its own sake, advances no further than an aesthetics or a hygiene, whereas I have recourse to the same means (laid bare) *in despair*" (p. 15). Or about Tantrism: "The *Tantric Buddhists* have recourse to sexual pleasure: they don't ruin themselves in it, but use it as a springboard. Games of virtuoso, of deliquescence intermingle and nothing is further from the will for laying bare" (p. 17).

In the following paragraph we understand Bataille's reticence: "But I know little, at bottom, about India . . . The few judgments which I abide by—more in antipathy than in receptivity—are linked to my ignorance. I have no hesitation about two points: the Hindus' books are, if not unwieldy, then uneven; these Hindus have friends in Europe whom I don't like" (p. 17). Bataille is quite right on both of these points. The Hindu books are forbidding, heavy, etc.: translators and specialists on India are solely responsible, especially because the sense of intellectual proprietorship in regards to this continent seems stronger than in the other fields of French specialization.

On the second point, Bataille raises a true historical problem. He began to write *Inner Experience* in 1941. At that time, Subra Chandas Bose—who was president of the Congress Party and a disciple of Gandhi—chose, because of his hatred for the British, to build what would later become the Indian army alongside Goering; Bose died in a plane accident on his way to Japan. In India today, despite this position, which would be hard to conceal, Bose is seen as a national hero; his statue overlooks a square in Calcutta, and the position of his arm is unmistakably Hitleresque. Romain Rolland, who died in 1943, also despaired of his Indian friends' advancement, and only with great difficulty prevented Rabindranath Tagore from making an alliance with Mussolini. Only Mahatma Gandhi, as always, behaved without any shadow of ambiguity.

3. This entire passage comes from the book by Sudhir Kakar, *Shamans, Doctors and Mystics: A Psychological Inquiry into India and Its Healing Traditions* (London: Oxford University Press, 1982). The commentaries here are not by Sudhir Kakar but Catherine Clément. The chapter on Tantrism as therapy is found on p. 171: "Tantra and Tantric Healing" and the testimony, which Kakar told me is less than ten years old, goes from p. 182 to p. 185. It was first published in Hindi in the book by the astrology professor.

4. Sudhir Kakar has begun to become well known in France, where several of his books have been published, including *Moksha* (Paris: Belles Lettres, 1985); *Les Pièges de l'amour érotique*, with John Munder Ross (Paris: PUF, 1987) (Tales of love, sex, and danger); and *Intimate Relations: Exploring Indian Sexuality* (Chicago: University of Chicago Press, 1989), published in France by Editions des Femmes, 1990.

He belongs to a small core of researchers who are in charge of analyzing the evolution of Indian mentalities at the Center for the Study of Developing Societies, which is financed by the state but whose members are free to choose their field of research, whether sociological, psychological, cultural, or political. Another member of this group is Ashis Nandy, the author of a remarkable and outspoken work on the interiorization of English colonization, *The Intimate Enemy: Loss and Recovery of Self under Colonialism* (London: Oxford University Press, 1983). Also see the interview with Ashis Nandy by Guy Sorman in *Les Vrais Penseurs de notre temps* (Paris: Fayard, 1989).

5. It is difficult to untangle what, within the puritanism of modern India, derives from England, the Mogul Empire, or Hinduism itself. The Indian intellectual usually shies away from this last question—that of Hinduism—by evoking the immodest eroticism of temple statuary, especially that of Khajuraho, but this position is so hackneyed that soon it will no longer be convincing.

In any case, Tantrism in its philosophical application is not popular with certain intellectuals, who have understood only too well the independent nature of this philosophy, its hostility to hierarchy and the moral order. But they are not too clear on Tantrism's uniquely mystical and ascetic applications. As far as popular practices themselves are concerned, they have apparently lost nothing of their influence, as witnessed by Sudhir Kakar's book.

6. An important reference for what is to follow is Michel Hulin's book *Le Principe de l'Ego dans la pensée indienne classique: La Notion d'ahamkara* (The principle of ego in Indian classical thought: The concept of Ahamkara) (Paris: Collège de France, Institut de Civilisation Indienne, 1978). An indispensable book, brilliant and sensitive, which avoids the "heaviness" dreaded by Bataille.

7. In *Benares, City of Lights*, by Diana L. Eck (London: Routledge and Kegan Paul, 1983).

8. M. Hulin, *Le Principe de l'Ego*, p. 291. The rest of the text: "This repossession of the self by the Heart, where the whole universe originates and is resolved, and which is present at the beginning and the end of the perception of objects, is called 'universal vibration' in the Treatises. Vibration: *Spandasastra*. Repossession: *vimarsa*, literally the act of 'finding the way.'"

9. See ibid., p. 302. Hulin notes the necessity of the image of Kali, which unites the more sophisticated Tantric practices with those that are by far the most popular in India today, especially in Bengal. He would thereby seem to justify the otherwise etymologically unjustifiable pun on *Kali*, the dark, and *Kala*, time.

10. Ibid., p. 331.

11. This magnificient passage is also by Michel Hulin, ibid., p. 331.

12. [Trans.: Clément writes "Parole Inter-dite," or "forbidden," but her use of the hyphen creates a neologism, "inter-said," that is lost in translation.]

13. *Sitkara*, the breath or muffled death-rattle, Hulin, *La Principe de l'Ego*, p. 333.

14. Ibid., 313–14.

15. "This is the impulse that is released in a region of the heart at the moment when one remembers something that must be accomplished, upon hearing good news or when one is frightened, when one sees something unexpected, in the spurt of sperm, when one speaks very fast, when one runs away with all one's might," quoted in ibid., p. 315.

16. *Kundalini*, the source of innumerable Western daydreams, is the name of this serpentine energy, a figure reducible to *shakti*, or the energy of the universe. The reason for the fascination of this image among Western daydreamers who are crazy about India is a topic worthy of study.

17. *Kramamudra*: "The yogi seals himself off through successive bends in the road to Consciousness through its aspects of emanation of conservation and of cosmic reabsorption; by means of *Kramamudra*, he appropriates that which [has lain dormant] inside himself. That is the 'energy of consciousness,' the fourth state. The yogi is completely immersed in himself, although he directs himself outward and the utilization of supreme energy remains an immediate reality. This is a yogi who is highly evolved. During this process, because of the feeling of being swallowed up that is progressively more pervasive, exterior objects are engulfed by an extremely dynamic consciousness and are devoured by it. Then there is a phase of vomiting, an immersion that now begins from within—the energy of consciousness—until the true nature of the external is discovered, that is, the totality of objects that have an appearance of *eccéité* (*Dasein*). And this immersion is demonstrated as a coagulation of the essence (*rasa*) of consciousness," quoted in Hulin, *La Principe de l'Ego*, p. 338. For more information on *rasa*, see below, chapter 16.

18. G. Bataille, *On Nietzsche*, *Oeuvres complètes*, vol. 6, (Paris: Gallimard, 1973), p. 202.

19. Lacan, "Propos sur la causalité psychique," p. 188.

20. Claude Lévi-Strauss, *Tristes Tropiques*, trans. John and Doreen Weightman (New York: Pocket Books, 1977), p. 223.

21. The actual figures, which do not take into account the 18 million Indians who are born each year, are as follows: Hindus, 700 million; Muslims, 100 million; Christians, 16 million; Sikhs, 12 million; Tribals, as they are known in India, a figure that is difficult to ascertain, several million; Jains, 3.5 million; Parsis, a community that is rapidly decreasing, 71,000 in 1990; Buddhists, 65,000.

22. In 1989–90, these clashes—a repeat of those that occurred after Partition in 1947 between Hindus and Muslims—especially those in Uttar Pradesh in October 1989 between Sikhs and Hindus, and in Delhi, where 3,000 Sikhs were massacred the night after Indira Gandhi was assassinated. But Buddhists have also taken up arms against Muslims in Ladakh.

23. J. Nehru, *The Discovery of India* (1946). It is this passage by Nehru that Sudhir Kakar quotes at the end of his introduction to *Moksha*, adding that "this search for an exclusively Indian spirit—an identity in contemporary terms—is a constant preoccupation of Indian intellectuals today" (p. 44).

24. Satyajit Ray spoke of his affiliation with the Brahmo-Samaj movement in the episode of the French television program *Océaniques* that Pierre-André Boutang devoted to him in June 1989. The movement's founder, Raja Ram Mohan Roy, was a Sanskrit scholar but also knew Persian, Arabic, English, Greek, Latin, and Hebrew. According to Nehru, he was the primary founder of the Indian press, and was instrumental in having the British ban *sati*, the burning of widows on their husbands' funeral pyres (see below, chapter 11). Mohan Roy died in the middle of the nineteenth century in Bristol, England, where he was on a mission for the Governor of Delhi.

25. As is often the case, but more so because of the funeral pyres.

26. Indian classical theater in its traditional form is mainly epic; then it leaped over history to meet up with more modern and Westernized forms.

11. Thought Burned Alive: Indian Philosophies

1. Contemporary Indian philosophy is remarkably faithful to the conceptual rules and moral principles of classical philosophies. I recall having heard one of the professors in the Department of Marxism at Grant University in the Spring of 1989; I asked one of the women philosophers present who among them could consider themselves to be an atheist, since after all Nehru had been one and didn't try to hide it. She answered, "You must understand that in a country where there are 700 million Hindus, it would be difficult for me to declare myself an atheist without cutting myself off from the masses." Even the most avant-garde (if this concept still has meaning) of Indian philosophers has but one goal: to invent a "grass-roots" philosophy, based in nature, that is in some ways "ecological." In a country where industrialization has wrought ecobiological and moral havoc, they are absolutely right.

2. This is the title of a recently published book by Roger-Pol Droit, who, for the first time in the history of French philosophy, poses the question: When and how was it decided to forget the philosophies of India? Why was this decided and by whom? For it is true today that this immense corpus appears nowhere, neither in secondary education nor in the common body of philosophical training; it is also true that the myth of the birth of Greek philosophy still encumbers the most celebrated and lucid minds, blocking the horizon; French philosophers are enormously ignorant in this field. I speak from personal experience: trained as a philosopher, I came to India to live and took stock of how much I didn't know about Indian philosophy, which was to say everything. I hope that Roger-Pol Droit will continue in his work as spokesperson and will succeed in convincing the French philosophical community. *L'Oubli de l'Inde* (Forgetting India) (Paris: PUF, 1989).

3. *Swaraj*: autonomy. Tilak independence slogan around 1915, when Gandhi returned from South Africa: "Autonomy is my birthright."

4. This chapter owes a lot to two important books: Lilian Silburn, *Instant et cause: Le Discontinu dans la pensée philosophique de l'Inde* (Discontinuity in Indian philosophy), 2nd ed. (Paris: De Boccard, 1989; first ed., 1955); and Charles Malamoud, *Cuire le monde: Rite et penseé dans l'Inde moderne* (Cooking the world: Ritual and philosophy in modern India) (Paris: La Découverte, 1989). Along with the book by Roger-Pol Droit, three important books in a year: not bad!

5. Quoted by Silburn, *Instant et cause*, p. 70. The rest of the passage: "In the same way, the sacrificer empties his own being in the form of a seed into the pot and obtains a person comprised

of poetic meter, hymns, breath, divinity, *brahman*, and immortality, and in a year, his physical body will have been constructed, whole and complete." Prajapati is then also the year.

6. *Purusa* is the name given to the golden statue of Prajapati that must be reconstituted in the image of man; it is also the figure of fire, Agni. See Malamoud, *Cuire le monde*, p. 77.

7. Ibid., p. 79.

8. Ibid., p. 81. Malamoud does it discreetly, in a footnote, but he finally does say it, regarding the phrase modestly translated as "The core of a person is made of droppings": "This scandalous formulation, if translated correctly, would read: 'the Center of the Self is shit.' This phrase does not come from an anthology of blasphemies, but is found in one of the most orthodox Vedic texts, which is, to a certain extent, the supreme authority for the Brahmanic ritual of *Taittiriya-Samhita*, Book V, 3, 5, 2."

9. Silburn, *Instant et cause*, p. 74. Person, soul, or self; the term is reputedly untranslatable.

10. Regarding the sand spread out by the priest, also see the passage quoted by Silburn, ibid.: "Endless are the days and nights and endless is sand; that is why, spread out by days and nights, sand becomes complete for the sacrificer, it is neither deficient nor excessive. Endlessly sand is spread, endless are the days and the nights, endless the oceanic rhythm. Prayer is thought, and thought that is equal to all of sand expresses infinite *brahman*" (pp. 81–82).

11. Ibid., p. 106. *Prana* is breath. *Dharman* is structure.

12. Ibid. Death and evil are *mrtyu*.

13. [Trans.: The same word in French, where "yoke" is *joug*.]

14. Breathing exercises are complex and lengthy; one can suspend breath while breathing in and holding four times the length of normal breathing, and then exhale for a period that is twice as long as it took to breathe in; breathing can be suspended when breathing out as well. Then there is the question of *how* one breathes: with or without noise, with or without vibrating the vocal cords, etc. It is a difficult art.

15. Sudhir Kakar, *Moksha* (Paris: Belles Lettres, 1986), p. 49.

16. Silburn, *Instant et cause*, p. 109.

17. Baudelaire, "La Mort des amants" (The death of the lovers).

18. Thus, quoted by Michel Hulin, a text from the *Advaita* in which blue and pleasure are linked instantly: "If objects, blue, pleasure, are led into the 'I,' the great ocean of consciousness . . . " In *Le Principe de l'Ego dans la pensée indienne classique: La Notion d'ahamkara* (Paris: Collège de France, Institut de Civilisation Indienne, 1978), p. 286.

19. Kakar, *Moksha*, p. 47.

20. Text by Ramana Maharishi, quoted by Kakar, *Moksha*, p. 49.

21. [Trans.: The French says *hystérie oblige*, playing on *noblesse oblige*; we have translated it with that in mind.]

22. Raja Ram Mohan Roy. See above, chapter 10, note 24.

23. Roop Kanwar was not yet eighteen when she climbed onto the pyre, in front of the villagers of Deorala, Rajasthan, on Sept. 4, 1987. A few days later, an immense crowd gathered to consecrate her as a goddess; by their very presence, notables and maharajas condoned the return of this sacrifice. The resulting polemic lasted for an entire year: was it better, in the name of secular tolerance (which in India is called secularism), to allow this to occur, or should this practice be forbidden, and if so, how? The problem of national identity, of an absorbing of differences and a defense of secularism, is indeed more serious when it involves issues of life and death. Again, there is the "chador question," which became an issue in India two years before it appeared in France, posed in a massive, brutal, bloody, and most of all spectacular way, since thousands of villagers witnessed the ritual.

On the history, ritual, and problems concerning the satis in India, see the forthcoming book by Catherine Weinberger-Thomas, who has been working on this extremely sensitive topic for a long time, in Europe, where it excited writers' imaginations, as well as in India and the other

Hindu countries, where its consequences are still felt. That is not including its filmography: two years before the Deorala affair, an impressively large cast of extras was used to film a sati sequence for *The Far Pavilions*, also filmed in Rajasthan. The scene is admirable; it undoubtedly affected the Rajputi extras.

24. Brünnhilde in *Der Götterdämmerung*, Norma, and Marfa in *Khovanschchina* are operatic "satis"; see Clément, "From Operatic Flames to Indian Pyres," in David Levin, ed., *Opera Through Other Eyes* (1990).

25. Silburn, *Instant et cause*, p. 115.

26. See Malamoud, *Cuire le monde*, pp. 35–70.

27. Kakar, *Moksha*, p. 60.

28. Directors of television series in India—for example, in the *Ramayana* (72 episodes)—portray with great gusto lessons on how to leave one's body being given by a guru to a group of adolescent boys. Special effects are perfect for this type of program.

29. Silburn, *Instant et cause*, p. 103.

30. Ibid., p. 178.

31. Ibid., p. 179.

32. From Kamalasila, quoted in Hulin, *Le Principe de l'Ego*, p. 103.

33. Silburn, *Instant et cause*, p. 214.

34. Without this weakness, the hero and his brothers would not have gone into exile in the forest, would not have accomplished their exploits, would not have obtained the powerful weapons that would perhaps allow them to win the Great War; in fact, without this weakness the hero would not have fulfilled his destiny.

35. Malamoud, *Cuire le monde*, p. 74.

36. See the *Theodicy* (Paris: Belles Lettres, 1992).

37. After the aesthetic stage, in *Either/Or*, comes the ethical stage and the continuity of marriage. That is how the seducer settles down after the seduction and becomes the knight of faith who saunters home, dreaming of his roasted lamb's head, etc.

12. Syncope Leaves for the Forest: The Renouncers

1. *Samyasin*, a renouncer. "There is an institution, *samnyasa* or renunciation, in fact a social state apart from society proper." Louis Dumont, *Homo Hierarchicus: The Caste System and Its Implications*, appendix B, p. 273; trans. Mark Sainsbury, Louis Dumont, and Basia Gulati (Chicago: University of Chicago Press, 1970). For Dumont, this institution of Hinduism is the only one that allows a sense of the individual to be developed.

2. "One of the great finds of Brahmanic ideology was to put into place, at the end of the Vedic period, a system of *asramas*, or stages of life. A man's life (or at least those belonging to one of the three upper classes of society, who are 'born twice,') is divided into several periods: upon leaving childhood, the young boy receives a Vedic initiation from a master who grants him a 'second birth'; he is now a Brahmanic student and spends several years in the master's house, serving him and studying the Veda. This stage is followed by that of 'master of the house': After all these years of study, chastity, and service, the young man returns to his village and gets married; he is now a *grhastha* and devotes himself to economic activities and to procreation, along with religious activities that can be summed up by the word *istapurta*, or sacrifice and gratification. This period in the village is not necessarily the last: when the master of the house has gray hair and has seen 'his sons' sons,' he is allowed (that is, in a manner conforming to the *dharma* he now attempts to transcend) to leave the village, to rid himself of his earthly goods and to take up the life of a renouncer." Charles Malamoud, *Cuire le monde: Rite et pensée dans l'Inde moderne* (Paris: La Découverte, 1989), pp. 106–7.

3. See Malamoud, ibid., the entire article entitled "Village et forêt dans l'idéologie de l'Inde brahmanique" (Village and forest in the ideology of Brahmanic India), particularly p. 96, note 8.

See also Louis Dumont, *Homo Hierarchicus*, appendix B, "Renunciation in Indian Religions," pp. 275 ff.

4. The touching story of this beautiful heroine is the delight of Indian television series. Shakuntala is frolicking in the forest with her companions when a king meets her, falls in love with her, and marries her on the spot. Before leaving, he gives her a ring. Then, due to a curse, he forgets Shakuntala, who chastely waits for him and carries his child. Renouncers recognize her purity through her truthfulness and charming surroundings, and her familiarity with animals. They take her to the king, across a lake, into which she loses the ring; the king, who no longer recognizes her, sends her away. Later, when he meets up with her again, the child has grown up and it is no longer the same story.

5. Especially in *Rêveries d'un promeneur solitaire*.

6. See Dumont, *Homo Hierarchicus*, appendix B, paragraph 5, "The Sect." "Practically all the sects have been founded by sanyasis and the greater part include, apart from wordly adherents, a sanyasi order constituting the nucleus of the sect. The link between both sides is provided by the ancient institution of the spiritual master or *guru*. Instead of the renouncer alone having his *guru*, he in turn serves as *guru* to whoever wishes it. The institution is thus most remarkably enlarged or democratized. . . . Of course there is scope here for degradation, but by this channel the religion and thought of the sects, that is of the renouncer, penetrate to the great mass of men-of-the-world" (p. 284). Note that Dumont spells 'renouncer' as *sanyasin*, while Malamoud uses *samnyasin*; I refuse to choose between them, and make each of them responsible for their own spellings.

7. Lilian Silburn gives an excellent description of their historical evolution of yogis, *sramanes* and *samana*, in *Instant et cause: Le Discontinu dans la pensée philosophique de l'Inde* (Paris: De Boccard, 1989), especially on p. 135. Non-Brahmans, merchants, warriors, sometimes kings, sometimes Untouchables, "*sudras*" are nihilists, sophists, logicians, "reasoners," "tonsured ones" or Tantric practitioners, who ignore traditional sacrifices and castes and practice universal compassion, or *ahimsa*, which later will be called "nonviolence."

8. This is the approximate scenario used by Mahatma Gandhi, who although president and active member of the Congress Party, was especially gifted in the art of consensus thanks to renunciation. See below, chapter 16.

9. The question of the Untouchables, whom Gandhi preferred to call "Harijans," or "Children of God," has not been resolved. In 1988, priests again began to forbid them entrance to temples, a practice that Gandhi had fought against long before Indian independence.

10. Henri Bergson, *The Two Sources of Morality and Religion*, trans. R. Ashley Audra and Cloudesley Brereton (Garden City, N.Y.: Doubleday/Anchor, 1954), p. 38.

11. Ibid., p. 39.

12. Ibid., p. 42: "From time immemorial woman must have inspired man with an inclination distinct from desire, but in immediate contact, as though welded to it, and pertaining both to feeling and to sensation. But romantic love has a definite date: it sprang up during the Middle Ages on the day when some person or persons conceived the idea of absorbing love into a kind of supernatural feeling, into religious emotion as created by Christianity and launched by the new religion into the world." *Two Sources* dates from 1932.

13. Also see "Real Duration and Prediction" in *Time and Free Will: An Essay on the Immediate Data of Consciousness*, trans. F. L. Pogson (New York: Harper, 1960). On this topic, see the famous metaphor of the hand and the iron filings: "So, if we took into account only what we saw, the simple act of an invisible hand plunged into iron filings would seem like an inexhaustible interplay of actions and reactions among the filings themselves in order that they might effect an equilibrium. If such is the contrast between the real working of life and the aspect it presents to the senses and intelligence which analyse it, is it surprising that a soul which no more recognises any material obstacle should feel itself, rightly or wrongly, at one with the principle of life?" (Bergson, *Two Sources*, p. 54).

14. In an important note in *Homo Hierarchicus*, appendix B, p. 434, note 21, Louis Dumont, without contradicting Silburn in *Instant et cause*, insists that the majority of renouncers were Brahmans; two exceptions are "great heretic *sanyasis*" from warrior or royal families: the Buddha, who was born a king, and Jina, founder of the Jain religion, which followed a path historically and ideologically parallel to that of Buddhism.

15. There was much lamentation in the cinema world in India in 1989; annual film production had dropped . . . from 850 to 800 films.

16. Bertrand Blier.

13. Educational Love at First Sight: The Lady, the Guru, and the Psychoanalyst

1. This is the case, for example, in the book by Dominique Lapierre, *La Cité de la joie* (published in English as *The City of Joy*), which portrays the poverty of a destitute peasant; he dies in the shantytown, penniless after his daughter's marriage, which was held not in the village but in the city. The peasant, who has become a "rickshaw-wallah" (rickshaw puller), has been rendered destitute by the ceremony, which was as sumptuous as his poverty would allow. Lapierre is careful to note that this story and its descriptions of Calcutta refer to a time when the Indian state of West Bengal was flooded by refugees from Pakistan (which became Bangladesh in 1971), which continued as the new country became progressively more Islamicized. The flow of immigrants to West Bengal that began in 1947 is being absorbed, slowly but surely. Calcutta, contrary to popular belief, is not an enormous shantytown; it is in fact the only city in India that has an underground subway system that works. It is by far the most interesting Indian city from an artistic or intellectual point of view; Satyajit Ray, who made his home there, explained it well. And it must be said again that India has been self-sufficient in terms of food for at least twenty years. The West undoubtedly has no idea of the harm done to its own reputation by its conventional images of India, made of horror and pity; India is all too aware of this. Calcutta is the key focal point of this mass-media imagery.

2. Sudhir Kakar, p. 117, *Mères et enfants* (Mothers and children); see the section devoted to the young bride: "[Her] status within her husband's family: it is not that of a wife, but of a daughter-in-law."

3. As a companion for reading and writing, I prefer Georges Bataille to Denis de Rougemont. The first reason for this choice is clear: Bataille, more so than de Rougemont, is a syncope hunter; he says it, writes it, never tries to escape from any question or obstacle, preferring instead to confront it with honesty, even if he must leave his pen in the air in suspense—syncopated. Denis de Rougemont's objective, against which I have nothing, is founded on the notion of the crisis in marriage, for which he seeks a solution. The idea of passionate love presents itself as an enormous counterpoint to an institution he sees as being menaced. The syncope of love at first sight appears only faintly. It is clear, however, that the same roads are being traveled, with the same references: Night, *The New Eloise*, Wagner, etc.

But the book by Denis de Rougemont troubles me. What he calls "the Orient" is mainly based on the poetics of Arab mystics; like Bataille, and they must have had the same sources, he writes a little about Tantrism, which he demolishes in four words as "this abtruse psycho-physiological technique" (*Love in the Western World*, trans. Montgomery Belgion [New York: Harper and Row, 1956], p. 117). Once again, Indian philosophy falls through the trapdoor, and it is clearly to Islam's benefit. That is not surprising: the entire book, to its credit, shows Islam's influence on the birth of courtly love. I quite agree; if I often quote from Djalâl ul-Dîn Rumi on one hand and *Le Fou d'Elsa* on the other, it is for similar reasons. But Denis de Rougemont's approach appears to be a good illustration of the separation between the West and India mentioned above by Lévi-Strauss, which is due to the violent confrontation between the West and Islam. Finally, I do not see the use of differentiating between Eros and Agape; Denis de Rougemont uses these to distinguish the burning love of the "pagan mystics" from the marriage between Christ and the Church;

but it is the same Eros that is at work in the ecstasies of the Christian saints and in love at first sight, whether or not mystical marriage is at issue. But it is also true that I do not feel very Christian; that, perhaps, created the rift.

4. Kakar, p. 211.

5. Pp. 192–93; from the book by Yogananda, *Autobiographie d'un yogi* (Paris, 1989). I would also like to render homage to the work of Dr. Jacques Vigne, who was kind enough to send me his fascinating manuscript on the relationship between master and disciple in India, comparing it with the relationship between psychoanalyst and patient in the West, which is entitled *Le Maître et le thérapeute* (The master and the therapist) (Paris: Albin Michel, 1991). Dr. Vigne did fieldwork in Benares, where I was fortunate to meet him. It is also in Benares that I was able to have long discussions on the condition of the renouncer with Mahantji Misra, as he is affectionately known, in the temple where he is the head priest (*mahant*). Dr. Vigne and Veer P. Misra also told me about a woman, Ma Ahandamayi, who was very influential in Benares, where she occupied a position between that of a yogini and a renouncer, a position Dr. Vigne analyzes in his book. As is often the case with spiritual masters of either sex, Ma Anandamayi had certain shamanistic attributes, not unlike those of Ramakrishna.

6. Sudhir Kakar, analyzing the effusive relationship between master and disciple, comments convincingly that it is automatically an aspect of political life in India; the politician must project an image that is both paternal and maternal, infinitely sheltering. "When Indians watch or meet these holy men or some political leader like Gandhi or Nehru, they are capable of letting themselves be overtaken by the propensity to idealize and transmute the banal into the miraculous, their 'objectivity' being wiped out by an overflowing of respect." Later on he adds, "The maternal mode of attention to the family safeguards an aspect of the continuity between the different stages of individual experience, whereas the insistence on the preeminence of relationships tends to neutralize *the narcissistic orientation of the individual and his investment of self, which, if it were not repressed, would seriously undermine stability and social cooperation*" (p. 194; emphasis added).

7. See the well-known speech given by Alcibiades at the end of the *Symposium*: the brilliant young man compares Socrates to a Silenus, a rather ugly and unattractive statue [Trans.: a statue that opens up, and has the figure of a god inside]. "I don't know whether anyone has ever opened him up when he's being serious, and seen the little images inside, but I saw them once, and they looked so godlike, so golden, so beautiful, and so utterly amazing that there was nothing for it but to do exactly what he told me," section 217a (trans. Michael Joyce, in *Collected Dialogues of Plato*, ed. Edith Hamilton and Huntington Cairns [Princeton: Princeton University Press, 1961]).

8. Sudhir Kakar's translation of a passage from the *Bhagavata-Purana*. In a note, Kakar writes that the "gift of tears" was recognized as a sign of holiness by medieval Catholicism. See below.

9. [Trans.: "To lose oneself there": the French is *s'y abîmer*, an unusual construction connoting a place—an abyss (*abîme*)?—and one is damaged (*abîmer*) by falling into it.]

10. See *Mira*, by Catherine Clément, published by Grasset.

11. Georges Duby, *Mâle Moyen Age: De l'amour et autres essais* (The male in the Middle Ages: On love and other essays) (Paris: Flammarion, 1988), "La Matrone et la mal mariée" (The matron and the unhappily married woman), pp. 50–73.

12. See especially, by Henri Rey-Flaud, "Le Rituel de l'Asag" (The ritual of Asag), in *La Névrose courtoise* (Courtly neurosis) (Paris: Navarin, Bibliothèque des Analytica, 1983), pp. 28–32. In it he quotes Andreas Capellanus (Andreas the Chaplain), who around 1185 expressed the rules of "purus amor" as follows: "*Fin amor* is that which unites the hearts of two lovers with a passionate strength. It consists of the contemplation of the mind and in the heart's feelings; it allows lovers to kiss each other on the mouth and to embrace one another and even permits the respectful contact of their naked bodies—but the supreme *jouissance* is prohibited; it is not allowed to those who seek to love each other with *fin amor*" (p. 31).

13. Georges Duby in *The Three Orders: Feudal Society Imagined*, trans. Arthur Goldhammer

(Chicago: University of Chicago Press, 1980), gives a brilliant description of how the cleric begins his ascent of the social ladder by means of courtly love. "Honesty" [*honnêteté*] requires exclusion: the "horrid, hirsute" peasant will not be allowed into the Garden of Love, according to the cleric Andreas the Chaplain, any more than the beggar in the public square or the prostitute. Duby comments: "Thus not only was the beggar excluded, but with him all men whose hands were callused but empty, cast out together among the beasts: these were the men who made love in the manner of horses and mules, unable to dominate the *impetus*. Why? Because they were poor. Physical suffering made them alien, kept them from sufficiently extricating themselves from the clutches of the carnal. Beauteous love was denied to any slave of labor" (p. 340).

14. Lacan said it often, but it is in Seminar XX that the most striking traces are found; for example, pp. 59 and 65. *Le Séminaire XX: Encore 1972–73* (Paris: Seuil, 1975).

15. See Duby, *Three Orders*, p. 342, describing how the cleric became "virtuous" (*prud'homme*).

16. Or "Folle-de-miel" (the honey-mad girl), a key character in Lévi-Strauss's *Du Miel aux cendres* (From honey to ashes) (Paris: Plon, 1967), p. 87.

17. Duby, *Three Orders*, p. 356.

18. [Trans.: The French says *le château de cartes du Tendre*, playing on *cartes* ("cards") and on *carte du Tendre*, the "map of Love" that appeared in Madeleine de Scudéry's seventeenth-century novel *Clélie* and that mapped out the course love takes in society.]

19. [Trans.: *Fou d'amour*, "love-crazed man," recalls *fou de dieu*, "religious fanatic," or "someone crazy about God," a term that appears several times in the text.]

20. See Lacan in *Encore* (p. 79), where there is a brief, elliptical passage on the homosexual undercurrent of courtly love: "I made an allusion to courtly love, which appeared at a time when homosexual amusement had fallen into extreme decadence, and into a kind of an impossible bad dream called feudalism": *âmusement* and *hommosexuel* [sic]. [Trans.: Clément is pointing out Lacan's puns: conflating *âme* (soul) and *amusement*, and *homme* (man) with *homosexual*.]

21. [Trans.: The French used here for "bring into the world" is *donner jour à*: literally, "to give day to."]

22. That is what Denis de Rougemont is talking about in *Love in the Western World*, when he develops the dialectic of the obstacle in "The Tristan Myth," pp. 36–37.

23. G. Bataille, *Inner Experience*, trans. L. Boldt (Albany: SUNY Press, 1988), p. 120.

24. Ibid., p. 17.

25. [Trans.: Clément uses the English word "insight."]

14. Jouissances: Between the Angel and the Placenta

1. I thank Jean-Jacques Brochier for teaching me this slang expression: the French, *s'envoyer à dame*, literally means "to send oneself to a lady"; the English is not so exclusively male.

2. See *Le Mahabharata*, selections translated into French from the Sanskrit by Jean-Michel Péterfalvi (Paris: Flammarion, 1987), vol. 1, pp. 91–92 ff. "At a time so pleasant for all creatures," complains the antelope, which is the sage Kimdana in disguise, "at such a perfect time, what wise man would kill an animal that was coupling in the forest?" In the shortened version, which is so well written by Jean-Claude Carrière, the antelopes have become gazelles, and it is quite possible that the complaining antelope is a woman. But here we feel the influence on Carrière of the myth of Tiresias, who is the only man, according to Greek mythology, to know that women experience more pleasure than men (*Le Mahabharata*, trans. Jean-Claude Carrière [Paris: Belfond, 1989]).

3. Lacan, *Encore 1972–73* (Paris: Seuil, 1975).

4. See the close of chapter 16.

5. Beginning in 1887, when he was a student at the Ecole Normale Supérieure, Romain Rolland worked on what he called his *credo*: "I feel, therefore it is." See especially pp. 107–8 in *Le*

Cloître de la rue d'Ulm (The cloister in the rue d'Ulm) (Paris: Cahiers Romain Rolland, Albin Michel, 1952). Ibid., p. 352, *Credo quia verum*. Romain Rolland was twenty-two years old.

6. About Beethoven's music, the same stress as in Bataille, regarding the Leonora Overture. "A feeling of divine intoxication invaded me which I could neither have described nor can describe in a straightforward way, which I have attempted to follow by evoking the suspended nature—and which brings me to tears—of the depth of being . . . " (Bataille, *Inner Experience*, p. 69).

7. In Romain Rolland, *Life of Ramakrishna*, trans. E. F. Malcolm-Smith (Calcutta: Advaita Ashrama, 1965), p. 33.

8. Lacan, *Encore*, p. 70.

9. Marcel Brion, *L'Allemagne romantique: Le voyage initiatique* (Paris: Albin Michel, 1976), pp. 12–13. Also see Georges Bataille, in *Inner Experience*, concerning a phrase from Nietzsche, "Be this ocean: there will be one" (Fragment 80–81). Bataille writes: "The so simple commandment: 'Be that ocean,' linked to the *extreme limit*, at the same time makes of a man a multitude, a desert. It is an expression which resumes and makes precise the sense of a community" (p. 27). Bataille understands the link between ecstasy, the ecstatic's loss of identity, and the founding of a utopian community—even if it is in the desert.

10. Excerpt from an unpublished text by Sudhir Kakar on Ramakrishna.

11. "I was following a narrow path between the rice fields. I raised my eyes to the sky as I munched my rice. I saw a great black cloud spreading rapidly until it covered the heavens. Suddenly at the edge of the cloud a flight of snow-white cranes passed over my head. The contrast was so beautiful that my spirit wandered far away. The puffed rice was scattered. Somebody picked me up and carried me home in his arms. An excess of joy and emotion overcame me. . . . This was the first time that I was seized with ecstasy" (Rolland, *Life of Ramakrishna*, pp. 22–23). Ramakrishna was six years old at the time.

12. [Trans.: The French *bouc émissaire* means "scapegoat"; the words are separated here as "goat" and "emissary," but the connotation still resonates in French.]

13. Janet, *De l'angoisse à l'extase*, vol. 1, pp. 109–10.

14. Ibid., p. 110.

15. I am thinking of Joris-Karl Huysmans's unbelievable hysteria, when he attacked Jews and Freemasons in *Sainte Lydwine de Schiedam* (recently republished by Maren Sell, with an excellent preface by Alain Vircondelet). Huysmans went so far as to regret that it was no longer possible, in order to fan Christianity's dying embers and to eradicate the Jews, to use "a few well-sulfured shirts and some nicely dried logs"; the interruption of these practices proves, he wrote, "the loose morals of our time." In a more subdued vein, there is the lovely book by Jean-Noël Vuarnet, *Extases féminines* (Female ecstasies) (Paris: Arthaud, 1980); a loving admirer, without furor.

16. Pupul Jayakar, *Krishnamurti: A Biography* (San Francisco: Harper and Row, 1986), p. 128. It is unfortunate that this book has not been seen for what it is: a contemporary view of Indian philosophy. It was labeled as occultist, nothing more.

17. Sanjay Gandhi, the younger brother of Rajiv Gandhi.

18. See the reproduction of this painting in Vuarnet's *Extases féminines*.

19. William James, *The Varieties of Religious Experience* (Cambridge, Mass.: Harvard University Press, 1985), p. 307.

20. As Gérard Depardieu's enchanting expression goes.

21. This is the wager in the game between Faust and Mephistopheles: in order to win the soul of the scientist, the devil must give him the desire to pronounce these words. Faust will only say them at the end of the second *Faust*, looking over the polders in Holland, for which he was the engineer and overseer.

22. Huysmans, *Sainte Lydwine*, p. 238; also see the description of the smell: "an exquisite musty

odor of shells and Levantine spices, a fragrance both energetic and delicate, something like the very Biblical and very Dutch scent of cinnamon" (p. 80).

23. Isolde at the end of the Liebestod: "Are these waves / of intoxicating scents? How they fill and surround me with sound! . . . / Shall I breathe? / Shall I listen? / Shall I get carried away / immerse myself / Sweetly dissolve myself / in scents?" (Paris: Aubier Montagne, 1974), p. 241. "Mystical jaculations" is one of Lacan's expressions.

24. Directed by Peter Sellars at the Maison de la Culture in Bobigny in the fall of 1989.

25. [Trans.: Playing on the homonym *omelette* and a diminutive for *homme*, "little man."]

26. Lacan, *Écrits*, *Position de l'Inconscient*, p. 845.

27. Literally, a lack of appearance, a disappearance.

28. Science fiction is, as always, wonderful; see, for example, Clifford D. Simak, *Le Principe du Loup-Garou* (The principles of werewolfism) (Paris: Editions Denoel, 1971). A man—or what appears to be a man—wakes up naked, far from his home, after a mysterious lapse in consciousness. The story will show that (a) he is not a man of flesh and blood, but a synthetic man created especially in order to appropriate the virtues of the other species in the universe; (b) in returning to his planet, he is no longer "one," he is "three"; or rather, they are three: Thinker, pure mind and absolute logic; Converter, which effectuates the metamorphoses; and Investigator, a being who has the appearance of a wolf. Suddenly, the hero of the story finds himself to be a wolf or a luminous pyramid. Then he returns to human form.

29. Heinrich von Kleist, *Marquise of O*, trans. David Luke and Nigel Reeves (Harmondsworth: Penguin, 1978), pp. 86–87.

30. Jambet and Lardreau.

31. See the superb book by Christine Buci-Glucksmann on the Baroque, *La Raison baroque: De Baudelaire à Benjamin* (Baroque thought: From Baudelaire to Benjamin) (Paris: Editions Galilée, Collection Débats, 1984), especially chapter 1, "Une Archéologie du moderne, Angelus Novus" (An archeology of the modern: Angelus novus). "If the allegorical figure of the Angel—its portrait—outlines strange networks in the midst of modernity which touch on 'something' horrible, frightening or bizarre; a fundamental contretemps where humanity meets with its own destruction 'by accident' (Poe); where history like a storm of progress reverts into a 'unique catastrophe' (Benjamin); or where beauty kills by being terrible (Rilke): these could be some of the themes of this rapprochement where Freudian uncanniness is played out over and over, like an echo" (p. 19).

32. From the cover of the fourth edition of *L'Ange* (Paris: Livre de Poche, Biblio-Essais, 1989; 1st ed., Grasset, 1976).

33. Jean Audouze, technical adviser to the French president and director of the Institute of Astrophysics in Paris, and Michel Cassé, astrophysicist at the Institute of Basic Research of the CEA (Sarclay).

34. Conversation, about not the invisible but the unusual, with Michel Cassé, the author of the quoted passage, in the presence of Jean Audouze.

35. Ibid.

36. Jean Audouze, Michel Cassé, and Jean-Claude Carrière, *Conversations sur l'invisible* (Conversations about the invisible) (Paris: Editions Belfond Sciences, 1988), pp. 157–58.

15. Ego Orgasm and the Indolence of the Subject

1. [Trans.: We have retained the French infinitive *jouir*, in keeping with Clément's ambiguity: *jouir*— "to enjoy, be in ecstasy, to have an orgasm"; *jouissance*—"ecstasy, orgasm, enjoyment.")

2. Text excerpted from "The Capacity to Be Alone" (1958) and quoted from extensively by Masud R. Khan, English psychoanalyst of Pakistani origin, in his splendid article, "Orgasme du moi dans l'amour bisexuel" (Ego orgasm in bisexual love), in *Bisexualité et différence des sexes*

(Bisexuality and sexual difference), in the indispensable *Nouvelle Revue de Psychanalyse* 7 (Spring 1973), p. 323.

3. Ibid.

4. See Lacan, in *Encore*: "What Aristotle called *philia*, that is to say a possibility of a bond of love between two such beings, manifesting the tension towards the Supreme Being, can also become transposed in the manner I have described—it is in their courage to endure the intolerable relation to the supreme being that the friends, the *philoi*, recognize and choose each other" ([Paris: Seuil, 1975], p. 78).

5. Quoted by Michel Hulin, *Le Principe de l'Ego dans la pensée indienne classique: La Notion d'ahamkara* (Paris: Collège de France, Institut de Civilisation Indienne, 1978), p. 342.

6. D. W. Winnicott, "The Split-Off Male and Female Elements to Be Found in Men and Women," in chapter 5 of *Playing and Reality* (London and New York: Routledge, 1986), pp. 72–85.

7. Shakespeare, *Hamlet*, act 3, scene 1.

8. Winnicott, "Split-Off Male and Female Elements," p. 85.

9. Michel de Certeau, *La Fable mystique* (The mystical fable), vol. 1, 16th-17th centuries (Paris: Collection Tel, Gallimard), 1987.

10. Ibid., p. 67, as is the quote from Evagrius.

11. Lacan, *Encore*, p. 70.

12. Hadewijch d'Anvers, seventh vision, *Visions* (Paris: L'Oeil, 1987), p. 46. Also see the commentary on poem XVIII, by Anne Dunand, *Ornicar* 47 (1988).

13. See Hubaux and Leroy's *Le Mythe du Phénix dans les littératures greque et latine* (The phoenix myth in Greek and Latin literature) (Liège: Bibliothèque de la Faculté de Philosophie et Lettres de l'Université de Liège, Fascicule 82, Droz, 1939).

14. Hadewijch was a Beguine; this is what the women living in these communities were called, the word deriving from the English word "beggar," because of their vow to renounce the world; this is the origin of the French expression *avoir le béguin pour*, "to have a crush on someone." Michel de Certeau comments, on p. 160 of *La Fable mystique*, that these communities were also real female republics.

15. Ibid., pp. 38–40.

16. Letter to Fliess, December 6, 1896: "At the boundary between two such epochs a translation of the psychic material must take place. I explain the peculiarities of the psychoneuroses by supposing that this translation has not taken place in the case of some of the material, which has certain consequences. For we hold firmly to a belief in a tendency toward quantitative adjustment. Every later transcript inhibits its predecessor and drains the excitatory process from it. If a later transcript is lacking, the excitation is dealt with in accordance with the psychological laws in force in the earlier psychic period and along the paths open at that time. Thus an anachronism persists: in a particular province, *fueros* are still in force; we are in the presence of 'survivals.'" In *The Complete Letters of Sigmund Freud to Wilhelm Fliess, 1887–1904*, ed. and trans. Jeffrey Moussaieff Masson (Cambridge, Mass.: Harvard University Press, 1985), p. 208.

17. Pierre Janet, *De L'Angoisse à l'extase* (Paris: Payot, 1975), pp. 1–419.

18. See Janet, "Le Délire psychasthénique" (Psychasthenic delirium), ibid., pp. 332–98.

19. Ibid., p. 365.

20. Ibid., vol. 2, p. 499.

21. Ibid., p. 497.

22. Ibid., p. 567. And again: "I am in a state of extreme languor, I am only half alive and I love this delicious sinking feeling, I have enough energy to accomplish only what is necessary, I do not have the courage to do more" (vol. 1, p. 61).

23. Laetitia slept for five years straight without any interruption, save the rude awakenings caused by Janet's hypnotic passes.

24. [Trans.: *Oubliettes* are tiny dungeons where people were put when they were imprisoned for life; from *aublier*, to forget.]

25. Ibid., p. 245. Laetitia's declarations on her lack of a past are on p. 70.

26. Ibid., p. 244.

27. Ibid., p. 508.

28. Ibid., p. 578.

29. See S. Kierkegaard, *Either/Or*, trans. Howard V. Hong and Edna H. Hong, vol. 3 of *Collected Writings of Kierkegaard* (Princeton: Princeton University Press, 1987). "And just as the beads in this wine, as it simmers with an internal heat, sonorous with its own melody, rise and continue to rise, just so the lust for enjoyment resonates in the elemental boiling that is his life" (p. 134). Kierkegaard designates this territory as "sensual geniality"; the champagne aria is its national anthem.

30. Dostoyevsky, *Notes from Underground*, trans. Andrew R. MacAndrew (New York: Signet/NAL, 1961), pp. 92, 104, 120.

31. Paul Valéry, *Théorie poétique et esthétique*, *Philosophie de la danse* (Poetic and aesthetic theory, philosophy of the dance), *Oeuvres complètes* (Paris: Pléiade, Gallimard), p. 1396.

32. Interview conducted in Delhi in January 1990; I thank Jean-Paul Montanari for making it possible for me to meet this dancer.

33. Valéry, *Théorie poétique et esthétique*.

34. Personal testimony given in Delhi in the fall of 1988. Françoise Adret is the artistic director of the Lyon-Opéra Ballet.

35. Philipe de Felice, *L'Enchantement des danses et la magie du verbe*, introduction (Paris: Albin Michel, 1957), p. 11.

36. Ibid., p. 217.

37. Quoted by Ananda Coomaraswamy, *The Dance of Shiva: Fourteen Indian Essays*, rev. ed. (New Delhi: Sagar Publications, 1968), p. 73.

38. Quoted by Jacques Boulenger in *De la Valse au tango* (From the waltz to the tango) (Paris: Devambez Editeur, 1920).

16. Syncope's Strategies: The Creative Act and the Un-Governing of the World

1. Pierre Janet, *De L'Angoisse à l'extase* (Paris: Payot, 1975), vol. 1, pp. 133–35: "Martial's" feeling of glory. Especially p. 134: "As many precautions as I took, the rays of light escaped from me and went through the walls; I carried the sun in me and could not prevent the spectacular flashing within me. . . . At that moment I experienced an incredible feeling of happiness; with one push of the shovel I had discovered a marvelous lode, I had won the most dizzying lottery. I was more alive at that instant than ever in my existence."

2. Ibid., pp. 137–38.

3. Anton Ehrenzweig, *The Hidden Order of Art* (Berkeley: University of California Press, 1967).

4. Ibid., p. 103, for the passage describing the three steps.

5. V. Woolf, *The Waves* (New York: Harvest/Harcourt Brace Jovanovich, 1978), p. 57.

6. Ehrenzweig, *Hidden Order*, p. 103.

7. Ibid.

8. Here is the passage that discusses the Jews in a historical context: "As marginal members they had to be cast out or burned in order to save the body social. In this sense there is below the schizoid-oral level of antisemitism also a depressive anal level of phantasy. There seems something in the Jewish fate which symbolizes an anal phantasy of voluntarily casting oneself out. It is sometimes forgotten that the Jewish dispersal all over the world was partly voluntary and antedates the destruction of the temple" (Ehrenzweig, *Hidden Order*, p. 247).

9. Quoted by Michel Hulin, *Le Principe de l'Ego dans la pensée indienne classique: La Notion d'ahamkara* (Paris: Collège de France, Institut de Civilisation Indienne, 1978), p. 334.

10. Ibid., p. 335.

11. See Gershom Scholem, the chapter entitled "Shekhina, les facteurs passif et féminin de la divinité" (Shekhina: The passive and feminine aspects of divinity), in *La Mystique juive* (Jewish mysticism) (Paris: Editions du Cerf, 1985), pp. 151–202. Scholem uses the spelling *Shekhina*, whereas Michel de Certeau uses *Sekina*. (See note 76, p. 187, referring to Geneviève Javary's *Recherches sur l'utilisation du thème de la Sekina dans l'apologétique chrétienne du XVe au XVIIIe siècle* [Studies in the use of the Sekina theme in Christian apologetics from the fifteenth to the eighteenth centuries] [Lille: Université de Lille III and Librairie Honoré Champion, 1978], pp. 361–527.) Here again, I refuse to choose between the two.

12. Georges Bataille, *Oeuvres complètes* (Paris: Gallimard, 1973), vol. 5, p. 221.

13. *Young India*, December 17, 1925.

14. *Oeuvres complètes*, vol. 7, p. 612. Notes for "A quoi engage notre volonté de gouvernement mondial" (What is involved in our desire for world government?) Club Maintenant, February 22, 1949.

15. Letter to Romain Rolland of January 19, 1930, in *Correspondance* (Paris: Gallimard, 1967), p. 428.

16. Ibid.

17. Quoted by Georg Lukács, *Young Hegel*, trans. Rodney Livingstone (Cambridge, Mass.: MIT Press, 1975), p. 103, still in regard to the crisis of 1797.

Conclusion: Deceiving Death and Embracing God

1. [Trans.: *Coup de soleil*, which can also mean "sunstroke."]

2. In *La Tradition secrète du Nô* (The secret tradition of Noh), Collection Connaissance de l'Orient (Paris: Gallimard, 1960). In particular, "L'Echelle des neuf degrés" (The scale of nine degrees), p. 175.

3. *A Complete Dictionary of Music*, trans. William Waring (New York: AMS Press, 1779, rpt. 1975). Article on "syncope," pp. 390–91. We have changed this eighteenth-century translation's use of "time" to "beat," in keeping with Clément's usage.

4. [Trans.: The French uses *train-train* for "routine," so that Clément can then make a pun about "derailing" routine.]

5. The story of the sage who was struck by King Pandu's arrow is interesting; in order to mate, he must move back into nature and metamorphose into an animal. As man, or Hindu sage, he would not have the right. Once again, the world is turned upside down; when one is in the human form, one couples—but quickly; but if one is a yogi, it is better to become an animal again in order to find pleasure.

6. [Trans.: *Dévoyés*: literally, "led astray," delinquents perhaps.]

7. On May 19, 1976, Claude Lévi-Strauss was invited by Edgar Faure to speak before the Commission on Human Rights of the National Assembly. He rewrote his speech and published it in *Le Regard éloigné* (Paris: Plon, 1983), p. 374. I never tire of quoting from this superb text, which is not yet well-known.

8. [Trans.: *La Pensée sauvage*, the title of a well-known book by Lévi-Strauss that has been translated as *The Savage Mind*.]

9. See Ernesto de Martino, *La Terre du remords* (The land of guilt) (Paris: Gallimard, 1966). Also Gilbert Rouget, *La Musique et la transe* (Music and trance) (Paris: Gallimard, 1980).

10. Rousseau, *Dictionary of Music*, pp. 266–67.

11. "Mejnun" or "madman" is the name that the pre-Islamic Bedouin poet Keis al-Nedji gave himself; his story was celebrated by other poets and became known as *Mejnun Leila* (Leila's Madman); he is the subject of a marvelous book by André Miquel.

12. Louis Aragon in *Le Fou d'Elsa* in turn names himself Keïs-Ibn-Amir an-Nadidji, also called "Elsa's Madman." "*Ils vont vieillir ensemble*" (They will grow old together), p. 309.

13. Ibid.

14. Ibid., in "*Ô impie*" (Oh impious one), p. 425, the last stanzas in the poem by Louis Aragon; italicized in the original.

Index

Compiled by Robin Jackson